Dietrich W. R. Paulus
Joachim Hornegger

Applied Pattern Recognition

Other titles in Computing

Books already in print:

The Efficiency of Theorem Proving Strategies
by David A. Plaisted and Yunshan Zhu

Recovery in Parallel Database Systems
by Svein-Olaf Hvasshovd

Efficient Software Development with DB2 for OS/390
by Jürgen Glag

Corporate Information with SAP®-EIS
by Bernd-Ulrich Kaiser

SAP® R/3® Interfacing using BAPIs
by Gerd Moser

Multiobjective Heuristic Search
by Pallab Dasgupta, P. P. Chakrabarti and S. C. DeSarkar

Intelligent Media Agents
by Hartmut Wittig

Scalable Search in Computer Chess
by Ernst A. Heinz

The SAP® R/3® Guide to EDI and Interfaces
by Axel Angeli, Ulrich Streit and Robi Gonfalonieri

Joint Requirements Engineering
by Georg Herzwurm, Sixten Schockert and Werner Mellis

Applied Pattern Recognition
by Dietrich W. R. Paulus and Joachim Hornegger

Vieweg

CONTENTS v

Part I Introductions 3

1 Pattern Recognition 5
  1.1 Images and Sound 5
  1.2 Applications of Pattern Recognition 6
  1.3 Environment, Problem Domain, and Patterns 7
  1.4 Characterization of Pattern Recognition 8
  1.5 Speech Recording 9
  1.6 Video Cameras and Projections 10
  1.7 From Continuous to Digital Signals 13
  1.8 Sampling Theorem in Practice 14
  1.9 Visualization and Sound Generation 15

2 From C to C++ 17
  2.1 Syntax Notation 17
  2.2 Principle of C++ Compilation 18
  2.3 Function Calls and Arguments 19
  2.4 Declaration and Definition of Variables 20
  2.5 Unix-File Access via Standard Functions 21
  2.6 Numeric Expressions 23
  2.7 Main Program 24
  2.8 Function Definition 25
  2.9 Scope and Lifetime 26

3 Software Development 29
  3.1 Software for Pattern Recognition 29
  3.2 Software Development and Testing 30
  3.3 Modular and Structured Programming 32
  3.4 Comments and Program Layout 32
  3.5 Documentation 33
  3.6 Teamwork 34
  3.7 Tools for Software Development 35
  3.8 Efficiency 35
  3.9 Approximation 36

4 Control and Data Structures 39
  4.1 Structures 39
  4.2 Enumerations 40
  4.3 Scope Resolution 40
  4.4 Unions 41
  4.5 Bit- and Shift Operations and Bit-Fields 41
  4.6 Logical Values and Conditionals 42
  4.7 Loops 44
  4.8 Exception Handling 45
  4.9 Switches 46

5 Arrays and Pointers 49
  5.1 Vectors and Matrices 49
  5.2 Pointers 51
  5.3 Vectors vs. Pointers 52
  5.4 Pointer Operations and Allocation 52
  5.5 Pointer to Structures 53

	5.6	Strings	55
	5.7	Pointer and Array Arguments	55
	5.8	Pointer to Pointer	56
	5.9	Command Line Arguments	57

6 C++ as a better C 59
   6.1 Type Declaration 59
   6.2 Type Conversion for Pointers 59
   6.3 Type Specifiers and Variable Declaration 60
   6.4 Type-Safe Linkage 62
   6.5 Overloaded Function Names 63
   6.6 Return Value and Arguments 63
   6.7 Macros and Inline Functions 65
   6.8 Function Pointers 66
   6.9 Comma Operator and Conditional Expressions 66

7 Statistics for Pattern Recognition 69
   7.1 Axioms 69
   7.2 Random Variables 70
   7.3 Moments of a Distribution 73
   7.4 Generating Random Variables 75
   7.5 Random Vectors 77
   7.6 Independence and Marginal Densities 78
   7.7 Mixtures 79
   7.8 Statistical Features and Entropy 80
   7.9 Signal-to-Noise Ratio 81

8 Classification and Pattern Analysis 83
   8.1 Classification 83
   8.2 Preprocessing 84
   8.3 Feature Extraction 85
   8.4 Learning 85
   8.5 Analysis 86
   8.6 Segmentation 86
   8.7 Pattern Understanding 89
   8.8 Active Vision and Real Time Processing 90
   8.9 Software Systems 91

Part II Object–Oriented Programming   93

9 Object–Oriented Programming   95
9.1 Object–Oriented Software Techniques 95
9.2 Basic Vocabulary 96
9.3 Data Abstraction and Modules 97
9.4 Inheritance 98
9.5 Templates 99
9.6 Abstract Classes 100
9.7 Object–Oriented Classification 100
9.8 Polymorphism 101
9.9 Object–Oriented Programming Languages 101

10 Classes in C++   103
10.1 Methods and ADT's 103
10.2 Class Declarations 105
10.3 Object Construction 106
10.4 Destruction of Objects 107
10.5 Operators 108
10.6 User-Defined Conversion 109
10.7 Advanced Methods and Constructors 110
10.8 Vector Class 111
10.9 Class Design 113

11 Representation of Signals   115
11.1 Array Class 115
11.2 Templates in C++ 117
11.3 Images 118
11.4 External Data Formats 119
11.5 Binary Images 121
11.6 Color Images 121
11.7 Subimages 123
11.8 Matrix Operations 124
11.9 Speech Signal Class 125

12 Signals and Images   127
12.1 Synthetic Sound 127
12.2 Geometric Patterns 128
12.3 Noise Signals 128
12.4 Combination of Signals 130
12.5 Simple Image Manipulation 131
12.6 2–D Views of 3–D Polyhedral Objects 131
12.7 Single Stereo Images 133
12.8 Textures 134
12.9 Audio and Video Devices 135

13 Fourier Transform   137
13.1 Introductory Considerations 137
13.2 Fourier Series 138
13.3 Fourier Transform 140
13.4 Discrete Fourier Transform 144
13.5 Complex Number Class 145

13.6 Inverse Discrete Fourier Transform	146
13.7 Fourier Transforms of Speech Signals	147
13.8 Fast Fourier Transform	148
13.9 2–D Fourier Transform	150

14 Inheritance for Classes 153
14.1 Motivation and Syntax 153
14.2 Access to Members of Base Classes 154
14.3 Construction and Destruction 155
14.4 Pointers to Objects 156
14.5 Virtual Functions 158
14.6 Abstract Classes 159
14.7 Image Class Hierarchy 160
14.8 Multiple Inheritance 161
14.9 Implementation Issues 163

15 Edge Images 165
15.1 Strategies 165
15.2 Discrete Derivatives of Intensity Functions 166
15.3 Mask Operators 168
15.4 Discrete Directions 169
15.5 Edge Class 171
15.6 Edge Images 173
15.7 Robert's Cross 173
15.8 Second Derivative 174
15.9 Color Edge Operators 176

16 Class Libraries 179
16.1 Stream Input and Output 179
16.2 National Institutes of Health Class Library 181
16.3 Input and Output for Objects 184
16.4 Frequently Used Classes 186
16.5 Collection Classes 187
16.6 Memory Allocation 189
16.7 Standard Template Library 191
16.8 Advanced C++ Features 194
16.9 Templates vs. Inheritance 196

CONTENTS ix

Part III Pattern Analysis   199

17 Filtering and Smoothing Signals   **201**
     17.1 Linear Filters 201
     17.2 Rank Order Operations 203
     17.3 Edge Preserving Filters 204
     17.4 Elimination of Noisy Image Rows 207
     17.5 Resizing an Image 208
     17.6 Resolution Hierarchies 209
     17.7 Geometric Distortions 210
     17.8 Polymorphic Image Processing 211
     17.9 Image Operator Hierarchy 214

18 Histogram Algorithms   **217**
     18.1 Discriminant Analysis Threshold 217
     18.2 Histogram Entropy Thresholding 220
     18.3 Multi-Thresholding 220
     18.4 Global Histogram Equalization 221
     18.5 Local Histogram Equalization 223
     18.6 Look-up Table Transformation 224
     18.7 Histogram Classes 225
     18.8 Color Quantization 226
     18.9 Histogram Back-Projection 227

19 Edges and Lines   **231**
     19.1 More Edge Detectors 231
     19.2 Edge Thinning 233
     19.3 Line Detection 238
     19.4 Hysteresis Thresholds 239
     19.5 Closing of Gaps 241
     19.6 Zero-Crossings in Laplace Images 241
     19.7 Hough Transform 243
     19.8 Circle Detection 246
     19.9 Optimal Line Detection 249

20 Image Segmentation   **251**
     20.1 Chain Code Class 251
     20.2 Edges 252
     20.3 Chain Code Algorithms 254
     20.4 Neighborhood 258
     20.5 Contours in Binary Images 259
     20.6 Polygon Representation 260
     20.7 Region Segmentation 261
     20.8 Point Segmentation 262
     20.9 Image Analysis 263

21 Spatial and Spectral Features   **265**
     21.1 Different Types of Features 265
     21.2 Frames and Blocks 266
     21.3 Spatial Features 268
     21.4 Short Time Fourier Analysis 270
     21.5 Cepstral Features 274

21.6	Mel Spectral and Cepstral Features	275
21.7	Linear Predictive Coding	277
21.8	Model Spectrum and Cepstrum	280
21.9	Implementation Issues	281

22 Numerical Pattern Classification — 283
22.1	General Notes on Classifiers	284
22.2	Design of Classifiers	285
22.3	Linear Discriminants	286
22.4	Polynomial Classifiers	290
22.5	Bayesian Classifiers	290
22.6	Properties of Bayesian Classifiers	292
22.7	From Bayesian to Geometric Classifiers	294
22.8	Nearest Neighbor Classifier	295
22.9	Implementation of Classifiers	297

23 Speech Recognition — 299
23.1	Classification of Speech Signals	299
23.2	Dynamic Time Warping	300
23.3	Mixture Densities	306
23.4	Hidden-Markov-Models	310
23.5	Topological and Statistical Variations	314
23.6	Incomplete Data Estimation	315
23.7	Learning from Multiple Observations	317
23.8	Hidden-Markov-Model Classes	320
23.9	Statistical and Neural Speech Understanding	322

24 An Image Analysis System — 325
24.1	Design of PUMA and ANIMALS	325
24.2	Hierarchy of Picture Processing Objects	327
24.3	Segmentation Objects	332
24.4	External Representation	334
24.5	Graphical User Interfaces	335
24.6	Display	337
24.7	Computer Vision	337
24.8	Object Recognition	338
24.9	Model-Based Image Analysis	340

Part IV Appendix   343

A   Software Development Tools   345
     A.1   Groups and ID's with Unix 345
     A.2   Program Building with `make` 346
     A.3   The Use of Libraries 347
     A.4   Version and Access Control 348
     A.5   Teamwork 349
     A.6   Shell 349
     A.7   SED 350
     A.8   AWK 350
     A.9   Perl 350

B   Source Code and Tools   351
     B.1   List of Tools 351
     B.2   Portable Image Format 351
     B.3   How to get the sources 352
     B.4   Image Display 352
     B.5   Course Material 352
     B.6   Addresses 353
     B.7   Headers and Source Files 353
     B.8   Images 355

C   Formulas   356
     C.1   Lookup Table Transformation 356
     C.2   Marginal Density 356
     C.3   Identity 357
     C.4   Property of the H–Function 357
     C.5   Lagrange Multiplier 358
     C.6   Notation 359

Bibliography   360

Figures   368

Tables   373

List of Programs   374

Index   375

Preface

This book emphasizes practical experiences with image and speech processing. It offers a comprehensive study of

- basics of image processing and image analysis,
- basics of speech processing and speech understanding,
- object–oriented software design and programming,
- programming in C++.

The theoretical background is introduced in an order respecting the requirements of programmers who have to deal with pattern recognition problems. The mathematical exposition is self-contained and the prerequisites are some basic calculus and probability theory.

In the first part we introduce speech and image processing, programming tools, elementary statistics, and the basics of C++.

In the second part we describe object–oriented programming in general and possible applications of object–oriented concepts to image and speech processing. The new features of C++ are introduced entirely by the use of examples. Some details are only mentioned in the exercises. Therefore, the book is not a manual of C++, but a guide of how to use it for pattern analysis.

The third part describes systems for image segmentation and speech understanding. We combine the data representation described in the second part with the algorithms that use and manipulate them here in the third part. We implement statistical models in C++ and show the applications to feature extraction and classification. Even those who are put-off by the mathematics in Chapter 21–23 should read Chapter 24 to get an idea of how to continue the projects proposed in the earlier chapters of the book.

In part four — the appendix — we give additional technical informations.

The introduction of the C++ programming language is done in an informal way. We do not specify all the language details.[1] However, everything the reader needs is described in sufficient detail to cover most applications of image and speech analysis programs. A basic knowledge of the C programming language is required. We assume that the readers of our book are interested in both pattern recognition and programming in C++.

The input of images or signals and the output to screen or sound devices are only briefly mentioned in Sect. 12.9. These strictly hardware-dependent issues have to be solved differently

---

[1] Some footnotes provide references for those who want to know the details.

on every computer. Some locations for sources of image display programs are also listed in the appendix.

Parts of this text were used for several years by students in a two-term undergraduate course in computer science at the University Erlangen-Nürnberg. The book was also used in several lectures on the graduate level (e.g. at Stanford University), for compact courses in applied programming, and for lectures on applied pattern recognition. The students had to prepare projects in small groups (2–4 students).[2] Some sections were used in a course in *computational engineering* at the University Erlangen-Nürnberg. This book teaches not only C++ but *real object–oriented* programming and algorithms for image and speech processing.

The authors wish to express their special thanks to all those who helped to make this book possible.[3] First of all, Prof. Dr. H. Niemann, the head of our department, for his constant advice and support. Furthermore, U. Ahlrichs, R. Beß, Chr. Drexler, Dr. J. Denzler (who is shown in Figure 24.6), F. Deinzer, A. Gebhard, B. Heigl, M. Reinhold, and M. Zobel helped to keep PUMA (the common system, Sect. 24.1) running. Dr. E. Nöth and S. Harbeck helped with the speech processing sections; J. Haas and V. Warnke computed the spectrograms and supported us when we wrote the chapters on spectral features and classification. Prof. E.-G. Schukat-Talamazzini's book on speech understanding was a rich source of ideas for our chapters 21-23. The Chapter 19 uses figures and text which were taken partially from [Brü90] – with permission of the author. From their experiences in the exercise classes, U. Ohler and G. Stemmer gave us many hints of how to improve the text.

Our special thanks goes to Carey Butler who carefully revised the text of the first version and did his best to improve our English and style. After a complete revision of the text and of the structure, Dr. Michael G. Brown again read the whole book; he corrected many errors and gave us most valuable hints to improve style and contents. Timothy Dodge corrected our changes for the latest revision of this book. All remaining errors are our own fault and we apologize for them. Last but not least we thank all of our students for their comments and suggestions for improvement.

Erlangen, Germany   D. Paulus and J. Hornegger
September 2000

---

[2]Some projects are included here as exercises. Further course materials (slides in Postscript or TeX as well as all programming examples) are available upon request (see page 351 for details).

[3]For the tools used see page 344.

Part I

"We must begin inquiring whether the distinction between what can and what cannot be seen in the pictures by 'merely looking at them' is entirely clear. (...) Does merely looking, then, mean looking without the use of any instrument? This seems a little unfair to the man who needs glasses to tell a painting from a hippopotamus."
Nelson Goodman, [Goo69]

The goal of this part of the book is to provide the basic background knowledge required for the more sophisticated applications in those parts that follow. Details are left to footnotes and to the references. Only those subjects relevant for part II and III are introduced.

In this part of the book we will cover three different topics:

- Principles of pattern recognition and their applications to image and speech processing,
- Mathematical techniques for image and speech processing,
- The conventional part of the C++ programming language with simple applications to image and speech processing,
- Software engineering principles and tools in Unix and PC operating systems, C++, and pattern recognition applications.

Chapter 1

Pattern Recognition

In this chapter we will briefly introduce the basic ideas and the models used in pattern recognition. We exclude biological aspects and treat only the mathematical and technical aspects of perception. This is done in a very informal way, since it is not within the scope of this book to present a rigorous discussion of pattern recognition theory. We put our main emphasis on explaining image and speech processing concepts. The research problems treated are motivated by practical examples. After a brief introduction to the applications of pattern recognition, a sketched mathematical description of patterns, problem domain, and environment is given. Due to the fact that modern computer systems need digital data, we will also discuss the central problem of how continuous, observable signals can be transformed into digital signals. More technical descriptions can be found in the literature (e.g., in [Bis95, Nie83, Rip96]).

1.1 Images and Sound

The basic input data to any pattern recognition system is recorded in the form of digitized signals. These digital signals are then processed by the system. Images as well as speech are typical examples of input data and represent the most important areas in the research and application of pattern recognition.

Digital images and speech signals are very common in today's computer and audio-visual equipment. Digital high-definition video is becoming a huge market. Almost all personal computers have video and audio capabilities and publishing programs now enable the mixing of digital images with text, thereby creating new, so called, *hypertext* documents. PC users are familiar with the JPEG and MPEG standards[1] which are often used for image transmission. Image data formats (like TIFF [Poy92]) are compatible across hardware borders. Special hardware for video conferences using personal computers and standard computer communication networks are also now available. Several types of media are commonly used in conjunction with each other: text, speech, pictures, movies, etc. The combination of these many media sources and their uses is called *multimedia*.

---

[1]see the reference website for MPEG http://www.bok.net/~tristan/MPEG/ for further information

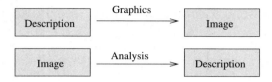

Figure 1.1: Graphics and image analysis

Digital signals can be *synthesized* by a computer based upon a description given to it; sound can be generated by a synthesizer or a voice generator and images can be created by *computer graphics*. Natural signals are *recorded* by special devices; sound, for instance, is recorded by microphones and images are captured by cameras. The quality of sensor data depends on the sensor used.

The treatment of sensor data is called *signal processing*. If a computer tries to "understand" what a natural signal "means", then we call this process pattern recognition and analysis. The terms "image processing" and "speech processing" are used as general terms for signal processing as well as the analysis of images and speech. The relation between graphics and image analysis is shown in Figure 1.1. In this book, we cover image and speech processing and the recognition of visual and audio signals: this is different from algorithms that treat visualization or sound generation.

1.2 Applications of Pattern Recognition

Applications of pattern recognition can be found in several areas. For instance, industry, medicine, and the military make extensive use of pattern recognition techniques. Image processing of satellite images [Jäh93], automatic and computer-aided medical diagnosis based on X–ray or MR–images e.g. [Udu91], robot control using visual information [Rim91], and autonomous vehicles [Tal93] serve as common examples. Other applications are automatic postal address reading systems [Sch78] or the development of an electronic appointment diary [Bub96], where the interface is a system for handwritten character recognition. Bar code readers are commonly used in banks and shopping centers.

Acoustic communications with computers, dialogue systems, and speaker recognition are potential applications of speech processing. Already car telephones are available with which you can dial using just your voice.

Other applications may be found, for example, in seismic processing where the input signal comes from a seismic sensor. Other signals are processed in medicine such as sounds of the heart or signals from the brain (which have more similarity to speech processing than to image processing).

1.3 Environment, Problem Domain, and Patterns

Human beings use their eyes, ears, skin, nose, and taste buds as sensors to perceive their environment. These sensors provide our brains with the stimulation necessary for perception. Technically speaking, we model the environment as a large number of variables or dimensions, whose values cover a specific range that can be recorded by sensors like CCD cameras or microphones. Dimensions will not be considered, if they are not measurable by sensors.

Algorithmic approaches to pattern recognition problems require the presentation of a mathematical framework and a formalization of each problem domain being examined. We now briefly provide a general mathematical approach to pattern recognition [Nie90a].

We describe the environment U by the following set

$$U = \{\boldsymbol{b}_r(\boldsymbol{x}) | r = 1, 2, \ldots\} \quad , \tag{1.1}$$

using vector functions $\boldsymbol{b}_r(\boldsymbol{x})$. The dimension D_r of $\boldsymbol{b}_r(\boldsymbol{x}) \in \mathbb{R}^{D_r}$ may be different for every r. The components are by definition real numbers. To give some examples:

- $\boldsymbol{b}_1(x,y)$: sea-level (x = geogr. degrees longitude, y = geogr. degrees latitude)
- $\boldsymbol{b}_2(x,y,z)$: temperature, (x,y,z) position in 3–D space
- $\boldsymbol{b}_3(x,y,z,t)$: wind-force / wind-direction (vector!) of the 3–D position (x,y,z) at a certain time t

The aim of pattern recognition is not the description of the *complete* environment. Instead, we limit ourselves to special application domains or parts of the environment, i.e., the so called *problem domain* (or *task domain*) Ω:

$$U \supset \Omega = \{\boldsymbol{f}_r(\boldsymbol{x}) | r = 1, 2, \ldots\} \tag{1.2}$$

The dimensions of $\boldsymbol{f}_r(\boldsymbol{x})$ and $\boldsymbol{x}$ are now fixed and adjusted for each application. Examples are color still images, movies (image sequence), and speech:

- color image (three color channels red = 1, green = 2, blue = 3):
  $f_1(x,y), f_2(x,y), f_3(x,y)$
- TV image sequence (time dependent): $f_1(x,y,t), f_2(x,y,t), f_3(x,y,t)$
- speech signal: $f(t)$

Elements of the problem domain Ω are called *patterns* $\boldsymbol{f}_r(\boldsymbol{x})$ and they are represented as multivariate vector-functions

$$\boldsymbol{f}_r(\boldsymbol{x}) = \begin{pmatrix} f_{r_1}(x_1, x_2, \ldots, x_n) \\ f_{r_2}(x_1, x_2, \ldots, x_n) \\ \vdots \\ f_{r_m}(x_1, x_2, \ldots, x_n) \end{pmatrix} \quad . \tag{1.3}$$

Figure 1.2: Simple pattern (left), complex patterns (right)

1.4 Characterization of Pattern Recognition

H. Niemann characterizes the field of pattern recognition in [Nie90a; p.4] as follows:

> "Pattern recognition deals with the mathematical and technical aspects of automatic derivation of logical pictures of facts. At the present state of the art this comprises classification of simple patterns as well as analysis and understanding of complex patterns."

In general, the patterns we are working with can be divided up into different categories. On the left of Figure 1.2 an example for a simple pattern is presented. In contrast, the other image shows a more complex pattern; the scene shown has far more details and it is not clear from the beginning, what to look for on that picture. One might be interested in finding the autonomous robot shown in the center of the image; it could also be the task to count the number of windows in this room.

During the *analysis* process, an *individual* symbolic description is computed for each pattern. This description may be different for any two patterns. In pattern classification, a fixed label (namely the class index) is assigned to every pattern. Formal details are provided in chapter 8.

If simple patterns are given, our primary interest is in classifying the complete image into one class. A typical example is the recognition of written characters. The decomposition of images and a symbolic description of the observed scene appear during the analysis of a complex scene. A simple classification of a complex pattern is usually not useful since this will not be sufficient for a complete description of the scene. For instance, satellite images can be decomposed into regions — like "forest", "street", "water", and "town" — before a subsequent processing step begins. In some applications a general classification can still be the ultimate goal, for example, for the classification of a complicated medical image into "critical" or "healthy". For the analysis facial imags, as shown in Figure 1.3,[2] the result may be either a classification into "may enter" or "access denied" at an automatic gate, or a more complex

---

[2]All input images can be found in the internet, see Appendix B.8.

1.5 Speech Recording

Figure 1.3: Facial images

analysis of the face can be desired, such as determining the mouth contour for automatic lip reading.

1.5 Speech Recording

Before we describe how digital signals are computed from continuous ones, we will briefly introduce some basics of the recording of speech signals and images. Speech signals are usually recorded using microphones. The quality of a recording device can be measured partially by the signal to noise ratio (cf. Sect. 7.9). Microphones try to copy the mechanism of the human ear (see Figure 1.4), where a membrane (approximately 0.1 mm thick) is used to transform the sound. The human ear consists of three main parts:

- the outer,
- the middle,
- and the inner ear.

The outer ear consists of the ear lobe and the meatus. The ear lobe channels sound into the ear and supports the localization of sound sources. The meatus transmits the received sound signal to the middle ear drum, and its length is approximately 2.7 cm. This transmission channel can be considered as an acoustic tube with a resonance frequency of about 3000 Hz. As the tympanic membrane moves, so does the three bone structure (the bone chain). This results in a movement of the stapes of the middle ear and transmits the signal to the inner ear. Inside the cochlea, the main part of the inner ear, there is the so-called basilar membrane. This membrane converts the mechanical signal into the corresponding neural signal. A very interesting and important feature is the fact that different frequencies excite different parts of the basilar membrane. This allows the analysis of frequencies. For that reason, the ear is considered to work like a spectrum analyzer, and the use of spectral features for speech recognition purposes seems advantageous. However, the conversion of mechanical signals into neural signals works in a way that is not yet understood completely. Indeed, little is known about how the brain decodes the acoustic information it receives.

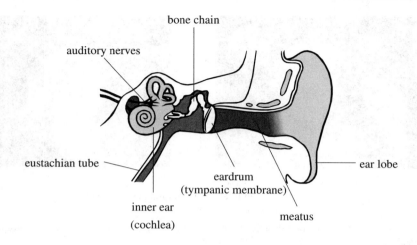

Figure 1.4: Human ear

In the case of microphones, a diaphragm is made to be stimulated by impulses in the frequency range from 10–25000 Hz. The diaphragm's physical movement is then converted to an electrical signal. Unfortunately, due to the mechanical parts in the transmission, the device does not respond to all frequencies equally. Digital filters can be used to compensate this effect. A typical speech signal recorded with a microphone is shown in Figure 1.5 (see [Ada83] for the meaning of that phrase).

1.6 Video Cameras and Projections

Many image processing systems use gray-level images as input data for their recognition and analysis algorithms. These images can be recorded by a video camera or similar sensors that project a three-dimensional scene onto a two-dimensional plane. We will consider two different kinds of projections here that are commonly used for modeling the real projection onto a CCD–chip. The most realistic way cameras capture images is by using perspective projection. This kind of projection is also the way that images are projected onto the retina of the human eye. The simplest model of a camera with perspective projection is the so-called *pinhole camera* (Figure 1.6).

In the pinhole camera model, we have a focal point lying behind an image plane. Three-dimensional points are projected onto points in an image plane in such a way that the lines starting from the focal point to the 3–D scene points intersect the image plane; this indicates the locations of the projected points. The resulting image coordinates (x_p, y_p) can be written in terms of the camera focal distance f and the three-dimensional object coordinates (x_c, y_c, z_c) in the following manner:

$$x_p = \frac{f\, x_c}{z_c} \qquad y_p = \frac{f\, y_c}{z_c}, \tag{1.4}$$

1.6 Video Cameras and Projections

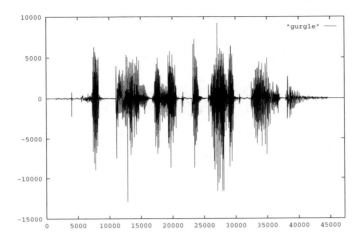

Figure 1.5: Part of the utterance "The pan galactic gurgle blaster".

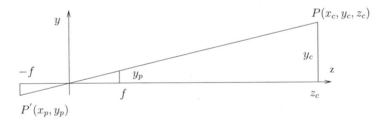

Figure 1.6: The pinhole camera model

where z_c represents the *depth* of the observed 3–D point. Of course, the pinhole camera model is only an approximation of the real physical system. The lens, for instance, may cause distortions such that straight lines of the real world do not appear as straight lines in the projection. Furthermore, the axes of the coordinate system associated with the CCD–chip are not necessarily orthogonal. All these parameters have to be considered within the projection equations. The computation of these intrinsic camera parameters is a highly nontrivial problem and a part of camera calibration procedures [Fau93, Tru98].

The so called *scaled orthographic projection* (or *weak perspective projection*) provides an approximation to perspective projection. Scene points are simply projected orthogonally from the observed three-dimensional scene onto the image plane. The projected point (x_p, y_p) of the 3–D point (x_c, y_c, z_c) is therefore (x_c, y_c). In fact, the orthographic projection results from the perspective projection by defining the focal distance to be infinite. This follows from (1.4) by

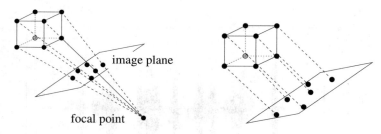

Figure 1.7: Perspective projection (left) and orthographic projection (right)

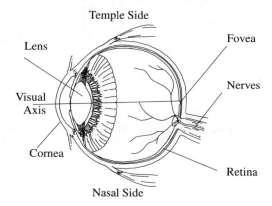

Figure 1.8: Human eye

setting $z_c := f + z$ and computing the limits:

$$x_p = \lim_{f \to \infty} \frac{f\, x_c}{f + z} = x_c \qquad y_p = \lim_{f \to \infty} \frac{f\, y_c}{f + z} = y_c \qquad (1.5)$$

In perspective projection, the size of the object in the image plane varies for different distances, so the resulting orthographic projection image has to be scaled by a factor to simulate the changes in perceived size. Nevertheless, weak perspective projection does not capture perspective distortion. Figure 1.7 shows the principles of perspective and orthographic projection in two dimensions.

Detailed discussions and comparisons of different projection models and their relationships can be found in [Alo90]. Due to the nonlinear projection equations in (1.4) many computer vision algorithms apply techniques from perspective geometry which allow the use of linear algebra to deal with perspective projections [Fau93, Kan93].

Human beings use their eyes for the perception of visual data. A cross section of the eye is shown in Figure 1.8. Indeed the projection model of eyes can by approximated by perspective projection. The image of the scene is projected through the pupil to the retina, which of course

1.7 From Continuous to Digital Signals

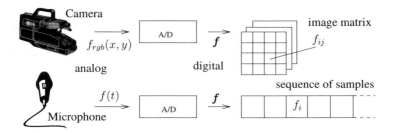

Figure 1.9: Analog/digital-conversion (A/D) for pattern recognition. The continuous signals $f(x, y)$ resp. $f(t)$ are converted to the discrete values f_{ij} resp. f_t.

is not plane; the resolution on the retina is also not constant, it is much higher in the area of the fovea. As in the case of microphones, the technical solution of image acquisition has many similarities in biology.

1.7 From Continuous to Digital Signals

The vectors (1.1) and (1.3) represent continuous signals. However, today's computer systems usually process digital data with finite precision. Therefore, we have to convert continuous to discrete signals by so-called A/D converters. Figure 1.9 shows an example of a color image converted to three discrete matrices and a transition of an analog speech signal to its digital version. For an obvious distinction between analog and digital signals it is necessary to introduce the following notation. For continuous signals we use $f(x, y)$ for two-dimensional and $f(t)$ for one-dimensional signals. For the discrete signals we make use of indices, i.e., f_{ij} resp. f_t for representing matrix and vector elements; for the vector we write $\boldsymbol{f}$.

In everyday life, we watch movies at the cinema which are composed of sequences of discrete images (25 images per second). Our brain does not recognize the discrete structure; we observe continuous sequences. This illustrates the aim of the so called *sampling theorem*. It seems to be sufficient to take a certain number of discrete states for the reconstruction, i.e., interpolation, of a continuous signal.

The conversion of continuous to discrete signals is characterized by two parameters:

1. The *sampling rate*, which follows immediately from the sampling theorem.
2. The *quantization* of the signal value, which is responsible for the quality of the sampled signal.

The quality of signals is measured by the *signal-to-noise-ratio* measured in decibels (dB). The sampling theorem states that after the transition of an analog signal to a digital version of a band limited signal with the frequency bound ω_G, the original signal can be exactly interpolated by a discrete sum, if the sampling period was lower than $1/(2\omega_G)$. The error of this quantization has to be zero. We will see more about this topic in Chapter 13 and Sect. 13.7.

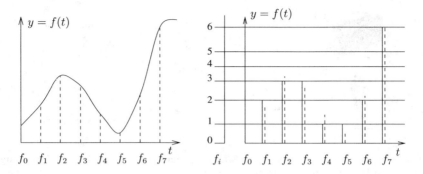

Figure 1.10: Sampling of a continuous 1–D signal (left); quantization (right): dashed lines illustrate sampling values, solid lines discrete values.

Of course for real signals, like natural speech, the band limitation is not generally satisfied. But band limitation can be forced artificially using band pass filters. If the sampling rate is too low, *aliasing* occurs.

The quantization aligns the range $\mathbb{R}$ of the continuous function to the discrete range $\{0, \ldots, N\}$. The discrete values result from the number of bits used in the binary representation of the discrete range. This situation is sketched in Figure 1.10. The sampling rate is the width of intervals on the time axis (Figure 1.10, left). The quantizations are the discrete steps on the y–axis and are determined by the characteristics of quantization (Figure 1.10, right). The characteristics can be expressed by the so called *characteristic line*, which does not have to be linear. Nevertheless, linear characteristics are satisfactory for practical purposes. The error of quantization can be computed using the distance between the continuous and discrete function values, e.g., the Euclidian distance. A more comprehensive mathematical discussion of the sampling theorem can be found e.g. in [Nie90a, Nie83].[3]

1.8 Sampling Theorem in Practice

For practical applications in image processing, quantization and sampling rate are usually nonparametric; the technical equipment, like CCD–chips or the resolution of a monitor, has fixed values for these parameters which cannot be modified by users. For images, the sampling rate is determined by the distance of the CCD elements on the chip. One additional difficulty is the fact that these pixels usually are not of quadratic shape (cf. Exercise 1.f).

In the field of speech recognition nonlinear quantization has noticeably improved the recognition quality; in many cases, logarithmic quantization is done as well [ST95].

For simplicity, we assume only linear quantization characteristics in the following chapters. The processed images will be gray-level images, i.e., they have just one channel.

---

[3]In the context of the Fourier transformation (Chapter 13) we will discuss this topic again.

1.9 Visualization and Sound Generation

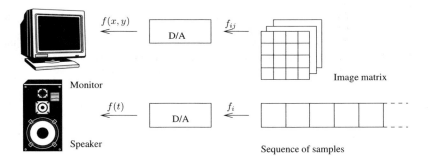

Figure 1.11: Digital/Analog-Conversion (D/A) for visualization and acoustic control. The discrete values f_{ij} resp. f_t are converted to analog signals $f(x,y)$ resp. $f(t)$.

The movie example introduced above is also suitable for showing the necessity of the sampling theorem and the connection between the sampling period and the limited frequency. Assume in a movie that shows 25 discrete images a second, you observe a wheel rotating with the frequency F. Everyone of us has observed the phenomenon: Depending on the speed of a car, the wheels rotate forward or backward. The explanation is simple using the sampling theorem. Only when the frequency F of the wheel is smaller than or equal to $25/2$, then it is possible to reproduce the continuous rotation of the wheel; if the frequency F is greater than the sampling rate of $25/2$, the continuous signals cannot be reconstructed. In these cases it is possible that the wheels seem to rotate backwards.

1.9 Visualization and Sound Generation

For visualization and acoustic control, e.g., in a multimedia application, we also need a conversion from digital to analog signals. This D/A–conversion is shown in Figure 1.11. Theoretically, the sampling theorem guarantees a faultless reconstruction of the continuous signal.

Typical problems occur, if the signal is visualized with another size than the original recording. In this case, care has to be taken that the sampling theorem is not violated.

Exercises

1.a   Verbally describe the pictures in Figure 1.3. What would be an appropriate symbolic description?

1.b   Which problems will arise with respect to the sampling theorem if a digital image has to be resized (shrunken or expanded)?

1.c   Let Ω be a discrete task domain of size n. How many different ways exist to define a k class partition on this set?

1.d   Which sampling rate is needed for a signal with a limited frequency of 10 kHz?

1.e Describe the effects of the sampling theorem on your audio, TV, and video equipment. Does the CD player obey the rules of the sampling theorem?

1.f Look up the horizontal and vertical size of your TV screen and your PC monitor in the technical documentation. Also check the number of pixels on these devices. Can these pixels have a quadratic shape? What is the ratio of width to height?

Chapter 2

From C to C++

In this chapter we start to do a quick transition from C to C++, treating C++ as an extension of ANSI–C [Joh93]. It will enable readers to write very simple C++ programs.[1] As stated in the introduction, the description of the language does not cover all the details: the syntax definitions are incomplete with respect to the language definition; they are complete, however, in the sense that they contain all the applications which can be found in this book. In Sect. 2.1 we introduce some notation to be used throughout this volume. In Sect. 2.2 we explain the basic principles for compilation and in Sect. 2.3 we show simple function calls. Some C++ extensions to C declaration syntax are listed in Sect. 2.4. Sect. 2.5 describes standard formatted input and output which is part of the C programming language and available in C++ as well. In the remaining sections of this chapter we describe basic features of C and set them in the new context for C++. Basic data types, the main program, function definition, and scope are described in the final sections.

2.1 Syntax Notation

The C programming language [Ker78] has become very popular and is used in many pattern processing systems. More recently, attention has shifted towards object-oriented programming. C++ is the natural choice for those who want to do object–oriented programming and have a C background or want to reuse their existing C program sources. Most ANSI–C programs will compile with the C++ compiler, i.e. they *are* themselves C++ programs. C programs of course, do not contain all the new object–oriented features which enrich the C++ language.

Some kind of notation has to be used when a new syntax for a programming language is to be introduced. We use the following simple syntactical conventions:

- syntactic structures in square brackets are optional,
- alternatives are separated by a bar " | ",
- an * indicates arbitrary repetition (including omission),

---

[1] ... as long as they don't ask too much about what's going on ... The new syntax will become clear later.

- if necessary, { } pairs are used to indicate what is to be repeated, or where the alternatives refer to
- a $^+$ indicates at least one repetition,
- terminal strings (i.e. those strings which will literally appear in the source code) are typed in `teletype` and are underlined.

An example including several of these features is shown in the syntax of floating point numbers. Verbally, it reads as "an integer number is a sequence of at least one digit, a real number can have either a sequence of digits before an optional dot followed by the fraction which may be omitted, or the integer part may be omitted, in which case the fraction must be present."

Syntax:
$digit := \underline{0} \mid \underline{1} \mid \underline{2} \mid \underline{3} \mid \underline{4} \mid \underline{5} \mid \underline{6} \mid \underline{7} \mid \underline{8} \mid \underline{9}$

$int\_number := digit^+$

$real\_number := \{int\_number^+ \underline{.} \ int\_number^*\} \mid \{int\_number^* [\underline{.}] \ int\_number^+\}$

$signed\_real\_number := [\{\underline{+} \mid \underline{-}\}] \ real\_number$

When an intuitive description is simpler than a formal definition, we either mix the style or use a verbal description only. The following is an example of a syntax definition for comments in C++.

Syntax: $comment := \underline{//} \ any \ text \ until \ end \ of \ line$

The syntax description do often not cover all variants but serve as a guideline for the most common cases. A complete formal definition of the C++ language can be found in the appendix of [Str97].

2.2 Principle of C++ Compilation

The source code of C++ programs and, similarly, of C programs is translated by a compiler. By convention, C source files have the extension .c and the C++ files end in .C.[2] Initially, sources are pre-processed by a program called cpp.[3] In this step all lines beginning with the symbol # are evaluated. Except for comments, no information other than pre-processor directives may be present on these lines.[4]

First, we consider the lines starting with #include followed by a filename in angle brackets as <system-file> or in quotes as in "personal-file". In both cases, a temporary file is generated by the compiler, where the corresponding system and personal files are explicitly inserted (gray box in Figure 2.1). By convention, included files usually have the extension

---

[2] Operating systems which do not distinguish upper and lower case letters in file names use .cxx and .cpp to denote C++ programs.

[3] Some non-Unix systems may call it differently or work without it. The principle of compilation is, however, the same. Usually, C code is pre-processed by a program called cpp; C++ compilers use the pre-processor as well.

[4] Some systems also allow compiler directives such as hints for optimization or parallel implementation here.

2.3 Function Calls and Arguments

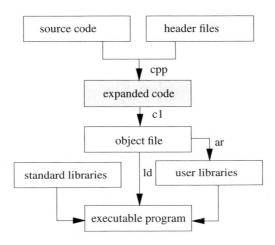

Figure 2.1: From source code to executable programs

".h"; they are called *header-files*. The path entries of the compiler are searched for the files included by #include <file>. When #include "file" is used, the compiler searches for the file in the current directory first, before looking at the default compiler path.

Most of the files searched for by <file.h> are part of the environment for the compiler or operating system. They may be found at a common place for all users of the system. Private files "file.h" will often be used by only one user.

The temporary file produced is then compiled successively by one or more programs contained in the compiler. Usually, two compiler passes produce an object module, which has the extension .o or .obj. Executables are then created by a linker which resolves external symbols from the system libraries and adds the interface to the operating system. Alternatively, the object module may be added to create or modify a library (usually with extension .a of .lib). Figure 2.1 shows the data flow of the compile process annotated by the required programs.[5]

2.3 Function Calls and Arguments

We now present a brief introduction to C and C++ functions and their arguments. In doing so, we concern ourselves solely with how to deal with constant arguments and function call syntax; the remaining details about functions are given later (Sect. 2.8). Here is a very simple example of a program (see Listing 1).[6] It consists of a main function (always called main) and a pre-processor directive (#include). The code is syntactically correct both in C and C++.

---

[5] If dynamic linkage is used (so called "shared libraries"), the resolution of external symbols from the libraries happens at program runtime or when starting the program. Building such libraries requires special treatment which is described in compiler manuals.

[6] The examples for programs are numbered consecutively. An index can be found on 374.

```
#include <stdio.h>      /* pre-processor include directive */
#include <stdlib.h>     /* pre-processor include directive */
main()                  /* definition of function: main */
{                       /* begin block */
    puts("hello\n");    /* function call of puts with
                           constant string argument */
    exit(0);            /* exit gracefully */
}                       /* end block */
```
1

The file stdio.h allows the inclusion of common input and output functions (I/O) by inserting their declarations into the source code.[7] The imported file is placed within the compiler environment and is inserted in the program by the pre-processor.

Input and output functions are not part of the *syntax* definition of C++. They are made available from standard *libraries* via function calls. The function call puts stands for *put string* and prints its sole argument on the screen; the program, when executed, will produce the output "hello" followed by a new line. The compiler "knows" about this function because it is declared in the file stdio.h. A call to the function exit with argument 0 ends the execution and flushes all open files. By convention, the argument 0 indicates proper program termination, whereas any other value would indicate some sort of error condition. The compiler knows about this function from the declaration found in stdlib.h.

Note that a function can be called by just giving its name.[8] The arguments that are passed to the function must be enclosed in parentheses. In Figure 1 we see a function with only one argument; later, we will use functions with several arguments separated by commas and sometimes even functions with a variable number of arguments.

Actually, main is also a function. The program above *defines* the function main; the other functions referred to are only called and but defined elsewhere. Their definitions are attached to the executable by linking it with the system libraries (see Figure 2.1).

2.4 Declaration and Definition of Variables

In C++, each identifier for either variable of function has to be declared before it can be used. The *declaration* merely introduces the name and its associated attributes to the compiler. The *definition* of a variable, however, requests a storage location for the value as well; the definition also serves as a declaration.

- In C, variables have to be declared and defined at the beginning of a block. C++ allows this nearly everywhere,[9] since declarations are now syntactically treated as statements. The declaration is valid only inside the current block.

- If identifiers are declared outside of functions, they are *global* and are valid in every function following the declaration. Global variables should be used very carefully.

---

[7]Of course, streams in C++ are safer and nicer (Sect. 16.3). But for teaching purposes we explain standard function calls rather than introducing things like cout << without proper preparation.

[8]As in Pascal and other languages based on the ideas of Algol 60.

[9]In the following chapters we will note occasional exceptions, where declarations are not allowed.

```
int i;                      // definition of i uninitialized!!
long l = 3, l2 = -4L;       // definition and initialization
char * str0 = "abc";        // string variables are char *
char * str1 = "cde",        // a string
     * str2 = "ax",         // another string
       c    = 'a';          // this is not a string!
const int ci = 3;           // regular integer
```

Fundamental data types in C and C++ are `char`, `short`, `int`, `long`, `float`, and `double` with their `unsigned` variants for the integer types. Variables of fundamental data types can be defined and initialized at the same time. The initialization's validity will not be checked by all compilers (i.e., uninitialized variables will not always produce a compiler warning).

The basic syntax of the variable definition is as follows:

Syntax: [`const`] *type* [*ptr*] *var1* [= *val*] [, [*ptr*] *var2* [= *val*]]* ;

This means that we first specify the type of an identifier, and optionally, *something* which will be introduced later (called `ptr` here) followed by the identifier's name. Optionally, we may then list any additional identifiers. Any of the variables in the list may be initialized to the value given after the "=" sign. It is recommended that all variables are initialized immediately along with the definition. The relaxed placement rules for declarations (with respect to C) simplify this task, since some computation can be programmed in between two subsequent declarations and definitions.

Listing 2 shows some definitions and declarations. Strings are denoted by `char *` and can be assigned a constant value; the `*` is repeated for the subsequent definitions; the `*` corresponds to the `ptr` in the above program fragment. Strings are explained in detail in Sect. 5.6. In the last line, `str1` and `str2` are strings, whereas `c` is a single character. Constant values — such as the variable `ci` in the example — can be declared as such with the keyword `const`; they have to be initialized immediately where they are declared. Long integer constants are given as a sequence of digits followed optionally by an `L`.

2.5 Unix-File Access via Standard Functions

Most (useful) programs need some sort of input and output. The C–language was developed together with the Unix operating system. Input and output were originally separated from the language definition. However, most programmers use the standard interface provided in the `stdio.h` header file.

The Unix naming conventions and the basic philosophy for file and terminal I/O were used when C was ported to other operating systems (even to MS-DOS). We may thus talk about files as if we all were using Unix.

Unix offers — as one of its remarkable features — a uniform file concept which includes directories and devices in a homogeneous way. Access of files in C is done by function calls. C++ encapsulates the I/O operations by streams.[10] The `stdio`–interface is, however, still

---
[10] This will be treated in Sect. 16.3.

```
const char * terminal = "/dev/tty";    // constant string
FILE * tty = fopen(terminal,"w");      // open console output
fclose(tty);                           // close the file
```
 3

%x	output of integer value hexadecimal
%d	output of integer value decimal
%ld	output of long-value decimal
%c	output of character
%s	output of string
%%	output of %
%f	output of double or float value as integer plus fraction
%e	output of double or float value scientific notation

Table 2.1: Format control strings

available in C++ allowing existing C routines to be reused. Three channels in Unix exist which are always ready for input and output; they are referred to as a FILE*:[11]

- stdout: this is the destination for regular output, (output may be delayed due to buffering)
- stdin: this is the primary source for input (e.g. from the keyboard),
- stderr: errors should be printed here; they will be printed instantly, i.e. no buffering.

New output and input channels are opened by a function call to fopen with two string arguments: the first is the file name and the second is the access mode ("w" for write and "r" for read).[12] Existing files will be destroyed by the use of "w"! The function fclose closes a channel which was opened by fopen; the argument is the FILE* (see Listing 3).

The function printf prints to the current standard output device (stdout). It provides a general facility for the conversion of data to text. The declaration of this function is included in the file stdio.h. The number of arguments to this function is dependent on the first argument, which is used to format the text. In this string, there may be several substrings beginning with a percent sign (%) which are treated specially. The characters immediately following the percent sign determine the format of the text and the type of the required arguments (Table 2.1). The actual arguments corresponding to those specified in that string are listed next. For every percent sign, except for %% which prints a percent sign (Listing 4), there is one argument.[13] Further options exist for the format string but are less commonly used.

The percent sign can be followed by a numerical value specifying the length of the output text. This value precedes the character of the specified type. The output length of integers and strings can be given as integer values. Negative values for width means left adjustment. Floats and doubles are formatted using float values; the number before the decimal point specifies the

---

[11] What type is a FILE? What does the * mean? As we told you, don't worry, if you do not know yet (see footnote 1 on p. 17)!

[12] Depending on the operating system, there may be more choices or the distinction for binary and text mode.

[13] Another exception is %* not mentioned in the table (cf., for example, [Str97; p. 357]).

```
int i = 30;   float f = 1.3;
printf("%d students were marked %f\n", i, f);
printf("%s%c %f %%\n", "that i", 's', 33.0);
```
4

```
printf("%5d students were marked %3.1f\n", i, f);
printf("%-20s %7.2f %%\n", "that is ", 33.0);
```
5

overall width and the value after the decimal point stands for the number of decimal places (Listing 5).

The additional first argument of the function `fprintf` specifies the output file. A function call to `fprintf(stdout,...)` and `printf(...)` is equivalent (Listing 4 and Listing 6).

One basic property of this input/output concept is that data transfered to files is buffered, i.e. not every read or write function call will immediately result in some disk access. As a consequence, an output to `stdout` will not directly show up on the screen. The error channel (`stderr`), however, is unbuffered.[14] Alternatively, the function call `fflush(stdout)` can be used to print all information currently accumulated in the buffer.

2.6 Numeric Expressions

For `short`, `int`, `float`, `long`, and `double` the binary operators `+`, `-`, `*`, `/` have their usual intuitive semantics. The operator precedence is identical to the operator rules of mathematics, i.e. `*` and `/` bind tighter than `+` and `-`; parentheses are used for grouping as well. Exponentiation does not exist as an operator in C++.

Mathematical operations are also admissible for variables of type `char`. Characters are converted to integers in C and treated as small integers in C++. Range checking and the overflow of integers are not detected by the system at runtime so if data-types are mixed in an expression, an automatic adjustment of types is performed.[15] This process is known as *implicit conversion*. Automatic type conversion is a complicated topic. We recommend, therefore, to use explicit conversion whenever in doubt.

The C++ syntax for type conversion is simple and looks like a function call:

Syntax: *type (expression)*

When the type cast to is not a simple type name, e.g. in `(byte **) ptr`, the old C–syntax can still be used:

---
[14]This is important and useful when you trace a program with control output!
[15]There exist different rules for conversion in C and C++, due to the fact that in C, for example, there is no `char`–valued expression.

```
int errno = -1;
fprintf(stdout,"%5d students were marked %3.1f \n", i, f);
fprintf(stderr,"Fatal Error %d\n",errno);
```
6

```
int     i = 3 * 5;                  // value: 15
float   f = 0.7 + 3;                // value: 3.7
int     j = int(f) * ( i + 2 );     // value: 51
int     k = static_cast<int>(f);    // value: 3
```
　　　　　　　　　　　　　　　　　　　　　　　　　　　　　　　7

```
#include <stdio.h>  /* will not C++ compile without it! */
main(int argc, char ** argv)
{
   int i = argc;
   char * progname = argv[0];
   FILE * of = fopen("/dev/tty", "w");
   fprintf(of,"Program \"%s\" %d args\n", progname, i-1);
   exit(0);
}
```
　　　　　　　　　　　　　　　　　　　　　　　　　　　　　　　8

Syntax:　　(*type*) *expression*

New compilers now support the `static_cast` syntax:[16]

Syntax:　　`static_cast<` *type* `>(` *expression* `)`

Conversion from `float` or `double` to integer types truncates to the appropriate range. When rounding is required, add 0.5 to the `float` value. Conversion and casts are shown in Listing 7.

Instructions are terminated with semicolons. The assignment operator is "=". Integer division is performed with "/" when the operands are integers; the modulus operation is "%".

2.7 Main Program

The function main has to be defined once in each complete C++ program. This function represents the main part of the program (see also Listing 1). Usually, it is defined with two arguments called `argc` and `argv`. Theses variables contain the arguments given by the operating system interface (e.g. the command line processor). The variable `argc` contains the number of arguments; `argv` provides the locations of the argument strings (cf. Sect. 5.9 for more details). The first value is the name of the program (as it is known to the operating system); it is referred to as `argv[0]`, i.e., `argc` is always greater than 0.

In Listing 8, the variable `i` is defined and initialized to the number of arguments. A string variable `progname` will be assigned the name of the program. An output file is opened with a fixed name (a device in Unix). The program name and the number of arguments are printed to this file which is then closed automatically before the end of execution of the program by the call to the `exit` routine. It is, however, good practice to close all open files explicitly. Also, note that \" in the format string of the `fprintf` function call enables " to print.

---

[16]For classes (Chapter 10) and other user-defined types, the `dynamic_cast` can be used which uses runtime type information (Sect. 16.8). For pointers (Sect. 6.2), the `reinterpret_cast` is used. The syntax of these conversion is the same as for the `static_cast`.

```
void printij(int i,int j)           // definition
{                                   // function body
    if (i < 0) return;              // conditional return
    printf("I is %d, J is %d\n", i, j); // print something
}                                   // return
main()                              // main function
{                                   // body
    printij(1,2);                   // call other function
}                                   // return
```
9

2.8 Function Definition

Modular programs split the code into functions and procedures which group a series of statements or expressions together. Functions are used in expressions and may return a value; procedure calls are considered statements in their own right. Their actions can be controlled by *parameters* called *arguments* for functions.

The `void` type is a key word and prefixes a `procedure`[17] declaration in C++. A procedure definition in C++ looks like the following:

Syntax: `void` *identifier* `(` [*type argument* [`,`*type argument*]*] | `void` `)` *block*

The block in the procedure definition is called the *body* of the function. A function may be called using its name followed by a possibly empty list of arguments included in parentheses; instead of an empty argument list, the key word `void` can also be written. The arguments have to correspond in number and type to the list given in the declaration. These arguments are passed to the function and their values are substituted for the variables in the function body.[18] The control returns to the location following the call after termination of the function. This happens when the last statement of the function body is executed or upon encountering a `return` statement, as shown in Listing 9. It is admissible for functions to call themselves, i.e., recursion is possible.

Functions may have a return value. This already happened in Listing 8 where the variable `out` was initialized with the return value from the call to `fopen`. The syntax for functions is as follows:

Syntax:

returntype identifier `(` [*type argument* [`,`*type argument*]*] | `void` `)` *block*

The execution of the function can be terminated at any point inside the function body with a `return` statement that now has to specify a value to be passed back:

Syntax: `return` *expression*

The expression has to be of the type given by the *return type* in the function declaration. The use of functions is demonstrated in Listing 10; this also shows how access is made to command line arguments. The (external) function `atoi` has one string argument taken from the

---
[17]The term *procedure* is used here as in Pascal. Procedures are functions that do not return a value.
[18]At this point we consider only passing arguments by value. Later we will see other possible mechanisms (Sect. 6.3).

```
int sign(int i)                    // sign function definition
{
    if (i < 0) return -1;          // case 1
    if (i == 0) return 0;          // case 2
    return 1;                      // otherwise
}
int main(int argc, char ** argv)   // main function
{
    int j=argc+sign(atoi(argv[1])); // function calls
    return 0;
}
```
10

```
void a(int);                             // declaration
void b(int,int);                         // declaration
void a(int i)      { /* ... */ b(i,1); } // definition
void b(int i,int j) { /* ... */ a(i); }  // definition
```
11

command line. It *returns* an integer value — namely the conversion of its string argument to a number. The return from the `main` function calls `exit` and terminates the program. For regular termination of the program this is the preferred method in C++ (cf. Sect. 10.4).

If the return type is omitted from a function definition (as in the previous examples with the functions `main`), it is assumed for historical reasons to be of type `int`. It would be better to replace all definitions of `main` by `int main` in the examples. If the use of a function is intended where no return value is needed, then the function should be declared as `void`; this will disallow its use in expressions.

Since procedures are just special cases of functions — returning the type `void` — in the following we talk about functions and arguments only and omit the terms *procedure* and *parameters*.

2.9 Scope and Lifetime

As already noted, identifiers have to be declared prior to their use. Functions, for example, may be declared first and then defined later. In this way it becomes possible for two or more functions to call each other mutually (Listing 11).

The name of a variable becomes known to the compiler as soon as it compiles the declaration statement. Variables declared inside a block are invisible from the outside. The value and the storage location of these variables is lost when the block is exited. It will be reallocated upon reentering the block where the declaration occurs.[19]

Declarations outside of any function are called *global*. These names are visible in any function following the declaration. It is considered bad programming style to use many global variables across different files.

As in many other programming languages, the name of a variable that has already been declared outside of a given block may be reused within this block for a completely different purpose.

---

[19]Depending on compiler implementations.

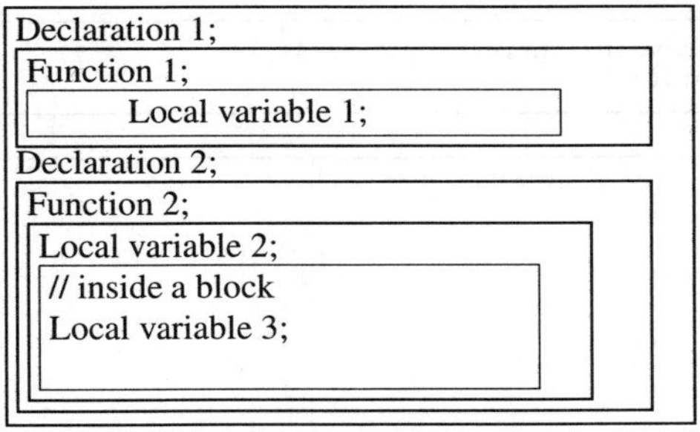

2.9 Scope and Lifetime

```
┌─────────────────────────────────────┐
│ Declaration 1;                      │
│ Function 1;                         │
│   ┌─────────────────────────────┐   │
│   │ Local variable 1;           │   │
│   └─────────────────────────────┘   │
│ Declaration 2;                      │
│ Function 2;                         │
│   ┌─────────────────────────────┐   │
│   │ Local variable 2;           │   │
│   │   ┌─────────────────────┐   │   │
│   │   │ // inside a block   │   │   │
│   │   │ Local variable 3;   │   │   │
│   │   └─────────────────────┘   │   │
│   └─────────────────────────────┘   │
└─────────────────────────────────────┘
```

Figure 2.2: Declaration inside blocks

```
int v, w, x;                  // global variables (bad style!)
void fct(int v, int w, int k) // global v,w will be invisible
{
  int x;                      // will overwrite global x
  { int w; }                  // will overwrite argument w
}
```
[12]

The closest declaration (with respect to scope) will be the one referenced to within the block. In Figure 2.2, we depict functions by two nested blocks; the first introduces the names of the arguments, the second corresponds to the function body. Inside a function, the argument names can overwrite global name bindings. Inside the function body, new declarations may then introduce new names. Declaration 1 will be known in Functions 1 and 2. Declaration 2 will be known only in Function 2. Local variable 1 will be visible only in Function 1. Local variable 2 will be visible only in Function 2. Listing 12 shows how variable names can be overwritten in nested blocks and by function definitions. Such style — of course — does not improve the readability of your code!

If a local variable is tagged `static`, it will keep its value even if the program control passes out of the block (Listing 13). When the block is entered again, the variable will be accessible with its old value. The name, however, is nevertheless invisible from the outside. If a global variable is tagged `static`, its name will be known only inside the current module.[20]

---

[20] Using namespaces (Sect. 16.8), this traditional feature can be avoided.

```
void fct()
{  static int counter = 0;                  // keep the value
   printf("fct called for the %d-th time\n", ++counter);
}
```
[13]

```
char*s="char*s=%c%s%c;main(){printf(s,34,s,34);}";
main(){printf(s,34,s,34);}
```
14

```
#define BEGIN {
#define END }
#define IF if(
#define THEN )
#define ELSE   else
main ()
BEGIN
     int i = 1;
     IF i < 0
     THEN BEGIN i = 0; END
     ELSE i = 1;
END
```
15

Exercises

2.a Write a program that prints your address including the date and place of your birth and your profession into a file named "my_address". Try different ways of formatting the output!

2.b Arguments can be passed from the command line to a program as program execution begins. The variable `argv` contains all parameters given on the command line when the program was called. The ith argument can be retrieved by `argv[i]`. Standard functions are provided for converting strings to integers or floats such as `atoi` and `atof` respectively.
The following line assigns the converted first argument string to the variable `i`:

`int i=atoi(argv[1]); // assign return value of call`

Similarily, `atof` can be used to convert to a `double`:

`double d=atoi(argv[2]); // assume float argument`

Write a program that prints its number of arguments and interprets the first argument as an integer `i`. Also print the ith argument.

2.c What happens if you provide an illegal value of `i` at runtime, (e.g. you provide the argument line "4 a b")?[21] Will the system warn you?

2.d What is the shortest complete C++ program?

2.e Try to understand the following C–program listed in Listing 14.
Run the program and send the output to a file! Can you invent something similar?
Why is it a C program and not a C++ program?

2.f *Syntactic Macros*
It is tempting for a Pascal programmer to write a program as in Listing 15. This is, however, bad programming style for C++ and C. In particular, some tools like the "C–beautifier" `cb` will not work with this code.
Rewrite this program to standard C++. Pascal programers also note the if—else syntax; there is no `then`!

---

[21] Be sure to remove the file `core` if you create one!

Chapter 3
Software Development

In this chapter we introduce the basic principles of software development with a special emphasis on pattern recognition programs and object–oriented programming. Basic concepts of documentation and program design are also explained.

3.1 Software for Pattern Recognition

Digital images, represented as matrices of fixed size, are the basic data for computer vision. Usually, gray-level images have 256^2 or 512^2 pixels with 256 different gray-levels, i.e. each image contains, 64 KBytes resp. 256 KBytes of data. For color images, such as RGB–images with three color channels, three-dimensional arrays are required for representing an image. The number of two-dimensional arrays needed for color images depends on the number of color channels. For motion analysis, an image sequence of 25 images per second has to be processed. If we use 512^2 color images, one second of the image stream requires 18.75 MBytes.

Speech recognition algorithms are based on a *sequence* of sample values. When considered as a certain interval of time, these sequences can be interpreted as vectors. Very often, the sample frequency of speech signals is 16 kHz with a quantization of 12 or 16 Bits. Consequently, the amount of information per second is 23.4 to 31.25 KBytes.

These examples show the large amount of data pattern that recognition algorithms have to process, i.e., the data segment of an executable program will be large. Implementations of pattern recognition systems are often huge programs with many lines of source code, i.e., the code segment will be large as well. Even if the systems described in this book seem to be small, they will rapidly grow in size if they are applied to real world problems. Therefore, it is essential that the rules of good software production be strictly obeyed.

Large systems must have a sufficient amount of documentation concerning their behavior in order to be useful for other users. To facilitate further improvements, the code should have been extensively commented by its implementors. The structure of such systems must be modular and this modularity should be based upon recent developments in the field of software-engineering. Each programmer contributes a small part of the complete system, using all implemented modules. It is crucial to guarantee compatibility between program code, documentation, and comments as well.

3.2 Software Development and Testing

Figure 3.1 shows the classical cycle of software development. CASE–tools (*C*omputer *A*ided *S*oftware *E*ngineering) make it possible to generate code automatically during the planning and design phases. Additionally, automatic code generation influences its own documentation.

With the analysis of the problem, we also start with the documentation of the software (box 0). The documentation is finished within the final version of the code (box 10).

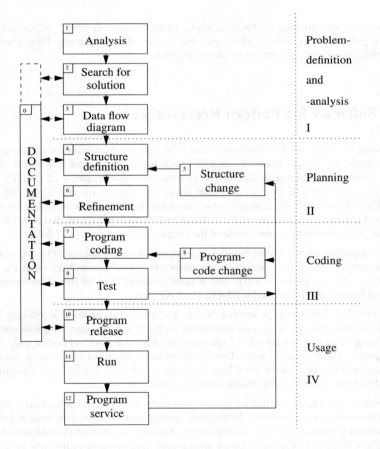

Figure 3.1: Classical cycle of software development

Small errors in the source code are taken into consideration in box 7–9. If errors are found (e.g. when debugging, box 9), we will proceed with box 8. More serious problems, e.g. logical mistakes, make a complete revision necessary, as depicted in box 5.

In the first phase of a project a computer is not needed. In the planning phase (box 4–6), the computer can be used for supporting the work because there are software tools available to generate structograms (see below) or flow diagrams. The test phase of the program is generally done in a development environment using *debugging* tools.

The common principle of *stepwise refinement* for software development can be seen in box 4 and box 6. Here we start with an abstract top-level description of the problem, e.g., a function interface with a dummy implementation, and then iteratively refine the implementation, adding new functions and supplying the code for the dummy functions.

Object–oriented programming is associated with the keywords "class", "object", and "inheritance" and will be discussed in more detail in Chapter 9. Several changes in the classical development cycle and the terminology were introduced in the course of object–oriented programming. In order to judge the improvement gained by object–oriented software, it is useful to know about the classical ideas and principles for software development.

The test phase is a very crucial part of software design and programming. It should not be ignored, neglected, or underestimated. Systematically organized tests will increase the reliability of software for real-world applications. Problems not considered during the analysis might be detected during tests. A general problem is the following fact:

> Tests can reveal the existence of errors, but tests cannot prove their non-existence.

The more you test, however, the lower will be the chance that there is a hidden bug in your code. Some general guidelines will help you testing your software:[1]

1. Each branch in the program should be activated at least once during the test. This comprises the parts for rare error conditions as well!
2. Every loop should be used at least twice.
3. Try to imagine irregular, unexpected, wrong, inconsistent input and test your routines with such data, for example, images of size 1×10000 or even of size 0×0; a speech signal sampled with 1MHz or 1Hz.
4. Use more than one data set for testing.
5. Use at least one data set as input for which you know the expected output of the program.
6. Test predictable special cases, such as discontinuities of functions, division by numbers close to zero, etc.
7. Keep in mind the limitations of resources, such as storage or execution time. Estimate the required resources.

There are some cases in which one can formally prove the behavior of functions and routines; this is called program verification. In real world problems, such proofs are usually very hard or even impossible.

---
[1]Collected from the world wide web, from lecture notes, and from personal experience.

3.3 Modular and Structured Programming

Obeying the principles of modular programming, we generally split program source code into several parts. Most often, implementation code is considered separately from the interfaces that will influence it. In C/C++, header files are used to share common interfaces between different modules.

Unfortunately, C++ does not enforce that the sharing of variables and data is controlled by a clean interface definition. Global variables used by several modules create dependencies which are often hard to understand.

The flow of information naturally follows the statements in the source code. Unconditional jumps (in C/C++ this means the use of `goto`) are bad practice. Function calls return to the statement following the calling statement. They modify only what is specified in the function definition. Modifications of global variables should be the exception (due to potential "side effects") and should be well documented.

We state the following default rules for programming:

- no `goto`'s,
- no side effects of function calls, and
- no global variables.

The aim of modularizing programs is guided by well defined interfaces (in C/C++: the use of header files). The principle of local changes states that as long as the interfaces are not involved in those changes, the changes have no (undesirable) influence on other modules. Well defined dependencies for source code fragments and interchangeability of modules are primary goals of modularization.

3.4 Comments and Program Layout

Comments in source code are neglected by many programers. Nevertheless, good and sufficient comments aid in the reuse and maintenance of software. Programs should at least contain text covering the following:[2]

- description of the module (description of the file, revision number, state of the project, name of the author, etc.)
- description of the functions, their arguments, and their semantics,
- description of the main part of the program including the command line options.

Mnemonic identifiers for variables and files as well as comprehensible comments should be used; this supports and facilitates documentation and the chance of producing reusable software.[3]

---

[2] Some of this information can be added automatically, e.g. by `rcs` (A.4, Sect. 3.7, Exercise 3.d).

[3] We once got a program, properly commented and documented, doing its job perfectly — but the variable names were all in a foreign language...

Proper indentation of code lines makes the code a lot more readable. Usually, statements in the same block of code are lined up vertically. New blocks are indented by one tab position.[4]

C++ assists commenting with its a syntax; comments can be added to the end of each line (see page 18). It is highly recommended to add terse and descriptive notes to each code line, or at least to each group of closely related lines (e.g. one comment for a small loop is usually ideal).

3.5 Documentation

The components of useful documentation are textual descriptions of the program semantics as well as the abstract structure of the modules and interfaces.

The flow of control can be visualized by structograms as introduced in [Jen85]. Be careful to avoid the use of C syntax within graphical visualizations of algorithms; this description should be an *alternative* to reading program code. The basic components of structograms are blocks which can be nested or stacked on each other. A sequence of statements is called a *block* and can be depicted as in Figure 3.2.

```
statement
...
statement
```

Figure 3.2: Structogram element for sequential execution

Three types of loops are shown in Figure 3.3. The FOR loop is used for iteration, the WHILE loop checks the condition before the loop is entered, and the UNTIL loop checks it at the end, i.e. the loop is executed at least once in an UNTIL loop.

Figure 3.3: Three types of loops

The graphical presentation of a branching in the flow of control shown in Figure 3.4 is not the standard form, but available in the strukto–TEX–style.[5] For more than two branches (i.e., for a switch), another component is available which is not shown here.

Algorithms designed using structograms will almost automatically result in well structured code. There is no way to express a goto in a structogram!

Data flow can be documented with data flow diagrams. Especially in object–oriented systems, special care has to be taken regarding the documentation of data structures. Entity-Relation

---

[4]For C and C++ two styles for indentation are common. Most Unix systems provide the program cb which is a C–beautifier. Therefore it makes little sense to invent your own style! See the manual of this program for the description of the styles.

[5]Available from most TEX–archives.

IF	condition
THEN	block
ELSE	block

Figure 3.4: Conditional execution

Diagrams (ER) which are common in data base design can be used. Modern object–oriented software development provides extensions of these ideas (Sect. 9.1).

When function definitions, variables, and data structures have to be documented, the problem of consistency arises, as descriptions have to be provided which refer to information in source files; often, programmers have to change the source code and forget to update the documentation. We experienced that program documentation which is kept in separate files from the source code almost never reflects the actual status of the project. Therefore we put all the documentation into the source and header files, as close as possible to the implementation. Consistency of documentation with the actual programs was enhanced considerably. There are programs which do this job nicely, e.g. a system called `doxygen` (Appendix B.1).

3.6 Teamwork

The design and implementation of large or huge software systems, such as for image analysis or speech processing, cannot be finished by a single person. Such work will only succeed if the project is properly coordinated and planned.

We have to partition the complete problem into independent parts, and define the interfaces of each partition. For implementation purposes, modules and classes are suitable concepts for information hiding. If more than one person modifies the files, we need to implement version and access control. This guarantees that no conflicts will occur – for example, when two partners edit the same file at the same time. Furthermore, all changes and their authors should be taken down.

Basically, ther are two strategies for administration. Either, each member of the team works on his private *copy* of the sources; at certain stages, he commits his changes to the global repository of the sources merging his updates with the changes of others which have occured since he made his private copy. Or, all members of the team work on the *same* sources.

The first solution requires mechanisms to resolve conflicts of changes. The CVS system (Appendix B.1) provides automatic tools for managing information in the described way. The second solution requires locking facilities, so users can change information without interfering with each other. This can be done with `rcs`, a system which will be describe further below. For beginners, we recommend to start with `rcs`.

Comments in the program will provide details on the version number, the status, the author, etc. of a module. Keywords will be used to denote these informations. Some of this information can be filled in automatically, as outlined in Appendix A.4.

3.7 Tools for Software Development

Unix is more than just an operating system kernel that provides an interface between the user and the hardware. Unix also includes several tools for program development which are not directly related to the hardware. For example, the operating system itself provides facilities for teamwork. Unix groups can be built who share rights on individual files or directories. File locking mechanisms are present to avoid conflicts. Such mechanisms are also available for other recent operating systems.

For software development, the following features and commands are useful for software production, especially in a team with shared resources:

- `groups` (ask your system administrator)
- `newgrp` (change your current group in system V based Unix)
- `umask` (can be set to grant access to a group by default)

The following tools are useful for every programmer. They should be used in any project, no matter whether in a team or working alone.

- `make` is a program maintenance tool. `make` will do all the required actions such as compiling or linking after a change in the program source code or generating new documentation automatically.
- `rcs` is the abbreviation for "revision control system". `rcs` will record your changes and in addition grant or deny access to source files shared by several users. Various related tools exist.

In appendix A we briefly describe these common Unix tools which are also available on almost any other computer operating system.

3.8 Efficiency

Efficient programming is often neglected by computer programmers. It is, however, very important for image and speech processing. Especially for real-time processing of images and speech, the huge amounts of data require efficient code. Efficiency has to be a major *design goal* for image and speech analysis programs and should almost never interfere with structured and clean programming. Any "dirty tricks" have to be well commented and should have only local influence on the program. [Sch90] gives some examples of efficiency considerations for segmented programs.

The test phase of a program (box 9 in Figure 3.1) reveals inefficient parts of a program which have to be changed. High modularity helps to keep the required updates local. On modern computer processors, the costs of calling a function and passing arguments to it are small and performed in few processor cycles. When the function called computes more than just a trivial expression, the relative computation time of the function body is high compared to the time needed for calling and returning. Thus, no reduction of the efficiency is to be expected if programs split the code in many small functions, which are in turn easier to be optimized.

C++ additionally provides functional syntax and semantics even for trivial computations, which can be executed *without* loss of efficiency (Sect. 6.7).[6] Efficiency is one reason for C to be used in so many image and speech processing systems. C++ seems to be the right extension as it keeps the speed and adds a lot to structuring and modularization.

Another general idea, the approximation of functions, influences the performance of a system. We describe this idea in a wider contex now.

3.9 Approximation

Efficiency of programs is a crucial issue and far too often neglected by programmers. Especially in image and speech processing, the overall runtime behavior of the final system is important for its success.

Many pattern recognition applications require rather complex computations and many evaluations of computationally expensive functions. For instance, in computer vision applications we have to evaluate trigonometric functions (see Sect. 15.4) or for classification purposes we need the computation of logarithms (see Chapter 22).

Commonly accepted and applied techniques to reduce the complexity of numerical computations are:

- The approximation of computationally expensive (uni– or multivariate) functions by simple (uni– or multivariate) functions like polynomials.
- The usage of a look-up table (LUT) where prior computed function values are stored.

The complexity of polynomals is well understood, for instance, and there exist highly efficient algorithms for the evaluation of polynomials [Knu73]. If there is enough memory available, look-up tables with an appropriate accuracy should be prefered because some functions cannot be approximated by a polynomial. A simple application of these techniques illustrates the following example.

Let us consider the perspective projection as introduced in Sect. 1.6. The projection of a single 3-D point $p = (x, y, z)^T$ into the image plane requires the computation of a fraction:

$$p' = \begin{pmatrix} fx/z \\ fy/z \end{pmatrix} . \qquad (3.1)$$

If the range of the depth z is known in advance, we might consider the approximation of the ratio $1/z$ by a linear function or by a look-up table. Multiplication and summation or the access of list elements are usually much more efficient than the computation of fractions.

Let us assume the depth of the considered 3-D points is in the range of $u = 10$ to $v = 11$, i.e. $z \in [u, v]$. The linear function $f = a \cdot z + b$ which is closest to $1/z$ can be computed by

---

[6]There exist tools which can be used to find the part of the program where most of the computation time is spent.

3.9 Approximation

minimizing the area enclosed by these functions:

$$\int_u^v \left(\frac{1}{z} - a \cdot z - b\right)^2 dz \to \min \quad . \tag{3.2}$$

A necessary condition for a and b is that the partial derivatives w.r.t. a and b of (3.2) have to be zero. Using this, we get the optimal parameters a and b:

$$a = 6\left(2(v-u) - (u+v)\ln\frac{u}{v}\right)\left(v^3 - 3uv^2 + 3vu^2 - u^3\right)^{-1} \tag{3.3}$$

$$b = 2\left(3(u^2 - v^2) + 2(v^2 + uv + u^2)\ln\frac{v}{u}\right)$$
$$\left(v^3 - 3uv^2 + 3vu^2 - u^3\right)^{-1}$$
$$\tag{3.4}$$

A look-up table for computing the required ratios for $u = 10$ and $v = 11$ is shown in Table 3.1. The function $1/z$ and its linear approximation are plotted in Figure 3.5 for the range $u = 10$ and $v = 11$.

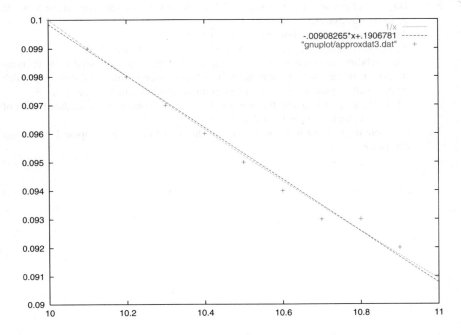

Figure 3.5: Function and its linear approximation

Index	0	1	2	3	4	5	6	7	8	9
x	10.0	10.1	10.2	10.3	10.4	10.5	10.6	10.7	10.8	10.9
$f(x)$	0.1	0.099	0.098	0.097	0.096	0.095	0.094	0.093	0.093	0.092

Table 3.1: Look-up table for function approximation

```
> co -l test.C,v
> co -l test.C
> ci Makefile
> chmod ugo-rwx *
> chmod +w test.C,v
> make love
> got a light?
```
16

Exercises

3.a Write a `Makefile` which compiles the C++ program `my_program.C`, adds the object file to the library, and generates an executable program `test` using the library.

3.b Decide and discuss which commands are useful or nonsense in Listing 16. Try them on your machine!

3.c Huge programs are divided up in modules and the C++ source code can be found in different directories.
Assume we have the following sub-directories:
`filters, segmentation, models, classification`.
Each subdirectory contains C++ code and a `Makefile` for compilation, building libraries and executable programs. Write a `Makefile` in the actual directory which automatically updates the complete program system by calling `make world`.

3.d Check the `rcs` manual and find out which of the information in the module header of a program (Sect. 3.4) can be added automatically.

3.e Compare the runtime behavior of the introduced techniques to compute $1/z$ on your computer.

Chapter 4
Control and Data Structures

In this chapter we briefly describe the data structure definitions which are already available in conventional C. We explain how these data structures and control statements can be used in C++. In Sect. 4.8 we introduce the new concept of exceptions in C++.

4.1 Structures

Like most modern programming languages, C++ has a mechanism for gluing already known data types together into a new data type. In C++ this is called a `struct` and usually has a type name.[1] The syntax is basically as follows:

| Syntax: | `struct` [*sname*] { *declaration** } [*vdef*] `;`

This introduces a new type name (*sname*). The semicolon at the end is very important and is a common source of errors, when it is forgotten. Declarations of variables inside the braces declare storage locations which are the *members* of the data structure; the names are called *structure tags*. Variables (one, or many separated by commas) may be immediately defined with a type declaration (*vdef*); more commonly, they are defined separately using the structure name (*sname*). Listing 17 shows the new data type `PointXY` for point coordinates. The variable `p0` in Listing 18 is defined using this new data type. Access to the members of a structure is possible via a variable followed by a dot and the member tag.

Static or global data can be initialized by values listed in curly brackets, as shown in Listing 17 for the variable p.

In contrast to C, the structure name can be used as a type without a `typedef` (cf. Sect. 6.1).

---
[1] Occasionally the name is left out; cf. Listing 146 for an example.

```
struct PointXY {            // declare new data type
    int x,y;                // members are x and y
};                          // do not forget the ;
```
17

```
PointXY p0;                // define a variable
p0.x = 1;                  // access member x
p0.y = 1;                  // access member y
static PointXY p = { 1, 2 }; // initialize a static variable
```
                                                                          18

```
enum Vt {
        voiced = 1,              // labels
        fricative = 2,           // for
        voiced_fricative = 3,    // speech (voice)
        stop = 0                 // segments
      } ;
Vt v = voiced;
enum ZoomSetting {wide = 0, portrait = 1, tele = 2};
ZoomSetting z = wide;
```
                                                                          19

4.2 Enumerations

Enumeration data types allow constant integer data with a very small range to be explicitly named. They are a handy feature to use, to associate several constant values with their own name. The syntax is as follows:

Syntax: enum [*typename*] { {*name* [= *int_value* ,] }* } [*vdef*] ;

Variables can be defined using the *typename*. If no initialization is specified with the *int_value*, the next free integer value is chosen by the compiler.[2] An example for labeling phonemes and lens positions is shown in Listing 19.

Enumeration data can be used in many cases where formerly defines were used in traditional C.

4.3 Scope Resolution

In Sect. 2.9 we saw how global names can be avoided when the declarations are inside a block or local to a file.

Enumerations, as in Listing 19, introduce many global names. This is generally bad software practice and may cause problems when linking different modules together. A solution is to declare enumerations within a structure scope. The names are now visible only inside the structure. They can still be used from the outside with the *scope resolution operator* "::".[3] An artificial example is shown in Listing 20; we will see more practical examples later. Of course, enum definitions do not require any storage during the run time of a program.

The scope resolution operator — like all other two character operators — may not be separated by a blank character.

---

[2] It is even possible to assign the same value twice to different names with explicit initialization.

[3] Another application of this operator is to access a name that was overwritten by the same name in a closer block, as we will see later in Listing 128. Various other sophisticated uses of this operator are possible but not treated in this book.

4.4 Unions

```
struct X {                        // artificial example
   enum A { i = 1, j = 2, k, l};  // enum within structure
   A a0;                          // variable of this type
} x;                              // structure variable
X::A a1;              // use type defined in structure scope
int i = X::i;         // use value defined in structure scope
```
20

```
union numbers { long a; double b; char c; };
numbers n;
```
21

4.4 Unions

Another language feature in C/C++ is called a `union`. Inside a union, several fields can be specified. The syntax looks exactly like the syntax for structures. Fields declared inside the union are accessed just like the fields inside a structure.[4]

Syntax: `union` [*sname*] { *declaration** } [*vdef*] ;

In contrast to structures, all the fields in a union share the *same* location in memory and can only be used alternatively. The overall memory requirement is calculated from the longest entry. In Listing 21 the size of the union `numbers` will be based on the length of the `double` field. There is no compiler generated run time information about which field is used and how many bits are valid.[5] If such information is required, it has to be coded explicitly.

Unions are in some sense a low-level language feature and should be used with care![6]

4.5 Bit- and Shift Operations and Bit-Fields

Often operations are defined on integer values so that they can be used to inspect data bit by bit. They are used this way mainly in operating system or hardware driver code or in highly efficient parts of a program. They are also useful for low-level image and speech processing.

Bit– and shift-operations for C and C++ are listed in Table 4.1. A zero value is inserted on left shift operations (LSH). A right shift (RSH) of an unsigned value will insert a zero in the highest bit. A right shift of a signed integer will do an arithmetic shift corresponding to a division by two; i.e., the highest bit is left unchanged and the second highest is filled with the value of the highest bit.[7] The operators & and | combine their operands bitwise. In contrast, the boolean operators && and || combine the values of their operands logically.

Binary bit and shift operations can be combined with an assignment as shown in Listing 22.

When dealing with hardware — e.g. the interface to a frame grabber — it is often required to request exactly a certain number of *bits* — for example, 8 or 16. One implementation

---
[4]Similarly, methods can be declared inside unions as with structures and classes of C++.
[5]In Listing 21 one can create illegal bit patterns for the `double` field when the union is written with the long field and then read using the double field.
[6]Inheritance in C++ (Chapter 14) can in many cases substitute unions in C.
[7]This behavior is machine dependent; you should not rely on it.

Syntax		Example
&=	AND	a &= 0xff
|=	OR	a |= 0x13ff
^=	XOR	a ^= b
<<=	LSH	a <<= 3
>>=	RSH	a >>= 2

Syntax		Example
&	AND	a & 0xff
|	OR	a | 0x13ff
^	XOR	a ^ b
<<	LSH	a << 3
>>	RSH	a >> 2
~	NOT	~0

Table 4.1: Bit operations on integer values

```
int b = -2;                 // not spectacular
int a = b | 0x33;           // bitwise OR connection
int c = a << 4;             // see the operator precedence
b ^= (a & 0xffff);          // parentheses look better
b = a || c;                 // logical connection
```
22

could use a structure containing a `byte` and a `short`. Since the size of a `short` may vary between machine architectures, it is better to request 16 bits. The language construct in C++ and C is a so called *bit field*. An example is shown in Listing 23. Inside a structure the number of bits for a field may be specified. There is no difference with respect to access to this structure members in comparison to regular members as in Sect. 4.1. Their type for the members is always `unsigned int`. Depending on compiler or hardware restrictions, there may be limitations on the number of bits which can be requested in bit fields.

Bit fields are, of course, also a low-level feature of C and C++. If they are used properly, they may be very useful for efficient programming — as is required for pattern recognition purposes. In combination with unions (Sect. 4.4) the use of bit fields can be even trickier; only if such tricks are properly encapsulated, they can add efficiency to a program while still maintaining its clarity.

4.6 Logical Values and Conditionals

The C language did not supply the data-type `boolean`; instead, integer values were used as truth values. The value 0 stands for `FALSE`, everything else is interpreted as `TRUE`. In standard C++, the data type `bool` is used as an integer type with values $\{0,1\}$. Operators for comparison are:

```
struct SubPixCoord {             // subpixel coordinates for images
    unsigned int x: 12;          // with size MxN
    unsigned int y: 12;          // M,N in [0..4095]
    unsigned int xfract: 4;      // subpixel accuracy 1/16 pixel
    unsigned int yfract: 4;
};
SubPixCoord p;                   // a variable
unsigned int x0 = p.x;           // access bit field as unsigned int
```
23

4.6 Logical Values and Conditionals

```
int i,j;
if (i > 2)                          // if #1
    if ((i == 5) || (j < 3))        // if #2
        j = 4;
    else
        j = 8;                      // belongs to if #2
```
24

Syntax: *expr1* $\geq$ | $>=$ | $\leq$ | $<=$ | $!=$ | $==$ *expr2*

The operator == checks whether two values are equal. A common mistake is to confuse the assignment operator = and the equality operator ==. Inequality can be tested using !=. The operator < (> >= <=) checks whether the expression on the left is smaller (greater, greater or equal, smaller or equal) than the expression on the right side.

Logical values — i.e., integer expressions — can be combined by operations as listed in Table 4.2. The precedence of operators is complicated and a common source for errors. We suggest the use of parentheses to make the wanted precedence obvious.

Operator	Explanation	Example
&&	AND	((i>1) && (i<2)) ...
||	OR	((i>1) || (i<-2)) ...
!	NOT	((i>1) && (!(i<2))) ...

Table 4.2: Logical operators

Often it is necessary to control a program through the use of validity tests with boolean expressions. Normally, statements are executed in the sequence given in the program. Expressions are evaluated from left to right. Conditional execution as well as loops and function calls can alter this sequence. Unconditional jumps (`goto`) are almost never needed and considered bad programming style. Jumps are often accepted in C to deal with exceptional cases (cf. the function `longjmp` in most C libraries). C++ provides alternatives such as exception handling as a more structured way of handling errors. We will see solutions in Sect. 4.8.

Conditional execution can be done using the `if` statement:

Syntax: `if (` *expression* `)` *statement1* [`else` *statement2*]

Statement1 is executed if the expression evaluates to an integer value other than 0. Otherwise if the `else` clause is present, *statement2* is executed. Nesting of conditional statements is possible. As in Pascal, the "else" is assumed to belong to the next possible "if". Listing 24 shows this situation.

Of course, the statements in the conditional branches can be blocks (cf. Listing 25). Also note the typical indentation style for `if` and `else` cascades in the following example (see also Sect. 3.4) which puts the last `else` under the previous `else`. Cascades of if-else-if-else etc. thereby can be aligned.

```
if (i > 2)
      j = 3;
else if ((i == 5) || (j < 3))    // if cascade
      j = 4;
else {                            // here we use a block
      j = 8;
      i = 2;
}                                 // we end the cascade
```
25

```
while ( i > 2) {
      printf("%d ", --i);
}
// next loop
do {
      printf("%d ", --i);
} while (i > 0);
```
26

4.7 Loops

Three types of loops exist in C++ corresponding to the structograms in Sect. 3.5. The syntax of the while and the do loops are as follows:

Syntax:

> *1)* while *(expression)* statement
> *2)* do *statement* while*(expression);*

We call the *statement* in the loop the *loop body*; it may of course be a block containing several statements. In the while–loop the statement is executed as long as the expression evaluates to something other than 0. The do–loop terminates when the expression evaluates to 0; the do–loop body is executed at least once. Since both loops use the keyword while, it is crucial to use proper indentation (Listing 26, see also Sect. 3.4)

The third loop syntax is the for–loop, which is a special type of the while–loop:

Syntax: for ([*statement1*] ; [*expression*] ; [*statement2*]) *statement3*

This is equivalent to a while loop

```
statement1; while(expression){statement3; statement2;}.
```

The for–loop contains two assignments and one boolean expression. The first assignment initializes the loop variable, the second assignment can be used to change the loop variable, and if the boolean expression becomes false (i.e., zero), the loop terminates. Any of the statements may be empty.

Since declarations are statements in C++, they can be used in the loop to introduce a new variable. This style of writing is very common in C++; it is exemplified in Listing 27. The variable will be valid only inside the loop.[8]

---

[8] To support programs which were written with older versions of C++ compilers, the variable might be also visible after the loop.

```
for (int k = 0; k < 10; ++k) {   // declare loop variable
    int j = random();             // get some value
    if (j == -1) break;           // exit the hard way
    if (j == 0) continue;         // skip the following
    printf("%d %d", i, j);        // otherwise: print
}
```
27

Any loop can be terminated by a `break` statement. The `continue` statement skips the rest of the loop body and continues with the next iteration. These constructs help to avoid `goto`'s. They are commonly used but in principle unstructured (no symbol exists in standard structograms, Sect. 3.5). Listing 27 shows these constructs.

4.8 Exception Handling

Exceptions are a new type of control structures introduced in standard C++ recently. The idea has been used in interpreted languages such as Lisp for a long time. The reason for this concept is that certain exceptional conditions require actions in the program that require passing the flow of control immediately to some distant place. Jumps by `goto` in C and C++ are possible only within a function. In C we could use the function `longjmp` for this purpose; this function deliberately modifies the contents of the stack. This was a function included in some library and was thus not part of the language definition. The use of this function in C++ will cause considerable problems.

The idea of exceptions is that in case of an error or exceptional condition, the control should be passed to a so-called *handler* in a structured way. The handler can then decide whether the program has to be finished — possibly after some cleanup — or whether the condition that caused the exception is not critical and the program can be continued. A typical example of an exception is an arithmetic overflow in a computation.

Three new key words are used to deal with exceptions: `try`, `catch`, and `throw`. An example is shown in Listing 28; we will explain some more details on exceptions in the following chapters whereever appropriate. We say that "an exception is raised" (by a throw) and that the "handler catches" the exception (by the catch). Whatever is written after the throw keyword is copied and passed as an argument to the handler. There may be several handlers for different exceptions which are tried in the order of appearance as shown in Listing 32; the handler is selected by matching the type of the expression thrown, with the expression given after the catch clause. Try blocks may also be nested. When an exception is thrown, control is transferred to that handler with a matching type whose try block was most recently entered and which was not yet exited. If no exception is presently being handled, executing a throw-expression with no operand will terminate the program.

Exception handlers are a very powerful tool and require that the compiler creates code for exception support. Of course there have to be special mechanisms, e.g. to catch exceptions

```
FILE * openOut(char * n)
{
   FILE * f = fopen(n,"w");
   if (f == NULL) throw "could not open file";
   return f;
}
int main()
{
   try { // use a block to combine a sequence of statements
      FILE * f = openOut("test");
      fprintf(f,"write to file\n");   // f will never be
      fclose(f);                       // NULL here
   } catch (char * s) {                // exception handler
      fprintf(stderr,"Error %s\n",s); // for type char *
   }
   return 0;
}
```

28

during exception handling.[9] The rule of thumb says that exceptions should only be used for those cases that are really exceptional.

4.9 Switches

Instead of cascading numerous levels of if else if else ..., a switch can be used when all the conditionals depend on the same integer variable. The value of this variable can be used to dispatch to several *constant* integer values. These values are used as case labels. The execution of such a branch can be terminated with a break statement. If the break is missing, the control continues with the next statement. When this is desired it should always be commented. Otherwise, it might look like one of many common programming errors in C. A default case can be specified which is applied if none of the switch values are matched (assuming switches contain a break). The most common form of the syntax is:

Syntax:

switch *(expression)* { *case_stms** [default:] *statement** }

case_stms: {case *const-expr:*}* *statement** [break;]

After the opening curly bracket of a switch, a declaration is possible. These variables cannnot be initialized. Inside the switch, declarations are not allowed, except when they are inside a new block.

A function including a switch is shown in Listing 29. Note, that some of the statements "fall into the next case", which is commented, as required. We will use this example later on (Sect. 20.1, page 251); then we will be able to understand the meaning of the error message in the default case of the switch.

---

[9]Since we do not rely on such features in the following programs, we do not describe these mechanisms here. Details can be found in the C++ reference manual.

4.9 Switches

```
void fct2(int c)        // function will modify global i and j
{   extern int i,j;     // GLOBAL VARIABLES
    switch(c) {
        char buffer[64];   // local variable
        case 1:   ++i;     // fall into next case
        case 0:   ++j;
            break;
        case 3:   --j;     // fall into next case
        case 2:   ++i;
            break;
        case 5:   --i;     // fall into next case
        case 4:   --j;
            break;
        case 7:   ++j;     // fall into next case
        case 6:   --i;
            break;
        default:
            sprintf(buffer,"Illegal direction (%d)\n",c);
            throw buffer;
    }
}
```
29

```
extern void fct(int f);              /* M.h */
extern int verbose;
```
30

Exercises

4.a Graphically show the dependencies of the files in Listing 30–32.

4.b Write and test a makefile for the shown examples. Include the dependencies for version control with rcs (Appendix A.4).

4.c How can the break and continue statements be avoided? Transform the code in Listing 27 into an equivalent program without break and continue and draw the structogram.

```
#include "M.h"                       /* M1.C */
void fct(int f)
{
  if (verbose) printf("fct() called\n");
  if (f < 0) throw "negative";   // just to show
  if (f > 0) throw f;            // possible throws
}
```
31

```
#include "M.h"                       /* M0.C */
int verbose = 0;            // global variable
main(int argc, char ** argv)    // nonsense example
{
    verbose = (argc > 1);       // verbose used as boolean
    try {
    if (verbose) fct(argc);     // conditional call
    } catch (char * s) {
        fprintf(stderr,"%s\n",s);
    } catch (int f) {
        fprintf(stderr,"thrown to int: %d\n",f);
    }
}
```

Chapter 5

Arrays and Pointers

In the first chapter we explained that discrete speech signals can be represented by vectors. Images are usually stored as matrices or as higher dimensional arrays. Therefore vectors and matrices are very important data-structures in the field of pattern recognition and should be discussed in detail. Vectors and matrices are directly related to the concept of pointers in C and C++.

5.1 Vectors and Matrices

In general, C++-arrays are indexed by unsigned integers beginning with 0. A one-dimensional array f of size N therefore has the elements $f_0, f_1, \ldots, f_{N-1}$. Neither the compiler nor the run-time system check the range of the subscripts; nasty errors may occur with the use of improper values (see also Exercise 2.b on page 28).[1]

A variable is declared as an array by placing the constant number of elements within square brackets following the variable name. With multidimensional arrays the size specification is repeated:

Syntax: *type ID [size]*;*

Examples of the declaration of arrays are given in Listing 33. For two-dimensional arrays, the first size specifies the number of rows, the second specifies the number of columns. Access to

---
[1] In Sect.10.8 we will learn how to avoid this "feature" in C++.

```
int    a[10];              // integer array size 10
char   c[20];              // character array size 20
float  f[20][10];          // float matrix size 20 x 10
int i = 9;                 // integer variable

unsigned char image[256][256];  // a typical image
a[4] = 3;      c[9] = 'c';      f[4][2]      = 4.33;
a[0] = a[4];   a[0] += 4;       image[1][i] = 0;

a[++i] = 10;  // syntactically correct, but wrong index! (i>9)
```

```
#define COLUMNS 256
#define ROWS    256
static unsigned char image[ROWS][COLUMNS]; // global image
main(int argc, char ** argv)               // main program
{
    int s = atoi(argv[1]);                 // should check argc!
    for (int i = 0; i < ROWS; ++i )        // loop over rows
       for (int j = 0; j < COLUMNS; ++j )  // loop over columns
          image[i][j] = (i * s) ^ j;       // ^ introduced later
    fwrite(image[0],COLUMNS,ROWS,stdout);  // ugly - raw write
    exit(0);                               // good exit code
}
```
34

single elements is done by supplying an index of range $0, 1, \ldots, N-1$ for each dimension,[2] as shown in Listing 33, which also shows how eight bit gray level images are represented in C and C++, i.e., pixels are unsigned char represented as byte. The size of the image is fixed to 256^2 elements. A change of image size would most likely cause many changes in the source code as the limits of the loop have to be adjusted. It is a little better to use macros (Listing 34), as it was common in traditional C. C++ also introduces constants which can be used as array sizes; we will learn about this feature later in Sect. 6.3.

The program in Listing 34 creates a fancy synthetic image and writes it — the hard way — to stdout.[3] It combines the indices i and j with the xor-operator ^ introduced in Sect. 4.5. The result for two different values of s is shown in Figure 5.1.

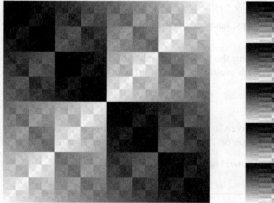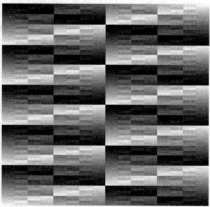

Figure 5.1: Result of Listing 34 with argument 1 and 5

---

[2]The expression image[2,4] is also syntactically correct, but is equal to image[4]! (Cmp. 6.9)
[3]We will see better ways of storing images in Chapter 11.

```
int * a, b, *c;    // Pointers to int a and c, normal int b
```
`35`

```
int b = 3;      char a = 'a';   // memory filled with values
int *bp;        char * ap;      // pointers (not initialized)
int *cp = NULL;                 // better: initialize
bp = &b;                        // *bp == b
cp = bp;                        // *bp == *cp
ap = &a;                        // *ap == a
*ap = 'x';                      // a == 'x'
ap = NULL;                      // NULL-pointer
```
`36`

5.2 Pointers

People often are very suspicious of using pointers. Especially those whose "native language" is Pascal. Nevertheless, the essence of C and C++ is in the usage of pointers.

"First of all, don't panic".

Pointers in C and C++ are declared as variables pointing to data of a known type, i.e. they are no pointers *per se*, but pointers to integers, pointers to floating point numbers, pointers to characters, etc.[4] The syntax was already introduced in Sect. 2.4.[5] The * declares the variable immediately following the asterix as a pointer to the type given first:

Syntax: *type* [***] *var1* [$\equiv$ *expr*] [*,* [***] *var2* [$\equiv$ *expr*]]* ;

Listing 35 shows the definition of two pointer variables to integers (a and c); the variable b is a normal integer variable.

After the definition of a pointer variable, the value of the variable is undefined (as it is the case with normal values), i.e. the address in the value cell is arbitrary and — in general — not valid. Pointer values can be set by assigning one pointer to another of the same type. Pointers can be set to any location in memory where data of the expected type is present. In contrast to Pascal, for example, this location can be assigned by the address operator & on a normal variable and does not have to be allocated dynamically. The access of the data pointed to by the pointer is done using a *. Listing 36 illustrates the various uses of pointers.

If a pointer is not initialized, it points *somewhere* – which is usually an illegal location. It is often required to have a pointer point *nowhere*; in Pascal this is done with the *nil*-pointer value. In C/C++ there is a macro in the file stdio.h or stdlib.h named NULL; we then call the pointer a "NULL-pointer".

---

[4] Pointers declared as void * can point to any data, see Sect. 6.2.
[5] There we did not specify what ptr was.

```
char carray[64];              // array of fixed length
char * cptr = carray, *cptr1;
cptr = &(carray[3]);
// carray = cptr ;            // ILLEGAL
carray[3] = *cptr;            // carray[3] == cptr[0]
cptr[3] = 'a';                // [ offset ] is legal for pointers
```
37

```
int iarray0[10] = {1,2,3,4,0,1,2,3,4,5}; // all values specified
int iarray2[10] = {1,2,3,4,5};           // remaining values 0
int iarray1[]   = {1,2,3,4,5};           // int iarray1[5]
```
38

5.3 Vectors vs. Pointers

Vectors and pointers are very similar in C/C++ and their syntax is the same in many cases. A vector can be seen as a constant pointer to the first element of an array. Some applications are shown in Listing 37.

Assignment to the whole vector with one operator is not possible (see the illegal line in the example), since an array is a *constant* pointer. However, a pointer can be set to an array. Assignment to single elements is obviously possible as well. Data pointed to by a pointer can be accessed using [index] as in an array.

Global or static arrays of simple types can be initialized during the variable's definition. The values assigned are listed in curly brackets separated by commas. The size of the array can be implicitly determined by the number of initial values. If a size is specified, it may not be smaller than the size indicated by the number of elements in the initialization (Listing 38).

Static multidimensional arrays are initialized by nested lists of values as shown in Listing 39. For two-dimensional arrays, the inner lists initialize the rows, one after another.

5.4 Pointer Operations and Allocation

Pointers can be manipulated by various operators; for example, they can be compared using the relational operators (> >= == != < <=, cmp. Sect. 4.6). If an integer is added to a pointer, the address is incremented by the given number of elements; i.e. if 4 is added to a pointer pointing to an integer (int *), the result of the addition points to the fourth integer following the previous position of the pointer. The same holds for subtraction. This can be understood best if we look at the index operator [index]; the expression carray[3] is

```
char image[4][3] =       // image variable
    { {  1, 0 ,  1},     // row 0
      { -1, 0 , -1},     // row 1
      { -1, 0 , -1},     // row 2
      {  1, 0 ,  1} };   // row 3
```
39

5.5 Pointer to Structures

```
cptr = &(carray[0]);         // some operations
*cptr = 'a'; cptr++;         // on pointers
*cptr = 'b'; *++cptr = 'c';  // ...
cptr = new char[10];         // allocate 10 characters
cptr1 = cptr + 3;            // third element of array
int d = cptr1 - cptr;        // number of elements between pointers
delete [] cptr;              // discard allocation
cptr = new char;             // allocate 1 characters
delete cptr;                 // discard allocation
```
40

```
void strcpy(char * to, char * from)
{             // zero character terminates string
    while((*(to++) = *(from++)) != '\0')
        /* empty loop body */ ;
}
```
41

identical to *(carray+3).[6] Subtraction of two pointers (of the same type) yields the number of elements between the two positions.

Like in addition and subtraction of numbers, pointers can also be incremented and decremented. These operations are often combined with * to access the element pointed to as can be seen in Listing 40. A pointer can be set to a legal address by assigning the address of a variable using the address operator. Alternatively, the pointer may be set to unnamed memory requested by the operator new; the memory will be sufficiently large and aligned for the requested data type. If memory allocation fails, an exception will be raised. The allocation can be discarded by the operator delete. When the type given to the operator is a structure (see below), sufficient storage is requested.

Syntax:

>   *ptr* = new *type* [[*nelem*]]
>   delete [[]] *ptr*

A summary of the operations on pointers is given in Table 5.1. When arrays are created with new type[size] the corresponding delete operation has to use the syntax delete [].

The function in Listing 41 is a very common application for strings. It also shows the combination of assignment and relational comparison. The first string had better be long enough! When a loop's body is empty (as in Listing 41), this should be marked and commented clearly, so other readers will not suspect an error there.

5.5 Pointer to Structures

As with standard data types, pointers may be set to user defined data types. Structure members can be accessed by the use of pointers to structures. The combination of pointer access and member ((*ptr).member) can be abbreviated by the operator -> (Listing 42, which uses the definition given in Listing 17).

---

[6]Together with the commutativity of addition, this implies a[i] == i[a]. This is not a joke!

operator	operand 1	operator	operand 2	Explanation
*	ptr			Dereference
&	var			Address of
++	ptr			Increment
--	ptr			Decrement
	ptr	=	ptr	Assignment
	ptr	=	& var	Assignment
	ptr	=	new type [number]	Array allocation
	ptr	=	new type	Allocation
delete	ptr			Disposal
delete[]	ptr			Array disposal
	ptr	[number]		Array access
	ptr	+	int	Addition
	ptr	-	int	Subtraction
	ptr	-	ptr	Distance
	ptr	rel-op	ptr	Compare addr.

Table 5.1: Operations on pointers; rel-op stands for any relational operator (Sect. 4.6).

```
PointXY p1 = { 1, 2 } ;      // variable
PointXY *pp = &p1;           // define a pointer variable
p1.x = 1;                    // access via variable
(*pp).y = 1;                 // access via pointer
pp->x = 2;                   // short hand for (*pp).x = 2;
```
42

Incrementing a pointer to a structure naturally advances the pointer by the number of bytes occupied by the structure. This value can be found by the sizeof operator, which returns the size (measured in byte) of its argument at *compile-time*. The argument can be a variable, an expression, or a type name. This operator again shows the difference between vectors and pointers. Applied to a pointer, the operator will give the number of bytes required for storing an address; applied to an array, it will give the size of the array. Listing 43 shows how to enquire the number of elements in an array at compile time. The result of the sizeof operator cannot be used in pre-processor directives, since it is evaluated by the compiler, not by the pre-processor (cf. Figure 2.1).

As can be seen in Listing 43, the sizeof operator may be used to write machine-independent programs which adjust their behavior according to the size of the same data type found on a different machine architecture.

```
static char s[] = "abc";                    // initialize static array
static char * cptr   = s;                   // pointer
static int   arrayp[] = {1,2,3,4};          // initialize static array
int as = sizeof(arrayp)/sizeof(int);        // number of elements
int sl = sizeof s;                          // no () required!
int pl = sizeof cptr;                       // pl != sl
```
43

```
char string0[10];                        // constant length 10
char string1[] = { 'a', 'b', 'c', '\0'}; // length 4
char string2[] = "abc";                  // also length 4
```
44

```
void swapint(int * a, int *b) {int tmp=*a; *a=*b; *b=tmp;}

void fct()
{   int i = 3, j = 4;
    swapint (&i,&j);             // now i == 4, j == 3
}
```
45

5.6 Strings

In Listing 43, the array s represents a string, i.e. strings are vectors (one-dimensional arrays) of characters. They are always delimited by the trailing '\0' character. Initialization of a string (i.e. an array of characters) can be done using the lists described in Sect. 5.3; it also can be simplified by supplying a string in double quotes (Listing 44). In the first case, the '\0' has to be added explicitly; in the later case, the '\0' is added automatically, the array will thus be one element longer than the number of characters provided in the initialization.

Useful functions on strings can be found in the standard libraries. Comparison and manipulation of strings is facilitated by the following routines: strcmp compares two strings, strlen returns the length of the string, and strcpy copies one string to another (Listing 41). These functions are declared in string.h and can be inserted into the program with #include <string.h>. Refer to the compiler or operating system manual for further information on these functions. The standard libary for C++ also contains strings and string functions (Sect. 16.7).

5.7 Pointer and Array Arguments

The C programming language passes *all* function arguments by value. Changes to the arguments in the function body are therefore local and have no global effect. We now discuss how functions can change data.

Functions can change data that is not declared inside of the function using pointer arguments. In Listing 41 the pointers to and from are incremented; this does not, however, change the value of the pointers provided in the call which are passed to the function by value! The changes occur in the data pointed to by the arguments! This is shown in Listing 45.

Of course, global variables may be accessed inside a block or function. This is generally not the best software practice. The return value of a function can be used in the calling sequence to promote the changes of a function. Later we will see other argument parsing facilities for C++ (Sect. 6.3).

When a multi-dimensional array is to be passed to a function, the size of the argument has to be provided to the compiler; only the first size of the argument may be left unspecified. An example is given in Listing 46. For image processing, this is of course completely unsatisfac-

```
void fct(unsigned char m[][3], unsigned char f[][256])
{    f[3][4] *= m[1][1];   }
```
46

```
int i = 3,            // integer
  * ip,               // pointer to integer
  ** ipp;             // pointer to pointer to integer
int ia [5][6];        // matrix of integers
ip = &i;              // assign pointer
ipp = &ip;            // assign pointer (to pointer)
*ip = 4;              // now i == 3
** ipp = 5;           // now i == 5
ia[3][4] = 1;         // (1) ok
ipp[3][4] = 1;        // (2) legal syntax, illegal address
```
47

tory. Several text books treat images as one-dimensional arrays and do pointer arithmetic for the interpretation of lines and columns. There is, however, a nice *trick* for circumventing the problems with multidimensional arrays (see e.g., [Pre92]) which we will exploit in Sect. 10.8; until then, we will keep the image sizes constant.

5.8 Pointer to Pointer

Pointers are tied to a given type. Naturally, the data the pointer points to can again be a pointer. The declaration and application of a pointer to a pointer to an integer is shown in Listing 47 for ipp.

Because of the dual nature of pointers and vectors, a twofold pointer can be seen as a two-dimensional array, i.e. it can be accessed using two indices. Although this looks similar as an array access (Listing 33), it has a different meaning to the compiler. For static arrays, indices are evaluated using the type sizes contained in the array declaration; after an arithmetic expression, this will result in the address of the array element. Generally, addition and multiplication is required here. We will use this feature later in Sect. 11.1 to access matrix elements efficiently.

For pointers to pointers, the indices are offsets to the pointer. The first index will be an offset to the pointer. This will yield an address to which the second offset is applied. No arithmetic other than addition is required here. The last line in Listing 47 shows that pointers to pointers and matrices (two-dimensional arrays) can both use the operator [] twice. The meaning to the compiler is different, however: The line (1) is interpreted as *(&(ia[0][0] + 3 * 6 + 4) - as the number of elements in a line is 6, and we want to access the 4th element in the third line; the line (2) is interpreted as (ipp[3])[4] which is equivalent to *((*(ipp+3))+4) - and an illegal address will be computed. For the matrix, the number of elements has to be known, which explains, why it has to be specified in the declaration of arguments to functions.

```
int main(int argc, char ** argv)
{
    while ( argc-- > 0 ) printf("%s\n", *(argv++));
    return (0);
}
```
<!-- 48 -->

```
/* defines for XS and YS  should be in some header file*/
unsigned char image[YS][XS];    // global definition of an image
main(int argc, char ** argv)
{
    char * in, * out;
    // get args
    readimage(in,image);
    // etc.
}
```
<!-- 49 -->

5.9 Command Line Arguments

In Sect. 2.7 we used the `main` function with two arguments `argc` and `argv`; `argc` is already known as the number of arguments on the command line; we can now explain `argv`.

The argument `argv` is an array of strings, i.e. a pointer to a pointer to a character. It is passed to `main` as a pointer to the first string which contains the name of the program. The length of each string is known by the trailing '\0' in the string. Listing 48 shows a program that prints its own arguments. When `argv` is declared as `char **`, it is common to scan all arguments by `*++argv` or by `*(argv++)` as shown in Listing 48.

There exist several handy functions for parsing the arguments of a program. In the following chapters we will use extensions of the functions defined in the following exercises.

Exercises

5.a   Declare, define, and initialize a static array of strings with its size determined by the number of initialization strings. Write a NULL string as the last string.

5.b   Write a routine `cmp_arg` with one string as an argument called `opt`. Compare `opt` to all the strings of Exercise 5.a. If the string is a unique prefix of a string in the list, return its index in the array. If it is a prefix, but not a unique one, return -1; if it is not found in the list, return -2.

```
/* defines for XS and YS  should be in some header file*/
void readimage(char*filename,unsigned char image[YS][XS])
{
    FILE * file = fopen(filename,"r");
    if (file == NULL) throw "Could not open input file";
    int t = (fread(image[0],YS,XS,file) < XS * YS); // ugly - raw binary read
    fclose(file);
    if (! t) throw "short file";
}
```
<!-- 50 -->

Hint: use the function `strncmp`.

5.c Write a routine `printargs` which prints all the strings of the list in Exercise 5.a.

5.d Write a routine `check_args(argc,argv)` which is called from `main`. Every command line argument starting with a '-' should be checked by the routine of Exercise 5.b. Skip the '-' for that purpose. Use a switch on the return value of `cmp_arg`. In case of failure, use `printargs` and print an appropriate error message.

5.e Write a simple function which generates a synthetic image containing a filled circle. Your main program could look similar to Listing 49. Use a fixed size for the image. Provide filename, center, and radius from the command line using the `cmd_arg` function and a switch. Write the image to a file using the raw write function in Listing 34 — but hide the call in a separate function `write_image` and put the defines for the image sizes in a separate header file as shown in Listing 50.

Make sure that your program works with arbitrary image sizes. Write a makefile and use `rcs` (cf. Appendix A).

5.f Write a program that applies a simple *filter* (cf. Chapter 17) to an image: replace every pixel by the mean of its left and right neighbor. For argument handling, input and output, proceed as in the previous exercise.

Chapter 6

C++ as a better C

In this chapter we conclude the description of the conventional programming part of C++. We include the new features of C++, which amend some of the defects of C. Most of the important features of C which are also valid for C++ will have been mentioned by the end of this chapter. The exercises in this chapter introduce some useful programming and debugging tools.

6.1 Type Declaration

New types can be introduced using already known declarations with the keyword `typedef`. Listing 51 shows common types declarations of the new types `byte`, `Cstring`, and `GrayValue`. For structures, a `typedef` — as in C — is no longer required in C++ (cf. Sect. 4.1).

Type definitions may enhance the readability and portability of a program. Imagine, for example, a change of your image data format from eight to sixteen bits.

6.2 Type Conversion for Pointers

As was already explained in Sect. 2.6, types can be converted to others through the use of a type cast. Numerical values are then adjusted to the given type. A change of size and value is sometimes necessary (e.g. when converting from an unsigned character to a double value). In C++, the `reinterpret_cast` is preferred to the old C-style syntax.[1]

Pointers can also be converted using cast expressions. Normally, the size of the result is the same as before, i.e. a pointer requires the same number of bytes for storing the address no matter to which type it points. An example of type conversion for pointers is shown in Listing 52.

---
[1] We will learn more about such pointer conversion operators in the following, in particular in Sect. 16.8.

```
typedef unsigned char byte;    // byte now identical to uns. char
typedef byte GrayValue;        // gray value identical to byte
typedef char * CString;        // string type
```
51

```
char * cpt;                              // some pointer definitions
int * iptr, i;                           // not initialized
void * anyptr;                           // can point anywhere
iptr = &i;                               // pointer to an int
cpt = (char*) iptr;                      // explicit conversion (C--style)
cpt = reinterpret_cast<char*>(iptr);     // explicit conversion (new)
anyptr = &i;                             // now points to an int
* (int*) anyptr = 3;                     // cast required
```

A special notation void * can be used for a generic pointer pointing to *any* type. Before the data pointed to can be accessed, however, the pointer has to be cast to the appropriate type. The cast thus tells the compiler that the pointer is set to data of another type than the one deduced from the syntax. This is a potentially dangerous thing! The result of a pointer cast may in some cases give illegal values of the address or may even change the value of the pointer. For example, on most machines you should not try to cast a character pointer to an integer pointer, if the character pointer has an odd address.[2]

6.3 Type Specifiers and Variable Declaration

Variables can be *specified* with additional keywords in the declarations. C++ offers several choices: const declares the variable to have a constant value,[3] & makes it a so-called reference, register is used for compiler optimization, extern, auto, and static control scope[4] and lifetime. These modifications are valid for function arguments as well. When a variable is declared extern, the statement is a declaration and not a definition.

Reference arguments in function declarations provide a twofold benefit. First, changes to a nonlocal variable can be done through the use of reference arguments. This introduces arguments with the "call by reference" semantics as found, for example, in Pascal or Fortran. An example is shown in Listing 53 (compare to Listing 45).

Secondly, it is often advantageous not to pass large objects to a function. Arguments passed by value require a copy operation on the data. Argument references are not copied when they are passed as arguments; only a reference to the object is passed to the function. To make this intention explicit, a combination of reference and const should be used as shown in Listing 54.

Reference variables provide alternative names for accessing data (Listing 55). They have to be initialized upon definition. The keywords auto and static are used as in C.

---

[2] Try for example:
```
float f=1, * fp=&f; char * cp=1 + (char *) fp; fp=(float*) cp; *fp=3;
```
Do not forget to remove the core file!

[3] Enumeration data types provide alternative ways for the definition of integer constants.

[4] The use of static to restrict the scope of a name to the file currently compiled is depreciated in new C++ compilers. It is now recommended to use namespaces instead. This applies for example to the variables globalint and the function fct in Listing 54.

6.3 Type Specifiers and Variable Declaration

```
void swapint(int &a, int &b)
{                       // swap the value of two integers
    int tmp = a; a = b; b = tmp;
}
void fct()
{   int i = 3, j = 4;
    swapint (i,j);      // now i == 4, j == 3
}
```
53

```
static int globalint = 0;   // local in this module
static void fct(int a,      // pass by value
        int & b,             // pass by reference
        const int & c,       // pass by constant reference
        int * d,             // pass as a pointer
        const int * e)       // pass as pointer to constant
{
    auto     int i = 0;      // same as int i = 0;
    register int k = 10;     // hint to the compiler
    static   int j = 1;
    const    int l = 0;
    a = i;                   // local effect
    b = i;                   // will change the referenced arg
    c = i;                   // **error**
    *d = 1;                  // global effect
    e = d;                   // ok, only data pointed to is const
    *e = *d;                 // **error**
}
```
54

We can now specify a more complex (but still incomplete, see [Str97]) syntax for a variable declaration; for simplicity we leave out initialization and multiple variables in one declaration statement.[5]

Syntax:

[extern | static | register | auto] [const] *type* [*_*_* | &_] *var1* [[*size*]]*

Various combinations of * and [] can result in cryptic sequences of characters. Through the use of typedef's it is often possible to reduce the complexity of such expressions. A declaration and an explanation[6] is shown in Listing 56.

---

[5] We still miss the possibility to express pointers to functions etc.
[6] The program c++decl is in the public domain (see Sect. B.1). It explains in clear English a given variable definition or declaration or cast expression for C or C++.

```
PointXY p2;                 // PointXY is a structure of int x; int y;
int & px = p2.x;            // set a reference to the member x
px = 3;                     // now: p2.x == 3
```
55

```
c++decl> explain int * const f[10]
declare f as array 10 of const pointer to int

c++decl> declare A as array 20 of pointer to const int
const int *A[20]

c++decl> explain const int & f(float &);
declare f as function (reference to float) returning reference to const int

c++decl> declare f as function (reference to double) returning \
pointer to function (reference to float) returning int
int (*f(double &))(float &)
```

56

```
extern "C" int verbose;
extern "C" int fct(int);
main(int argc, char **argv)
{
   if (verbose) printf("%d\n", fct(argc)); // call C function
}
```

57

6.4 Type-Safe Linkage

When using different modules, inevitably names for functions and variables have to be shared between different files. In C, only the name of the variable or function is exported to the linker. For example, if a function f is defined in one module and used as an integer f in another module, this will not result in a linkage error. The runtime system will, however, show the disastrous effects.

C++ introduces type-safe linkage and treats the integer f different from the function f(). The technique used generates function names that include an encoding of the function's argument types into the external name. It does this through the use of a unique naming scheme (called "name mangling"). Occasionally, the linker will report such unresolved symbols. A program called demangle can then be used to decode these cryptic messages into more readable ones.

A special notation extern "C" can be used to circumvent the coding of arguments into the external name. This is useful when modules compiled in the C language have to be linked with C++ modules. Listing 58 and Listing 57 show a C and a C++ program which can be linked together into one program which will most likely *not* print what the programmer expects. Since the C++ system has no information about the argument's type for the function fct, it will just put an integer number on the stack.[7] The C function will not "know" about the type of the data on the stack and will just handle it as if it were a floating point number. Name mangling ensures that such errors can be detected by the compiler and linker. However, differences in the return value between declaration and definition will still not be detected.

It is also possible to include complete files as C code into a C++ program such as the stdio.h file in Listing 59.

---

[7]Most compilers pass arguments to a function via a stack pointer which is not directly accessible to the user.

6.5 Overloaded Function Names

```
/* ANSI C Program */
int verbose;                             /* global variable */
int fct(float f) { return (int) f; } /* converts its argument to int */
```
58

```
/* C++ subroutine */
extern "C" {
#include <stdio.h> /* should be C anyhow ... */
int c_function(int);
}
extern "C" int cplusfcn(int i) { return i*i; }
main(int ac, char **av)
{
    printf("%d\n",c_function(ac));
}
```
59

If you want to provide a C++ function for a C subroutine, you will have to circumvent name mangling as well. Using the prefix `extern "C"` this is also possible. These techniques are shown in Listing 59 and 60.

6.5 Overloaded Function Names

Several different functions may share one common name as long as each function can be uniquely identified by its arguments either by their type or by the number of arguments. Of course this only makes sense for groups of functions which essentially do the same thing, e.g. as those in Listing 61. Name mangling ensures that such functions can be distinguished by the linker. This technique of selection upon the type is similar to the selection of the `catch` clause in Sect. 4.8.

Two functions of the same name which differ in the return type alone, i.e. with no difference in the argument lists, are not allowed since this would cause no change in the mangled names. A distinction could be made neither by the compiler, nor the linker. Some functions which cannot be distinguished by the compiler are shown in Listing 62.

6.6 Return Value and Arguments

A function can have a variable number of arguments in the call syntax, such as the function `printf`. The implementation of such functions in C is possible using macros from an include file `varargs.h`. This is, however, error prone, since the compiler cannot check whether a sufficient number of arguments is provided when the function is called. A safe and easy

```
/* C Subroutine */
extern int cplusfcn(int);
int c_function(int i) { return cplusfcn(i); }
```
60

```
double  square(double a)  { return a*a; }  // square for double and float
int     square(int a)     { return a*a; }  // for int
```

```
typedef unsigned char byte;
double  square(unsigned char a)  { return a*a; }
int     square(byte a)           { return a*a; }  // **error**
```

solution in C++ is to provide default values for the arguments in the *declaration* of the function. These values can then be left out when the function is called. Only the trailing arguments can have initial default values. Another possibility is the use of "...". which declares the function with an unspecified number and type of arguments.[8] This should be avoided in general; but it is necessary for both C and the Unix interface of the language. Listing 63 shows these features.[9] This syntax is also used for exceptions to specify a handler that will catch any throw; naturally this handler should be the last in the list of handlers after a try block.[10]

The specifiers described in Sect. 6.3 are valid when declaring the return value of a function as well. Returning a reference is rather interesting, because the return value of the function can be assigned a value as if it were a variable (Listing 64); this example also shows the use of the macro assert which is very useful during program development. If the expression passed to the macro evaluates to false, the program stops at this point and gives a message that the assertion failed at this point in the source code.[11]

The above example also shows a new return type: a reference to an integer. It is an error to return a reference to a function's local variable, which is not static, upon its return, since the memory location is no longer valid after the return from the function that was called. This is a common mistake, but usually compilers print warnings, which give hints to programmers.

---

[8]The function then has to use varargs to recover the argument list.

[9]See varargs and [Str97] for details of a possible implementation for fct2.

[10]Functions which will throw an exception which is not handled inside the function, shall specify this in the function declaration: For example, void f() throw (int, double); is a declaration of f() for which in the definition we can use throw 1; or throw 1.0;. We will not need this feature in the following.

[11]The macros can be defined to an empty statement when the program is compiled with -DNDEBUG; see your local compiler manual. Compare also Exercise 6.c.

```
void fct0(int i, int j = 3) {}              // definition
void fct1(int i, char c = ' ', float f = 0.0);  // declaration
int  fct2(int i ... );                      // declaration

void fct1(int i, char c, float f) {}        // definition

main()
{
    fct0 (1);              // call fct0(1,3)
    fct2 (1,2,3,4,5);      // fct2 will have to take care of the args
    fct0 (1,2);
}
```

```
#include <assert.h>              /* useful macros for debugging */
int & elem(unsigned int i)
{
    static int f[10];      // must be static
    assert(i < 10);        // check index
    return f[i];           // return reference to local data
}
void fct(int i)
{
    elem(i) = 3;           // see the function call on the left!
}
```

```
#define square(a) a*a          /* a dangerous macro */
main()
{
    int   i = 3;
    float g = 3.0;
    int   j = square(++i);     // surprise
    float f = square(g+2);     // surprise
    printf("%d %f\n", j, f);   // prints 20 11.0
}
```

6.7 Macros and Inline Functions

Macros are often a source of nasty errors, especially if they have side effects as shown in Listing 65.

Although it looks like a function call, square in Listing 65 is just a textual substitution and has no function semantics. C++ introduces inline functions, which in many cases replace the use of macros with a safer tool.

Inline functions provide the runtime efficiency of macros and the flexibility of functional semantics including local variables and scoping rules. Listing 66 shows the new version of Listing 65 which now works as expected. However, we need two function definitions in order to provide the square of integral numbers and of floating point numbers. Of course, inline functions can be overloaded just as regular functions.

The function atof in Listing 66 works like atoi but returns a floating point value. Inline functions are "expanded" like macros but provide functional semantics. They should be used in C++ instead of macros wherever possible.

```
#include<stdlib.h>
inline int    square(int a)    { return a*a; }   // square 1
inline double square(double a) { return a*a; }   // square 2
main(int argc, char ** argv)
{
    int   j = square(atoi(*++argv));             // call square 1
    float f = square(atof(*++argv)+2);           // call square 2
    printf("%d %f\n", j, f);                     // works as expected
}
```

```
static int fct1(int i) { return i; }
static int fct2(int i) { return i*i; }

static int (*fptr) (int)    // declare fptr as ptr to function
         = fct1;             // and initialize to fct1

main()
{
    printf("%d\n", fptr(2)); // indirect function call to fct1
    fptr = fct2;
    printf("%d\n", fptr(2)); // indirect function call to fct2
}
```
`67`

```
extern "C" void
qsrt(                          // extern C quick sort function
    void *base,                // pointer to start of data
    int nel,                   // number of elements
    int size,                  // size of an element
    int (*compar)(const void *, const void *) // compare function
);
```
`68`

6.8 Function Pointers

In Chapter 5 we introduced pointers to data. Pointers may also be set to functions. The syntax of the declaration is basically as follows:

Syntax: *return_type* (*<u>*</u> name) (arguments)

This means that a function pointer variable *name* is declared that can be set to a function of a given type; this declaration includes the return type and the argument declaration of the function. It is possible to circumvent this kind of type checking by a cast, but in general this can introduce problems during run time of a program.

Functions can be called *indirectly* via pointers as shown in Listing 67. This technique is very powerful and used in large C programs. In C++, other mechanisms exist which are safer with respect to type checking and simpler in terms of programming. We will hear more about that in Part II.

Since C++ provides better features than function pointers, we will not go into details here. This language feature is, however, required if functions from the system libraries are to be used, for example, a quick-sort function as declared in Listing 68 and used in Listing 69.

A complicated cast of the function pointer `compare` is required to bypass C++ argument type checking. Such casts can occasionally be made more readable by a `typedef` for a function pointer.

6.9 Comma Operator and Conditional Expressions

Two minor features of C and C++ conclude this chapter. The *comma operator* is mostly used in tricky macros and should be avoided in general. Only the common use in a `for`–loop is

6.9 Comma Operator and Conditional Expressions

```
static int cmp(const int* i1,const int* i2) {return (*i1)-(*i2);}
main()
{
    int * ia = new int[20];
    // do something with ia
    qsrt(ia,20,sizeof(int), (int(*)(const void*,const void*))cmp);
}
```
69

```
int i = 1, j = (i > 2) ? 2 : 0 ;
for (i = 0, j = 0; i < 10; ++i, ++j) {}
```
70

recommended (in Listing 70 the two expressions left and right of the comma are evaluated both). The result of the first expression is discarded.

The *conditional expression* is used more often. Depending on the result of the expression before the "?" the result is either the value of the next expression or of the one following the ":".

Syntax:

expression ? expression1 : expression2

It is clearly defined what happens if the comma operator and conditional expressions have side effects. However, such things are very hard to read and understand; they should thus be avoided.

Exercises

6.a **The Functions** `sscanf` **and** `fgets`

The function `sscanf` extracts values from a string and is part of most C libraries. This function can be used when `atof` and `atoi` are not sufficient.

In combination with the function `fgets` which reads a string into a buffer, simple formatted input can be parsed. The formatting parameters are essentially the same as for `printf` (Table 2.1). However, the arguments have to be provided as pointers to be filled with values. An example is shown in Listing 71.

The functions `fscanf` and `scanf` read directly from a stream and are not as safe as sscanf and fgets. C++ provides safer facilities for input from streams ([Str97], cf. Sect. 16.3).

Declare the functions `fgets`, `fscanf`, and `sscanf` with their argument lists. Check your result against the declarations in the file `<stdio.h>`.

```
int i; char c; float f;
char buffer[256];
fgets(buffer,sizeof(buffer),stdin);
sscanf(buffer,"I = %d, F = %7.2f, c = %c",&i,&f,&c);
```
71

```
int main (int argc, char** argv)
{
    DEBUGMSG(("starting main %s\n", *argv));
    // do something
    if (argc == 1)
        DEBUGMSG(("argc == 1\n")); // make sure this works
    else
        DEBUGMSG(("argc <> 1\n"));
    DEBUGMSG(("End of main\n"));
    return 0;
}
```
72

6.b *Repeat Macro*

One syntactic macro — in contrast to Listing 72 — will make code more readable,[12] since the multiple use of the keyword `while` is avoided:

Write a macro `repeat` and `until ( expression )` which will work as expected (refer to the Pascal manual). Use proper parentheses for the expression!

6.c *Debug Macro*

Even if your system has a nice debugger, messages for debugging a program are often very handy. On the other hand, it is a nuisance to remove them for the final run. Efficiency requires that such lines disappear completely from the code after debugging.

Define a simple macro called `DEBUGMSG`.

It should have one (!) argument which is used for the function `printf`. Since `printf` directs its output to `stdout` — which is a buffered file — messages are delayed until the buffer is full. Use the function `fflush` to avoid this behavior. The macro should expand to *one* statement so it can be used in an `if-then-else` sequence as shown in the example program.

Hints:

- Create two files:
  - `debugmsg.h` containing the macros
  - `debugmsg.C` containing the functions

  Write a test program, use a makefile and `rcs`.

- The resulting lines in the program should look as in Listing 72.

- Check the file `<assert.h>` for further ideas. Try `man assert` as well.

Then, conditionally redefine the macro in a way that

- No output is printed
- No code is generated for this line

---

[12]This is at least the opinion of the authors of this book.

Chapter 7

Statistics for Pattern Recognition

Applications of image and speech processing have to deal with uncertainty and noise effects. Probability theory and statistics provide a mathematical framework to handle these phenomena. As outlined in Sect. 1.4, pattern recognition and analysis deal with the *mathematical characterization of perception*. It is, therefore, natural to use all kinds of mathematical tools for solving pattern recognition problems.

The subsequent sections briefly introduce the basics of probability theory and statistics that are useful for understanding the algorithms and principles applied later in this book. For more mathematical details, we refer to the monographs [Bre88, Pap91].

7.1 Axioms

Many concepts of probability theory are inspired by numerical phenomena. You can, for instance, *measure* the energy of a speech signal or the intensities for each pixel of a gray-level image. Such measurable quantities are called *random variables*.

The basic object in probability theory is the *probability space* $(\mathcal{S}, \mathcal{F}, p)$, where $\mathcal{S}$ represents the set of all possible outcomes of an experiment, $\mathcal{F} \subseteq 2^{\mathcal{S}}$ is the family of events, i.e. a set of subsets of $\mathcal{S}$, and p is a function assigning to each event $A \in \mathcal{F}$ its probability $p(A) \in [0, 1] \subset \mathbb{R}$.

The probability space introduced must satisfy the axioms of probability theory summarized in Table 7.1.

Depending on the applications, the range of random variables can be discrete or continuous. Both cases are important for pattern recognition applications and are discussed in the following section.

> **Axioms of Probability Theory:**
> 1. $\mathcal{S} \in \mathcal{F}$
> 2. if $A \in \mathcal{F}$, then $\bar{A} \in \mathcal{F}$
> 3. if for all elements of the sequence $(A_n)_{n \geq 0}$ we have $A_n \in \mathcal{F}$, then $\bigcup_{n \geq 0} A_n \in \mathcal{F}$.
> 4. $p(\mathcal{S}) = 1$
> 5. for any sequence $(A_n)_{n \geq 0}$ of pairwise disjoint events the following additivity condition is valid
>
> $$p\left(\bigcup_{n \geq 0} A_n\right) = \sum_{n \geq 0} p(A_n) \quad .$$

Table 7.1: Axioms of probability theory

7.2 Random Variables

The probability to observe a discrete random variable X is written as $p(X)$; similarly, the probability that the value of X is in the interval $[A, B]$ is denoted by $p(A \leq X \leq B)$. Using above axioms of probability theory the following equation obviously holds:

$$p(X \leq A) = 1 - p(X > A) \quad . \tag{7.1}$$

In many practical situations it is necessary to *estimate* the probability $p(X)$ for each random variable X from a set of training samples. Estimates of probabilities are denoted by $\hat{p}$. This is done using the relative frequency of the observed random variables. Let M be the set of observed random variables and $|M|$ the cardinality of the training set. For each random variable $X \in M$ we can compute

$$\hat{p}(X) = \frac{|\{Y \in M \mid Y = X\}|}{|M|} \quad . \tag{7.2}$$

This quotient is called the *relative frequency* of X.

The *cumulative distribution function* (c.d.f.) for the random variable X is defined by

$$P(x) = p(X \leq x) = \sum_{X \leq x} p(X) \quad . \tag{7.3}$$

A cumulative distribution function is monotonic and increasing; its maximum value equals 1.

One fundamental result of probability theory states that the relative frequency converges to the real probability for $|M| \to \infty$. The difference between the real probability $p(X)$ of observing X and the estimated relative frequency is less or equal to an arbitrarily small positive number; this number converges to zero for an infinite sample set (see e.g. [Bre88]).

7.2 Random Variables

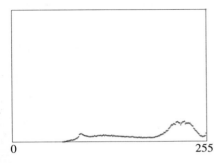
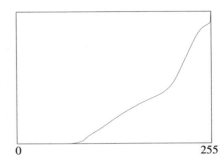

Figure 7.1: Frequencies and the associated cumulative distribution function for gray-level image shown on p. 3

The following example will clarify some of the introduced concepts: In image processing applications, random variables often are the gray-levels of image pixels. Figure 7.1 shows a gray-level image, its frequencies of gray-levels, and the associated distribution function. The relative frequency of each gray-level can be computed by dividing the value of the level in the histogram by the number of image pixels. Each gray-level in the histogram is related to the number of pixels having this value. You can also see that the distribution has the value 1 for the gray-level 255, i.e. the probability to observe a gray-level less or equal to 255 is 1.

Suppose now that we are working on analog image data. In this case the random variable *gray-level* will have a real value, i.e. we have a set of random variables of infinite cardinality. From the axioms of probability theory we conclude that the probability of observing a specific gray-level equals zero. Of course, for each point in the image plane, we can measure a gray-level; nevertheless the probability of observing exactly this gray-level is zero. The sum over the probabilities of all possible outcomes has to be equal to one. Due to the fact that the cardinality of the set of random variables is infinite, the summands cannot be nonzero.

In analogy to the discrete case, we define the cumulative distribution function

$$F(x) = p(X \leq x). \tag{7.4}$$

If there exists a nonnegative function f such that,

$$F(x) = \int_{-\infty}^{x} f(z)\, dz, \tag{7.5}$$

then we call $f(x)$ the *probability density function* (p.d.f.) of the continuous random variable X.

One of the most famous probability densities is the *Gaussian density*

$$f(x|\mu, \sigma^2) = \frac{1}{\sigma\sqrt{2\pi}} \exp\left(-\frac{1}{2}\frac{(x-\mu)^2}{\sigma^2}\right). \tag{7.6}$$

This density function defines a parametric family of densities $\{f(x|\mu, \sigma^2)|\mu, \sigma^2 \in \mathbb{R}\}$. The parameters μ and σ^2 are called the *mean* and *variance* of the given distribution. A probabilistic

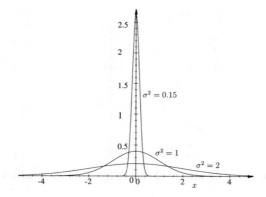

Figure 7.2: Gaussian densities with $\mu = 0$ and $\sigma^2 = 0.15, 1, 2$

interpretation of these two parameters will be given in the next section. Figure 7.2 shows some examples elements of this parametric family. It is fairly easy to see that the value of the density function $f(x)$ for $x = \mu$ can be greater than 1, if $\sigma < 1/\sqrt{2\pi}$. So $f(x)$ should not be confused with the probability function p of the probability space (Sect. 7.1).

The cumulative distribution of normal, or Gaussian, distributed random variable is

$$F(x) = \frac{1}{\sigma\sqrt{2\pi}} \int_{-\infty}^{x} \exp\left(-\frac{1}{2}\frac{(z-\mu)^2}{\sigma^2}\right) dz \quad . \tag{7.7}$$

For the integral in (7.7) there exists no closed form solution. That is the reason why numerical methods are used to evaluate this integral.

In the field of pattern recognition, Gaussian densities are widely used [Nie83, Dud73]. Normally distributed random variables are mathematically easy to handle, and most applications take advantage of the approximation of density functions by Gaussian densities or variations [Nie83]. Gaussian distributions are suitable to model noise effects (Chapter 12, [Bel89]). In speech recognition Gaussian distributions describe the statistical behavior of features [ST95]. The probabilistic modeling of point features for object recognition purposes is often based on normally distributed random vectors [Sar94]; this probabilistic model leads to reliable recognition results.

The support of mathematical functions and operations in the language definition of C++ is small compared to other languages, like e.g Fortran. For the computation of function values with e.g. the formula in (7.7) we need the constant π, exponentiation, etc. These values and functions can be found in a header file math.h and a mathematical library which has to be added by the linker (Sect. 6.4).[1] Listing 73 shows an implementation of the Gaussian density function $f(x|\mu, \sigma^2)$ as defined in (7.6).

---

[1] Usually, a flag has to be passed to the linker like -lm to inform it that this library is needed.

```
#include <math.h>              // import constants and functions
inline double sqr(double d) { return d*d; }
double gauss(double x, double sigma, double mu)
{
   return ( 1 / (sigma /
           sqrt(              // sqrt: square root function
              2 * M_PI        // M_PI: from math.h
           )) *
           exp ((             // exp(..) exponentiation function
              - 0.5 *
              sqr(x - mu)     // sqr: square function
           ) / sqr(sigma)));
}
```

73

```
double mean(double *v, int s)
{
    double S = 0;
    while (s-- > 0) S += *(v++);
    return S;
}
double variance(double *v, int s)
{
    double V, m = mean(v,s);
    while (s-- > 0) V += sqr(*(v++) - m);
    return V/s;
}
```

74

7.3 Moments of a Distribution

In general, the underlying statistics of gray-levels or other observable sensor data is not known. Nevertheless, the statistical quantities mean and variance can be estimated from k observed random samples. The *mean* of given samples can be computed by

$$\hat{\mu} = \frac{1}{k} \sum_{i=1}^{k} f_i \quad , \tag{7.8}$$

and the *variance* is estimated using

$$\hat{\sigma}^2 = \frac{1}{k} \sum_{i=1}^{k} (f_i - \mu)^2 \quad . \tag{7.9}$$

To prove that mathematical formulas can often simply be translated to programs, we give an implementation of (7.8) and (7.9) in Listing 74.

Although, these formulas are often used for arbitrary distributions of random values, the estimates are true only if they are normally distributed. Both values can be computed assuming that the gray-levels f_i, $1 \leq i \leq k$, are normally distributed or not. A proof of the estimation formulas (7.8) and (7.9) can be done by a so called *maximum likelihood estimation* of the parameters μ and σ^2 (cf. [Fah94, Tan96]). If a random generator is given and if it is known that all generated observations are normally distributed (see the "black box" in Figure 7.3), the parameters μ and σ^2 can be estimated by maximizing the likelihood function

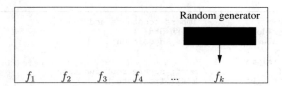

Figure 7.3: Random generator for normally distributed variables

$$L(\{f_1, f_2, \ldots, f_k\}, \mu, \sigma^2) = \prod_{i=1}^{k} f(f_i|\mu, \sigma^2)$$

$$= \left(\frac{1}{\sigma\sqrt{2\pi}}\right)^k \exp\left(-\frac{1}{2\sigma^2}\sum_{i=1}^{k}(f_i - \mu)^2\right) \quad (7.10)$$

for the observed set of gray-levels. Here, we assume that all observations are pairwise statistically independent (see Sect. 7.6). Thus, the density function of observing the training set $\{f_1, f_2, \ldots, f_k\}$ is the product over all single density values $f(f_i|\mu, \sigma^2)$.

A common way for the optimization of continuous functions, such as the likelihood function or its logarithm, with respect to some parameters is the computation of zero-crossings of the partial derivatives with respect to the unknown parameters μ and σ^2.

To give an example, the computation of mean and variance of the gray-levels of the video image shown on p. 3 yields $\mu = 190.961$ and $\sigma^2 = 2739.55$. This is kind of obvious, since the image has a balanced ratio of dark and light gray-levels.

The cumulative distribution or the density function characterize the distribution completely. The mean and variance introduced above can be computed using the estimators introduced above. Even if the underlying distribution of the observed sample data is not Gaussian, we can get a result for μ and σ. Therefore, we cannot conclude from these values the underlying distribution of the sample data. The mean and variance are coarse measures of the distribution. Therefore, we generalize these measures.

Let k be a natural number and $f(x)$ the density function of a distribution. If the function $g(z) = z^k f(z)$ is absolutely integrable [Bre88], then we call

$$m_k(p) = \int z^k f(z) dz \quad (7.11)$$

the k–th absolute moment of the distribution p. Analogously, we call

$$\widehat{m}_k(p) = \int (z - m_1(p))^k f(z) dz \quad (7.12)$$

the k–th central moment of the distribution p, if $g(z) = (z - m_1(p))^k f(z)$ is absolutely integrable.

The first absolute moment is called *expectation* and we commonly write $E[X]$ for the expectation of the random variable X. Above definitions are valid for continuous random variables.

7.4 Generating Random Variables

In the discrete case, one has to substitute the integral sign with a discrete summation.[2] The first absolute moment and the second central moment are the mean and variance in the discrete situation.

The definition of moments is not only restricted to univariate density functions. Moments can also be computed for higher dimensional arbitrary functions. For instance, assume a discrete gray-level function $(f_{i,j})_{0 \leq i,j \leq 255}$, where $f_{i,j} \in \{0, 1, \ldots, 255\}$. The discrete sum

$$m_{r,s} = \sum_{i,j=0}^{255} i^r j^s f_{i,j} \qquad (7.13)$$

introduces the (r, s)–moment of the given gray-level image. The center of gravity (x_S, y_S) of $f_{i,j}$, for example, can be computed by first moments, i.e.

$$x_S = \frac{m_{1,0}}{m_{0,0}} \quad \text{and} \quad y_S = \frac{m_{0,1}}{m_{0,0}} \ . \qquad (7.14)$$

Normalization of geometric patterns is usually done by pattern transforms based on moments (7.13) for various values of r and s [Nie83; p.64].

7.4 Generating Random Variables

Often it is required to generate random variables of a certain distribution. Most libraries provide only functions to generate random variables which are uniformly distributed in some interval: the density function of a random variable X uniformly distributed in $[a, b]$ is defined as

$$f_X(x) = \begin{cases} \frac{1}{b-a} & ; \quad \text{if } a \leq b \\ 0 & ; \quad \text{otherwise} \end{cases} \qquad (7.15)$$

For discrete random variables this means that the probability of a certain value in the given interval is the same for all values; the probability is one divided by the number of possible outcomes. A typical example is throwing a dice where the probability is $1/6$ for all six digits.

Now let X be a random variable with an arbitrary distribution. If we consider in a second step the value of its cumulative distribution as a random variable U (either discrete or continuous), i.e. $u = F_X(x)$, we observe that this random variable is distributed uniformly over $[0, 1]$. Here we use the subscript X to denote which c.d.f. is considered. The monoticity of $F_X(x)$ assures that $U \leq u$ if and only if $X < x$ and thus we get:

$$F_U(u) = p(U \leq u) = p(X \leq x) = F_X(x) = u \ . \qquad (7.16)$$

This shows $F_U(u) = u$ and obviously the density function is the first derivative that is (7.15) where $a = 0$ and $b = 1$.

We can also use the above argument the other way round and get: a uniform distribution can be used to generate arbitrary distributions. Given a random variable U which is uniformly

---
[2] As in Listing 74, a sum is mostly implemented by a loop in programming.

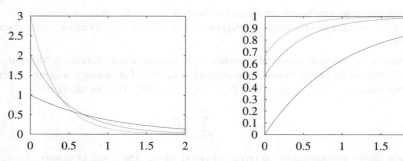

Figure 7.4: Exponential distribution for $\lambda = 1, 2, 3$: p.d.f. (left), c.d.f. (right)

```
extern int random() ;    // generate uniformly distributed in [0,RAND_MAX]
static double Rand()     // generate uniformly distributed in [0,1]
{
    return double(random())/RAND_MAX;
}

double expdens(double lambda)
{
    return - (1.0/lambda) * log(lambda * (1 - Rand()));
}
```

distributed in the interval $[0, 1]$ we can compute a function $g(u)$ such that the random variable $x = g(u)$ has a required distribution $F_X(x)$. It turns out that the solution is surprisingly simple (see (7.16)): $g(u)$ is the inverse of the F_X and thus

$$x = F_X^{-1}(u) \quad . \tag{7.17}$$

Now we can use (7.16) and (7.17) to state the general transform from a random variable X with distribution F_X to a random variable Y with distribution F_Y. The random variable defined by $u = F_X(x)$ is uniformly distributed and thus for $y = F_Y^{-1}(F_X(x))$ we get:

$$p(Y \leq y) = F_Y(y) \quad . \tag{7.18}$$

Now we demonstrate this technique and generate samples of another famous density, the so-called exponential distribution. A random variable is called exponentially distributed if

$$f(x) = \begin{cases} \lambda e^{-\lambda x} & ; \text{ if } x \geq 0 \\ 0 & ; \text{ otherwise} \end{cases} \quad . \tag{7.19}$$

Figure 7.4 shows this distribution and cumulative distribution for several values of λ.

The c.d.f. is $F_X(x) = 1 - \frac{1}{\lambda}e^{-\lambda x}$ and its inverse is $F_X^{-1}(u) = \frac{-1}{\lambda}\ln(\lambda(1-u))$. According to (7.17) we can generate exponentially distributed random variables as shown in Listing 75.

The above introduced transforms of random variables are very important for many image processing applications. For instance, in Sect. 18.4 we will use these techniques to enhance contrast of gray-level images or to reduce the total number of gray-levels.

7.5 Random Vectors

The definition of random variables can be used for generalization purposes. We call a vector $\boldsymbol{X} = (X_1, X_2, \ldots, X_n)$ a *random vector* of dimension n, if the components $X_1, X_2, \ldots, X_n$ are real valued random variables. The multivariate cumulative distribution function of $\boldsymbol{X}$ is similar to the one-dimensional case. It is defined as

$$F_{\boldsymbol{X}}(x_1, x_2, \ldots, x_n) = P(X_1 \leq x_1, X_2 \leq x_2, \ldots, X_n \leq x_n). \tag{7.20}$$

The nonnegative multivariate density function $f_{\boldsymbol{X}}(x_1, x_2, \ldots, x_n)$ can be computed from the following n–dimensional integral equation

$$F_{\boldsymbol{X}}(x_1, \ldots, x_n) = \int_{-\infty}^{x_n} \ldots \int_{-\infty}^{x_1} f_{\boldsymbol{X}}(y_1, \ldots, y_n) \, dy_1 \ldots dy_n. \tag{7.21}$$

The formulas for discrete random vectors follow immediately, if the integral signs are substituted with sums over all possible values of the discrete random variables.

For example, a gray-level image of size $M \times N$ can be viewed as a discrete random vector of size $n = M * N$, where the gray-levels of the image represent the components of the vector.

Let $\boldsymbol{X} = (X_1, X_2, \ldots, X_n)$ be an n–dimensional random vector. The *mean vector* $\boldsymbol{\mu} = E[\boldsymbol{X}]$ is now defined by the means of all components, i.e.

$$E[\boldsymbol{X}] = \begin{pmatrix} E[X_1] \\ E[X_2] \\ \vdots \\ E[X_n] \end{pmatrix}. \tag{7.22}$$

The generalization of the variance is done by the *covariance* of two random variables X_i and X_j by

$$\sigma_{i,j} = E[(X_i - E[X_i])(X_j - E[X_j])]. \tag{7.23}$$

Obviously this results in the variance, if $i = j$. The *covariance matrix* is now given by

$$\boldsymbol{\Sigma} = \begin{pmatrix} \sigma_{11} & \ldots & \sigma_{1n} \\ \vdots & & \vdots \\ \sigma_{n1} & \ldots & \sigma_{nn} \end{pmatrix}. \tag{7.24}$$

It is symmetric (see (7.23)) and positive definite.

To continue with the famous Gaussian density function, its generalization to n dimensions is

$$f_{\boldsymbol{X}}(\boldsymbol{x}) = \frac{1}{\sqrt{2^n \pi^n |\det \boldsymbol{\Sigma}|}} \exp\left(-\frac{(\boldsymbol{x} - \boldsymbol{\mu})^{\mathrm{T}} \boldsymbol{\Sigma}^{-1} (\boldsymbol{x} - \boldsymbol{\mu})}{2}\right), \tag{7.25}$$

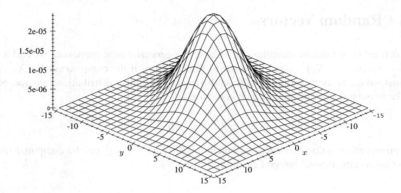

Figure 7.5: 2–D Gaussian density

where $\boldsymbol{x} = (x_1, x_2, \ldots, x_n)^\mathrm{T}$, $\boldsymbol{\mu}$ is the n–dimensional mean vector, and $\boldsymbol{\Sigma} \in \mathbb{R}^{n \times n}$ is the covariance matrix. To simplify the formula of multivariate Gaussian densities, many authors use the identity

$$2^n \pi^n |\det \boldsymbol{\Sigma}| = |\det(2\pi \boldsymbol{\Sigma})| \quad , \tag{7.26}$$

to eliminate the explicit appearance of the the variable n, the dimension of the random vectors considered. Figure 7.5 shows an example of a two-dimensional Gaussian density.

In general, arbitrary one-dimensional densities $f(x)$ ($x \in \mathbb{R}$) can be lifted to higher dimensional density functions $\tilde{f}_{\boldsymbol{X}}(\boldsymbol{x})$ ($\boldsymbol{x} \in \mathbb{R}^n$). For that, we define an $(n \times n)$–dimensional matrix $\boldsymbol{\Sigma}$, which can be any positive definite symmetric matrix, and an n–dimensional mean vector $\boldsymbol{\mu}$, compute the quadratic form

$$\boldsymbol{x}^\mathrm{T} \boldsymbol{\Sigma} \boldsymbol{x} \in \mathbb{R} \quad , \tag{7.27}$$

and get the n–dimensional density function

$$\tilde{f}_{\boldsymbol{X}}(\boldsymbol{x}) = \frac{\alpha}{\sqrt{|\det \boldsymbol{\Sigma}|}} f((\boldsymbol{x} - \boldsymbol{\mu})^\mathrm{T} \boldsymbol{\Sigma}^{-1} (\boldsymbol{x} - \boldsymbol{\mu})) \quad , \tag{7.28}$$

where the variable α has to be chosen such that

$$\int_{\boldsymbol{x}} \tilde{f}_{\boldsymbol{X}}(\boldsymbol{x}) \, d\boldsymbol{x} = 1 \quad . \tag{7.29}$$

For the n–dimensional Gaussian density, we have $\alpha = (2\pi)^{-\frac{n}{2}}$.

7.6 Independence and Marginal Densities

Axiom 5 (Table 7.1) shows that for pairwise disjoint events the additivity condition is valid. Real valued random variables $X_1, X_2, \ldots, X_n$, or the components of a random vector $\boldsymbol{X} =$

$(X_1, X_2, \ldots, X_n)^{\text{T}}$ are said to be statistically independent, if for all $x_1, x_2, \ldots, x_n \in \mathbb{R}$

$$f_{\boldsymbol{X}}((x_1, x_2, \ldots, x_n)) = \prod_{i=1}^{n} f_{X_i}(x_i) \quad . \tag{7.30}$$

If random variables do not satisfy the independency condition, the probability function can be factorized using conditional probabilities:

$$\begin{aligned} f_{\boldsymbol{X}}((x_1, x_2, \ldots, x_n)) &= f_{X_1}(x_1) f_{X_2|X_1}(x_2|x_1) \\ & \quad f_{X_3|X_1,X_2}(x_3|x_1, x_2) \\ & \quad \vdots \\ & \quad f_{X_n|X_1,X_2,\ldots,X_{n-1}}(x_n|x_1, x_2, \ldots, x_{n-1}) \quad , \end{aligned} \tag{7.31}$$

where the conditional probabilities are defined as

$$f_{X_i|X_j}(x_i|x_j) = \frac{f_{X_i,X_j}(x_i, x_j)}{f_{X_j}(x_j)} \quad . \tag{7.32}$$

Assume that the bivariate density function $f_{X_1,X_2}(x_1, x_2)$ is given, and we are looking for $f_{X_1}(x_1)$. If X_1 and X_2 are statistically independent and if f_{X_2} is known, a simple division gives us $f_{X_1}(x_1)$. In general, these prerequisites are not satisfied. A common way to compute the unknown density function is *marginalization*. We integrate in the continuous domain and sum in the discrete case over all admissible values of x_2 and get

$$f_{X_1}(x_1) = \int_{x_2} f_{X_1,X_2}(x_1, x_2) \, dx_2 \quad . \tag{7.33}$$

The process of marginalization will play a central role within the theory of Hidden-Markov-Models, which will be introduced in Chapter 23 for solving single-word recognition problems.

7.7 Mixtures

A useful combination of discrete probabilities and continuous random variables can be achieved by so-called mixture densities. A mixture density is a linear combination of N density functions $f_1(\boldsymbol{x}), \ldots, f_N(\boldsymbol{x})$

$$f(\boldsymbol{x}) = \sum_{i=1}^{N} p_i f_i(\boldsymbol{x}) \tag{7.34}$$

where the weighing factors hold the probability constraint, i.e., they sum up to one (cf. Appendix C.2):

$$\sum_{i=1}^{N} p_i = 1 \quad . \tag{7.35}$$

Obviously the mixture (7.34) is a probability density function because

$$\int f(\boldsymbol{x})\,d\boldsymbol{x} \;=\; \sum_{i=1}^{N} p_i \int f_i(\boldsymbol{x})\,d\boldsymbol{x} \;=\; \sum_{i=1}^{N} p_i \;=\; 1 \quad . \tag{7.36}$$

Mixture densities are widely used in pattern recognition [Dud73, Nie83]. They are mostly applied to approximate arbitrary densities for which no density function can be given. The most common mixture density is the so-called *Gaussian mixture* which is a convex combination of (possibly multivariate) Gaussians:

$$f(\boldsymbol{x}) \;=\; \sum_{i=1}^{N} \frac{p_i}{\sqrt{|\det 2\pi \boldsymbol{\Sigma}_i|}} \, \exp\left(-\frac{(\boldsymbol{x} - \boldsymbol{\mu}_i)^{\mathrm{T}} \boldsymbol{\Sigma}_i^{-1}(\boldsymbol{x} - \boldsymbol{\mu}_i)}{2} \right) \quad . \tag{7.37}$$

It is, however, difficult to choose the number N of mixture components properly [Jel98]. The parameters $p_i, \boldsymbol{\mu}_i, \boldsymbol{\sigma}_i$ can be determined by an maximum likelihood esitimation, as shown in Sect. 7.3: this requires the maximization in a high-dimensional parameter space which is computationally hard. In practice, an iterative algorithm is applied which results from the EM-algorithm; we will introduce this important technique in Sect. 23.6.

7.8 Statistical Features and Entropy

The defined statistical distribution characteristics constitute possible features of patterns as we will learn later. For example, a speech signal is divided into intervals of fixed size, usually at a sampling rate of 10 kHz or disjunctive windows of a duration of about 12.8 ms. In general, the interval size should be motivated by phonetics and has an averaged duration of 10–20 ms. For each signal frame, features like the mean number of zero-crossings can be used. Images can be decomposed into blocks of fixed size, for example, 16×16 pixels. Statistical measures like moments can be computed for subimages. These are suitable features for the given patterns and can be applied to pattern classification (Sect. 8.1).

When we observe a random measure x_i of the random variable X_i, the information derivable from the outcome will depend on its probability. If the probability of observing the random variable is small, a large degree of information can be concluded, since the occurrence of this random variable is very rare. In contrast to that, random variables with a large probability of being observed have a very small degree of information. In coding and information theory the amount of *information* is defined as

$$I(x_i) \;=\; -\log p(x_i) \quad . \tag{7.38}$$

The important property of a randomized information source is the *entropy* which is defined as the average amount of information, i.e.

$$H(S) \;=\; -\sum_{x_i \in S} p(x_i) \log p(x_i) \quad , \tag{7.39}$$

where S denotes the set of observations. The entropy is the measure of the amount of information required in specifying which random variable has occurred on average. The entropy $H(S)$

holds the inequality $H(S) \geq 0$, if and only if $p(x_i) = 1$ for some $x_i \in S$. A probability is called *degenerated*, if $p(x_i) = 1$ for some x_i and $p(x_j) = 0$ for all $x_j \in S$, where $i \neq j$. Thus, the entropy is minimal for degenerated probabilities. The maximum value of $H(S)$ depends on k, where k denotes the cardinality of S. Obviously, $H(S) = \log k$ if and only if $p(x_i) = p(x_j)$ for all $1 \leq i, j \leq k$.

7.9 Signal-to-Noise Ratio

For the representation of a real value f_i in the computer we have to use the discrete value f_i'. The error between the discrete and the real value is called *quantization noise* (cf. Figure 1.10) and is given by

$$n_i = f_i - f_i'. \qquad (7.40)$$

A measure for the accuracy of this quantization is the *signal-to-noise ratio* (SNR). For the quantization of continuous signals the SNR is defined by a quotient of means:

$$\text{SNR} = \frac{E[f^2]}{E[n^2]}, \qquad (7.41)$$

where f denotes the random measure of the sampling value and n a random variable for the quantization noise.

The assumptions that the quantization error is uniformly distributed, the quantizer is not saturated, and the quantization is fine enough, leads to the following formula for the SNR:

$$\text{SNR} = 12 \cdot 2^{2B-6}, \qquad (7.42)$$

where B is the number of bits used for quantization, i.e. we have 2^B different values for the digital range [Nie83; p. 29]. B is typically greater than 6. Thus, an additional bit improves the quantization error by 6 dB. The signal-to-noise ratio is used as an objective measure for the "quality" of a signal. It may happen, however, that a signal with high SNR looks resp. sounds worse than one with a lower ratio.

Exercises

7.a Compute the probability that in a gray-level image of size $N \times M$ all pixels have the same gray-level. Assume that the discrete gray-levels are uniformly distributed on the integers $[0, g]$.

7.b Usually, mathematical function libraries provide a random function which generates uniformly distributed random numbers from a fixed interval $[\min, \max]$.[3] Sketch an algorithm which permits the computation of uniformly distributed numbers out of a parameterized interval $[l, u]$ using the available random generator.

---
[3] Try `rand()` or `random()` on your machine.

7.c   Write a program which plots one special function: the *Cauchy probability density*

$$f(x) = \frac{1}{\pi} \frac{1}{1+x^2} \tag{7.43}$$

and compare the graph with the Gaussian density.[4] Show that there exist no mean and variance for the Cauchy density! Do you think Gaussians should be approximated by Cauchy densities?

7.d   Give a proof of (7.8) and (7.9) as suggested in the text!

7.e   Compute the SNR for music with CD quality (16 bit).

---

[4]The program `gnuplot` is a great tool for plotting data.

Chapter 8

Classification and Pattern Analysis

Depending on the input data and the problem to be solved, there exist three major areas in pattern recognition and pattern analysis:

1. classification of simple patterns,
2. classification of complex patterns, and
3. analysis of complex patterns.

We saw examples for those cases already in Figure 1.2.

In the subsequent parts of this book we will concentrate our discussion on the first and third point above, even though we will briefly introduce all of them. A comprehensive discussion is presented in [Bis95, Nie83, Rip96]. In this chapter we give an overview of the architecture of pattern recognition and analysis systems and motivate the other chapters of this book. We outline the relation of knowledge based pattern understanding systems to the general problems of artificial intelligence.

8.1 Classification

The goal of pattern classification is to associate a class with the given input pattern (Sect. 1.4). With respect to the classification process, the task domain (see Sect. 1.3) is partitioned into k disjoint classes Ω_λ ($\lambda = 1, \ldots, k$), i.e. $\Omega_\mu \cap \Omega_\nu = \emptyset$ for $\nu \neq \mu$. The classification assigns each observed pattern to exactly one class of this partition. Several applications suggest the insertion of a *reject class* Ω_0; for example, for those applications where rejection will bring about lower costs than misclassification. For classification, patterns are usually first reduced to features, as we will see in Sect. 8.3.

Some examples illustrate the goal of classification:

1. classes $A - Z$ and "unknown" for character recognition,
2. forest, street, field, water for the automatic generation of maps using satellite images,
3. the phoneme classification of the classes vowel, plosive, fricative, nasal, and silence for word recognition.

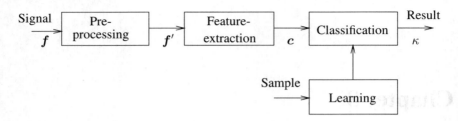

Figure 8.1: The architecture of a simple classification system [Nie83] together with the notation for signals, feature vectors, and class index

The classification algorithms can be divided into two groups: syntactical classifiers and numerical classifiers. If features of patterns are real numbers, vectors, sets or other structures on the field of reals, the resulting classification system will be a numerical one. Typically, statistical principles are used for the design and implementation of numerical classifiers. In speech recognition a signal is considered as a sequence of random measurements and the decision making is based on statistics [Jel98]. Due to the geometric nature of objects, numerical classifiers in computer vision require the computation of distances between geometric representations [Mar82]. This is why we introduced basic statistical methods in Chapter 7. Alternatively, artificial neural networks can be used for classification purposes. We briefly mention this subject in Sect. 23.9.

Syntactical classification uses the results of parsing a syntactic description of the pattern using a formal language. Examples of syntactical image classification can be found in [Bun92]; syntactic classifiers for speech recognition are used in [Nie83].

Figure 8.1 shows the modules of a classification system for simple patterns. The classification module decides which class fits best to the computed features. Usually, a training set (sample) is used so that the parameters of the classification process can be adapted by a learning module.

8.2 Preprocessing

Before features can be extracted, the signal is *pre-processed* (Figure 8.1). Usually, pre-processing operations are problem-independent. Patterns are transformed into patterns, i.e. an image matrix into an image matrix or a speech signal into a speech signal. In other words, the type of representation does not change; as in Figure 8.1 a signal f is pre-processed to f'.

The goal of pre-processing is to simplify the computation which will have to be done in later stages of the analysis. The signal may be enhanced, normalized, filtered, etc. in order to reach this goal. For example, smoothing of patterns represents a typical operation in the pre-processing stage. Smoothing will eventually reduce unnecessary details or noise and may thus speed up succeeding processing. Other examples of pre-processing operations are things such as filters or changes of the size of images or the duration of speech signals.

Another common pre-processing technique is the normalization of the input signals. Energy normalization, for example, would adjust the loudness of speech signals or the darkness of an image. Size normalization of patterns or rotation of a given sub-pattern into a normal position is common, e.g. in character recognition.[1] These factors can be partially suppressed by suitable pre-processing operations. You can, for example, normalize the intensity of light, which is ordinarily different under varying illumination conditions, or the energy of speech signals.

8.3 Feature Extraction

After pre-processing, patterns are transformed to lower dimensional feature sets or feature vectors; the pre-processed signal f' is now converted to a feature vector $c \in \mathbb{R}^n$ in Figure 8.1.

Numerical features can be vectors of real numbers or a set of vectors which characterize the class of a pattern. For speech signals one can use information about frequencies in the signal; we will learn how to compute this in Chapter 23. The average gray-level of a region in an image can be significant in the classification of objects. Some simple statistical features are, for instance, the average intensity in a local spatial neighborhood of a picture region or the variance in the temporal proximity of a speech sampling value. An intuitive assumption is that an increase of features' dimensions will lead to more accurate recognition results; the more features, the better. Surprisingly this conclusion is false. Bellman could show that with increasing dimensionality of feature vectors the discriminating power decreases [Bel61]. The *curse-of-dimensionality* is basically characterized by the following properties:

- in high dimensional spaces it is impossible to get big sample sets, i.e., with increasing dimension an exponentially increasing number of data points is required to guarantee a densely sampled Euclidean space,
- all inter-point distances are large and rather equal, and
- all data points are close to the boundary of the considered space.

The choice of the right balance between the dimension of feature vectors and their discriminating power is one of the main concerns of pattern recognition. In some applications, however, numerical features are not appropriate and it might be advantageous to use symbolic features instead.

Symbolic features once extracted are fundamental for syntactical classifiers [Bun92].

8.4 Learning

Now we have outlined all blocks in Figure 8.1 except for "Learning". A crucial problem is the acquisition of information on pattern classes. This is done in the learning stage of a classifier. The classifier has to provide methods which allow the automatic learning of pattern classes and its associated features. Basically two major issues have to be solved:

---

[1] This is not a trivial problem. Consider the sampling theorem!

1. Signals are noisy and instances of the same class generate different feature vectors. There is an obvious need to introduce some mathematical concept that characterize features belonging to the same class.
2. If the number of pattern classes and classes itself are unknown, then classes and the implied partition of the feature space have to be determined in the learning stage.

Many applications provide an intuitive definition of classes, for instance, the classification of digits implies 10 classes. If the assignment of features to classes is known, and only the distribution of features of a single class has to be computed from samples, we call this process *supervised learning*. If classes of training samples are unknown, both class assignment and class-specific distribution have to be computed. This is the so-called *unsupervised training*.

8.5 Analysis

The analysis of complex pattern searches to obtain the *individual* symbolic description of an input pattern rather than the class index obtained from classification. In general, this requires a knowledge-based processing of the patterns, i.e. the system is based on knowledge about the range of the application. The first part of the analysis requires no application dependent knowledge. The general structure of the analysis is shown in Figure 8.2. Preprocessing can be done problem-independently as in Figure 8.1. The parameter setting and selection of the appropriate pre-processing method may, however, be based on assumptions about the signal, i.e. on knowledge about the problem. The pre-processing operations correspond to those used for the classification of the simple patterns. The search for the characteristic and simple parts of patterns is called *segmentation*.

Model driven analysis (the upper two blocks in Figure 8.2) can be understood as a search and optimization process during which optimal correspondences between the knowledge about the given scene — represented as models in the knowledge base — and a segmented image are found [Nie90a, Sag97].

8.6 Segmentation

Like pre-processing, image segmentation algorithms are mostly data driven and require no knowledge about the application domain. In image procession, there is no need to know anything about the objects in the scene. Speech can be segmented solely based on the information in the signal. The choice of the optimal segmentation algorithm can be guided by knowledge. This is called model driven segmentation which is not considered in this book.

Segmentation is frequently a data driven process where knowledge about the application domain is not required. In this book, we mainly cover these problem-independent segmentation techniques. In a model driven approach, problem dependent knowledge for segmentation can be used.

Image segmentation can be based on homogeneities; namely, homogeneous regions that are detected in the image; we briefly discuss this later in Sect. 20.7. Alternatively, discontinuities

8.6 Segmentation

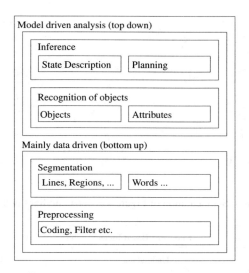

Figure 8.2: Structure of a knowledge based system for pattern analysis. The left part represents the image analysis process, the right one the speech analysis (from [Nie90a]).

can be used for the detection of primitives. It is assumed that these correspond to contours in the real objects. Line based segmentation is the result of this way of looking at images. We will cover techniques for line segmentation in Chapter 15 and 19.

The resulting primitives of segmentation depend on the methods used. Common examples are lines, regions, or vertices: the latter being a result of the intersection of two or more lines.

Studies show that simple geometric objects are an important part of human visual perception. Usually, the segmentation into lines is carried out in a series of computational steps. First the edge candidates are extracted from the image as we will see later in Chapter 15. Second, these candidate points are then linked together to form lines. The corners and intersections (vertices) are localized and the lines are approximated by circular arcs or straight lines (Figure 8.3). All of these objects are represented and stored in a common interface for image segmentation called a *segmentation object* (Sect. 24.3). We will cover the representation of such data in Part II; in Part III we describe algorithms for the computation of such data.

Every segmented part has to be weighted for its reliability; this measure will be used by the image analysis module (Sect. 8.7) in advanced recognition tasks.

Data abstraction of these objects yields a series of processing steps, which are shown in Figure 8.4. Proceeding from one level to the next means the introduction of a new class of data. We start with the image data, search for meaningful geometric parts, compute their relations that we store in a data structure for segmentation results, and finally obtain a symbolic description of the input data. This idea is further pursued in Part III. As denoted in Figure 8.4, processing

Figure 8.3: Segmentation of Figure 1.3 (left) into lines and corners

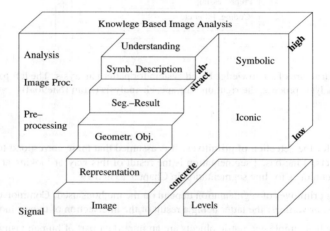

Figure 8.4: Levels of Abstraction with respect to data structures in image processing [Pau92b]

close to the input data is called "iconic", processing close to the description is called "symbolic processing".

The segmentation of speech signals corresponds to a decomposition of the time ordered signal into linguistic units. Each unit represents an interval of the signal and can be, for instance, a single word or a syllable of a continuous spoken utterance. In general, those units computed by segmentation operators symbolize parts that are either homogeneous in some sense when they are compared to their neighbors – this is the case for region segmentation in Sect. 20.7, or they are heterogeneous regarding some other criterion – this is used for edge detection in Chapter 15. Different approaches for the segmentation of speech signals can be found in [Nie90a, Nöt90].

With the impressive impact of Hidden-Markov-Models to speech recognition and analysis (see Chapter 23) segmentation of speech signals is of minor interest. It turned out that statistical

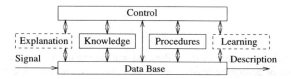

Figure 8.5: General structure of pattern analysis systems [Nie90a].

methods give better recognition results than structural analysis of the speech signal. The speech signal is divided into frames of equal length. For each frame features are computed. We introduce some algorithms for feature extraction in Chapter 23. The features are the input of statistical decision methods. We introduce basics of statistics for this purpose in Chapter 7 and apply them to speech processing in Chapter 23.

8.7 Pattern Understanding

Understanding a pattern within the present context requires knowledge stored explicitly in a knowledge base.

When the steps shown in Figure 8.4 are implemented, a modular architecture is recommended in [Nie90a]: image processing methods are applied to the data and images are eventually transformed into a description as shown in Figure 8.5. This process is controlled by a separate *control* module that selects algorithms to be executed by the module *procedures*. The analysis of the input signal is generally performed by *matching* of model data from the knowledge base to the segmentation data.

It is essential for the control module that the results of the segmentation are judged according to their quality and reliability. This problem dependent measure has to be provided by the segmentation methods. The search problem mentioned in Sect. 8.5 can then be solved by general search strategies in the control module, like the A^*-graph search or dynamic programming (see e.g. [Nie90a], Sect. 23.2).

Knowledge based pattern analysis as well as pattern understanding is related to problems of artificial intelligence (AI). In fact, speech understanding and vision were one of the first major ideas for machine intelligence. One of the important journals for speech and image analysis is called "Pattern Analysis and Machine Intelligence". For such systems, automatic acquisition of knowledge by a "learning" module is useful; it is recommended that the system can comment its own actions using an "explanation" module.

The following problems are directly connected to AI and refer to its central ideas (knowledge representation, searching, matching):

- representation scheme for the knowledge base,
- matching of patterns with models ,
- search for best matching object,
- dealing with uncertainty and false assumptions, and

- planning.

In image analysis, the recovery of three-dimensional information from the visual data can be assisted by spatial or geometric reasoning. Speech analysis will use linguistic knowledge and dialogue strategies.

Object–oriented programming can assist to keep track of software dependencies in a large knowledge based system. C++ provides the extreme computational efficiency which is also required for pattern understanding. Matching and optimization can be nicely implemented with object–oriented techniques; we will see an example in Sect. 23.2.

It should be noted that current research explores alternatives to "traditional" AI. Instead of an explicit model for speech or objects, statistical information is gathered and used for understanding. AI methods are left to dialogue strategies or to planning, which are also required in active vision tasks.

8.8 Active Vision and Real Time Processing

Instead of, or in addition to a symbolic description (which was the result of the system in Figure 8.4 and Figure 8.5), in active vision systems a series of commands for the active device is required. This will result in a top-down data flow all the way from control to low-level image processing (Figure 8.2), as the analysis influences the image input or the parameters of image processing.

Typical active methods change the focal length of a zoom lens or the aperture (Sect. 1.6). Different viewing directions are also possible if the lens is mounted on a robot. Examples can be found in [Den94]. One idea motivated by the human eye is to use a higher resolution in the area where interesting objects are expected (see the fovea in Figure 1.8). Technically, this can be achieved by two cameras with different focal length, or by changing the zoom setting of a single camera.

Active vision usually requires a response of the system within fractions of a second; otherwise a feedback of the information cannot be accomplished. It is crucial that the response delay is guaranteed not to exceed a maximum period. This is commonly called real-time processing if the time period is reasonably short. Of course, this again relates to efficiency (Sect. 3.8). Typically, the images are captured at 25 frames per second (Sect. 1.7). A delay of less than 40 ms is therefore usually sufficient for real-time processing. Since common algorithms require more computing time, other control algorithms with a shorter delay period have to be found.

In real-time speech analysis, the maximum computation time is determined by a human's senses while communicating with a machine. This can be used as an upper limit for the analysis of a complete utterance.

8.9 Software Systems

Software engineering in the field of image processing has been an important topic for several years. Data structures and more recently object–oriented programming have been proposed e.g. in [Car91, Cog87, Dob91, Pau92b, Pip88, Jak94]. A somewhat longer summary can be found in [Pau94]. Since this problem is currently discussed widely, the list of references above and systems below can of course not be complete.

Several commercial and free software systems are available for image processing; some of them we will now briefly introduce.

A very popular system is the Khoros system [Ras92] which has a large library of image processing functions and a nice graphical interface. It now also has a C++-interface.

The book [Zim96] comes with a CD ROM for image processing on a PC. The system described in [Koe96] is said to be available from a company. Both systems are written in C++ and encompass large hierarchies for image processing.

The so called "Image Understanding Environment" (IUE) has been discussed and planned for several years, e.g. in [Har92]. It is now available on the internet in the public domain (cf., for example, various articles in the proceedings of the *Image Understanding Workshop*, e.g., [Mun92]). It provides a large C++ library and has a graphical user interface. Real time processing was explicitly excluded [Har92].

All those systems have nice user interfaces; none of them is dedicated to real-time applications or high efficiency (cf. Sect. 3.8). In this sense, the very basic approach presented in this book differs from all of them.

In contrast to image processing there are fewer free software packages for speech processing. Most of the currently available systems were free several years ago and became commercial, as, for example, the Entropic's HTK toolkit[2] which provides utilities for building speech recognition systems using Hidden-Markov-Models. Another product offered by Entropics is the ESPS/Waves package with basic signal processing functions and visualization tools.

The ISADORA system (Integrated System for Automatic Decoding of Observation Sequences of Real-values Arrays) [ST95] is another toolset for working with one-dimensional signals, especially for the use with HMM based speech recognition. It integrates Markov modelling and hierarchical representation of phonetic, lexical and syntactic knowledge into one network.

The OGI Speech Tools are free software and provide a set of speech data manipulation tools developed at the Center for Spoken Language Understanding (CSLU). They can be used to compute and display signal representations and train neural networks.[3]

There are, of course, several systems for knowledge representation used in image and speech understanding. Most of them result from some AI project. Only one general system is known to the authors which is tailored for its application in pattern analysis (upper part of Figure 8.2): the system is called ERNEST [Nie90b] which was used in our work on knowledge-based image analysis. The principles of our system for image segmentation and image analysis (lower part of Figure 8.2) are the subject of part II and III of this book.

---

[2] http://www.entropic.com
[3] http://www.cse.ogi.edu/CSLU

```
main(int argc, char **argv)  // first approach to speech recognition
{                            // analyzes sequence of single words
    int word;                // words may be identified by numbers
    init_micro();            // start up recording
    wait_for_speech();       // record speech frames until
                             // speech is observed
    do {
        get_frames();        // record until a pause is observed
        preprocess();        // filter frames
        features();          // extract features
        word = classify();   // find word number from frames
        action(word);        // show some reaction on the input
    } while(word!=0);        // 0 means "QUIT"
    return 0;
}
```

76

Exercises

8.a Explain differences and similarities of feature extraction and segmentation!

8.b Think about formalisms for representing domain knowledge. Which techniques would you prefer?

8.c Discuss the objectives of classification and analysis in detail!

8.d Define a vector for the speech signal locally in the main function. Pass the vector and its length as arguments to all the functions which need it.

If your computer has an audio input device, put all the device dependent code into a separate module and run the program. Try to recognize three different, isolated spoken words: "Start", "Stop", and "Quit". Use simple features, like the duration of the speech signal, or try the features learned in Chapter 7.

8.e **Top-Level Loop for Speech Analysis**

Start writing a program using the control structures introduced in Listing 76 that waits until a speech signal is recorded by a microphone and then tries to analyze the data until a spoken end command is heard. Assume that isolated words are spoken (in contrast to a continuously spoken language), and that each word is analyzed separately. Use your function of Exercise 8.e as a test.

Following the idea of stepwise refinement (Sect. 3.2) and the structure of Figure 8.1, specify a top-level loop (see Listing 76) and leave some details to be filled in later.

Fill in data structures and variables needed for the speech signal. In the initialization, the actual settings of the device and the noise level in the background should be measured. Waiting for the word to start can be done simply by adding up the absolute values of all sampled values in the present frame. If the computed number is considerably higher than a comparable computation for a frame in the initialization, we assume that a word has been spoken.

Use separate files for the function dummies which are called from the main program. Make sure that a header file defines all the required interfaces. Use a Makefile to build the program.

Part II
Object–Oriented Programming

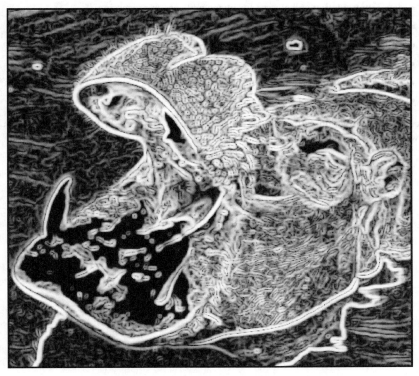

Edge strength computed on the image on page 3.

Part II of the book introduces C++ as an object–oriented language. We describe class hierarchies for general object–oriented programming and for object–oriented image and speech processing. This part of the book focuses on the coding of algorithms, whereas part III will emphasize the algorithms and the construction of pattern analysis systems.

This part of the book will teach

- object–oriented programming principles
- C++ classes
- data representation and classes for image and speech processing
- how to create useful test data
- Fourier transform which is the basis of most speech processing systems
- inheritance and its syntax in C++
- edge detection and its efficient implementation in C++
- class libraries for C++

Except for the function call operator, which we include in Sect. 17.8, this part contains our view of object–oriented programming in C++.

Chapter 9

Object–Oriented Programming

In this chapter we introduce the object–oriented programming paradigm and other related subjects for object–oriented software construction. The term "object–oriented programming" has become very popular. Many applications of object–oriented programming and software design principles exist, and there are many journals and scientific publications which are specialized in the philosophy and the possibilities of object–oriented systems. The following sections can only summarize the fundamental concepts of object–oriented programming languages. The interested reader may find more information in the references.

9.1 Object–Oriented Software Techniques

The object–oriented programming style involves the decomposition of a problem domain into a hierarchy of classes and a set of communicating objects which are themselves instances of classes. The object–oriented programmer then specifies *what* is done with the objects. The procedural way of programming uses aspects of *how* something gets done. The advantage of object–oriented software design is that a one-to-one correspondence between objects of the real world and the objects in the program can be made. Even the analysis of the problem domain has to be involved in this mapping. Analysis and program design are no longer separated in the software development process (cf. Chapter 3); object–oriented analysis and design share the same terminology and tools.

The first phase of object–oriented software development is to define the requirements (RD). In the object–oriented analysis (OOA) stage of a problem, concepts of the problem domain and their correspondences are identified and specified. Hierarchical relations between the concepts are used; information which can be shared by several special concepts will be included in a general concept and passed to the special cases through *inheritance*. In the object–oriented design (OOD) phase, the conceptual class hierarchy is overlayed with additional links which are meaningful for the implementation only. This provides a transition from the problem domain to the *solution* domain. After analysis and design, the object–oriented coding can take place (object–oriented programming, OOP). Whereas conventional software engineering is mostly sequential with some optional loops (Figure 3.1), object–oriented software development has a main stream from RD to OOP, with possible feedback at every stage (Figure 9.1).

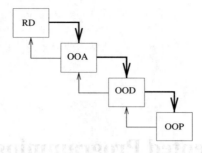

Figure 9.1: Object–oriented software engineering techniques (explained in the text)

Several graphical representations and mechanisms have been proposed for OOA and OOD in the past. The proposals of Booch [Boo91], Jacobson [Jac92], Rumbaugh et al. [Rum91], Coad & Yourdon [Coa91], and Shlaer & Mellor [Shl88] used similar ideas, each with its own flavor and with different notation. G. Booch, I. Jacobson, and J. Rumbaugh joint their efforts and created the "Unified Modeling Language" (UML) which includes three essential parts [Bre97]:

- guidelines for the vocabulary,
- fundamental modeling concepts and their semantics,
- notation for the visual rendering of the concepts.

Several diagrams for the description of the static and dynamic behavior of a system are provided. The method was accepted as a standard by the OMG (Object Management Group). We will use it in the following and briefly introduce the very basic notation.

9.2 Basic Vocabulary

According to [Weg87], the characteristical features of the object–oriented programming paradigm are:

- objects,
- classes,
- inheritance,
- data abstraction,
- polymorphism,
- message passing,
- methods,
- types, and
- durability.

Objects can be, for example, integers, real values, gray-level images, lines, addresses, or any other concept conceivable in the problem domain. Objects are *instances* of classes. Classes consist, in general, of data (member variables) and methods (functions) which can be used to manipulate the member variables. Classes describe the layout of objects.

For example, a class "gray-level image" has member variables like a matrix including intensity-values and the focal length of the camera used to capture the image (cf. Chapter 11). Necessary methods are, for instance, selectors for reading a gray-value at a certain location and a method which returns the focal length of the camera. The matrix can also be an instance of a class. The image class for gray-level images is derived from a more general class where the information common to all types of images is specified. The technique provided for the implementation of such dependencies is inheritance (Sect. 9.4). Data and common methods shared by all variants of images — e.g. a recording time stamp — can be defined in the common so-called base class.

Function overloading, where functions with the same function name are distinguished by their arguments, is also a common technique in object–oriented systems. This can be extended to operator overloading; for instance, addition and multiplication are denoted by + and ∗ for arbitrary numbers like integer, real or complex numbers. The implementation used depends on the arguments' type.

Another basic feature of object–oriented paradigm is the concept of *polymorphism* which we will elaborate in Sect. 9.8. In combination with inheritance, objects may exhibit "polymorphic" behavior and react to messages differently depending on the class the object actually belongs to. In the following sections we will elaborate on the above features a little further and relate them to C++.

9.3 Data Abstraction and Modules

One of the aims of object–oriented software design is to provide an abstract interface for programmers using the technique of *information hiding*. The user of a class only needs to know the methods of a class and their semantics. The internal data representation and the implementation details of several methods should not be in the scope of the user. The method of information hiding renders a high degree of modularity and supports the teamwork required in large programming projects.

Data abstraction facilitates modular programming. For example, you want to add two matrices in a part of a function. Since the matrix class provides a method for the addition of two matrices, you will not have to reimplement the addition using the components of the matrix. Furthermore, the code becomes more readable and thus reusable for other programmers (supposing that the code is well documented). Changes in a special operation, e.g. addition of matrices, can be done locally in the method's definition. The code which uses this function has only to be recompiled or linked.

Computer scientists invented the concept of *Abstract Data Types* (ADT). In this concept, data and the operations which read or alter the data are strongly connected. The data representation is no longer relevant. All access to the information is done using the operations provided by the data type. This is what we mean by information hiding. The definition of ADT is a more theoretical concept that combines data representation with formal aspects of implementation and representation. Some programming languages have implemented this concept; abstract data types are defined in some programming structures together along with the appropriate functions which define the interface for the given data type. Variables of this type can now be defined. The programmer can operate on these variables using only the methods which were associated with the ADT.

The central element of the method is the class diagram. Classes are represented as boxes that are divided up into three fields; the upper field contains the class name,[1] the middle field contains data fields called attributes, and the lower field contains method names. Except for the class name, the fields may be empty. Types and arguments are listed as well, as we will see in the examples below.

Using the graphical elements of UML, an ADT can be depicted as in Figure 9.2. If one data type A is associated to another type B, this can be visualized by an arrow connecting the two corresponding boxes, with the arrow head pointing to A. If C has A as a part, a line ending in a filled diamond at C connects these two boxes. Type C has to apply the operations associated with A in order to access data of A.

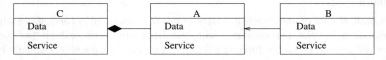

Figure 9.2: Three related abstract data types (ADT)

9.4 Inheritance

Classes, as well as ADTs, may be understood as descriptions of terms which describe the problem domain. Objects result from classes by aligning special values to their descriptions. Classes can arise by inheritance from one or more base classes. This process is called the derivation of a new class. In the terminology of object–oriented programming the base class is often called a *superclass* and a derived class a *subclass*. We call this inheritance graph a *hierarchy*, no matter whether it is actually a directed acyclic graph or really a tree.

The use of class hierarchies and inheritance forces programmers to think about an ordered structure of the underlying problem domain. The resulting source code is more structured and has a higher degree of reusability. Since the implementor of a class should provide a complete definition, i.e. not only those functions needed immediately but all reasonable functions for future uses of the class, the number of code lines may increase for object–oriented programming. This is compensated by the use of inheritance which reduces the number of lines needed for the implementation.

Inheritance can appear in two different ways: on the one hand we have *simple* inheritance. If each class is derived from at most one super-class, we call the inheritance simple. If at least one class has more than one base class, multiple inheritance is being used. Derived classes inherit both the methods and the members of their superclasses. Furthermore, inheritance grants more insight to a class than the usage relation in Figure 9.2. Many authors suggest the use of simple inheritance because there exist fewer conflicts, which occur e.g. if a member of the same name is inherited from two classes.[2]

---

[1] Instead of the technical name in the syntax of the programming language, we will occasionally use a descriptive term in the following figures.

[2] We will not further elaborate this problem here.

One object may contain members whose type are from other classes. We call the classes of the member objects *clients*. Instead of inheriting classes we may also in some cases use a client and define all the methods of the client in the new class. These methods will just pass the arguments to the corresponding methods of the clients. This is called *delegation*. In many cases multiple inheritance can be avoided using delegation.

Artificial intelligence tries to organize knowledge in some structured formalism. Most frameworks use special/general, concrete/abstract, and has-a/part-of relations. The semantic network system ERNEST [Nie90b] imposes restrictions on these links, e.g. that concepts related by a part-of relation must be on the same level of abstraction. For class design and inheritance planning, such thoughts are also very useful. Class hierarchies are understood best if derivation is used for classes that are in a 'is-a' relation; for example as a *line* "is a" *geometric object*, we derive the class `Line` from the class `GeoObject`.

9.5 Templates

Often, a system contains several classes that are identical except for the type or class of some member variables, such as sets of integral numbers or linked lists of lines. *Parametric types* allow class creation from a description including parameters. A general scheme is expanded to the actual classes. In C++, this can be done with templates (Sect. 11.2). For instance, matrix classes can be defined using parametric components. In contrast to classes created by inheritance, two classes created from templates have no explicit relation at run time in a C++ program.

To summarize, a provisional and simplified characterization of object–oriented programming can be itemized as follows:

- classes (represent abstract units),
- inheritance of classes (abstract generic terms), and
- objects (concrete terms associated with values).

Using the the UML notation, inheritance of two classes `Integer` and `Real` from `Number` can be depicted as in Figure 9.3. An arrow connects derived classes and the base class; the arrow head is an empty triangle. In UML, an extra small box in the upper corner of a class marks a template; the actual type is inserted here for template instantiation. This is shown in Figure 9.3 for a vector template and a vector of real numbers.

To summarize the relations of classes in UML notation:

- An arrow with an empty triangle as arrow head relates two classes by inheritance.
- Template instantiations use a dashed line to relate to the template.
- A line with a filled diamond at the head denotes composition.[3]

In the following sections and chapters we will see several examples.

---

[3] An empty diamond is used for aggregation. We will not use this concept in the following.

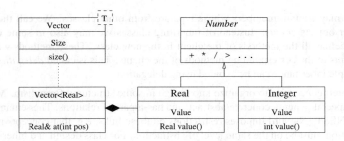

Figure 9.3: Inheritance for numbers

9.6 Abstract Classes

The examples explained so far were concrete classes including methods that are explicitly suitable for implementation purposes. Assume you have to implement a class for lines. Obviously there are different possibilities for representing lines. For instance, you can use polygons, arcs, or a set of affine functions. Furthermore, you have to distinguish between lines of different dimensions. Independent of the internal representation, a class for lines should include methods for the determination of its length or for traversing the points along the line. It cannot be the aim of an object–oriented programming system to implement all different classes for lines without the use of the more abstract concept of lines. Abstract classes provide the declaration of a class where no concrete members have to be specified and the methods can be declared in an abstract manner. In these abstract classes no implementation of the methods must be made. The concrete definition of the methods must then be developed in derived classes where the explicit representation is known. The advantage of abstract classes lies in the development of modular and well structured software, where classes which depend on each other in an abstract way are reflected within the network of classes. Abstract classes may additionally declare concrete members that are shared by all derived classes — as in the case of concrete classes.

The class Number in Figure 9.3 is an abstract class since an object is not simply a "number" but either a real number or an integer or whatever class of concrete numbers are used in the program. In UML, class names for abstract classes are printed in *italics*.

9.7 Object–Oriented Classification

The term "classification" was introduced for pattern analysis in Sect. 8.1. This term is also used in the description of object–oriented systems. Object classes can be defined as representatives of a class of objects. The universe of objects is divided into classes by a partition. Objects of similar purpose are grouped into equivalence classes. Object–oriented classes in this sense correspond to the term "class" in set theory.

A class is a set of objects that share a common structure and a common behavior.

This definition allows for the distinction of types and classes.[4] Classification is thus a fundamental problem of OOA. Objects have to be grouped according to their behavioral and structural similarity. However, the kind of behavior that is regarded as similar. is context-dependent. Class boundaries in the real world tend to be fuzzy rather than clear.

9.8 Polymorphism

Another basic concept of object–oriented programming languages is the use of polymorphism:

> A concept in type theory, according to which a name (such as a variable declaration) may denote objects of many different classes that are related by some common superclass; thus, any object denoted by this name is able to respond to some common set of operations in different ways.
>
> [Boo91; p. 517]

Sometimes an algorithm can be formulated in an abstract manner independent of the data types it operates on. Mathematicians are well versed in those problems. For example, the determination of the maximum element of a set or a sort algorithm on a set of elements depends only on the ordering of the elements' domain. So, routines are needed which can be applied to many different data types, for instance numbers, letters, or vectors. These functions are called *polymorphic* and they serve for sparing source code. Another consequence of polymorphism is a compact and more easily surveyed source code which can easily be reused by others.

Together with dynamic binding and inheritance, polymorphism is a key concept in object–oriented programming. Often operator overloading is called weak polymorphism. Examples for overloaded operators are addition and multiplication of integers, reals and complex numbers which share the same symbol.

Polymorphism in C++ can be either *compile time polymorphism* or *run time polymorphism*. The first is provided by templates (Chapter 11), the latter is supported by virtual functions (Chapter 14).

9.9 Object–Oriented Programming Languages

The ideas of Smalltalk [Gol83] should be familiar to everyone who wants to do object–oriented programming. Simula [Bir83] and Smalltalk can be seen as the 'parents' of object–oriented programming. Both language definitions describe the syntax and provide extensive class libraries for various applications. Most object–oriented concepts such as classes, objects, methods, inheritance, polymorphism, etc. were introduced in Smalltalk. The even older root of object–oriented programming can be found in Simula which introduced virtual functions and the class concept which are now similarly available in C++.

---

[4]Objects belonging to one class may still have separate types. However, this is relevant only in some object–oriented programming languages. In C++ we can handle classes as types.

The ancestor of object–oriented languages – Smalltalk – did not allow multiple base classes. Several modern object–oriented programming languages do, however, implement this concept. It is by far more complex to maintain a class hierarchy with multiple inheritance than one with single inheritance.

Another major influence on the new standard C++ library originates from Ada which was said not to be an object–oriented language, since it missed inheritance in its first revision. The generic modules in Ada have a similarity to templates in C++. The new revision of the ADA language standard supports single inheritance [Kem97].

C++, like Simula, is a compiled language and thus has to omit some features which can be realized only in interpreted languages like Smalltalk. C++, as defined in [Str97], provides no such environment as Smalltalk. C++ combines several features from various languages in a mixture of conventional and object–oriented ideas which can be used to write highly efficient yet modular programs and modules for pattern processing and analysis.

The first descendents of C++ exist already. The programming language Java is mostly used in world-wide-web applications but its application for other purposes is increasing.

The programming language Java [Lyo97] promises a new era in programming[5]. It is defined as a portable language where the portability extends down to the level of binary programs. This is achieved by the so called "Java virtual machine" which interprets the compiled programs. This interpreter has to be present on the host machine, or hardware support has to be provided. Java is an object–oriented language with a clean and simple syntax definition, much simpler than C++ although with a similar appearance. Several features of C++ have not been included in Java, such as operator overloading. The language has no pointer variables which is somewhat unusual. The language is type safe which helps creating reliable programs. Many deficiencies of C++ have been cured in this new language, for example, it supports automatic garbage collection. The compilers come with a rich library of general purpose classes which greatly simplifies sharing code with others.

Although the first highly efficient implementations exist and applications to signal processing have been proposed [Lyo97], Java currently lacks the required runtime efficiency for image processing applications.

Exercises

9.a Develop a class hierarchy for lines. Which methods should be declared in the abstract class? Is it useful to use multiple inheritance? Where can concepts like polymorphism and operator overloading be used in this example?

9.b Check the advertisements in your favorite computer journal for occurrences of the term "object–oriented". Try to find out whether this term is correctly applied there.

9.c Compare different other graphical descriptions of object–oriented programming with those mentioned in the text.

---

[5] e.g. http://rsb.info.nih.gov/ij/

Chapter 10
Classes in C++

C++ is not an object–oriented language. It *allows* for object–oriented programming. The concepts of object–oriented programming introduced in chapter 9 can be mapped to features of the C++ language. In this chapter we introduce the design of classes in C++ and show the use of abstract data types for encapsulation.

10.1 Methods and ADT's

Listing 17 (p. 39) showed the data structure PointXY consisting of two data entries. This basically looks like Pascal. No restrictions on the access, modification, and use of the structure members were specified. Good programming practice requires the definition of functions which use the new data type (Listing 77). In an implementation in C, all these functions have been prefixed with the data type name to avoid name conflicts.[1] Misuse or failure to use the new functions cannot, however, be controlled by the compiler. The use of these functions can be recommended but not enforced. Information hiding — as required in ADT's (Sect. 9.3) — is thus only partially possible. In C++, this is less critical, since argument types and argument number can be used to disambiguate functions as well.

In C++, in addition to data members, functions can be declared *inside* the structure. These functions are used only in conjunction with the data of the structure type. Listing 78 shows a structure for complex numbers consisting of a real and an imaginary part.[2] This already looks more like an ADT, since operations on the data type are declared with tight adherence to the data specification. These functions are called "methods" or member functions (cf. Chapter 9).

---
[1]This is a common technique which was used in e.g. the X11 windows system for Unix.
[2]A class for complex numbers can be found in the STL libarry, Sect. 16.7.

```
void PointXY_setXY(PointXY& p, int x, int y)  { p.x = x ; p.y = y; }
int  PointXY_getX(PointXY& p)                 { return p.x; }
int  PointXY_getY(PointXY& p)                 { return p.y; }
```
77

```
struct Complex {                      // structure declaration
   float re,im;                       // two data members
   Complex set(float,float);          // member function declaration
   float real() {return re;}          // member function definition
   float imag() {return im;}          // member function definition
};
float abs(const Complex &);           // function declaration
```
`78`

```
Complex c, *cp = &c;                  // variable definition
c.set(3,3);
float f = cp->real();
Complex c1 = c, c2 = *cp;
```
`79`

Functions *defined* within the body — the method `real` in Listing 78 — are automatically inlined (Sect. 6.7). The `inline` keyword can be used for better readability.

Methods can be accessed like data members using a variable and a tag — the method name — separated by a "." or a "->" in the case of a pointer. In addition, a parameter list can be given. As can be seen from Listing 79, structures can be assigned as a whole; they can also be returned from functions.

Definition of methods outside the structure use the structure name followed by `::`[3] and the method name (Listing 80). The complete name of a variable or a function consists of the scope (mostly the structure name), the double colon, and the variable name. We now see that the type name in the enumeration definition in Sect. 4.2 fits logically into this concept (e.g. `Complex::set` in Listing 80); the structure name prefix is a scope resolution which uniquely determines the name space where the function name has to be searched for by the compiler. Inside the methods, other methods and data members are known without explicitly mentioning the structure name. They can be accessed explicitly by the `this` pointer, which points to the actual object for which the method is invoked. This variable is declared and initialized by the C++ compiler in each and every (non-static) member function.[4] In some cases, the `this` pointer is required to access the actual object as a whole (`return` statement in the second implementation of the method `Complex::set` in Listing 80).

---

[3] cf. Sect. 2.9
[4] The compiler implicitly prefixes all the access expressions to class members by a `this->` pointer.

```
#define USE_THIS
Complex Complex::set(float x, float y)
{
#ifndef USE_THIS
    re = x; im = y;    // will give a warning (no return value)
#else /* alternatively */
    this->re = x;      // just to give an example
    (*this).im = y;    // just to be different
    return *this;      // this is returned
#endif
}
```
`80`

10.2 Class Declarations

```
class assoc_int {         // association between integer and string
 private:                  // can be omitted: classes start private
   int value;
   char * key;
 public:                   // the following defines the interface
   const char * Key() { return key; }   // read access to data
   void Key(char * k) { key = k; }      // set key
   int Value() { return value; }        // read access to data
   void set(int v, char * k);           // set value
};
```
[81]

```
assoc_int ai1;                    // object definition
ai1.set(8527894,"Paulus");        // legal use of method
ai1.value = 33;                   // **error**, value is private
char * n1 = ai1.key;              // **error**, key is private
char * n2 = ai1.Key();            // **warning, constant assigned
                                  // ** to char *
const char * n3 = ai1.Key();      // ok
```
[82]

Note also the pre-processor statement for conditional compilation depending on the existence of a defined (in terms of the pre-processor) macro in Listing 80. This kind of definition is often passed to the pre-processor from the compiler command line, e.g., with `CC -DUSE_THIS -c prog.C`.

10.2 Class Declarations

Structures as introduced in Sect. 4.1 partially satisfy the requirements of ADT's. The primary feature that is missing is "Information Hiding". This is possible with the `class` declaration in C++. Variables of a class type are called *objects*.

Classes are structures with access regulations. Data members and methods can be excluded from external usage; they are then accessible only inside other methods. Three keywords are used for access regulations: The label `public:` introduces unrestricted parts of the class. The label `private:` restricts the following entries for internal class use only. The label `protected:` will be introduced in Sect. 14.2. These labels can be repeated and can occur in any order. Listing 81 shows a class declaration of a so-called `assoc_int`.[5] A key (e.g. a name) is associated with an integer (e.g. a telephone number). The data members are accessible only by the public methods.

Structures as well as unions in C++ are exactly the same as classes except for one small difference; the initial access mode for structures is public; the initial mode for classes is private. Several uses, both legal and illegal, of the class `assoc_int` are shown in Listing 82. Making the return value of `Key` a `const char *` protects the string from manipulation after a call to the method.

---
[5] We will see applications of this class later.

```
class assoc_int {
 private:
    int value; char * key;    // private
 public:                       // the following defines the interface
    assoc_int();              // default constructor
    assoc_int(int,char*);     // alternative constructor
    const char * Key();
    int Value();
};
```
83

```
assoc_int ai1;            // definition and call of default constructor
assoc_int ai2(10,"a");    // definition and call of second constructor
assoc_int * aip1 = new assoc_int;           // use default constructor
assoc_int * aip2 = new assoc_int(11,"b");// use second constructor
```
84

10.3 Object Construction

It would be tedious and error prone if every class or structure had a method for initialization (as in Listing 77–81 the method `set` or `...setXY`) which had to be called explicitly for every object (Listing 82, 79).

C++ introduces special methods for classes called *constructors*.[6] These — usually overloaded — functions share the name as their class. They are used upon definition of an object and can initialize internal and external data automatically. Syntax and usage is best seen through an example. Listing 83 shows a modification of the class introduced in Listing 81. The method `set` is now left out.

Listing 84 is a modified version of Listing 82. Instead of explicitly initializing the objects we use constructors. The example also shows the use of the `new` operator on classes. The so-called "default constructor" is used if no argument list is provided. If no default constructor is implemented, it is provided by the compiler. As for overloaded functions, the choice of the appropriate constructor depends on the argument list. Listing 85 shows the definition of the default constructor for this class.

Arrays of objects can be defined in a similar way to arrays of simple types (Sect. 5.1). The default constructor is called for every object in the array (Listing 86). If no default constructor is defined for the class, the compiler will give an error message.

It is often useful to initialize one object with the contents of another object of the same type. The *reference constructor* (copy constructor) is used for this purpose. Declaration and use is shown in Listing 87 which extends Listing 17. If there is no declaration of a reference construc-

---

[6]This is also more flexible than the initializtion of structures, as it was shown in Listing 17. For classes, such initialization is prohibited.

```
assoc_int::assoc_int()         // default constructor
{                              // initialize members
    value = -1; key = NULL;    // by default
}                              // values
```
85

```
assoc_int aia[10];            // definition and call of default constructor
assoc_int * aip3 = new assoc_int[11];  // default constructor 11 times
```
`86`

```
class PointXY {               // declare new data type
  private:
    int xa,ya;                // members are xa and ya
  public:
    PointXY();                // default constructor
    PointXY(const PointXY &); // reference constructor, always const arg.
    PointXY(int, int);        // third constructor
    int x();                  // read access to member xa
    int y();                  // read access to member ya
};
```
`87`

tor, the compiler will automatically create one which copies all components recursively. This constructor is used when an object is returned from a function or passed to it as an argument. Note, that it is *not* called if the argument is passed as a reference; i.e., to avoid unnecessary copying, function arguments should be declared as constant references!

Listing 88 shows the definition of the constructor methods declared in Listing 87.

Constructors never have a return type. However, they can be terminated by a return statement like any other `void` function.

10.4 Destruction of Objects

Similar to object construction, the destruction code of an object is generated automatically by the compiler if it is not declared explicitly: The "destructor" is a special method; its name is the class name prefixed with a tilde (resembling the unary `not` operator, Table 4.1). A string class with destructor is shown in Listing 89.[7]

Typically, destructors release any memory which was allocated in the constructor (Listing 90). Other examples can be found in the following sections.

The destructor is called on an object when this object goes out of scope (and is not static, of course). Objects created by `new` can be destroyed by `delete`. This will call the destructor as well (Listing 91). For arrays, the destructor is called automatically for every element. There is only *one* destructor per class which always has no arguments and no return type. As with constructors, a return from the destructor with a `return` statement is possible. Static objects are also deleted, when the function `exit` is called from any point in the program. This feature

---
[7]A class for strings can also be found in the STL library, Sect. 16.7, and in the NIHCL library, Sect. 16.4.

```
PointXY::PointXY() { xa = 0; ya = 1; }
PointXY::PointXY(const PointXY & p) { xa = p.xa; ya = p.ya; }
PointXY::PointXY(int i, int j) { xa = i; ya = j; }
```
`88`

```
class string {                  // declare new data type
 private:
   char * st;                   // internal pointer
   int len;                     // number of characters
 public:
   string();                    // default constructor
   string(const char *);        // constructor
   string(const string &);      // copy constructor
   ~string();                   // destructor
   int length();                // return string length
};
```

```
string::string() {st = NULL;len=0;}   // default constructor
string::string(const char * s)        // copy char *
{
    st=new char[1+(len=strlen(s))];
    strcpy(st,s);                     // copy
}
string::string(const string & s)      // copy constructor
{
    st = new char [1+(len=s.len)];    // allocate
    strcpy(st,s.st);                  // copy
}
string::~string() { delete [] st; }   // will work with NULL pointer
int string::length() { return len;}   // information
```

can be useful, for example, for files which have to do some cleanup on permanent storage: like removing temporary files or locks on devices as the program terminates.

Objects defined in the main program will naturally be deleted when a return statement is encountered. They will not be deleted when the main function is terminated by a call to the function exit.

10.5 Operators

Several operators were introduced in C for fundamental types. They all have their fixed association rules. Some operators can be redefined for classes. The syntax of operator declarations is as follows:

Syntax: *return-type* <u>operator</u> *op (argument-list)*

```
void fct(char * sa)
{
    string s0;                          // empty string
    string s(sa);                       // allocate string
    string *sp = new string("ab");      // constructor call
    delete sp;                          // delete using destructor
    return;                             // quit function
}                                       // s will be destroyed
```

10.6 User-Defined Conversion

```
Complex Complex::operator= (const Complex& c)    // assign Complex
    {re = c.re; im = c.im; return *this;}
Complex Complex::operator=(double d)             // assign float
    {re = d; im = 0; return *this; }
Complex Complex::operator+ (const Complex& c) const
    {Complex nc(c); nc.re += re; nc.im += im; return nc;}
```
`92`

```
Complex r, q, s;     // declare
r = s;               // assign
s = q = r;           // assign twice
s = q + r;           // addition and assignment
```
`93`

where user definable operators are, for example; +,*,-,=,[ ],( ), or ==.[8]

Redefinition of an operator is called "operator overloading" which is one type of polymorphism (Sect. 9.8). We will not treat this topic in all details. We only give some clarifying examples for commonly used operators such as [ ], =, ( ) and leave the rest to the references. When used with care, operator overloading can facilitate programming and make programs easier to read. When misused, the results may be disastrous.[9] Operator overloading is possible only for classes.

Listing 92 shows the definitions of the assignment and addition operators for the class Complex (Listing 87); this operator is applied in Listing 93. By passing the actual object as a return value, sequences of assignments are possible.

Other overloaded operators will be explained and applied in later sections (cf. Chapter 16). One of them is the conversion operator explained in the next section.

10.6 User-Defined Conversion

Several conversion rules are defined for fundamental types; for example, a floating point number is truncated when it is assigned to an integer. Explicit type conversion takes place with a type cast. It can now be specified how this conversion to a given type should be performed on a user-defined data type. In order to do so, a conversion operator can be declared in a class as shown for the complex numbers in Listing 94. Note, that no return type is specified, since this type is known from the type the class is converted to (in this case a float).

---

[8]For a complete list refer to the manual [Str97].
[9]Imagine a program with + defined as multiplication on some numeric class ...

```
Complex::operator double () const
{                           // conversion of a Complex to a float
    assert(im==0);          // assert that it is no Complex number
    return re;              // return the real part
}
```
`94`

```
Complex a;
float f0 = (float) a;      // C style cast
float f1 = float(a);       // conversion function
float f2 = a;              // implicit conversion
```
95

```
class A {                  // artificial example
  private:
    int a;                 // some member
  public:
    A(int i) { a = i; }    // constructor definition
};
class B {                  // some other class
  private:
    int b;                 // with some member
    A   a1, a2;            // uses the first class
  public:
    B(int, int, int);      // declares a constructor
};
```
96

A constructor of a class which has exactly one argument is also used for automatic conversion to that class from the type of the argument. For example, the constructor `string(char*)` in Listing 89 will be used to convert a character pointer to a string object.[10]

Such type conversion can shorten expressions and in many cases be useful and simplify programming. As always, side effects have to be strictly avoided. Three examples for the invocation of the conversion function are shown in Listing 95. Especially with the implicit conversion, all side effects would be disastrous for the readability of the program.

10.7 Advanced Methods and Constructors

If a class contains data members of class type as shown in Listing 96, the question arises how to provide constructors for these objects.

The solution is shown in Listing 97. After a colon, a list of constructor calls for member objects can be given before the *definition* of a constructor function body. The member objects are constructed before the body of the constructor function for B is executed.

---

[10]This feature can be excluded by marking the constructor as `explicit`.

```
B::B(int i, int j, int k)
    :             // start member constructors
    a1(j),        // constructor for first object
    a2(k)         // constructor for second object
{
    b = i;        // assign a value to the member
}
```
97

```
class bytevector_V0 {                       // first version
private:
   byte * row;                              // the actual data
   unsigned int size;                       // number of elements
public:
   bytevector_V0();                         // default constructor
   bytevector_V0(int);                      // constructor (length)
   bytevector_V0(const bytevector_V0&);     // copy constructor
   byte   operator [] (int i) const;  // access also for const objects
   byte & operator [] (int i);              // access as usual
};
#if defined(BV_VERS) && (BV_VERS == 0)
typedef class bytevector_V0 bytevector;
#endif
```

`98`

It is sometimes important to know the order of member and base class construction. This order is not determined by the sequence of calls, for example in Listing 97. Instead, the base classes and members are called in the order of their declaration in the class!

10.8 Vector Class

We now introduce a simple vector class which will reveal several new features for classes and methods. We first restrict our class to a vector of `byte` elements (Listing 98).

In Listing 98, note the following things:

1. the overloaded operator `[]`: this operator has one argument of type `int`. We can now access `bytevector_V0` objects like arrays with an index in square brackets.

2. the `const` method (or a `const` operator): methods can be declared as `const`. This indicates to the compiler that the method will not change any data internal to the object. In particular, these methods are used when the object is itself a `const` object.

   Since the compiler can decide a constant from a variable object, the two declarations of the operator `[]` in Listing 98 are legal.

3. reference as return value: to allow for an indexed expression of a `bytevector_V0` on the left side of an expression, we use a reference to the element as a return value.

Listing 99 shows the implementation of the vector access methods. The meaning of the `const` operators and the reference return value will be demonstrated in the following.[11]

We now extend Listing 98 to a complete simple and efficient vector class. We define constructors and introduce a conversion `operator byte*` which greatly increases the efficiency of this class (Listing 100). This operator method is invoked when an object (not a pointer)[12] is cast to a `byte *`.

The implementation of the constructor and destructor methods is shown in Listing 101. The use of this class and its methods can be seen in Listing 102.

---

[11]Rather than calling `exit`, an exception could be raised here.

[12]It is a very common error to cast the pointer instead of the object itself. The compiler will think this is intentional and will not give a warning!

```
static void checkit(int i, int s)      // local helper function
{
    if (i >= s) {
      char buffer[64];
      sprintf(buffer,"Index %d out of range (max is %d)\n",i,s);
      throw buffer;
    }
}

byte bytevector_V0::operator[](int i) const // access also for const objects
    { checkit(i,size); return row[i]; }     // return byte

byte & bytevector_V0::operator [] (int i)   // read/write access
    { checkit(i,size); return row[i]; }     // return reference
```
99

```
class bytevector_V1 {
  private:
    byte * row;                         // the actual data
    unsigned int size;                  // number of elements
  public:
    bytevector_V1();                              // default constructor
    bytevector_V1(int);                           // constructor
    bytevector_V1(const bytevector_V1&);          // copy constructor
    ~bytevector_V1();                             // destructor
    byte   operator [] (int i) const;  // access also for
                                       // const objects
    byte & operator [] (int i);        // access as usual
    operator byte * () { return row; }
    int Size() const { return size; }
};
#if defined(BV_VERS) && (BV_VERS == 1)
typedef class bytevector_V1 bytevector;
#endif
```
100

The function fct1 in Listing 102 uses the index operator [] and allows assignment to vector elements, since this operator returns a reference to the indexed byte. In contrast, the function fct3 has a constant argument. The index operator on this object uses the method for constant objects which returns a byte instead of a reference. Assignment and modification of the object is thereby disabled. Read access is, however, possible. The method Size() can be used, since it is also declared as a constant method. The vector access in fct2 is unprotected; when the function is called in the main program, the compiler already knows the argument type of the

```
#include <assert.h>
bytevector_V1::bytevector_V1(int i) // constructor
{
    assert(i>0);
    size = i;
    row = new byte[i];
}
bytevector_V1::~bytevector_V1()        // destructor
{
    delete [] row;
}
```
101

10.9 Class Design

```
void fct1(bytevector & bv)
    { for(int i = bv.Size() - 1; i >= 0; --i ) bv[i] = 0; }
void fct2(byte * bp, int s)
    { for(int i = s - 1; i >= 0; --i ) bp[i] = 0; }
void fct3(const bytevector & bv)
    { for(int s =0, i = bv.Size() - 1; i >= 0; --i ) s += bv[i]; }
main(int argc, char ** argv)
{
    bytevector bv(10);
    byte * bp = (byte *) bv;   // call operator byte *
    fct1(bv);                   // pass array by reference
    fct2(bv,bv.Size());         // convert to byte * using operator
    fct2(bp,bv.Size());         // equivalent
    exit(0);
}
```
102

function which is a `byte*`; the actual argument is the object `bv` which will be converted to a `byte*` using its conversion operator.

An explicit cast to a `byte *` as in the main function body of Listing 102 will also invoke the cast operator.

10.9 Class Design

We conclude this chapter with several useful hints for class design in C++. Some of them are not obvious from the language definition but are required because of compiler limitations. The goals for class design in pattern analysis applications have to be:

- efficiency (due to the time limitations) *and*
- clean design (due to general software rules and the particular difficulty of the problem).

Classes or data structures should be declared for every complex unit in the description of the problem for which you have a clear idea in mind. Internals should be hidden to provide a clear interface in a modular programming style. It is good practice to put all data members in the private section of a class and to provide read only access methods for those values which should only be changed in a controlled way. Often the same message (i.e., function name) is used for read and write access with two overloaded functions as in Listing 81. However, during the class design care is needed. If you use objects for every small detail, you lose efficiency. For example, it is not useful to represent each image point by an instance of a class for pixels. The resulting image processing and analysis programs will show a lot of overhead and will not be efficient enough with such a degree of granularity.

If you split the program source for the methods of one class into several files, this can in some cases increase the time for the program to be linked. On the other hand, it can also reduce the program size.[13] Stay in the middle between high granularity (i.e., many small files) and a monolith (i.e., one huge program source file). Generally, definitions (except for inline functions) should be separated from declarations. Class, variable, and function declarations

---
[13] Think of a call of a little function in a large module that contains other functions which you will not call.

should be put into a header file (.h); definitions should be put into several modules (.C) which are independent of each other in the sense that they do not contain functions that mutually call each other.

Inline constructors for objects should in general be avoided for non-trivial construction tasks. Some compilers will generate a lot of code for each construction and the overhead of a function call will be small in comparison to the overall time for object construction.[14] The same holds for destructors.

Memory allocation and release in C++ is partially the task of the compiler which will call the destructor for automatic objects when they go out of scope. Objects allocated with the operator new have to be discarded explicitly by the user. Programs which allocate at one point (e.g., in a deeply nested function) and release memory at another point (e.g., in another function) are often hard to understand and thus a possible source of errors. We recommend that wherever possible, the function which allocates an object with new should also release the object with delete.

Exercises

10.a Implement a String class with useful methods for substrings, modification, indexing etc. Extend Listing 89 accordingly.
Include overloaded operators (operator+) for assignment and concatenation. Which other operators can you think of?

10.b Implement a class for points as a modification of Listing 87.
Include overloaded operators for assignment and vector addition. Which other operators can you think of?

10.c Implement an alternative complex number class with a representation using r and ϕ (cf. Eq. (13.10)).

10.d Extend the arithmetic operators for complex numbers. Which internal representation is best suited for multiplication?

---

[14]Look at Listing 96; what will the compiler have to generate in the case of an inline constructor?

Chapter 11
Representation of Signals

Intensity based images are the most common input data structure for image processing and analysis. In practice, matrices are used for the representation of these discrete gray-level images. Each element of the two-dimensional matrix describes the gray-level of the digital image at its associated location. These "picture elements" are called *pixels*.

In this chapter we define a simple class for images. Motivated by the given examples, we introduce the concept of templates for classes in C++ and demonstrate their advantages with respect to software engineering projects. We also implement a class for speech signals using these templates.

11.1 Array Class

In Chapter 5 we introduced the representation of images using two-dimensional arrays. It was explained in detail how these arrays are declared and used in C and C++ programs. The declaration of a matrix as an argument to a function requires that the fixed size of the arrays is known at compilation time. In general, it is expected that image processing modules are suitable for images of arbitrary size. A compilation for each image size is – obviously – unreasonable. Hence, other ways of dealing with images have to be found.

As it has been shown when the definition and implementation of the class `bytevector` was presented (Listing 98), the use of the C++ `new` operator allows the dynamic allocation of storage for arbitrary arrays during the execution of programs. For the same purpose we now define a class `byteArray2d`. The class declaration for the abstract data type `byteArray2d` is designed to provide a constructor, whose arguments are the size of the two-dimensional array. The size of an array is thereby no longer required to be known during compilation. Parts of the header-file of the required class `byteArray2d` are shown in Listing 103.

The implementation of the constructor `byteArray2d(int, int)` is shown in Listing 104. Note that a vector is first allocated to hold the complete array in consecutive memory locations. Then, a pointer array is allocated by `new` and initialized to the starting positions of each row in the array in the `for`-loop. The internal representation of a matrix is illustrated in Figure 11.1.

```
class byteArray2d {
private:
  int xsize;                            // number of columns
  int ysize;                            // number of rows
  byte** matrix;                        // array
public:
  byteArray2d();                        // default constructor
  byteArray2d(int, int);                // constructor
  ~byteArray2d();                       // destructor
  const byte* operator[] (int) const;   // access to vector with
  byte*&       operator[] (int);        // ... index check
};
```

`103`

```
byteArray2d::byteArray2d(int x, int y) : xsize(x), ysize(y) {
  byte * array = new byte[x*y];     // vector of size x*y
  matrix = new byte*[y];            // generate byte matrix
  for (int i = 0; i < y; ++i)       // all rows
    matrix[i] = & (array[i*x]);     // fill in vector pointers
}
```

`104`

This example also shows that members of a fundamental type can be initialized in the same syntactic style as member objects (cf. Sect.10.7).

This technique allows for index checking of the first index in an array access operation (Listing 105). If instead of a `byte**`, a vector of byte-vectors (see Listing 98) is used, which provides access control, the indices can be checked for both dimensions. This idea, however, requires changes in the class `bytevector`. In order to allocate a variable length vector of bytevectors, the `new` operator has to be used in the `bytearray2d` construction. Thus, the bytevector class has to provide a default constructor. In addition, after creation with the default constructor, the actual length has to be set and the internal pointer has to be allocated. These extensions are left as an exercise (Exercise 11.a).

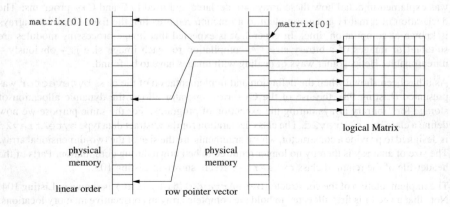

Figure 11.1: Internal representation of a two-dimensional array.

```
const byte * byteArray2d::operator[] (int i) const
{
  if (i > ysize) fprintf(stderr,"out of bounds\n"); // need smarter routine!
  return matrix[i];
}
```
105

```
byteArray2d::~byteArray2d()
{
  delete [] matrix[0];    // allocated by array = new byte[..]
  delete [] matrix;       // allocated by new byte*[..]
}
```
106

The destructor of this class just has to release the memory allocated in the constructor (Listing 104). The memory allocated in the variable `array` is accessible as `matrix[0]`. This is shown in Listing 106.

11.2 Templates in C++

We now have a matrix class for components of the type `byte`. This class is sufficient for the representation of gray-levels in intensity images. What happens, if we need a class of matrices with real numbers? We have to implement the class `realArray2d`. The only difference between `byteArray2d` and `realArray2d` is that we have to substitute the data type `byte` with `float` or `double`. It would be annoying, if we had to program the matrix classes for different types of elements over and over again. Thus, it would be advantageous to have the possibility of "parameterized types" (Chapter 9). Operations like multiplication or addition are reduced to multiplications and additions of the components which are parameterized. The arithmetic of matrices would not depend upon the special types of the entries. Fortunately, C++ offers a feature to realize these parameterized classes automatically. This concept is called a *template*. The basic syntax for declaring a class template is

Syntax: `template < class` *T* `>` *class-declaration*

A declared template specifies that an argument of type `T` will be used in the declaration of the parameterized class immediately following the template prefix. Formally expressed, type `T` is used within the declaration in exactly the same way as other types are. It does *not* have to be a class; it may as well be a simple type like an `int`. The concrete type of the parameter `T` is specified when a variable is declared. The name of the template class followed by the type in brackets < > can be used exactly like the conventional classes.

Listing 107 shows the implementation and the use of a template class for matrices. It directly extends Listing 103. The template class for matrices is used in a C++ program as shown now in Listing 109. The implementation of methods uses the class template as shown in Listing 108. The allocation is done exactly as in Listing 104.

The compiler and linker have to take care that code for every parameter type is generated. This should be transparent to the user.

```
template<class T> class Matrix {
  unsigned int xsize,ysize;             // sizes
  T ** matrix;                          // parameterized array
 public:
  Matrix();                             // default constructor
  Matrix(const Matrix&);                // copy constructor
  Matrix(int, int);                     // constructor with matrix size
  ~Matrix();                            // destructor
  T* operator[] (int);                  // access to vector
  void operator= (const Matrix&);       // assign matrix
  void operator= (const T& v);          // assign v to each element
  const T* operator[] (int) const;      // read only access
  operator T**(){ return matrix; }      // efficient access
  int SizeX()const{return xsize;}       // size information x
  int SizeY()const{return ysize;}       // size information y
};
```

```
template <class T> Matrix<T>::Matrix(int x, int y)
{
   xsize= x; ysize= y;
   T * array = new T[x*y];              // vector of size x*y
   matrix = new T*[y];                  // generate T matrix
   for (int i = 0; i < y; ++i)
      matrix[i] = & (array[i*x]);       // fill in vector pointers
}
template <class T> T* Matrix<T>::operator[] (int i)
   { return matrix[i]; }
template <class T> const T* Matrix<T>::operator[] (int i) const
   { return matrix[i]; }
```

11.3 Images

We now introduce image classes as the primary data structure for image processing and analysis. It quickly turns out that intensity images are not simply byte matrices. In real applications, we need further information about the image generation process. For example, it is necessary for recognition and classification purposes to know the camera geometry, i.e. the focal length or other parameters. Matrices are used as an internal representation of the image signal. Most common imaging devices use gray-level images with 256 gray-levels which can be stored in one byte (see Figure 11.2 or Figure 11.2 for examples). The components of the image's byte-matrix represent intensity values.

Another type of signals used for three-dimensional image processing are *range images*. Each component of the image matrix no longer represents an intensity value; instead, the *distance* of the scene points with respect to a given reference plane are stored within the matrix. The matrix elements in a range image can be any of the types byte, int, float, or double. It depends only upon the discrete step-sizes chosen for the depth values. Additional information

```
Matrix<int> m1(256,256);        // define a matrix of integers
Matrix<float> m2(512,256);      // define a larger matrix of floats
int c1= m1[2][100];             // access one element (secure,
float c2= m2[5][120];           // since the indices are checked)
```

11.4 External Data Formats

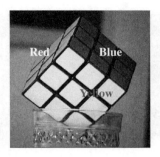

Figure 11.2: Examples of Color image (left) a gray-level image (center) and the corresponding range image (right)[3]

in the class range image could include the position of the reference plane or the scaling of the depth values. Figure 11.2 shows an example of a range image.[1] The depth values of the industrial part are encoded as gray-levels. The higher the gray-level, the lower is the distance of the scene point with respect to the optical sensor. Black pixels denote locations with undefined, i.e., unknown distance.

The declaration in Listing 110 introduces our first version of the abstract data type `GrayLevelImage` for gray-level images, wherein the defined template class for matrices is used, i.e. the class `Matrix` is a client of the abstract data type `GrayLevelImage`. Additionally, we have members which represent the focal length and the aperture of the camera lens as well as a scaling factor which describes pixel characteristics.[4] Later, we will enhance this class definition (Listing 211).

Pixel access is simply delegated to the image array with an inline operator `[]` which again checks the validity of the first index. We commonly choose the origin of the image coordinate system in the left upper corner. Therefore the first index of an image matrix corresponds to the y–coordinate axis, the second index belongs to x.[5] The method `isEqual` tests whether two images are equal.[6]

11.4 External Data Formats

Images require a large amount of external storage due to the large number of pixels. The image in Figure 11.2 has a dimension of 511×491 which requires 250901 bytes on disk. The simplest

---

[1]Due to the optical measurement device used in this case, there are areas on the object for which no range value is computed (like a shadow on the left).

[3](Ref. to Figure 11.2) Range images by the Institute for Physics, University of Erlangen-Nürnberg

[4]Pixels may be either quadratic (the rare case), or rectangular depending on the layout of the CCD. The relation of the sides is stored in the scaling factor (cf. Exercise 1.f).

[5]This means that $f(x,y) = f_{yx} = f_{ij}$. You should try to be consistent in your programs with respect to argument orderings and variable names!

[6]The test for equality is a complicated topic which will not be discussed here. It is different from the test for identity (`isSame`).

```
class GrayLevelImage_V0 {
  float focus;           // focal length
  float aperture;        // lens aperture
  float scaling;         // pixel side relation
  char * description;    // textual information
  Matrix<byte> image;    // the pixels
 public:
  GrayLevelImage_V0(int,int);                    // constructor
  ~GrayLevelImage_V0();                          // destructor
  int isEqual(const GrayLevelImage_V0&);         // test equality
  // etc.
  byte * operator [] (int i) { return image[i]; } // delegation
  int SizeX() const { return image.SizeX(); }
  int SizeY() const { return image.SizeY(); }
  float focalLength() const { return focus; }
};
#if defined(GLI_VERS) && (GLI_VERS == 0)
typedef class GrayLevelImage_V0 GrayLevelImage;
#endif
```

110

form of storage is the so called raw format (cf. Listing 34). For asymmetric image sizes, raw format may be insufficient; the image can only be read when the dimensions are known. How should the computer decide whether the image is 511×491 or 491×511?

Normally, various information about sizes, contents, resolution etc. is stored in the image files (e.g. in the common TIFF **T**ag **I**mage **F**ile **F**ormat, see [Poy92]). If the image elements are of a more complex data type than bytes, the external storage has to be conforming machine dependent internal formats. Machine independent storage is essential for the exchange of images between different computer architectures. Byte order of integral data types and floating point format are the major problems that have to be dealt with. Several standards exist for data representation, either by a standard committee (ISO/ANSI/DIN, cf. for example, [Pra95]) or as a "de-facto" standard imposed by the leading market position of some company (see also IIF e.g. in [Cla92]).

Images often contain a lot of redundancy. For that reason, image compression algorithms and strategies are of major importance. The JPEG (Joint Photographic Expert Group, [Wal90]) image compression standard and the MPEG (Motion Pictures Expert Group, [Gal91]) are commonly used for image transmission. Since the data compression using these algorithms discards information, these techniques are not always useful for image analysis. However, under appropriate parameterization, JPEG coded images can be used for image analysis and camera control in active imaging [Wal90].

One comon and very simple format is the `pgm` format in which images can be stored in binary or printable format. Because of its simplicity, we recommend that you use this format first (Exercise 11.g, Appendix B.2).

The program `compress` which is distributed with most Unix systems is designed for text compression. The same holds for `gzip` which is part of the GNU project. These programs are also applicable to images without loss of information, but of course with lower compression rates than JPEG or MPEG.

An image format suitable for object–oriented programming will be introduced in Chapter 16 and Chapter 24.2.

11.5 Binary Images

Figure 11.3: Gray-level image and two binary images with different thresholds

11.5 Binary Images

When each pixel in an image may be only black or white, then we are talking about *binary images*. This class of images is particularly useful in many areas as the speed of computation is generally higher e.g. with respect to gray-level images.

Logically, binary images and gray-level images are different image classes, since different operations are applicable to them. However, internally, they may both use a byte matrix, since only few computers allow efficient direct bit access. Most often, the smallest addressable unit is a byte.

The question arises how the bipartition of gray-levels must be selected such that an intensity image can be converted into a binary image in an *optimal* manner. We will learn about this in Chapter 18. Figure 11.3 shows a gray-level image and two binary images computed with different bipartitions.

11.6 Color Images

The human retina (cf. Figure 1.8) has three types of color receptors called *cone* cells. This justifies that color is usually represented through the combination of the three colors red, green, and blue (RGB). An example is shown in Figure 11.4.[7] For each basic color we need a matrix. Our first version for the declaration of a class `ColorImage` is shown in Listing 111.[8]

---

[7] Of course, the color images are printed here as gray-levels. They are available in full color together with the course material (Appendix B.8).

[8] Would you prefer a matrix of a structure containing three bytes for each pixel? Discuss advantages and disadvantages!

Figure 11.4: Three color channels (red, green, blue) for image Figure 11.2

```
struct ColorImage_V0 {          // Version 0
  Matrix<byte> * r;             // color channel red
  Matrix<byte> * g;             // color channel green
  Matrix<byte> * b;             // color channel blue
};
#if defined(COLImg_VERS) && (COLImg_VERS == 0)
typedef class ColorImage_V0 ColorImage;
#endif
```

The class for color images should include conversion to *color spaces* of other kinds, for instance, XYZ or HSL (see e.g. in [Wys82, Poy95]). These conversions are mappings from one three-dimensional vector to another. The transform of RGB to XYZ is a linear transformation, i.e. a multiplication by a matrix (11.1).

$$\begin{pmatrix} X \\ Y \\ Z \end{pmatrix} = \begin{pmatrix} 0.412 & 0.357 & 0.180 \\ 0.212 & 0.715 & 0.072 \\ 0.019 & 0.119 & 0.950 \end{pmatrix} \begin{pmatrix} R \\ G \\ B \end{pmatrix} \qquad (11.1)$$

The conversion to HSL (hue, saturation, luminosity) is much more complicated and non-linear. The YUV color space is used primarily for PAL or NTSC video [Poy95]. Cameras usually apply a non-linear conversion of intensity values called a *gamma-correction* which will be described in Sect. 18.6.[9] Also, a conversion to gray-level images seems to be useful as shown in (11.2) for RGB color images.[10] Within the color space XYZ, the conversion from colors to gray-levels results from a simple projection. Indeed, the Y–channel of the XYZ color space represents the gray-level image in (11.1), i.e.,

$$f_{i,j} = 0.212\, r_{i,j} + 0.715\, g_{i,j} + 0.072\, b_{i,j} \quad . \qquad (11.2)$$

Color images can also be created from gray-level images by *pseudo coloring*. A color vector has to be generated for every gray-level. This can easily be accomplished with histogram mappings (cf. Chapter 18).

---

[9]This mapping is often not exactly known and has to be determined by color-calibration.
[10]The image in Figure 11.2 was created from the color image in Figure 11.4 using this formula.

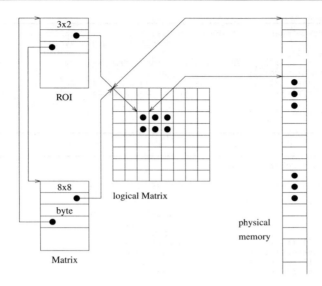

Figure 11.5: Logical and physical matrix mapped to a conventional linear storage. There exists no connected allocated storage for subimages (from [Pau92b]).

11.7 Subimages

Logically, image elements are accessed by the indices of the image array. In practice, however, pointers are often used which are set once and then incremented to gain speed. Therefore, it is essential for reliable programs to know something about the memory layout of images.

It is convenient, if an algorithm can be applied to a subimage, i.e. only a rectangular section of the image, without knowing about the size and offset to the enclosing image. For active vision, this is often called a "region of interest" (ROI). If we assume continuous allocation of pixels in the large image, the rows of the subimage will be split in memory as indicated in Figure 11.5.

The implementation of subimages is straightforward when using the technique introduced in Listing 104 ([Pau92b]). A subimage sets its line vector to the appropriate starting points in the master image. Images have to use reference counters in order to release memory correctly in the destructors.

Subimages provide a source of great performance gain in real-time image analysis, since only the relevant portion of the information has to be processed, as proposed also by the active vision approach. For subimages to work properly, it is essential that all image operations make the only assumption that elements in the image rows are allocated consecutively. Only then it is possible to use pointer access. When skipping from one row to the next, the pointer has to be initialized again using the subimage information. This is shown in Listing 112 for the computation of the mean of an image or a subimage. Implementation of subimages is left as Exercise 11.c.

```
extern "C" double mean(byte** image, int xs, int ys) // C-callable
{                                           // computes mean gray-value
   double res = 0;
   for (int i = ys-1; i >= 0; --i) {  // first index is i / y
      byte * ptr = image[i];          // use [ ]
      for (int j = xs-1; j >= 0; --j) // second index is j /x
         res += *(ptr++);             // may use pointer
   }
   return res / (xs * ys);
}
```
112

```
template<class T> class Vector {
 private:
   unsigned int xsize;              // number of elements
   T * vec;                         // parameterized array
 public:
   Vector();                                  // default constructor
   Vector(int);                               // constructor
   ~Vector();                                 // destructor
   T & operator[] (int);                      // access to vector
   const T& operator[] (int) const;           // read only access
   operator T*(){ return vec; }               // efficient access
   int SizeX()const{return xsize;}            // access
};
```
113

11.8 Matrix Operations

We now want to do basic mathematics with matrices and vectors. First, we need a template version of Listing 100 which is shown in Listing 113. For linear algebra, it is useful to tag a vector as a row vector or as a column vector. We leave out this detail at this point. Using the new vector declaration we can now implement operations such as the multiplication of a matrix by a column vector or multiplication of a row vector by a matrix.

Listing 114 shows a template *function* which is neither part of the class for vectors nor matrices. This function overloads the operator * for the operands Matrix and Vector. The use of this function requires that the operator * is defined on the actual type which is substituted for <T>. If this is not the case, the compiler will produce an error message.

```
template <class T> Vector<T> operator* (const Matrix<T>& m, const Vector<T> &v)
{
   assert(m.SizeX() == v.SizeX());            // check sizes
   int xsize = m.SizeX(), ysize = m.SizeY();  //
   Vector<T> r(m.SizeY());                    // local result vector
   for ( register short y=0; y < ysize;y++) { // loop over lines
      T s = 0;                                // sum over lines
      for( register short x=0; x < xsize; x++) // loop over columns
         s += v[x] * m[y][x];                 // sum up
      r[y] = s;                               // new vector element
   }
   return v;                                  // return copy
}
```
114

11.9 Speech Signal Class

```
void fct() {
  Matrix<int> m(3,3);        // integer matrix
  Vector<int> v0(3);         // integer column vector
  Vector<int> v1   = m * v0; // use copy constructor
  v0 = 2 * v1;               // use operator=
}
```
115

```
template <class T> Matrix<T> operator*(const Matrix<T>&, const Matrix<T>&);
template <class T> Vector<T> operator*(const Matrix<T>&, const Vector<T>&);
template <class T> Vector<T> operator*(const T&,         const Vector<T>&);
template <class T> T operator*(const Vector<T>&, const Vector<T>&);
```
116

Analogously we can now implement the following mathematical ideas for a scalar s, vectors $x, y \in \mathbb{R}^3$ and matrices $A, B, C \in \mathbb{R}^{3\times 3}$ in a way that Listing 115 is syntactically correct:

$$C = AB \qquad (11.3)$$
$$y = A\,x \qquad (11.4)$$
$$y = 0.12345\,x \qquad (11.5)$$
$$s = x \cdot y \qquad (11.6)$$

The declaration of these operations is shown in Listing 116 (in the same order as for the previous mathematical equations). The implementation is left as exercises (Exercise 11.f). The multiplication of a vector by a scalar explains why the functions in Listing 116 are not member functions of any class: the choice of an overloaded operator is done by the compiler from left to right in an expression, so there must be an overloaded operator for a scalar (an integer in Listing 115) which obviously cannot be a member function, since integer numbers are not instances of a class.

11.9 Speech Signal Class

Not all speech processing algorithms will split the sample values into frames of equal length. However, many computations can easily be described using such vectors of samples. Using the new `Vector` template we now proceed to define a speech frame class `SpeechSignal` and `SpeechFrame`. Operations are delegated to the vector template class. A basic structure is given in Listing 117. The speech frame references an object `SpeechSignal` for the representation of a whole speech signal. Similar to the image class, we include additional information for the sample values. Since we often want to use positive sample values, we provide a member `bias` which is added to each sample value. A time stamp marks the start of the speech signal and of each speech frame. In Chapter 21 we will see how the frames are computed from the speech signal. The class `Time` is left unspecified here; a possible source of implementation will be shown in Chapter 16. Data that is common to all speech frames, such as the duration, is not replicated in each object; instead, it is kept once in the referenced `SpeechSignal` object.

We choose a vector of short integers for the internal representation of the sample values. Thereby signals quantized with 12–16 bits can be represented. The `SpeechSignal` class

```
class SpeechSignal {            // small example - to be extended
   short bias;                  // added to each sample value
   long duration;               // frame length in [ms]
   float rate;                  // frame sampling rate
   Time  start;                 // Time class to be defined later
   Vector<short> signal;        // the sampled signal
 public:
   SpeechSignal();              // default
};
class SpeechFrame {
   SpeechSignal * origin;       // input sample data
   Time  start;                 // Time class to be defined
   Vector<short> samples;       // windowed sample values
 public:
   SpeechFrame (int s) : samples(s) {};
   Time Start();                // compute start time from index in signal
   short & operator [] (int i) { return samples[i]; }
};
```
117

also gives us the freedom to discard frames; in this case, the class will have to be extended by a representation of the sample values as a sequence, directly.

Exercises

11.a Implement a matrix template class using a vector of bytevectors (Listing 98). Extend the class Vector<T> (Listing 113) as indicated in Sect. 11.1.

11.b Write a program to convert to and from your favorite image format.

11.c Implement the concept of subimages for the image classes introduced in this chapter. Use a reference count in the image class to decide whether the destructor should release the allocated memory, or not.

11.d Implement the color transformation (11.1) using matrix multiplication by a color vector as in Listing 115. Integrate a member into the vector class for row and column vectors.

11.e Compute reverse transformations for (11.3) and (11.1). Apply the transformation back and forth several times. What kind of error will you get?

11.f Extend matrix and vector operations as indicated in Sect. 11.8.

11.g Write two functions for image input and output. The format is described in Appendix B.2.

    (a) Store a gray-level-image object in pgm format
    (b) Read a gray-level-image object from a pgm file

11.h Using the functions of Exercise 11.g, write a program that reads an image and computes some statistical features as described in Chapter 7, such as mean, variance, entropy, and median.

Chapter 12
Signals and Images

When testing new algorithms, it is often useful to start experiments using synthetic data for which the result of the processing is known (cf. Sect. 3.2). Image synthesis is part of computer graphics (cf. Sect. 1.1), and also the generation of realistic speech signals using text input is an area of research. In this chapter we mostly establish regular patterns or global features which are useful in pattern recognition for testing low-level algorithms.

Many algorithms in the field of low-level image and speech processing are concerned with noise reduction in the data (cf. Chapter 17). These techniques are often based on assumptions about special noise distributions. For the experimental evaluation of algorithms, it is useful to have synthetic image generators for different noise effects, i.e., special distributions of noisy pixels.

In the following sections we describe some algorithms for synthetic image and sound generation. We describe how to create *magic 3–D* images and conclude the chapter with a special case of synthetic texture images.

12.1 Synthetic Sound

For the evaluation of the correctness of programs, it is often useful to have an undisturbed input signal with well-known features. We select a sampling frequency and a linear quantization using 16 bit. For a simple sound generator, we need to set the loudness of the sound and use the `sin` function to generate samples. Also, rectangular and triangular signals can be generated.[1]

If we want to create a sound signal consisting of overlayed components, in general, we have several choices. We can either create a program with lots of arguments for the various parameters; or, we can interactively ask for the signals to be generated; or, we can create a set of tools for the composition of sound files.

The last choice has several advantages. Imagine, you want to test your large program, and you need some sound pattern in order to verify the correctness of the behavior of your code.

---
[1] Listen to them on your sound device!

You simply write a sequence of sound generation commands in your `Makefile`, compose the outputs, and then run your program on them. This way, you will not even have to record in your notes which signal is in which file, since this can easily be seen from your `makefile`.

The required tools are programs for sound generation, a program which takes an arbitrary number of input files and creates an output signal which contains an additive superposition of the input files,[2] and a program which modifies the amplitude of a given input signal.

12.2 Geometric Patterns

Similar to periodic sound signals, images of two-dimensional geometric objects with known position and shape are often used to test image processing methods. In contrast to computer graphics, usually no realistic image is necessary. Instead, lines, points, circles, and rectangles — either filled or the outline only — have to be positioned in the synthetic image. Lattices of variable width or chess board patterns are also frequently used, for instance, to check edge detectors. Some examples are shown in Figure 12.1 (see also Exercise 12.b).

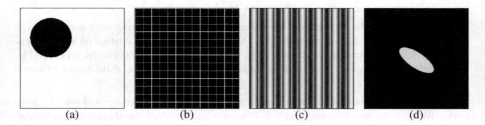

Figure 12.1: Examples of synthetic images

As in Sect. 12.1, these objects are simply created by a set of functions. For the combination of several images to a new one, additional and appropriate tools are required. Common combinations are image addition, bitwise *exclusive or*, bitwise *and*, logical *and*, logical *or*, and multiplication of an image with a factor to reduce or increase intensity. Also, the combination of three gray-level images to a color image can be a nice tool. All operations require modulo arithmetics due to the quantization involved.

12.3 Noise Signals

Many disturbances in real images are often due to pixel noise. Let us assume that statistically each n–th pixel is disturbed by noise, i.e. every pixel will be disturbed by noise with probability $1/n$ [Pra91].

---

[2]The input signals do not have to be combined with addition; there exist cases where a convolution of one with the other makes sense. Also, multiplication can be used in some cases.

12.3 Noise Signals

We use a program which generates a homogeneous black or white gray-level image as in Sect. 12.2. and add on average to each n–th pixel a uniformly distributed gray-level from the interval $[a, b]$ using modulo arithmetic. In the implementation, the parameters n, a and b are initialized by default values, and the user has the possibility to adjust these parameters during the function call. In Figure 12.2 examples are shown for three different choices of parameters.

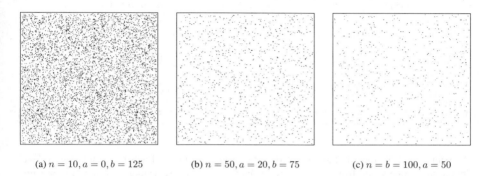

(a) $n = 10, a = 0, b = 125$ (b) $n = 50, a = 20, b = 75$ (c) $n = b = 100, a = 50$

Figure 12.2: Examples of pixel noise for different parameter values

Gaussian noise is often assumed to be an adequate modeling of real noise effects occurring in images recorded by CCD cameras or other sensors. As an alternative to the general principle introduced in Sect. 7.4 the famous algorithm of G. E. P. Box, M. E. Muller, and G. Marsaglia [Knu73, Joh87] can be used for generating normally distributed gray-levels with the mean zero and a variance of one. For normal distributions this method is preferred to the formulas introduced in Sect. 7.4, as (7.17) requires a closed-form solution for the inverse cummulative distribution F_X which does not exist for Gaussians. The described method is based on two $[0, 1]$ uniformly distributed random numbers u_1 and u_2. Using both numbers we introduce the following transformation of random variables:

$$v_1 = 2\,u_1 - 1 \quad , \tag{12.1}$$
$$v_2 = 2\,u_2 - 1 \quad , \text{ and} \tag{12.2}$$
$$s = v_1^2 + v_2^2 \quad . \tag{12.3}$$

If the value of s is greater or equal to one, the algorithm starts again with the computation of both uniformly distributed random numbers u_1 and u_2. Otherwise, it can be shown that the random variable

$$X = v_1 \sqrt{\frac{-2\ln s}{s}} \tag{12.4}$$

belongs to a normal distribution using the algebra of random variables [Spr79]. Using this idea we are able to create a sound signal of Gaussian noise or a noisy image (see Figure 12.3 left, below). Implementation issues are discussed in Exercise 12.i.

```
#define ImageOps(fn,op)                         /* function definition macro */   \
  static void image_##fn (Matrix<byte> & out,            /* result    */   \
                          Matrix<byte> const & in1,      /* operand 1 */   \
                          Matrix<byte> const & in2) {    /* operand 2 */   \
    for (int i = 0; i < in1.SizeY(); ++i)                                   \
      for (int j = 0; j < in1.SizeX(); ++j) {                               \
        int r = int(in1[i][j]) op int(in2[i][j]);                           \
        out[i][j] = (r<0) ? 0 : ((r>255) ? 255 : r); /* clip result */      \
      }                                                                     \
  }                                                                         \
  Option opt_##fn(#fn,"choice is " #fn,0);      /* command line option */   \

ImageOps (add,+)     ImageOps (sub,-)       // define functions for
ImageOps (mul,*)     ImageOps (div,/)       // the binary operators
ImageOps (bor,|)     ImageOps (band,&)      // + - * / | &
ImageOps (lor,||)    ImageOps (land,&&)     // || && ^ %
ImageOps (xor,^)     ImageOps (mod,%)       // xor and modulus
ImageOps (lsh,>)     ImageOps (rsh,<)       // comparison
ImageOps (eql,==)    ImageOps (neq,!=)      // equal and not equal
```
118

A special type of noise is the so-called *salt-and-pepper noise*. Each pixel in the gray-level image takes one value from a set of two values $\{a, b\}$. These values appear with the same probability of $1/2$ (cf. Figure 12.3 middle). For the implementation of a function which generates salt-and-pepper noise, the gray-levels a and b are parameters of the function call. We can also apply the same idea to sound signals and use the same random generators for both tasks.

12.4 Combination of Signals

In Listing 118 we show a macro that defines functions for binary operations on images.[3] Each macro expansion creates a function for image addition, multiplication, etc. In Listing 118 we pass one part of the function name as the first argument to the macro and an operator as the second argument. The function name results from a concatenation (expressed by ## for the pre-processor) of `image_` and the first argument; a command line option (cf. Sect. 16.7) is created by the concatenation of `opt_` and the same argument; the argument is passed to the command line option constructor as a string for the first argument, and it is concatenated with a constant string in the second argument.

Such tricks with macros are not possible with templates. A similar macro can now be defined for unary operations. The functions clip values greater than 255 and less than 0.

Together with the geometric patterns generated in Sect. 12.2 we can now create, for example, a circular mask and *and* it to an image, to mask out only the image portion inside the circle.

A similar macro and function can be defined to combine speech signals (Exercise 12.j).

---

[3]Note that comments are written in C notation since `cpp` may otherwise confuse comments and the trailing backslash.

Figure 12.3: Examples of Gaussian (left) and Salt-and-Pepper noise (middle) and combination of both (right) (see text in Sect. 12.5)

12.5 Simple Image Manipulation

A simple macro similar to the one in Listing 118 can be defined so that each pixel in an image is changed by a constant value, e.g. by adding a constant or multiplying with a constant.

Two other programs are very usful; one that has three input images and combines them to one output color image; another has one input (color) image and creates three output gray-level images from the color channels of the input image.

If we know how to write batch or shell programs, we can now simply combine these tools to generate nice test images. The rightmost image in Figure 12.3 is created by a combination of synthetic images introduced so far using the functions discussed in Sect. 12.4: first, a filled circle is created (Figure 12.1). Two images are created using the algorithms for Gaussian and salt-and-pepper noise, respectively. The circle image is combined with the Gaussian noise by a bitwise *and* as in the function which is created by the macro expansion `ImageOps(and,&)` in Listing 118, creating an image A. Subtracting each pixel value from the constant 255 inverts the circle image. Again, a bitwise *and* creates an image B containing the data to be filled into the circle. A pixelwise *or* using `ImageOps(or,|)` of A and B creates the image in Figure 12.3 (right).

12.6 2–D Views of 3–D Polyhedral Objects

Figure 12.4 shows different views of a polyhedral object. Synthetic views of polyhedral objects can be used in model-based image analysis when 3–D models are used and the recognition of such objects has to be verified in the image. A projection of the model to the estimated position is performed; the projected lines are matched to the lines in the images. To this effect, we outline three steps to implement a program for the generation of synthetic views of 3–D objects, where we do not care about hidden lines or occluded parts of the object.

First, we write a program which creates a synthetic white image including black points at specified locations. The coordinates of three-dimensional points and their gray-level in the

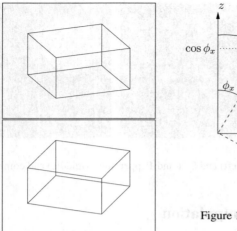

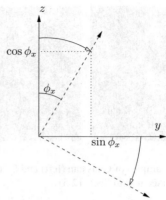

Figure 12.5: Rotation of unit vectors in 3–D

Figure 12.4: Views of a polyhedral object

projection are parameters of the function call, as well as the transformation from the 3–D world coordinates to the 2–D image plane. The transformation consists of a 3–D rotation, a 3–D translation, and a projection. There exist various representations of 3–D rotations. It depends on the given application which mathematical representation is appropriate [Kan90]. From a mathematical point of view, the easiest way is to multiply rotations around the axes of the world coordinate system.

The columns of the rotation matrix $\boldsymbol{R}_{\phi_x}$ which rotates 3–D points around the x–axis by the angle ϕ_x are defined by the images of the three unit vectors. Obviously, a rotation around the x–axis does not change the vector $(1, 0, 0)^T$, but the vector $(0, 1, 0)^T$ is transformed to $(0, \cos\phi, -\sin\phi)^T$ and the vector $(0, 0, 1)^T$ to $(0, \sin\phi_x, \cos\phi_x)^T$ (cf. Figure 12.5). The resulting matrix is thus

$$\boldsymbol{R}_{\phi_x} = \begin{pmatrix} 1 & 0 & 0 \\ 0 & \cos\phi_x & \sin\phi_x \\ 0 & -\sin\phi_x & \cos\phi_x \end{pmatrix} \qquad (12.5)$$

The matrices $\boldsymbol{R}_{\phi_y}$ and $\boldsymbol{R}_{\phi_z}$ are computed in a similar manner, and the complete rotation $\boldsymbol{R}$ is

$$\boldsymbol{R} = \boldsymbol{R}_{\phi_x} \boldsymbol{R}_{\phi_y} \boldsymbol{R}_{\phi_z} \ . \qquad (12.6)$$

Note, that matrix multiplication is not commuative and that the order of the rotations is relevant. The projection onto the 2–D image plane of a rotated and translated 3–D point can be done using several mappings. The perspective and the orthographic projection have been discussed already in Chapter 1.

Therefore, the remaining problem is the construction of digital straight lines which are defined by pairs of 2–D points. The easiest way of computing digital lines is to compute the analytical form of the corresponding straight lines, i.e., the 2–D coordinates (x, y) have to satisfy

$$y = mx + t \quad . \tag{12.7}$$

The digital points can be computed using the closest digital points in the image grid. The results are usually not convincing and computationally expensive. A more efficient algorithm to compute digital lines is the method attributed to Bresenham, which requires only integer arithmetics. This is a standard algorithm in the field of computer graphics, and is therefore not discussed here [Bre87].

12.7 Single Stereo Images

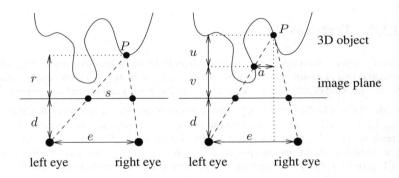

Figure 12.6: One 3–D point gets two points in the image plane (left); hidden point removal (right)

Recently, so-called *single stereo images* (SIS) have become very popular. They look very mysterious on the first glance. Nevertheless, the idea those images are based on is fairly simple. Humans have two eyes. If someone looks at a point in the three-dimensional space, this point can be seen by each eye — if no occlusion occurs. The projection of this point on an image plane along the eye's ray causes a separate two-dimensional point for each eye. In autostereograms the corresponding points are elements of *one* image and get the same gray-level. Figure 12.6 (left) shows the geometrical relations. Since we have similar triangles, the distance between both projected points is

$$s = \frac{r \cdot e}{r + d} \quad . \tag{12.8}$$

If a range image is used as input data, formula (12.8) yields for each 3–D surface point the corresponding coordinates of the two-dimensional image points.

Technically speaking, it is incorrect to plot a stereo pair into the image plane which corresponds to a 3–D point on the object, being visible to one eye only, Figure 12.6 (right). If we do so, we will get ambiguities close to depth steps in the range values. Let (x_l, y_l) and (x_p, y_p) be the 2-D coordinates of the left eye and the object point P. The distance u is computed by

$$u = \frac{a \cdot (d+r)}{|x_p - x_l|}, \qquad (12.9)$$

where $r = u + v$ is the depth value known from the range image. This equation can be used to decide, whether a point is visible by both eyes by comparing u and the corresponding range value for all admissible values of a. If the depth exceeds or is equal to $v = r - u$, the ray is intercepted and thus the point is not visible.

The geometric relationships needed for the implementation of a SIS generator can easily be derived. We can then compute the corresponding points for each of the range values. These correspondences are visualized by the assignment of identical gray-levels to each pair of pixels. The gray-levels necessary for coloring can be taken from a random image (see Sect.12.3).

12.8 Textures

Natural objects often have a structure which looks regular when seen from a large distance and irregular in a close-up view. Imagine, for example, an image of a corn field or a carpet on the floor. This kind of structure is called *texture* in computer graphics and image processing.

In [Kle95; p. 45–48] a simple algorithm for texture generation is described. Given parameters a_{lu}, a_u, a_{ru}, and a_l, with values from the interval $[-50, 50]$, and a parameter $n \in [50, 200]$, we create an $M \times N$ gray-level image f with G gray-levels. We define $H := (G-1)/2$. The gray-values of the image are computed sequentially line by line as shown in the structogram of Figure 12.7. Let Z be a uniformly distributed random variable in the range $[0, G-1]$. The function $r(x, y)$ creates noise with uniform distribution by

$$r(x, y) = (Z - H)\frac{n}{100} \qquad (12.10)$$

$\forall x, \forall y : f(x, y) = 0$
FOR $y \in [1 \ldots N-2]$
FOR $x \in [1 \ldots M-2]$
$q := \quad (f(x-1, y-1) - H)\,0.01 a_{lu} + (f(x, y-1) - H)\,0.01 a_u +$ $(f(x+1, y-1) - H)\,0.01 a_{ru} + (f(x-1, y) - H)\,0.01 a_l + r(x, y)$
$p := \begin{cases} H+q, & \text{if } 0 \leq H+q \leq G-1 \\ 0, & \text{if } H+q < 0 \\ G-1, & \text{otherwise} \end{cases}$
$f(x, y) := \min\{H+p, G-1\}$

Figure 12.7: Simple texture generation

Examples of synthetic images generated using this technique and natural textures are shown in Figure 12.8.

Figure 12.8: Example of synthetic (left, middle) and natural textures (fabric, right)

```
class FrameGrabber {
    int sx, sy;
public:
    FrameGrabber () ;         // establishes connection, initializes
    void resize(int,int);     // set size of grabbed matrix
    int Grab(GrayLevelImage &); // read into image
};

int FrameGrabber::Grab(GrayLevelImage& g)
{
    int xs = g.SizeX();
    int ys = g.SizeY();
    if ((xs != sx) || (ys != sy)) {
        resize(xs,ys);
    }
    // ... do the grabbing
}
```

12.9 Audio and Video Devices

Natural speech signals are usually recorded by a microphone which is connected to an audio device (cf. Figure 1.9). The speaker (cf. Figure 1.11) is connected to the same device. One option for processing is to record using a program that comes with that device, store the signal to file, and read that file with your program. A similar strategy is possible with frame grabbers and video devices.

If these devices are to be accessed directly by your program, we recommend to encapsulate the hardware dependent parts into a separate module. A simple interface for image grabbing is given in Listing 119. When an image is captured by the grabber, the size of the image determines the number of pixels transferred from the frame grabber. If the hardware does not support capturing smaller images, a software solution can be used, e.g. by resizing the image captured (cf. Sect. 17.5). This way, a program that requires such a feature can be compiled and run on a computer that just emulates this behaviour. As there are many different frame grabber types and many different camera types, it makes sense to set up a frame grabber class and a separate camera class. In the camera class we will have the parameters of the optics, such as the zoom setting, or the shutter time. Reading this information will send a request to the camera controller which may be connected e.g. to the serial line of the computer.

For audio signals, a similar approach can be taken. The digitalization hardware will be encapsulated by a class and its settings, such as sampling rate and bits per sample, will be stored in this class. Microphones currently do not offer computer controlled operations. It might, however, still be wise to provide different classes for different microphones, as they vary widely in the way they record sound. One entry in such a record might be the opening angle of the area inside which sound will be recorded, which can be taken from the technical description of the device or determined experimentally.

Exercises

12.a Write a program that creates
- a circle
- an ellipse
- a rectangle (optionally rotated)

The figures should optionally be filled.

12.b Use the functions in Sect. 12.3 and build a program `CreateImage` where options allow the generation of different noisy images with different parameters.

12.c Generate a synthetic range image of a polyhedral object.

12.d Write a program which reads a range image, a noise image, and computes a single stereo image.

12.e Implement a class which allows the generation of speech signals representing parameterized trigonometrical functions. The class should also provide methods for additive superposition and other operations on these speech signals.

12.f Using the algorithms given in Sect. 12.8, extend your main program to create textured images.

12.g Extend Listing 118 to a complete program which reads images and does arithmetic on the pixels.

12.h Extend Exercise 12.g to color images.

12.i Use the textual description of the algorithm in Sect. 12.3 for an implementation of a random number generator for normally distributed numbers with zero mean and variance one.

Use this function to generate a Gaussian image where the mean gray-level is determined by the parameter m. The variance can be modified by choosing different quantization steps of the continuous density function or by scaling the generated random values to the appropriate range.

12.j Similar to the macro in Listing 118, write a macro that combines speech signals.

Chapter 13

Fourier Transform

In the field of image processing, a sampled signal usually serves directly as input data for algorithms which extract geometric features or segmented images (Sect. 8.6, see also Chapter 19). Gray-level images, for instance, are used to compute point or line features or to extract regions of homogeneous intensity values.

In speech recognition it is necessary to derive a set of features for the sampled signal that are convenient for the subsequent processing steps. There are many different types of parameters to represent a speech signal. You can take, for example, the sample values of the speech and compute features like the zero crossing rate, the energy of the signal, or the slope at selected points [Nie90a, Rab88]. Usually features are not computed in the *spatial domain*, but in the *frequency domain* of the signal, i.e., a transform of the signal is required. Spectral features have some characteristics which are not directly evident in spatial data [Dud73]. Therefore, it has proven advantageous to do a spectral analysis of speech signals. A more detailed motivation, introduction, and definition of spectral features for speech processing will follow in Chapter 21.

In the subsequent sections we will give an introduction to the computation of Fourier transforms for signals of arbitrary dimensions including both the continuous and the discrete case.[1] The famous algorithm of Cooley and Tukey [Coo65] for the fast computation of Fourier transforms will be discussed. This is, in addition to algorithms for sorting, one of the most important and most cited algorithms in computer science and engineering. Some hints for the implementation in C++ of this basic technique will be given in the final sections of this chapter as well as some new features of the C++ language, which will be applied to a class for complex numbers.

13.1 Introductory Considerations

In linear algebra it is shown that a set of linear independent vectors can be used as a basis for a vector space. Linear independency says that no vector of the basis can be expressed as a linear combination of other basis vectors. The vector space is defined by all linear combinations of available basis vectors. A well-known example is the two-dimensional plane $\mathbb{R}^2$, where possible basis vectors are $e_1 = (1, 0)^T$ and $e_2 = (0, 1)^T$. All vectors $v \in \mathbb{R}^2$ can be written as

---

[1] Jean Baptiste Joseph Fourier (∗ March 21, 1768 - † May 16, 1830)

a linear combination

$$v = a_1 e_1 + a_2 e_2 \;, \tag{13.1}$$

where the coefficients $a_1, a_2 \in \mathbb{R}$. Obviously the basis vectors are not unique, but for a given set of basis vectors, all elements of the vector space can be uniquely identified by the coefficients of the linear combination. The cardinality of the basis is not necessarily finite. The vector space for polynomials, for example, is generated by the infinite set of monomials $\{x^n | n \geq 0\}$. A polynomial

$$h(x) = \sum_{k=0}^{n} h_k x^k \tag{13.2}$$

of degree n is uniquely given by its $n+1$ coefficients $h_0, h_1, \ldots, h_n$.

An interesting question is, whether there exits a finite or infinite set of basis elements for the space of signals. Indeed, every *periodic* signal can be written as a linear combination of sine and cosine functions. Figure 13.1 shows, for example, some plots of one-dimensional functions which are sums of trigonometric functions.

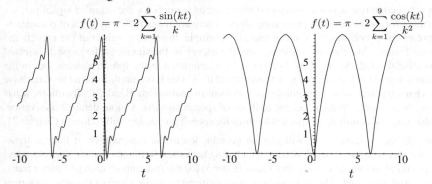

Figure 13.1: Linear combinations of trigonometric functions

13.2 Fourier Series

The basic idea of using the frequency domain of speech signals is founded on the mathematical result that an arbitrary 2π–periodic function[2] $f(t) \in \mathbb{R}$, where $t \in \mathbb{R}$, can be approximated by a — possibly infinite — Fourier series

$$f(t) = \frac{a_0}{2} + \sum_{k \geq 1} a_k \cos(kt) + b_k \sin(kt) \;, \tag{13.3}$$

---

[2]i.e., $f(t) = f(t + 2\pi)$

13.2 Fourier Series

i.e., a superposition of weighted sine and cosine terms. The scalar weights a_k and b_k are called the *Fourier coefficients* and can be used for the unique mathematical description of periodic functions. This result shows that $\{\cos(kt), \sin(kt) | k \geq 0\}$ forms a basis for the vector space of all 2π–periodic functions.

The convergence properties of this — in general infinite — sum were developed by Dirichlet and are summarized, for example, in [Bro85]. The behavior of Fourier series and the associated Fourier coefficients with respect to the symmetry properties of the periodic function $f(t)$ is remarkable and important for practical computations. The cosine function is an even function and the sine function is symmetrical to the origin of the coordinate system. This is the reason why the approximation of odd functions ($f(t) = -f(-t)$) using (13.3) includes only summands of sine functions and analogously, even functions ($f(t) = f(-t)$) are superpositions of cosine terms. Thus, whenever an odd or even function is developable in a Fourier series, we know that $a_k = 0$ or $b_k = 0$, $k \geq 0$, for the involved Fourier coefficients.

It should be clear to the reader, that if a *finite* sum of sine and cosine functions approximates a function without any errors, the *continuous* function can be exactly recomputed, if the discrete values a_k and b_k of the frequencies of sine and cosine terms occurring are known. This observation constitutes the basis for the informally introduced sampling theorem of Sect.1.7. However, there are, in general, infinitely many non-zero Fourier coefficients for arbitrary, not band-limited functions.

Let the function $f(t)$ be a given 2π–periodic function that should be approximated by a Fourier series. Now the practical question arises, how can we analytically or at least numerically, compute the Fourier coefficients $a_k \in \mathbb{R}$ and $b_k \in \mathbb{R}$ for $k \geq 0$ of (13.3). Indeed, there exist closed form solutions for the computation.

For this purpose, we multiply both sides of (13.3) with $\cos(lt)$ and determine the integral over the interval $[-\pi, \pi]$ of the resulting function. Applying the orthogonality property of the trigonometric sine and cosine functions, i.e., for integer k and l, it is

$$\int_{-\pi}^{\pi} \sin(kt) \cos(lt)\, dt = 0 \quad \text{and} \tag{13.4}$$

$$\int_{-\pi}^{\pi} \sin(kt) \sin(lt)\, dt = \int_{-\pi}^{\pi} \cos(kt) \cos(lt)\, dt = \begin{cases} 0, \text{if } k \neq l \\ \pi, \text{if } k = l \end{cases}, \tag{13.5}$$

we get

$$a_k = \frac{1}{\pi} \int_{-\pi}^{\pi} f(t) \cos(kt)\, dt \quad . \tag{13.6}$$

The multiplication of equation (13.3) with $\sin(lt)$ and subsequent integration results in a similar formula for b_k, i.e.,

$$b_k = \frac{1}{\pi} \int_{-\pi}^{\pi} f(t) \sin(kt)\, dt \quad . \tag{13.7}$$

These formulas are called *Euler's formulas*.

Let us, as an example, compute the Fourier series for the step function defined by

$$f(t) = \begin{cases} 1, & \text{if } 0 \leq t < \frac{\pi}{2} \\ -1, & \text{if } \frac{\pi}{2} < t < \frac{3\pi}{2} \\ 1, & \text{if } \frac{3\pi}{2} < t \leq 2\pi \end{cases} \quad . \tag{13.8}$$

Due to the symmetry of this function, we conclude $b_k = 0$ for all k. The coefficients a_k are computed by the evaluation of (13.6); herein, the integrals occurring over cosine functions are fairly elementary to compute, and we get

$$a_k = \begin{cases} 0, & \text{if } k \text{ is even} \\ \frac{4}{k\pi} \sin\left(\frac{k\pi}{2}\right), & \text{otherwise} \end{cases} \quad . \tag{13.9}$$

Figure 13.2 shows the first summands of the resulting Fourier series, and Figure 13.3 illustrates the superposition of these functions.[3] This example illustrates (but does not prove) the theoretical results of Dirichlet concerning the convergence properties of Fourier series, even in the case of non-smooth periodic functions.

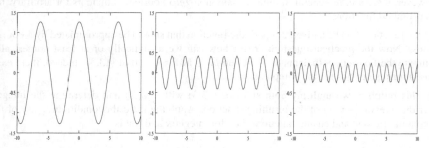

Figure 13.2: First three summands of the Fourier series for the step function defined in (13.8)

13.3 Fourier Transform

The Fourier series will now be used for the introduction and derivation of the Fourier transform. For this purpose, Fourier series will be written in complex form. By the introduction of the Eulerian formula

$$\exp(\pm i\phi) = \cos\phi \pm i\sin\phi \quad , \tag{13.10}$$

where $\exp(\pm i\phi) \in \mathbb{C}$ and i is the imaginary unit, the trigonometric functions can be written in terms of complex exponential functions, i.e.,

$$\cos(kt) = \frac{1}{2}(\exp(ikt) + \exp(-ikt)) \tag{13.11}$$

---

[3] The asymmetrical look of the function is due to a bug in the graphical tool used for visualization.

13.3 Fourier Transform

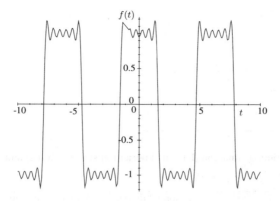

Figure 13.3: Superposition of the functions in Figure 13.2 and three further summands

and

$$\sin(kt) = \frac{1}{2i}(\exp(ikt) - \exp(-ikt)) \quad . \quad (13.12)$$

If we put these identities into the Fourier series (13.3), we can approximate univariate, real-valued functions $f(t)$ using the infinite complex series

$$f(t) = \frac{1}{2\pi} \sum_{k=-\infty}^{+\infty} c_k \exp(ikt) \quad , \quad (13.13)$$

where

$$c_k = \begin{cases} \pi(a_k - i\,b_k), & \text{if } k \geq 0 \\ \pi(a_{|k|} + i\,b_{|k|}), & \text{otherwise} \end{cases} \quad . \quad (13.14)$$

The formula for computing the weights c_k of each complex summand is shown to be

$$c_k = \int_{-\pi}^{\pi} f(t) \exp(-ikt)\, dt \quad . \quad (13.15)$$

Obviously, even functions have no complex parts in their complex Fourier series, because there are no sine terms, i.e., $b_k = 0$ for all k.

Let us now assume that the interval of periodicity for the function $f(t)$ is infinite. The sum of (13.13) will become an integral and the coefficients c_k will result in a continuous weight function $c(k)$ with respect to the real-valued variable k, i.e.,

$$c(k) = \int_{-\infty}^{+\infty} f(t) \exp(-ikt)\, dt \quad . \quad (13.16)$$

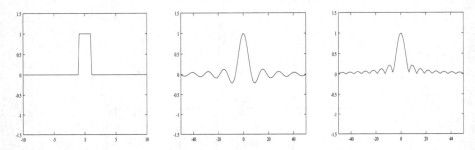

Figure 13.4: Continuous function (left), its Fourier transform (middle) and the absolute values (right)

	spatial domain	frequency domain
scaling	$f(at)$	$\frac{1}{|a|} F(\frac{\xi}{a})$
shifting	$f(t - t_0)$	$\exp(-i\xi t_0) F(\xi)$
symmetry	$-1/(2\pi) \cdot F(t)$	$f(-\xi)$
differentiation	$d^n f(t)/dt^n$	$(i\xi)^n F(\xi)$

Table 13.1: Some properties of the Fourier transform

The weight function $c(k)$ is called the *Fourier transform* of the function $f(t)$. In the following we will denote the Fourier transform of $f(t)$ by

$$F(\xi) = \int_{-\infty}^{+\infty} f(t) \exp(-i\xi t) \, dt = FT\{f\} \quad . \tag{13.17}$$

The Fourier transform of a function represents the amplitude of each frequency found in the signal. For example, Figure 13.4 shows the continuous function

$$f(t) = \begin{cases} 1 & \text{if } |t| < t_0 \\ 0 & \text{otherwise} \end{cases} \tag{13.18}$$

and the absolute values of the corresponding Fourier transform.

Some useful and often needed properties of this transform are summarized in Table 13.1. The proofs are elementary and left as exercise 13.k to the reader. The symmetry character shows that the inverse of the Fourier transform is again a Fourier transform. Thus, the computational complexity of the inverse Fourier transform is identical to the calculation of Fourier transform itself. Indeed, we have

$$f(t) = \frac{1}{2\pi} \int_{-\infty}^{+\infty} F(\xi) \exp(i\xi t) \, d\xi \quad . \tag{13.19}$$

13.3 Fourier Transform

Figure 13.5: Application of the convolution theorem

One fundamental property of the Fourier transform is the *convolution theorem*. It states that for the functions $f, g,$ and h and for their Fourier transforms $F, G,$ and H

$$h(t) = f(t) \star g(t) = \int_{-\infty}^{+\infty} f(x)\, g(t-x)\, dx \qquad (13.20)$$

the Fourier transform satisfies the equation

$$H(\xi) = F(\xi)\, G(\xi) \quad, \qquad (13.21)$$

since due to the shifting property of the Fourier transform we get

$$\begin{aligned}
H(\xi) &= \int_{-\infty}^{+\infty} h(t) \exp(-i\xi t)\, dt = \int_{-\infty}^{+\infty}\int_{-\infty}^{+\infty} f(x)\, g(t-x)\, dx\, \exp(-i\xi t)\, dt \\
&= \int_{-\infty}^{+\infty} f(x) \left(\int_{-\infty}^{+\infty} g(t-x) \exp(-i\xi t)\, dt \right) dx \\
&= \int_{-\infty}^{+\infty} f(x)\, \exp(-i\xi x)\, G(\xi)\, dx = F(\xi)\, G(\xi) \quad. \qquad (13.22)
\end{aligned}$$

This theorem shows that the computation of the convolution of two functions can be done by the multiplication of the Fourier transforms $F(\xi)$ and $G(\xi)$ of both functions and a subsequent use of the inverse Fourier transform.

The most common application of the convolution theorem in the field of signal theory is the determination of the function $f(t)$ from equation (13.20), if $g(t)$ and $h(t)$ are known. The principle of this process is shown in Figure 13.5. Only a division is required after the transformation into the frequency domain. Without the convolution theorem, we have to solve a complicated integral equation for the computation of $f(t)$. The convolution theorem is widely used in different fields of mathematics, computer science or electrical engineering. Fast multiplication algorithms for polynomials or integers [Aho74], for example, use the convolution as well as time-invariant linear systems [Nie83].

The application of the Fourier transform for speech or image processing requires some extensions in our software environment: First, all signals we can deal with are discrete rather than continuous. A discrete version of the Fourier transform and its inverse is needed (Sect. 13.4). Second, the introduction of the Fourier transform implies the necessity of complex numbers; we need an elaborated class for complex numbers, which provides methods like addition and multiplication (Sect. 13.5). Third, an extension of the one-dimensional case is required, because images represent two-dimensional signals (Sect. 13.9).

13.4 Discrete Fourier Transform

If we have to compute the Fourier transform of a recorded speech signal represented by the sequence of M sampling values $f_0, f_1, \ldots, f_{M-1}$, we need the discrete version of the Fourier transform. Following (13.16) we define

$$F_\nu = \sum_{t=0}^{M-1} f_t \cdot \left(\exp\left(-i2\pi \frac{\nu}{M}\right)\right)^t = \text{DFT}\{f\} \quad . \tag{13.23}$$

The computation of the *discrete Fourier transform* (DFT) and its inverse can easily be done, because it is a linear transform which thus can be written in matrix form. The discrete Fourier transform F_ν, $\nu = 0, 1, 2, \ldots, M-1$, is a linear combination of complex numbers which are solutions of the equation

$$x^M - 1 = 0 \tag{13.24}$$

and powers of these numbers. Let

$$m = \exp\left(-i\frac{2\pi}{M}\right) \tag{13.25}$$

and

$$m^{t\nu} = \exp\left(-i2\pi \frac{t\nu}{M}\right) \tag{13.26}$$

denote powers of the solutions of above equation. The root m is usually called the *M-th root of unity* and we know from the theory of complex numbers

$$\sum_{t=0}^{M-1} \exp\left(-i2\pi \frac{t}{M}\right) = 0 \quad . \tag{13.27}$$

Using definition (13.23) for $\nu = 0, 1, 2, \ldots, M-1$, we get the following linear system of equations for discrete Fourier coefficients:

$$\begin{pmatrix} F_0 \\ F_1 \\ F_2 \\ \vdots \\ F_{M-1} \end{pmatrix} = \underbrace{\begin{pmatrix} 1 & 1 & 1 & \cdots & 1 \\ 1 & m & m^2 & \cdots & m^{M-1} \\ 1 & m^2 & m^4 & \cdots & m^{2(M-1)} \\ \vdots & \vdots & \vdots & \vdots & \vdots \\ 1 & m^{M-1} & m^{2(M-1)} & \cdots & m^{(M-1)^2} \end{pmatrix}}_{D_m} \begin{pmatrix} f_0 \\ f_1 \\ f_2 \\ \vdots \\ f_{M-1} \end{pmatrix} \quad . \tag{13.28}$$

13.5 Complex Number Class

```
class Complex {                             // structure declaration
   double re,im;                            // two data members
public:
  Complex ();                               // to allow for arrays
  Complex (const Complex &);
  Complex (const double& r, const double i = 0);  // real and img. part
  Complex operator* (const Complex &) const;
  Complex operator+ (const Complex &) const;
  Complex operator- (const Complex &) const;
  Complex operator= (const Complex &);      // assign complex number
  Complex operator+ (const double &) const;
  Complex operator= (const double);         // assign real number
  operator double() const;                  // convert
  const double & real() const {return re;}; // read
  const double & imag() const {return im;}; // read
};
```
120

```
Complex power(const Complex&, unsigned int) ;  // compute complex power

inline double abs(const Complex & c)
{                                              // compute absolute
   return sqrt(c.real()*c.real()+c.imag()*c.imag()); // value for a
}                                              // complex number
inline Complex log(const Complex& c)           // (magnitude)
{
    return Complex(log(abs(c)),c.imag()/c.real()); // complex logarithm
}                                              // used and explained
                                               // later
```
121

This result shows that a straightforward implementation of the discrete Fourier transform requires one multiplication of a M–dimensional vector of sample data and a $(M \times M)$–matrix with complex components. Consequently, the complexity of the discrete Fourier transform is bounded by $\mathcal{O}(M^2)$.

13.5 Complex Number Class

For implementation purposes, we need complex numbers, operations on complex numbers, and the possibility to define matrices as well as vectors with complex components. Listing 120 and 121 show a class for complex numbers and some functions.[4]

The required multiplication of complex numbers is shown in Listing 122. For the computation of the discrete Fourier transform, it is necessary to compute powers of complex numbers. Due to the importance of Fourier transform with respect to real-time speech recognition ap-

---

[4] The interface of this class is compatible with the complex numbers provided in the standard C++ library, cf. Sect. 16.7.

```
Complex Complex::operator* (const Complex& c) const  // multiply
{                                                     // two complex
    return Complex(re * c.re - im * c.im, re * c.im + im * c.re); // numbers
}
```
122

```
Complex power(const Complex & c, unsigned n) // compute the power of a
{                                             // complex number
    if (n > 1) {
        Complex h = power (c,n/2);            // recursive call using
        return (h * h * power(c,n%2));        // divide and conquer-principle
    } else if (n > 0)
        return c;                             // end of recursion
    else return Complex(1);                   // Complex(1) for n == 0
}
```
123

```
#include "Matrix.h"
void DFTM_init(Matrix<Complex> & dm)
{
        Complex m(cos(2 * M_PI/dm.SizeY()),   // real part
                 -sin(2 * M_PI/dm.SizeX()));  // imaginary part
        for (int i = 0; i < dm.SizeY(); ++i)  // lines
            for (int j = 0; j < dm.SizeX(); ++j) // columns
                dm[i][j]= power(m,i*j);       // compute value for element
}
```
124

plications, the computation of powers of complex numbers has to be as efficient as possible. Listing 123 shows a power function that can be applied to complex numbers. The basic idea herein is the observation that for even exponents $n = 2n'$, the power can be decomposed into the computation of a square and an n'–th power of the square, i.e.,

$$z^n = z^{2n'} = \left(z^2\right)^{n'} , \qquad (13.29)$$

for arbitrary numbers z. Obviously, the complexity is reduced by dividing up the original problem into smaller sub-problems. But, this *trick* does not provide the optimal way of computing powers of complex numbers. As we have already seen in Eq. 13.10, each complex number z can be written using the Eulerian formula, i.e.,

$$z = a + ib = \sqrt{a^2 + b^2} \exp\left(i \arctan(b/a)\right) , \qquad (13.30)$$

where a denotes the real part of z and b the complex part. Using this identity, the power of complex numbers reduces to the computation of a power of reals, and one additional multiplication of reals, since

$$z^n = \left(\sqrt{a^2 + b^2}\right)^n \exp\left(i \arctan(b/a) \cdot n\right) . \qquad (13.31)$$

The extension of the class `complex` with respect to this method is left as an exercise. Using this power function we can compute the required M–th roots of unity in (13.28). The complete so-called "Vandermonde matrix" $\boldsymbol{D}_m$ (13.28) is computed by Listing 124.

13.6 Inverse Discrete Fourier Transform

The inverse discrete Fourier transform DFT^{-1} can be computed by inverting the matrix $\boldsymbol{D}_m$. Due to the fact that the components of $\boldsymbol{D}_m$ are $(\boldsymbol{D}_m)_{u,v} = m^{uv}$, we conclude using (13.27)

$$(\boldsymbol{D}_m \cdot \boldsymbol{D}_{m^{-1}})_{u,v} = \sum_{t=0}^{M-1} m^{ut} m^{-tv}$$

$$= \sum_{t=0}^{M-1} \exp\left(-\frac{2\pi i}{M} \cdot t(u-v)\right)$$

$$= \begin{cases} M, & \text{if } u = v \\ 0, & \text{otherwise} \end{cases} \qquad (13.32)$$

The inverse discrete Fourier transform is thus given by a linear mapping defined by the matrix

$$(\boldsymbol{D}_m)^{-1} = \frac{1}{M}\boldsymbol{D}_{m^{-1}}, \qquad (13.33)$$

where

$$\boldsymbol{D}_{m^{-1}} = \begin{pmatrix} 1 & 1 & 1 & \cdots & 1 \\ 1 & m^{-1} & m^{-2} & \cdots & m^{-(M-1)} \\ 1 & m^{-2} & m^{-4} & \cdots & m^{-2(M-1)} \\ \vdots & \vdots & \vdots & \vdots & \vdots \\ 1 & m^{-(M-1)} & m^{-2(M-1)} & \cdots & m^{-(M-1)^2} \end{pmatrix} \qquad (13.34)$$

The properties of the Fourier transform shown in Table 13.1 are also valid for its discrete version. In summary, the straight-forward computation of the inverse discrete Fourier transform as well as the Fourier transform require $\mathcal{O}(M^2)$ operations of addition and multiplication. The function shown in Listing 124 can be used analogously to compute $\boldsymbol{D}_m^{-1}$.

The efficiency and numerical stability of algorithms is often influenced by the ordering and sequence of applied operations. For instance, the Horner scheme is one of the most famous examples, where the reorganization of arithmetic operations decreases the problem's computational complexity. In fact, the reorganization of mathematical operations is also useful for the computation of the Fourier transform, as we will see in Sect. 13.8.

13.7 Fourier Transforms of Speech Signals

It is time to apply the discrete Fourier transform for practical experiments. Using concepts introduced above, we can now proceed with spectral analysis of discrete speech signals. We have already implemented a class for speech signals (see Sect. 11.9). Using the Vandermonde matrix $\boldsymbol{D}_m$, a discrete speech signal can be transformed into a complex vector by a simple multiplication of a matrix with a vector. This multiplication is already provided by the template classes for matrices and vectors (Listing 116). Speech signals, however, were represented by real numbers or integers. We could now define a conversion from vectors of doubles to vectors of complex numbers in order to use the matrix operations. Alternatively, we can define an operator for the multiplication of a complex matrix with a double vector, as shown in Listing 125; this operator is not declared inside the template class and can thus use only the methods `real()` and `imag()` for access to the internal data.

In practice, the complete speech signal will not be transformed, but only subsequent parts of it. For this purpose, the *Short-time Fourier* analysis will be introduced later in Sect. 21.4. For the practical usage of the Fourier transform (possibly satisfying real-time requirements), an efficient method for DFT computations is desirable and crucial. In Listing 125 we already did

```
Vector<Complex> operator*(Matrix<Complex> A, Vector<double> x)
{
    Vector<Complex> r(A.SizeY());            // vector (0,0,...,0)
    for (int i = 0; i < A.SizeY(); ++i) {    // lines
        double R =0, I = 0;
        for (int j = 0; j < A.SizeX(); ++j){ // columns
            R += A[i][j].real() * x[j];      // simplified arithmetic
            I += A[i][j].imag() * x[j];      // since multiplicand is
        }                                    // complex(x,0)
        r[i] = Complex(R,I);            // set element
    }
    return r ;                               // return vector
}
```

125

some improvements for efficiency reasons and did not use the operator for multiplication of a complex number by a real number. Of course, further improvements are possible for the DFT; we could, for example, omit the multiplications by the constant one which is present at various places in the matrix D_m. A highly accelerated version of the Fourier transform is introduced in the following section.

13.8 Fast Fourier Transform

We now turn to a highly efficient method for calculating the discrete Fourier transform of a given discrete signal $[f_t]_{0 \leq t < M}$. For the reduction of the complexity two main principles are commonly used:

1. the *application of homomorphisms* (compare, for example, the convolution theorem for the FT), and
2. the *divide-and-conquer* principle, where the decomposition of the original problem into smaller sub-problems speeds up the computation.[5]

The divide-and-conquer principle is the basic idea that the Fast Fourier Transform (FFT) algorithm is based on. We show how a recursive decomposition of a larger Fourier transform in terms of smaller ones can be performed. The complexity of determining the discrete Fourier transform will be reduced from $\mathcal{O}(M^2)$ to $\mathcal{O}(M \log M)$ using the remarkable idea of Cooley and Tukey [Coo65].

We restrict our discussion to the fast Fourier transform of radix two. For a more general and detailed discussion of this topic we recommend the books [Aho74] and [Kro79] which emphasize the algebraic background, and the books on signal theory [Opp75] and pattern recognition [Nie83] which concentrate on implementation details and practical aspects.

The first assumption is that the number of discrete sampling values is $M = 2n$. From (13.29) we know that

$$F_\nu = \sum_{t=0}^{M-1} f_t \, m^{t\nu} = \sum_{t=0}^{n-1} (f_t + f_{t+n} \, m^{\nu n}) m^{t\nu} \quad .$$

---
[5]An example is the fast computation of powers as shown in Listing 123.

13.8 Fast Fourier Transform

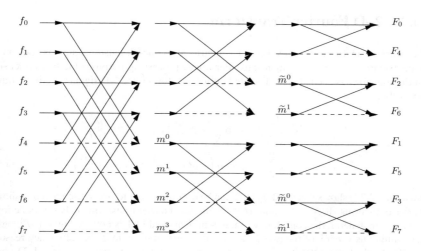

Figure 13.6: Principle of the FFT ($M = 8$)

Now we define the n–th root unity $\widetilde{m} = m^2$, and take into consideration that $m^{vn} = 1$, if v even, and $m^{vn} = -1$, if v odd; thus we get for $0 \leq u < n$ the following formulas for the values of the discrete Fourier transform divided into even and odd indices:

$$F_{2u} = \sum_{t=0}^{n-1}(f_t + f_{n+t})\widetilde{m}^{ut} \qquad (13.35)$$

$$F_{2u+1} = \sum_{t=0}^{n-1}(f_t - f_{n+t})\, m^t\, \widetilde{m}^{ut} \ . \qquad (13.36)$$

If we put extra parentheses into (13.36) to get $((f_t - f_{n+t})\, m^t)\, \widetilde{m}^{ut}$, we see that (13.36) as well as (13.35) are again Fourier transforms of sequences $[f_t^+ = f_t + f_{n+t}]_{t=0...n-1}$ and $[f_t^- = (f_t - f_{n+t})\, m^t]_{t=0...n-1}$ of n samples each, i.e., half the number of samples as the original sequence. These two Fourier transforms can now again be decomposed into even and odd terms, etc. Figure 13.6 illustrates this recursive decomposition of the DFT computation applying the symmetry properties; the new sequences $[f_t^+]$ and $[f_t^-]$ can be easily identified. Solid lines indicate an addition, dashed lines subtraction. Remarkable is the permutation of the indices on the right side. We conclude that for the computation of the DFT with $M = 2n$ sampling points we have to do $2n$ operations of addition, n operations of multiplication, and finally two discrete Fourier transforms of order n. Finally, we set $M = 2^n$ and apply above idea recursively for the involved smaller Fourier transforms. This algorithm for computing the DFT is thus bounded by $\mathcal{O}(M \log M)$ and yields an impressive decrease of the original complexity. Assume we set $M = 2^{10}$, then the Fourier transform using matrix multiplication requires 2^{20} complex multiplications. In contrast, the fast Fourier transform needs *only* $2^{10}/2 \cdot 10$ multiplications.

13.9 2–D Fourier Transform

The Fourier transform introduced so far is restricted to one-dimensional signals and can easily be extended to arbitrary dimensions. For image processing purposes the two-dimensional Fourier transform is needed. The discrete Fourier transform for a 2–D signal is defined straightforwardly as

$$F_{\mu,\nu} = \sum_{u=0}^{N-1}\sum_{v=0}^{M-1} f_{u,v} \exp\left(-i2\pi\frac{u\mu}{N}\right)\exp\left(-i2\pi\frac{v\nu}{M}\right)$$
$$= \sum_{u=0}^{N-1}\left(\sum_{v=0}^{M-1} f_{u,v}\exp\left(-i2\pi\frac{v\nu}{M}\right)\right)\exp\left(-i2\pi\frac{u\mu}{N}\right) \quad . \quad (13.37)$$

Equation (13.37) shows that the 2–D DFT can be decomposed into two subsequent one-dimensional Fourier transforms. If $N = 2^{n'}$ and $M = 2^n$ the fast Fourier transform is also suitable for the 2–D case. In general, the complexity of the d–dimensional FFT is bounded by $\mathcal{O}(M^d \log M)$. The continuous version of the two-dimensional extension is obvious. For efficiency reasons it is useful to implement the 2–D Fourier transform separately, instead of using a 1–D Fourier transform twice (Exercise 13.g).

The result of the DFT applied to the image shown in Figure 12.1 (b) is shown in Figure 13.7. The left image illustrates the real part, the middle the imaginary part, and the right one the magnitudes of the discrete Fourier transform. Herein, the DFT values are coded as gray-levels normalized to $\{0, 1, \ldots, 255\}$.[6]

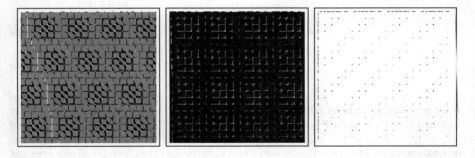

Figure 13.7: Fourier transformed image (Figure 12.1 (b)): real part, imaginary part, and absolute values visualized by gray-levels

The discrete Fourier transform of an image shows the so-called *spatial frequencies*. Many rapid gray-level changes mean high frequency in the direction of these changes. Implementation issues are discussed in Exercise 13.g.

Examples, where the discrete Fourier transform is applied to low-level image processing, are shown in Figure 13.8 and 13.9. The operations shown there can be performed on complex images or matrices with functions similar to the tools described in Sect. 12.5. The typical

---

[6]The problem, how to compute this mapping, will be discussed in Exercise 18.i.

13.9 2–D Fourier Transform

cross in Figure 13.8 results from gray-level quantization. The basic idea of filtering operations using Fourier transforms is the elimination of selected Fourier coefficients. The reduced Fourier transformation is re-transformed to the spatial domain. High pass filters, for instance, remove low frequencies, whereas high frequencies pass. This is important for edge detection algorithms (cf. Chapter 15), where we look for parts of the image which show large changes in gray-levels. For smoothing signals, however, it is necessary to eliminate high frequencies of the signal. This can be done using low-pass filtering operations. The elimination of selected frequencies is easy to implement, if the Fourier transform is available. You just leave out the Fourier coefficients of the non-required frequencies. The results of high- and low-pass filtering operations are shown in Figure 13.8 together with the related 2–D Fourier transforms (magnitudes gray-level encoded). The origin of the coordinate system is the image's center.

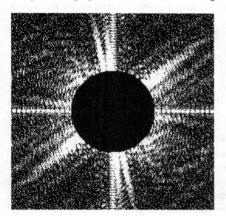 

Figure 13.8: High and low pass filter on the Fourier transform of the image shown in Figure 1.2 left

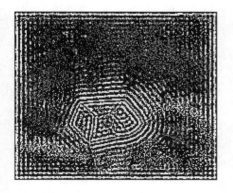 

Figure 13.9: Result of high- and low-pass filter: inverse of the transformations shown in Figure 13.8

Exercises

13.a Extend Exercise 8.e using features computed from the Fourier transform.
13.b Prove the properties listed in Table 13.1.
13.c Compute the Fourier transform of function (13.8).
13.d Implement the 1–D DFT/FFT using the classes for complex numbers and the template classes for vectors and matrices.
13.e Compute the Fourier transform of $[0, 1, 2, 3, 4, 5, 6, 7]$ using DFT and FFT algorithm.
13.f Write a program which computes the Fourier transforms of gray-level images.
13.g Find arguments for why it is not advantageous to implement the two-dimensional Fourier transform as two subsequent 1–D Fourier transforms. Can we use the functions implemented in Exercise 13.d? Do we need any extra operators for the matrix and vector classes?
13.h Compute the discrete Fourier transform of the following binary image:

$$\begin{pmatrix} 1 & 1 & 1 & 1 \\ 0 & 1 & 1 & 0 \\ 0 & 1 & 1 & 0 \\ 0 & 0 & 0 & 0 \end{pmatrix}$$

13.i The graphical visualization of the FFT algorithm induces a permutation on the indices of the FFT result (cf. Figure 13.6 where $f_0, f_1, f_2, f_3, f_4, f_5, f_6, f_7$ is mapped to $F_0, F_4, F_2, F_6, F_1, F_5, F_3, F_7$). Use a binary representation of the incoming and outcoming indices and find an easy rule for describing these permutations! (Classical variants of the resulting algorithm are discussed in [Opp75, Pre92]).
13.j Write a program for generating synthetic sound signals using Fourier series. The parameters of the Fourier series should be parameters of your program.
13.k Prove the properties of the Fourier transform which are summarized in Table 13.1.
13.l Create a textured image using the algorithms in Sect. 12.8. Compute its FFT. Can you determine a relation of the FFT and the parameters of the texture algorithm?

Chapter 14
Inheritance for Classes

As already explained in Chapter 9, object–oriented programming is mainly characterized by encapsulation, dynamic binding, and inheritance. The classes introduced in Chapter 11 showed implementations of abstract data types. In this chapter we give a detailed description of the fundamental and powerful principle of inheritance and its implementation in C++. We introduce the concepts for both *simple* and *multiple inheritance*. With the use of inheritance, the real world dependency structure of objects can be mapped into C++ class hierarchies in a natural manner.

14.1 Motivation and Syntax

The task of implementing a new function can often be simplified by inheritance of a new class from an existing class. When the new class is an extension of an existing class and has additional members, some additional functions, or possibly a redefinition of an already implemented function, programmers have only to define the differences in the new class with respect to the old class. Using inheritance, a complete reimplementation can be avoided. With inheritance we can provide a high degree of reusability for code and concepts.

Rectangles, for example, are a special kind of a geometric shape which can be also useful for object recognition purposes. Consequently, the class `Rectangle` is derived from the more general class `Shape`. Other related concepts are circles and triangles which can also be derived from the general class. Squares are a special case of rectangles and should therefore be derived from the for the rectangle class.

The derivation of a class from one base class is syntactically written in the following manner:

Syntax:	`class` *name* `:` [`public`|`private`|`protected`] *base*
	`{` *class-members* `}` `;`

The class derivation may be repeated, i.e., a class may be derived from an already derived class as shown in the abstract Listing 126.[1] In Sect. 10.2 we mentioned the similarity of structures, unions, and classes. One syntactic difference between unions and classes with respect to inher-

---

[1] It is impossible to have a circular sequence of derivations.

```
struct A              { int i; int f(); };  // base class
struct B : public  A  { int j; int g(); };  // derived with public base
struct C : private B  { int k; int h(); };  // derived with private base
```
126

```
void test()
{
  A a; B b;          // define local objects
  a.i = a.f();       // we have seen such things already
  b.j = b.g();       // this should be no surprise, either
  b.i = b.f();       // i and f() are available in B as well!
}
```
127

itance is that unions can be derived from structures or classes, but nothing can be derived from unions, i.e., unions are always leaves of an inheritance graph.

Members, operators, and methods of a superclass are inherited by the subclass, except for the assignment operator `operator=`. This property is shown in Listing 127 for the classes declared in Listing 126: functions, data, and operators defined in the public section of the base class are available for the derived class automatically.

The keywords `public`, `protected`, and `private` control the accessibility of base class features in the derived class; these topics are discussed in the next section. Since we used structures in Listing 126 and Listing 127, all members were public.

14.2 Access to Members of Base Classes

A class can be declared as a base class of another class either as `public`, `protected` or as `private`. The new keyword `protected` is also introduced for class members in addition to `public` and `private` which we already saw in Sect. 10.2. Protected information is accessible in the derived classes but hidden from the outside.

Public derivation provides the natural way of refining concepts from the general to the more specific. Private members of the base class are not accessible in the derived class. Public and protected members of the base will be public and protected members of the derived class.

Private derivation can be seen as a certain syntactic way of expressing the "part of" relation. The ideas of specialization and generalization (Sect. 9.4) do not apply here. If the base class is declared as `private`, the public and protected members of the superclass become private members of the derived class. Private derivation has a more technical application (see the examples in [Str97]). Public base classes are far the more frequent than private base classes.

As in the case of members, protected derivation is a mixture of public and private derivation and leaves its internals accessible to further derived classes.

These rules for accessibility are summarized in Table 14.1. The base class members get new access rights in a derived class depending on whether the base class is private or public. This is of particular importance when another class is derived from an already derived class. Also, private parts of the base class can be excluded from access by using private derivations.

14.3 Construction and Destruction

base class members	base		
	public	protected	private
private	no access	no access	no access
protected	protected	protected	private
public	public	protected	private

Table 14.1: Access rules of base class members inside the derived class. To give an example, if a protected member of a private base class is treated similar to a private member of the derived class.

```
class A             { public: int i,j; void f(); };  // base class
class B : public A  { public: int    j; };            // first derivation
class C : public B  { public: int i  ; void f(); };  // second derivation

main()
{
  B b; C c;           // Objects       ** Artificial
  b.i = 1;            // from base A   ** example
  b.j = 1;            // B's j         ** for
  c.j = 1;            // B's j         ** demonstration
  c.i = 1;            // C's i         ** of inheritance
  c.A::i = 1;         // A's i         ** and scope
  b.f();              // A's f()
  c.f();              // C's f()
  c.A::f();           // A's f()
}
```
128

As can be seen in Listing 128, the same name can be used for data and function members in both the derived and base classes. The data or function accessed by default is always the closest in the inheritance hierarchy.

14.3 Construction and Destruction

We now outline a small hierarchy of classes for geometric objects which is graphically depicted in Figure 14.1. Inheritance is used to provide special classes with notions valid for general classes. For example, each shape has an area; this is declared in the general base class. A square is a general case of a rectangle and has a special formula for computing its area; this is defined for the class representing squares. The general interface remains the same and is inherited from the general base.

Constructors are overloaded functions; the choice of the constructor depends upon the types of its arguments. In the definition of a constructor for a derived class, the choice of the base class constructor is done using the arguments provided to the base class constructor. Like the constructors for members, the base class constructor and its arguments are given following a colon. The construction of class objects is done from the top down in the inheritance graph. First, the base class constructors are called, then the constructors for member variables, and finally the derived class itself.

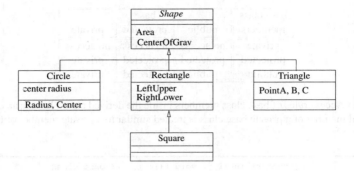

Figure 14.1: Small hierarchy of geometric shapes

```
struct Shape {            // simple base class for shapes
   Shape();               // constructor 1
   Shape(int i, int j);   // constructor 2
   ~Shape();              // destructor
   void rotate(double);   // rotate a geometric figure
};
```
129

An example of a base class for geometric shapes is given in Listing 129. The definition of a base constructor in a derived class is shown in Listing 130.

The destructor of a class deletes an object from the main storage. In a hierarchy of classes, the destructor of the base class will be called after the destructor of a derived class, i.e., the execution of destructors will be in the opposite order of the constructor calls. In the destructor definition we do not have to mention the destructors of the base classes; they are called automatically (Listing 130).

When error conditions occur during construction or destruction, exceptions can be used to manage partially constructed or destructed objects.

14.4 Pointers to Objects

It is necessary for pointers or references to specify the type of objects they reference. This regulation is slightly relaxed for classes that are related by public inheritance. A pointer declared

```
struct Circle : public Shape {
   Circle() : Shape() {}    // will use constructor 1 of base class
   Circle(int k);           // choice of base constructor unknown
   ~Circle()         {}     // inline destructor
};
Circle::Circle(int k)              // define constructor
: Shape(k,0)                       // choose base class constructor
{ /* more initialization */ }      // do what is left to do
```
130

14.4 Pointers to Objects

```
void fct(Rectangle & r)
{   /* Shape -> Rectangle -> Square */
    Shape      * sp;                    // base class pointer
    Rectangle  * rp;                    // pointer to derived
    Square     * qp;                    // pointer to derived from derived
    rp = &r;                            // natural
    sp = &r;                            // ok. every rectangle is a shape
    qp = (Square*) &r;                  // cast required
    qp = static_cast<Square*> (&r);     // new syntax
    qp->rotate(30.0);                   // rotate by 30 degrees
}
```
131

```
void fct1()
{
    Rectangle r;      // define object
    Square    s;      // define object of derived class
    fct (s);          // ok
    fct (r);          // cast in fct will be wrong!
}
```
132

to an object of a type found in a base class can point to an actual object of another type found in a derived class, if the base class is declared *public*.[2] A pointer declared as a pointer to an object of a derived class, however, cannot be set to an object of a base class; if such an assignment is required, an explicit pointer conversion has to be used. These rules are also applicable to references to objects.

Listing 131 shows pointers to objects. The cast in the last statement is required because not every rectangle object is a square. This cast can be disastrous if the object passed to `fct` is *not* a square (Listing 132) since then the function `rotate` might use features available in a square which are not present in a rectangle.

We now inspect the different functions `f()` in Listing 128 with respect to pointers to objects. In Listing 133 it is determined *at compile-time* from the pointer's type which function `f()` is called, similarly to the data member access in Listing 128. Using the scope resolution operator `::`, the function to be called can be specified explicitly. Virtual functions introduced next will provide even more flexibility for member function calls.

---
[2]Cf. Exercise 14.e

```
void FctS(C & c)        // compile time binding
{                       // A -> B -> C
    A * ap = &c;        // pointer to base A*
    C * cp = &c;        // pointer to derived C*
    c.f();              // call C::f()
    ap->f();            // call A::f()
    cp->f();            // call C::f()
    cp->A::f();         // call A::f()
}
```
133

```
struct A          { virtual void f(); int g(); };  // base class
struct B : public A {                  int g(); };  // 1st derivation
struct C : public B { virtual void f(); };          // 2nd
```
134

```
void FctV(C & c)           // run time binding
{ /* A -> B -> C */
  A * ap = &c;
  C * cp = &c;
  c.f();                   // call C::f()
  ap->f();                 // call C::f() !!
  cp->f();                 // call C::f()
  cp->A::f();              // call A::f()
}
```
135

14.5 Virtual Functions

The powerful concept of virtual functions facilitates the realization of dynamic binding, message passing, and polymorphism in C++. Classes that have virtual functions are called *polymorphic*. Functions in class scope can be declared virtual using the following syntax:

Syntax: | `virtual` *type function* `(` *arguments* `)` `;`

If a function is declared `virtual` in the base class, a function with exactly the same name and type of arguments declared in the derived class will also be virtual even without explicit repeated specification as a virtual function. Virtual functions allow the overriding of a definition of the base class function, i.e., if a virtual function is called via pointer to an object, the function associated with the object will be invoked, no matter whether the pointer is to a base object or to the actual object.

The described override mechanism implies that virtual functions have to be declared as non-static member variables. They cannot be declared as global non-member functions.

We now extend Listing 128 by virtual functions to Listing 134 and declare the function `f()` as virtual. The function to be used is determined *at runtime* by the actual type of the object to which the method is applied. In contrast to Listing 133, `ap->f()` now calls `C::f()`.

A virtual function in a derived class may not redefine another return type for the same virtual function in the base class, i.e., a function with the same name and the same argument list. A virtual function in a derived class which differs from one in the base class with specification `const` is considered a different function! As outlined in Sect. 10.7, the compiler will choose the function marked `const` for constant objects.

Destructors may be declared virtual. The use and syntax of this idea is shown in Listing 136. If the destructors were not virtual, the last line of the function `fct()` would not call the destructor of the derived class. Instead, due to the type of the pointer `Bp` only the base class destructor would be called.

14.6 Abstract Classes

```
class base              { public: base(); virtual ~base(); };
class derv : public base { public: derv(); virtual ~derv(); };

void fct()
{
   { base(); }          // ~base() will be called
   { derv(); }          // ~derv(), then ~base() will be called
   base * bp = new base();
   delete bp;           // ~base() will be called
   base * Bp = new derv(); //
   delete Bp;              // watch this!
                        // ~derv(), then ~base()
}                       // will be called
```
136

```
struct Shape {
   virtual void rotation() = 0; // pure virtual function
};
```
137

14.6 Abstract Classes

Many classes provide a common abstract structure where no instances of objects can exist. These abstract classes are only useful for structuring a class hierarchy and providing common interfaces. We did so already in Figure 14.1. For example, we can easily define a new class for lines derived from a common base class for geometric objects. The methods in this class depend on the concrete representation of the line and therefore must be implemented in derived classes. For instance, for each line a method should exist that returns the length of a line. Since the explicit representation of the line is unknown at the point when the class Line is compiled, we need a new language feature.

We can force the redefinition of a virtual function by the use of *pure virtual functions* in the class definition part. A virtual function becomes pure virtual, if the function is initialized by =0. No other definition is allowed then.

Syntax: virtual *type function (arguments)* = 0;

In Listing 137 the pure virtual function for the rotation of geometrical objects in general is shown. Since the class for geometric shapes is an abstract class, no instances can be generated and no concrete implementation of the method rotation is possible. No implementation of this function can be programmed for the class Shape. For this reason, we declare the method pure virtual. The compiler will disallow the creation of an object of the types Shape, only objects of these derived classes are possible which define rotation.

If a virtual function is not declared to be pure virtual, an explicit definition of this function has to be provided (see Listing 138). If inside a derived class all inherited functions are at some point of the derivation declared as no longer pure virtual, the class becomes concrete and objects can be instantiated.

Another way to declare an abstract class is to provide no public constructors, as we will see in the next section.

```
struct Rectangle : public Shape {
  virtual void rotation();  // has to define the virtual function
};
void Rectangle::rotation() { /* ... */ }
class Square    : public Rectangle { /* ... */  };
```
`138`

```
class Image_V0 {
    unsigned short xsize, ysize;   // filled by the constructors
    float focus;                   // filled by the constructors
  protected:                       // abstract class
    Image_V0();                    // all methods can be used in the
    Image_V0(int,int);             // derived classes
    // ops's etc.
  public:
    float focalLength() const { return focus; }
    int SizeX() const { return xsize; }
    int SizeY() const { return ysize; }
};
#if defined(IMAGE_VERS) && (IMAGE_VERS == 0)
typedef class Image_V0 Image;
#endif
```
`139`

14.7   Image Class Hierarchy

In Chapter 11 we saw different classes for images. Gray-level images and color images both need the members for their size and the camera parameters. It is therefore natural to create a common base class `Image` and put all the shared information there; the information is passed to the new classes via inheritance (Listing 139). Since many functions will provide interfaces for gray-level images, (e.g. filters, etc.), we now use image objects as representations for the three color channels in color images (cf. Listing 111). Listing 140 and Listing 140 contain a new declarations for gray-level and color images that extend Listing 110; some implementation is shown in Listing 142.

The base class declares all methods as "protected"; no object of the abstract class `Image` can thus be directly created since no operations could be performed on it.

In the following chapters we will derive more new image classes from class `Image`. The class sub-tree for images is shown in Figure 14.2. These images will use elements other than bytes. Therefore the image matrices are declared in the derived image classes. Since the return type of

```
class GrayLevelImage_V1 : public Image {
    // etc.
    Matrix<byte> image;   // 256 gray levels
  public:
    GrayLevelImage_V1(int xs,int ys) ;           // constructor
    // etc.
    byte * operator [] (int i) { return image[i]; } // delegation
    // other op's
};
#if defined(GLI_VERS) && (GLI_VERS == 1)
typedef class GrayLevelImage_V1 GrayLevelImage;
#endif
```
`140`

14.8 Multiple Inheritance

```
class ColorImage_V1 : public Image {           // Version 2
public:
   GrayLevelImage *r, *g, *b;  // color channels
   // op's
};
#if defined(COLImg_VERS) && (COLImg_VERS == 1)
typedef class ColorImage_V1 ColorImage;
#endif
```
141

```
GrayLevelImage_V1::GrayLevelImage_V1(int xs,int ys) :
Image(xs,ys),       // Base class construction
image(ys,xs)        // Member (Matrix) construction
{}                  // done already
```
142

a virtual function must be unchanged in the redefinitions inside the derived classes, no common access function to pixels can be declared in the class Image, although we would like to have them there.

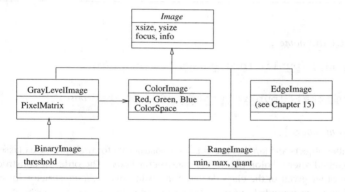

Figure 14.2: Hierarchy of image classes

14.8 Multiple Inheritance

The problems concerning multiple inheritance were already mentioned in Sect. 9.4. A class can be derived from two or more classes; each base class can be declared public, protected or private. Assume all base classes have member functions with the same name. When those functions are used, they have to be disambiguated. This can be explicitly done using scope resolution, or implicitly, based on different parameter lists.

Sometimes a base class is reached by more than one path in the inheritance graph. This will result in multiple instances of the base object. If this is not desired, a base class can be declared as virtual in addition to the keywords public, protected or private. The syntax is as follows:

```
struct visible {
    void display();                     // all public
    visible(int color);
};
struct RectangleMi: public Shape,       // first base
                    public visible {    // second base
    RectangleMi() : Shape(), visible(3){};  // NB: the base class construction
    ~RectangleMi();                     // destructor automatically ...
};                                      // ... deletes base objects
```
`143`

```
class GrayLevelImgage_V3: public Image, private Matrix<byte> {  // just a try
    // ...
public:
GrayLevelImgage_V3(int xs, int ys) :    // constructor
    Image(xs,ys),                       // base class1
        Matrix(xs,ys)                   // base class2 (no <byte> !)
        {};                             // empty body
};
```
`144`

Syntax: class *name* :

[virtual] [public |protected |private] *base*

{ , [virtual] [public |protected |private] *base*}* {

class-members };

As for member objects and single base classes, constructors for multiple base classes are listed comma-separated after a colon before the constructor body. The order of construction is defined by the order given in the class declaration. Additionally, a constructor for each virtual base class has to be provided, even in further derived classes. New aspects of a given idea can be programmed by multiple inheritance. Imagine a class visible which adds display capabilities to a graphics device. The interface to graphics routines can be inherited on top via inheritance from general to specific classes (Listing 143). In the constructor definition, the constructors for all bases have to be specified.

Another more C++ specific use of multiple inheritance using private base classes can be seen in Listing 144. This shows how the *has-a* relation can be implemented using private inheritance. This approach will, however, fail for the class ColorImage since there we need three instances of the matrix object. Almost always it is possible to avoid multiple inheritance, and this is generally to be recommended. The class for images, for example, was not derived from class matrix (Listing 139); rather, it includes a matrix as a member and delegates important operators or methods to the matrix class by inline functions.

Casting of pointers as in Sect. 14.4 is much more complicated when multiple inheritance is used. The type of the pointer to a polymorphic class in a cast can be checked when a dynamic_cast is used. Further information about multiple inheritance can be found in the manual [Str97]; in the following we will use single inheritance only.

14.9 Implementation Issues

The most difficult problem in object–oriented software design is the mapping of the structures and dependencies of the objects in the problem domain. First, natural dependencies of objects and classes have to be formalized. Always have in mind whether two different classes relate to each other in terms of inheritance, or whether a part-of relation (client) would be more appropriate. For example, gray-level images are represented using a matrix for the internal representation; matrix and images are not related by inheritance in the sense of specialization, however.

The goal of object–oriented software design is the development of compact, readable programs. The programs should be easy to understand and easy to modify. For users of your programs who are not interested in algorithmic details, an abstract and well documented interface should be provided. Furthermore, the algorithms have to be implemented in an efficient manner. Often it is not easy to implement algorithms efficiently and at the same time to satisfy the needs of concepts like modularity and readability. The implementor has to find a compromise among these conflicting goals.

Virtual functions are treated by the compiler in a different way from non-virtual functions. A function table is generated for every class having virtual functions. Virtual functions are called indirectly from this table. The table is constructed by the compiler in certain modules that define constructors. It is thus a wise idea *not* to use inline constructors since some compilers might then have to create many tables for one class instead of only one. Virtual inline functions are allowed by the syntax. In many cases they will, however, not be inlined. With respect to efficiency, virtual inline functions should therefore be used carefully (cf. Exercise 14.c).

A general guideline is that destructors should be virtual when there are virtual functions in a class.

Exercises

14.a Extend the template class for matrices and vectors. Derive the template class from a non-template base-class holding the size and access functions to the sizes. This is generally a nice idea since the non-parameterized parts can then be completely compiled at an earlier stage of compiler processing.

14.b Implement an abstract class for lines in C++ using the concept of pure virtual functions. Derive a class for straight line segments.

14.c Define a class in a header file and include this file in two source files. Turn `virtual` on and off for some methods. Also change methods or constructors to `inline`. How does the code size vary? Use a `Makefile`!

14.d Compare direct and indirect function calls with respect to execution time on your processor.

- Use a trivial function without arguments.
- Use a realistic function with three arguments and a non-trivial function body.

14.e If a cast from a derived class to a private base class were allowed, we could circumvent the access restrictions (Table 14.1). Explain why and how!

Chapter 15
Edge Images

Perception studies show that lines, vertices, and other features based on lines, are very important for perception [Mar80]. A typical part of image segmentation is the detection of edges (cf. Sect. 8.6). The automatic detection of line features in images usually requires several processing stages. Edge detection operators are applied to every pixel in the image. These operators check the local neighborhood for evidence of an edge. They return a measure for the likelihood of an edge at this point in the image as well as a guess of its orientation. The result is called an "edge image" (Sect. 15.6). In Chapter 19 we will further process edge images to obtain lines. This will transform edge images into more abstract geometric objects. This chapter gives a first insight into edge detection methods in gray-level images, partially based on [Brü90].

15.1 Strategies

The basic idea behind edge detection is to localize discontinuities of the intensity function in the image. Figure 15.1 shows an artificial cross section, i.e., a one-dimensional function of an edge. Figure 15.2 shows a plot of the gray-level function in the neighborhood of an edge in a real image.

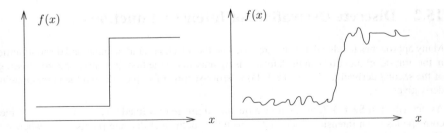

Figure 15.1: Ideal step edge (a) and real edge (b), where the x–axis is perpendicular to the edge.

 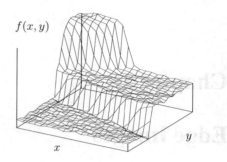

Figure 15.2: Intensity function in a real image in the neighborhood of an edge. On the left: gray-level image (Figure 1.3); with marked frame; on the right: 3–D plot of the intensity in the frame.

Several types of edge detectors can be found in the literature:

- derivatives of the intensity function (discrete approximation),
- edge masks,
- parametric models for edges,
- combinations of the above.

The first two strategies work with local masks; the first and second derivative as well as edge masks will be treated in this chapter. The other two methods, parametric models and combined methods, are dealt with in chapter 19.

In the following sections, we introduce a common edge image class which will be used for the representation of arbitrary edge operators. The resulting edge images can then be further inspected and lines will be segmented in Chapter 19.

15.2 Discrete Derivatives of Intensity Functions

Many approaches to edge detection are based on the idea that rapid changes and discontinuities in the gray-level function can be detected using maxima in the first derivative or zero-crossings of the second derivative. Figure 15.3 shows cross-section of step edges and the corresponding derivatives.

As described in Sect. 1.7, we assume a quantized image of a fixed size — $N \times M$ — which corresponds to an intensity function $f(x, y)$ that is defined at discrete points (i, j), where $i \in \{0, 1, \ldots, N-1\}$ and $j \in \{0, 1, \ldots, M-1\}$. The more rapidly the gray-level function changes over small changes in the location, the more likely an edge is at this location. Since the gradient points to the direction of highest gray-level changes, the gradient vector and its magnitude are

15.2 Discrete Derivatives of Intensity Functions

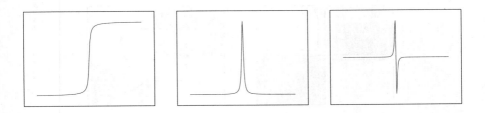

Figure 15.3: Edge (left), first derivative (center) and second derivative (right) in a cross-section.

the fundamental measurements for edge detection. The magnitude of the gradient defines the *edge strength*, and the direction of an edge at a certain point in the image is called the *edge orientation*. The edge orientation is usually defined to be orthogonal to the gradient. This, however, can be shown to be not always true by counter-examples (cf. Exercise 15.d), but most edge detectors are based on this widely used definition. The computations of edge strength and orientation are based on discrete derivatives of the intensity function. The *gradient* of a continuous function $f(x,y)$ is defined as the vector

$$\nabla f(x,y) = \begin{pmatrix} f_x(x,y) \\ f_y(x,y) \end{pmatrix} = \begin{pmatrix} \frac{\partial f(x,y)}{\partial x} \\ \frac{\partial f(x,y)}{\partial y} \end{pmatrix} \qquad (15.1)$$

consisting of the partial derivatives of the intensity function in the horizontal and vertical directions, and the gradient vector at position (i,j) points to the steepest ascent in its immediate neighborhood. Discrete approximations use central differences instead of differentials for the computation of f_x and f_y

$$f_x(i,j) = f(i+1,j) - f(i,j) \quad \text{and} \quad f_y(i,j) = f(i,j+1) - f(i,j) \qquad (15.2)$$

which simply result from setting h to the smallest possible discrete value (namely one) in the well-known derivative

$$f_x(x) = \lim_{h \to 0} \frac{f(x+h) - f(x)}{h} \quad , \qquad (15.3)$$

where instead of $f(x)$ we use the next pixel $f(x-1)$ to obtain a symmetric mask.

Edge strength (15.4,15.5) and *edge orientation* (15.6) can now be calculated from the gradient using vector calculus and basic trigonometry. The edge strength is computed as the length of the gradient vector. It is often convenient to use the sum of absolute values (15.5) instead of the root of the squares (15.4) since it is normally not the exact value that is important, but the value in comparison to the neighborhood.[1] This is another example, how approximations (Sect. 3.9) can simplify computations.

---

[1] Approximations of the values for f_x, f_y, s', and r can thus then be calculated using integer arithmetic and without use of the square root function.

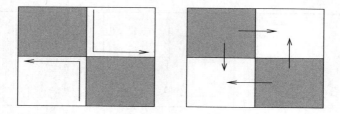

Figure 15.4: Definition of the edge orientation (left) and gradient (right)

$$s = \sqrt{f_x^2 + f_y^2} \qquad (15.4)$$
$$s' = |f_x| + |f_y| \qquad (15.5)$$
$$r = \arctan(f_y/f_x) \qquad (15.6)$$

Using definition (15.6), the approximative edge orientation can be computed from the direction of the gradient by a rotation of 90°. Figure 15.4 shows an image with black and white areas and the directions of the gradient along the edges, as well as the edge orientation.

15.3 Mask Operators

Figure 15.5 shows an interpretation of equation (15.2) as a symmetric mask. The derivative g can be estimated by a discrete convolution (cf. Eq. 13.20)[2] of the image f with the mask h

$$g = f * h \qquad (15.7)$$

with the components

$$g_{i,j} = \sum_{\mu=-m}^{m} \sum_{\nu=-n}^{n} h(\nu, \mu) f(i - \nu, j - \mu) \quad , \qquad (15.8)$$

where the indices of $h_{i,j}$ are defined in the range $i \in \{-m, \ldots, m\}, j \in \{-n, \ldots, n\}$ Since the distance from the central point where the derivative is estimated, is one pixel to the left and one to the right, the computation yields only half of the derivative (using Eq. 15.3). In the following, we only use the relative magnitudes of these values and can thus ignore this formal inconsistency.

Only a few pixels are taken into account when the discrete differential is computed using the simple operators in Sect. 15.2. As a consequence, these operators are very sensitive to noise. The usual cure for this problem is to apply a low-pass filter before the derivatives are calculated. Alternatively, a larger neighborhood can be taken into consideration for the computation of the derivatives, which then includes an averaging operation on several values of f_x and f_y.

---

[2]This means that derivatives of the intensity function can be computed using a linear filter, Chapter 17.

15.4 Discrete Directions

Figure 15.5: Masks for computation of the central differences in a point marked by a circle.

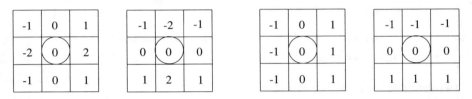

Figure 15.6: Masks for Sobel (left) and Prewitt (right) operator. Masks on the left: f_x, masks on the right: f_y. Note that these masks may be flipped with respect to other literature since we choose the origin of the coordinate system on the left top.

Well known operators of this type are the Sobel operator [Dud73] and the Prewitt operator [Pre70], which are shown in Figure 15.6. In [Dan90] it is shown that the Sobel mask is an approximation of the first derivative.

The more pixels that are taken into account in the computation, the lower is the sensitivity to noise. Small edges may, however, be missed by large operators. This trade-off situation is sometimes called the "uncertainty relation" of edge detection.

15.4 Discrete Directions

The application of the gradient operator on a gray-level image yields two values: f_x and f_y. The steepest possible edge in a gray-level image is the change from 0 to 255. The values for f_x and f_y for the Sobel operator can thus be in the range of $-1020\ldots 1020$. The edge strength computed as the sum of the two values will, however, only be in the range $0\ldots 1530$ for this using (15.5); the proof is left as an exercise. Other operators have similar behavior. This range can be represented using two bytes (usually a `short`).

Computation of the gradient's direction from f_x and f_y requires the evaluation of `atan2`. This function evaluates the `arctan` library function and treats the four quadrants properly so the range of the result is $[0, \pi]$ for $y \geq 0$ and $[-\pi, 0]$ for $y < 0$ instead of $[-\pi/2, \pi/2]$ for arctan. The result is a `double` value which now has to be quantized. A value of 144 directions seems to be more than sufficient where one step corresponds to $2.5°$. This number has the advantage that directions of $5°, 10°, 30°, 60°, \ldots$ can be represented as integers. 144 values

```
static double atan_0_8(double x, double y)  // returns 0 .. 8
{
  if(x == 0 && y == 0) return 0;
  if(y > 0)                                 // upper half
    if(x > 0)                               // 1st quadrant
      return (x > y) ? y / x : 2 - x/y;     // octant 0 1
    else                                    // 2nd quadrant
      return (y > -x) ? 2 - x/y : 4 + y/x;  // octant 2 3
  else                                      // lower half
    if(x < 0)                               // 3rd quadrant
      return (-x>-y) ? -4 + y/x : -2 -x/y;  // octant 4 5
    else                                    // 4th quadrant
      return (-y > x) ? - 2 - x/y : y / x;  // octant 6 7
}

double approx_atan(double x,double y)       // same range as atan2
{
    return (M_PI / 4) * atan_0_8(x,y);
}

unsigned char disr_atan(double x,double y) // 0..143
{
    return int(atan_0_8(x,y) * 36);
}
```

145

can be represented in one byte (an `unsigned char` in C++). Figure 15.7 (left) shows the line directions graphically.

The function `atan2` tends to be relatively slow on most computers. In Sect. 3.8 we saw that either a look-up table or an approximation of the computationally expensive function increases performance. A possible approximation is introduced in [Cap91]: By only three comparisons we can determine the octant for an (x, y) value pair. As shown in Figure 15.7 (right), value of $z = -x/y$ is computed in octant 1,2,5,6, which is $-\cot \alpha$; the ratio $z = y/x$ is computed in octant 3,4,7,0, which is $\tan \alpha$; these computations yield a value in the range $[0, 1]$:

$$z = \begin{cases} -\cot \alpha , & \text{if } \alpha > \frac{\pi}{4}, \text{ i.e. in octant 1,2,5,6} \\ \tan \alpha , & \text{otherwise} \end{cases}, \quad (15.9)$$

where we approximate cot and tan by the fractions above. Finally, the offset listed for the octants in Table 15.1 has to added to z and we get a value u; the reason for the sign change between octant 3 and 4 is that the library function `atan2` has a discontinuity at $\alpha = \pi$. To get the angle α from this value, we would need the arctan or arccot function. If we use a linear approximation $\alpha = \frac{\pi}{4} u$ instead, we will have a maximum error of 4.1° [Cap91].[3] The complete functions for this computation are given in Listing 145.

The accuracy of this approximation is illustrated in Figure 15.8 which shows a plot of the functions for the first quadrant (i.e. octant 0 and 1) for $u = \frac{4}{\pi}\alpha$ and

$$u = \begin{cases} 2 - \cot \alpha , & \text{if } \alpha > \frac{\pi}{4}, \\ \tan \alpha , & \text{otherwise} \end{cases}, \quad (15.10)$$

Obviously, the differences between the functions are small.

---
[3] This value could also be quantized and then used for table look-up.

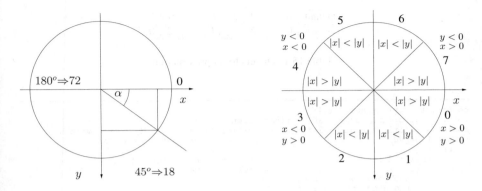

Figure 15.7: Discrete directions and quantization

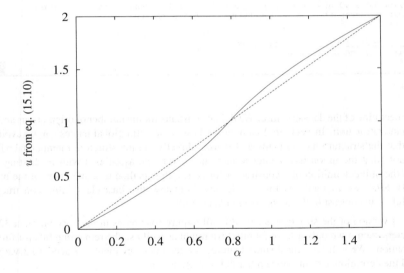

Figure 15.8: Discrete direction function

15.5 Edge Class

One implementation for edges could use a structure containing a `byte` for the edge orientation and a `short` for edge strength. Since the size of a `short` may vary between machine architectures, it is better to request exactly 16 bits using bit fields (Sect. 4.5).

In Listing 146 we combine several C++ features to implement a class for edges; the macro `M_PI` which expands to the value of π is taken from `math.h`. The methods hide the internal

Table 15.1: Offsets for approximation

Octant	0	1	2	3	4	5	6	7
Offset	0	2	2	4	-4	-2	-2	0

```
const int    orient_num = 144;
const float  orient_dunit = 360 / float(orient_num);
const float  orient_runit = 2 * M_PI / float(orient_num); // M_PI from math.h
struct Edge_V0 {                       // first version of a edge class
    union {
        unsigned int all;              // assume 32 bit architecture
        struct {                       // need no name
            unsigned int f_strength : 16;
            unsigned int f_orient   :  8;
        } fields ;                     // use member directly
    };                                 // union has neither name nor variable
    Edge_V0()                { all = 0; }   // clear
    inline Edge_V0(unsigned s, unsigned o); // set strength and orientation
    unsigned strength() const { return fields.f_strength; }
    // etc.
};
#if defined(EDGE_VERS) && (EDGE_VERS == 0)
typedef class Edge_V0 Edge;
#endif
```
146

implementation of the data structure. We define constants for the number of orientations and for the quantization unit. In Sect. 16.2 we will see how these extra global names can be avoided. Note that the structure has no name and is used directly via the structure member `fields`. Also note that the union has neither a name nor a variable associated with it: Listing 147 shows the inline definition of a constructor for edges; this method uses members of the union directly. Since we do not derive this simple class from any other base class, inline construction is useful — in contrast to the hints given in Sect. 14.9.

Our first version of the structure `Edge_V0` will require four bytes in memory on most 32 bit computers even if we only ask for 24 bits;[4] we might as well use the remaining bits for further information. We will later need some features for each edge element. In Sect. 19.3 we will extend the definition and introduce other fields in the union.

---

[4]Try this on your machine with the `sizeof` operator!

```
inline Edge_V0::Edge_V0(unsigned s, unsigned o)
{
    fields.f_strength = s;
    fields.f_orient   = o;
}
```
147

15.6 Edge Images

```
class EdgeImage : public Image {
   Matrix<Edge> image;
   unsigned short max_s;   // maximum strength in the edge image
public:
   EdgeImage();                             // default: empty image
   EdgeImage(const EdgeImage &);            // copy constructor
   EdgeImage(int,int,int maxs = -1);        // sizes and maximum strength
   Edge* operator[] (int i) { return image[i]; }
   const Edge* operator[] (int i) const { return image[i]; }
   void Max(int);                           // set maximum strength
   int Max() const;                         // request maximum strength
   // etc.
};
```

148

15.6 Edge Images

The application of an edge operator on every pixel of a gray-level image will produce an *edge image*. Like the image classes in the previous section, edge images share the information of the class Image (Listing 139) by inheritance. Edge images can thus extend the image hierarchy shown in Figure 14.2. A code fragment is shown in Listing 148. The operator [] maps the access operation to the matrix object by delegation. Again, it turns out to be useful that the matrix operators in Listing 116 were not members; matrix multiplication would make no sense for edge matrices.

Since different operators create edge images with different ranges for the edge strength, an entry max_s is useful. This entry has to be set to the maximum possible value by the edge operator creating the edge image. For example, the Sobel operator will set it to 1530, since this is the maximum possible value for the edge strength using Eq. 15.5 and the masks in Figure 15.6 (Exercise 15.h).

Visualization of edge images is shown in Figure 15.9. Edge strength is coded as gray-level;[5] orientation can be directly coded as gray-levels in the range of zero to 144 (Figure 15.9, right).

15.7 Robert's Cross

Edge detection using the first derivation was motivated by the differences in (15.2). An implementation using this idea will make use of the four out of eight neighbors of a given pixel. The so called *Robert's Cross* operator which also uses only four pixels (15.11) is even simpler than (15.2) and uses a smaller neighborhood.

$$f_1(i,j) = f(i,j) - f(i+1,j+1) \text{ and } f_2(i,j) = f(i,j+1) - f(i+1,j) \qquad (15.11)$$

Since the differences are computed diagonally (as a "cross"), the values f_1 and f_2 are not the horizontal or vertical derivatives, but instead they are the approximations of directional

---
[5]The range of the edge-strength is histogram equalized to 256 bit, i.e., a gray-level image, using the algorithms described in Sect. 18.5.

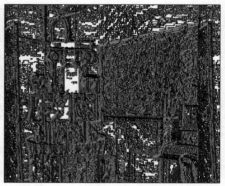

Figure 15.9: Gradient image computed with the Sobel operator on the test image shown in Figure 1.2.

Figure 15.10: Robert's image: strength and orientation

derivatives. The results of this operator are shown in Figure 15.10. This operator is very sensitive to noise but very simple to compute.

15.8 Second Derivative

Instead of searching for maximal edge strength in the first derivative of an intensity image, the zero-crossings of the second derivative can also be used. Figure 15.3 already showed this idea for continuous one-dimensional functions.

15.8 Second Derivative

0	-1	0
-1	4	-1
0	-1	0

-1	-1	-1
-1	8	-1
-1	-1	-1

1	-2	1
-2	4	-2
1	-2	1

Figure 15.11: Mask definition for the discrete approximation of the second derivation (Laplace operator)

The second derivative can be computed by the *Laplace operator* for discrete images. The Laplace operator for continuous functions is defined by

$$\nabla^2 f(x,y) = f_{xx} + f_{yy} \quad . \tag{15.12}$$

For the discrete Laplace operator we consider the derivative operator defined by

$$D_x f(x,y) = \lim_{h \to 0} \frac{f(x+h,y) - f(x,y)}{h} \quad . \tag{15.13}$$

In the discrete case the closest we can get to zero is $h = -1$ and $h = 1$. For that reason we define the difference operators ∇_i and Δ_i by

$$\nabla_i f(i,j) = f(i+1,j) - f(i,j) \quad , \quad \text{and} \tag{15.14}$$
$$\Delta_i f(i,j) = f(i,j) - f(i-1,j) \quad . \tag{15.15}$$

The definition for ∇_j and Δ_j are analogous. The discrete Laplace operator results from the twofold application of the difference operators, i.e.,

$$\begin{aligned}\nabla^2 f(i,j) &= \nabla_i \Delta_i f(i,j) + \nabla_j \Delta_j f(i,j) \\ &= 4f(i,j) - f(i-1,j) - f(i+1,j) - f(i,j-1) - f(i,j+1) .\end{aligned} \tag{15.16}$$

Three variations of this operator are shown in Figure 15.11, where the left matrix corresponds to (15.16). These operators are mostly similar, but have slightly different sensitivity to noise. Another possible definition uses larger neighborhoods, i.e.,

$$g(i,j) = \sum_{\mu,\nu} (f(\mu,\nu) - f(i,j)) \quad . \tag{15.17}$$

A major disadvantage of this operator is its sensitivity to noise as with all methods based on the discrete second derivative. Usually, the Laplace operator will detect amongst the correct edges various scattered edge points. Additionally, the definitions in Figure 15.11 and (15.17) will compute no edge direction, in contrast to the other edge operators introduced so far.

Various edge operators are based on Laplace operators (cf. for example [Mar80]). Usually, the intensity image is filtered with a Gauss filter[6] in order to reduce the sensitivity of the operator to noise. The result of Laplace edge detection on the un-filtered intensity image is shown in Figure 15.12, where all negative values are mapped to gray-level zero, all positive values are mapped to 255, and values close to zero resulting from the operator are mapped to 128.

---
[6]This filter will be introduced in Sect. 17.1.

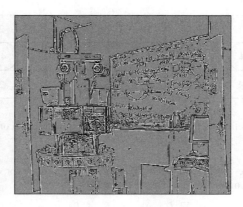

Figure 15.12: Laplace image of Figure 1.2, gray-level encoded

15.9 Color Edge Operators

Edge detection is possible on color images as well as gray-level images. The differences (15.2) or the Sobel operator can be generalized for several channels. We can reorganize the definition in Figure 15.6 as a three-fold weighted (with factor 1 or 2) sum of differences (one to the left/up subtracted from one to the right/down).

For the implementation of edge detectors we therefore need a scalar difference value for color vectors. According to [Shi87] the following distances of color pixels $\boldsymbol{f}_1 = (r_1, g_1, b_1)^\mathrm{T}$ and $\boldsymbol{f}_2 = (r_2, g_2, b_2)^\mathrm{T}$ can be used:

$$D_1(\boldsymbol{f}_1, \boldsymbol{f}_2) = \{(r_1 - r_2)^2 + (g_1 - g_2)^2 + (b_1 - b_2)^2\}^{\frac{1}{2}} \qquad (15.18)$$
$$D_2(\boldsymbol{f}_1, \boldsymbol{f}_2) = |r_1 - r_2| + |g_1 - g_2| + |b_1 - b_2| \qquad (15.19)$$
$$D_3(\boldsymbol{f}_1, \boldsymbol{f}_2) = \max\{|r_1 - r_2|, |g_1 - g_2|, |b_1 - b_2|\} \qquad (15.20)$$

The disadvantage for our purpose is that these distances are all positive. In order to compute the edge direction properly, we need negative values as well. One simple possibility is shown in (15.21). The different channels can be weighted with $\omega_r, \omega_g, \omega_b$; there may, however, be color vectors, for which the function D_0 will be zero although they look different to the observer.

$$D_0(\boldsymbol{f}_1, \boldsymbol{f}_2) = \omega_r(r_1 - r_2) + \omega_g(g_1 - g_2) + \omega_b(b_1 - b_2) \qquad (15.21)$$

The gradient image can now be calculated using (15.21). The resulting edge image can be further processed with the same programs as edge images resulting from gray-level images or other edge operators. The result of (15.21) on the color image in Figure 11.2 (left) is shown in Figure 15.13

15.9 Color Edge Operators

 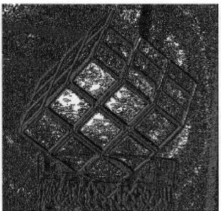

Figure 15.13: Gradient image computed with the color Sobel operator on the color image shown in Figure 11.2.

Exercises

15.a   Calculate the number of operations required by the various edge operators introduced so far. Try to reduce multiplication to additions and shifts. Do runtime measurements on the operators.

15.b   Show how the second derivative of the image intensity function may be computed using equation (15.2) twice.

15.c   Create a program which has an edge image as an input and creates a gray-level image as an output from either the edge strength or the edge orientation. Add that program to your toolbox of Sect. 12.5.

15.d   Consider the artificial, real-valued image defined by the intensity function:

$$f(x,y) = (50 - 20\cos(y/10))\left(\frac{\pi}{2} + \arctan(2x)\right)$$

(a) Plot the function in the rectangle defined by $-20 \le x \le 20$ and $0 \le y \le 30$.

(b) Show experimentally that the edge direction is not orthogonal to the gradient vector by plotting the angle that the gradient forms with the x–axis along the edge.

15.e   Implement a program which generates a table of the 144 discrete direction values for the arctan function atan2. The number of directions (e.g. 144) should be a parameter of the program.

15.f   Create a program which has a color image as an input and creates an edge image as an output. Use a color–Sobel operator with the difference D_0 in equation (15.21).

15.g   How can edge strength and edge orientation consistently be derived from the Robert's Cross definition?

15.h Show that the the maximum edge strength for the Sobel operator using (15.5) is 1530. What is the maximum strength for the Prewitt operator?

Chapter 16

Class Libraries

The implementation of large software systems and class hierarchies using C++ obviously requires to agree on a common class library whose implemented classes are useful, convenient, and necessary for a majority of applications. In this chapter we describe stream classes that are part of the standard C++ library supplied with the compiler and header files.

We give an overview of the NIHCL class library. This software package is in the public domain and satisfies the requirements of a general purpose C++ class library. We describe the basics in simplified form — just to enable the use of the library or to re-implement some of the basic ideas. Details of NIHCL can be found in the book of K. Gorlen et al. [Gor90]. We discuss abstract and very general classes, which are the super classes of all classes implemented in the system. We introduce static class members for C++ and also survey the Standard Template Library (STL) [Mus96]. STL and NIHCL, both provide container classes and some classes commonly used in many programs, such as strings. Since STL is described in many textbooks, we put our emphasis on NIHCL here. We also introduce the concept of friends in C++.

16.1 Stream Input and Output

Input and output operations like reading or writing data from a file are necessary for many programs. In C++ we implement input and output operations on objects which are instances of user-defined classes. The *syntax* of the C++ programming language does not provide the facilities for input and output of built-in objects. Those operations are implemented in an object–oriented environment using so-called *streams* which are part of the C++ *library* definition. The resulting function calls for I/O–operations are safer than the use of stdio, since all function calls are checked by the compiler for correct argument number and type (see below in Listing 151).

The classes for input and output streams are istream and ostream. Predefined global static objects are cerr, cout, and cin which are attached to standard error, standard output and standard input respectively (though can be redirected, of course). These C++ classes become available when the header file iostream.h is included. The class ostream has an overloaded operator << which writes an object to a stream. Analogously, istream provides

```
#include <iostream.h>           /* interface for streams */
main()
{
  int i;                        // integer to be read from standard input
  cout << "Type a nonnegative integer!\n";
                                // write to standard output
  cin >> i;                     // read i from standard input
  if (i >= 0)                   // input correct
    cout << "Your number is: " << i << "\n";
  else                          // wrong input, type error message
    cerr << "Your number is a negative integer!\n";
}
```
149

```
ostream& operator<<(ostream& strm, const Image_V0 & i)
{                                          // function which
  strm << "focal length: "                 // outputs all
       << i.focalLength() << "\n";         // information
  strm << "image size   : " << i.SizeX() << "," // attached
       << i.SizeY() << "\n";               // to image
  return strm;                             // objects
}
```
150

overloaded methods >> for reading data. Listing 149 shows a simple program that reads an integer and writes it to standard output. If the value of the given integer is negative, an error message will be written to standard error instead.

The definition of operators << and >> for built-in abstract data types can be extended in the following way: assume you want to write the member variables of the given class Image_V0 to stdout or some other stream. For that purpose, you have to define an operator <<; the operator in Listing 150 outputs the data of an image which we saw in Listing 139. As in Listing 116, we use a function rather than a member.

Listing 151 contrasts the stream concept to the stdio concept of traditional C; endl causes a new-line to be printed and the buffer will be flushed.[1] The program shows function calls with too many or wrong arguments. Even the C++ compiler can not check these errors since the interpretation of the format string is semantic information; this information may in addition not be available at compile time since the format string may be a variable defined or initialized elsewhere in the program.

The operator << can be used for the output of user-defined objects. This operator maps the arguments to the overloaded virtual function put which — depending on its arguments — stores the given data to the output stream in an appropriate format. An input function reading into an existing image object can be defined analogously.

---

[1] For details of the mostly obvious meaning of precision and endl we refer to [Str97].

```
char formatstr[] = "%d %4f\n";             // format string
fprintf(stderr, formatstr, "test", 2.0, 'a');  // no warning !!!
cout.precision(4);                         // valid until next call
cout << "abc " << 4.12345 << endl;         // endl will call flush
```
151

These mechanisms have to be extended to object–oriented programming; this was one key issue of NIHCL which is introduced in the next session. For more information about C++ streams, we refer the interested reader to the manual [Str97].

16.2 National Institutes of Health Class Library (NIHCL)

As outlined in Sect. 9.9, Smalltalk was the most important ancestor for object–oriented programming languages. The NIHCL class hierarchy [Gor90] re-implements some of the Smalltalk ideas for C++ using the same identifiers for methods and classes. Figure 16.1 shows the important classes of the NIHCL-class tree which are outlined shortly in the following. This tree illustrates that concrete classes can exist (e.g. a Set) which have derived classes, i.e. not every class having subclasses must be abstract.

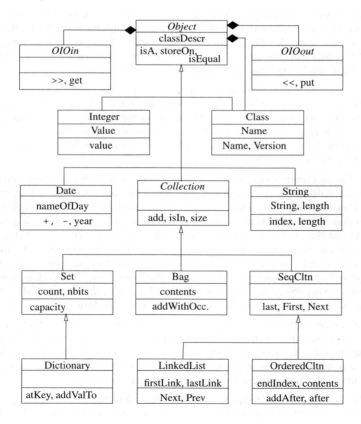

Figure 16.1: Essential classes of NIHCL. Method names are abbreviated.

Conceptually, the most general class in NIHCL is the abstract class Object.[2] This class provides the general interface by member functions that have to be implemented in the derived classes, where the explicit representation of an object is known. The general member functions of the class Object can be divided into three main categories: functions for identifying and testing the class of an object at runtime (like isA) functions for comparing objects (like isEqual) and finally functions for input and output operations of objects (like storeOn). A comfortable interface to input and output of objects (OIO) is provided by abstract classes (OIOin and OIOout); derived classes specify possible sources and destinations and data representation as binary or ASCII.

The implementation of a derived class of the class Object must include the declaration and definition of about 20 functions of the above mentioned three categories to be compatible with other NIHCL classes. Nevertheless, the implementation of these functions is elementary and fairly easy. NIHCL provides some macros which support the declaration and definition of these functions.

In many situations it is advantageous to have the capability to check the type of a given object, i.e. to determine the class to which the object belongs. For this purpose, Smalltalk provides a "meta class". C++ provides this information directly (Sect. 16.8); in the following, we show how NIHCL solved this task before this language feature was available in C++, since several other C++ ideas can be explained in this context.

In NIHCL, a class Class is implemented, which allows access to runtime information of the objects derived from class Object. The information, contained in the class Class, is the name of the class the object belongs to, the classes of the member variables, the size of its instances, inheritance information, and the version number. A simplified version of a class Class is shown in Listing 152. The structure of the class hierarchy is also stored by a pointer to a base class description object.

To ensure that all classes supply this information, a virtual member function isA() in the class Object is declared, which returns a pointer to a member variable classdesc of type Class. This function is redefined in every class derived from Object; each such class provides a new class description. Since the member variable classdesc is equal for all instances of one class it can be shared by these instances. It is not necessary that each object of the class has its own copy of this member variable. For this purpose, C++ provides the declaration of static members, where all instances of the class share those static variables; i.e. the keyword static indicates to the compiler that this member is allocated *once* for every *class* — not for every object. Such variables are called *class variables* in Smalltalk – in contrast to *object variables*. Listing 152 outlines this idea in a simplified form.

Class variables are syntactically like regular data members and obey the visibility and scoping rules. The only difference is that they exist only once and that they have to be initialized *once* in the program. Naturally, this initialization cannot be done in the constructors; instead, the variable is defined outside of all functions (Listing 153). The C++ runtime system will guarantee that such objects are created before the function main starts.

Member functions, as well as member variables, can be declared static, such as the function Object::desc() in Listing 152. The function definition in Listing 153 looks exactly

---

[2] For technical reasons, a class NIHCL is put on top of the hierarchy which is not shown in Figure 16.1.

16.2 National Institutes of Health Class Library

```
class Class;
class Object {                            // root of the object tree
   static Class classdesc;                // once in the program
public:                                   // enquire class membership
   Object();                              // default constructor
   Object(OIOin&);                        // constructor from stream
   virtual ~Object();                     // virtual for all obj's
   virtual const Class* isA() const;      // { return & classdesc; }
   virtual void storer(OIOout&) const;    // external representation
   void storeOn(OIOout&) const;           // will call storer
   static const Class * desc();           // static function!
   static Object * readFrom(OIOin&);      // will be discussed later
};
class Class : public Object { // simple version
   const Class * base;                    // here: only single inheritance
   char * className;                      // what's my name
   int version;                           // store my version
public:
   Class(char *, const Class *, int);
   const char * ClassName() const { return className; }
   int Version() const { return version; }
   const Class * Base() const { return base; }
};
```
152

```
Class Object::classdesc ("Object",NULL,0); // static member definition
const Class* Object::isA() const { return & classdesc; } // virtual
const Class* Object::desc()      { return & classdesc; } // static
Object::Object() {};
Object::~Object() {};
```
153

like a normal member function. However, static member functions can be called without an associated object just by the complete name consisting of the class name, scope operator, and the function name. A static member function can not be declared constant.

Each NIHCL class redefines isA and defines its own classdesc, i.e., there exists exactly one class description per class. The different static variables classdesc can be accessed by the prefix e.g. Time:: (Listing 154).

Since all classes which use NIHCL have to define these members and methods, and since all these definitions are textually identical, NIHCL provides macros for their definition. Again, a

```
class Time : public Object {              // one typical example
   static Class classdesc;                // again, one object
public:                                   // isA() looks similar
   virtual const Class* isA() const;      // { return & classdesc; }
   static const Class * desc();           // again a static function
   Time();
   Time(Date&,int,int,int);
};

Time::Time() {};
const Class* Time::isA() const { return & Time::classdesc; }
Class Time::classdesc ("Time",Object::desc(),0);
```
154

```
#define DECLARE_MEMBERS(c)                                         \
  private: static Class classdesc;                                 \
  public:  static const Class * desc();                            \
  public:  static c * readFrom(OIOin&); /* not virtual */          \
  public:  virtual const Class* isA()  const;                      \
  public:  virtual const char* ClassName() const;                  \
           virtual void storer(OIOout&) const;                     \
  public:  static c * castdown(Object*);                           \
  public:  static c & castdown(Object&);                           \
  private:
#define DEFINE_CLASS(c,b,v)                                        \
  const Class* c::isA() const { return & c::classdesc; }           \
  const Class* c::desc()      { return & c::classdesc; }           \
  const char*  c::ClassName() const                                \
     { return c::classdesc.ClassName(); }                          \
  c* c::readFrom(OIOin&) { /* dummy here */ return NULL; }         \
  Class c::classdesc(#c,b::desc(),v);
```

155

```
class String : public Object {
    char * str;
    int len;
    DECLARE_MEMBERS(String)           // define members
public:
    String();
    String(const char*);              // copy char *
    String(OIOin&);                   // construct from string
    char& operator [] (int);          // access to characters
    operator const char* () const;    // conversion
    String& operator= (const String&); // assignment
};
```

156

simplified version is shown in Listing 155;[3] the real macros in NIHCL have more parameters. The token #c expands to a string containing the macro argument c, if an ANSI pre-processor is used. The first macro is used in the class declaration. The second macro is used in the module that defines the methods. The second argument uses the static function desc() to access the class description of the base class. In cases such as Listing 155, macros are required, or at least considerably easier than templates. An example for these macros is shown in Listing 156.

The methods readFrom and storeOn reference the OIO classes. These classes are special *streams* for input and output of objects in an object–oriented environment. The virtual function storer is called from storeOn declared in class Object. We will introduce these streams next.

16.3   Input and Output for Objects

The method readFrom() in Listing 155 is declared static in the class, and can thus be called without having an object of that type. This function reads *and creates* an object.[4]

---

[3] Multi-line macros use a backslash to continue on the next line.
[4] This is a complicated problem which is described in [Gor90].

16.3 Input and Output for Objects

```
main()
{
    OIOin   in(cin);                        // object's input stream
    OIOout  out(cout);                      // object's output stream
    Object * o = Object::readFrom(in);      // static readFrom
    o->storeOn(out);                        // virtual storer
    String * i = String::readFrom(in);      // static readFrom
    o = i;
    o->storeOn(out); // will call virtual Image::storer
}
```
157

The mechanisms for input and output of objects in NIHCL extend the notion of streams (Sect. 16.1) and add methods for storing arbitrary objects (with the methods `storeOn` resp. `storer`) and construction from streams. An example for the class `Image` is shown in Listing 157 which we will further inspect now. The abstract base classes for object input `OIOin` and output `OIOout` are shown in Figure 16.1. The major difference to standard C++ streams is that these streams automatically recognize type and version of the object during a read operation and create the required objects, whereas using the streams of Sect. 16.1 an object has to be created first, before data can be read into it.

Here, we only give an overview of the interface allowing the user to store and read objects in NIHCL.[5] NIHCL uses two types of streams; one of them uses binary and one uses textual representation of objects. The usage is basically the same; we describe binary storage, since images and speech data has to be stored in binary format to save space.

Objects are stored via the `storeOn` method which has to be defined for each class that will eventually call the method `storer`. Arbitrary objects can be read using `readFrom`; this function is defined by the DEFINE_CLASS macro. The actual code for reading has to be provided in a constructor that has an input stream as an argument.[6] Clearly, when an object is read, its base class has to be initialized as well. This is simply done by the base class constructor which is executed before the object is initialized. An example is shown in Listing 158.

This automatic mechanism is not available for the opposite direction, the storage operation by the method `storer`. The `storer` method of the base class has to be explicitly called; this is done using the name of the base as a prefix. It is convenient to define a macro for the actual class name and base (Listing 158); for the DEFINE_CLASS we cannot use the THIS macro since otherwise the argument would expand to "THIS" instead of the desired "Image" in the expansion of #c in Listing 155.

The class `Object`'s input and output functions provide consistency checks and version control. In addition, the class name is stored; thereby, arbitrary objects can be read from a stream without knowing in advance exactly which object will be read.

Interfaces of OIO streams to the streams in Sect. 16.1 are shown in Listing 157. In Sect. 24.4 we derive our own special classes for object input and output from the NIHCL classes. We will show there how to open a stream and how to close it.

---

[5]Again, the reader is referred to [Gor90] for details.
[6]A tricky mechanism is used to call a constructor from the `readFrom` function.

```
#define THIS String
#define BASE Object

DEFINE_CLASS(String,BASE,0)              /* cannot use THIS here */

THIS::THIS(OIOin& strm) : BASE(strm)     // constructor from stream
{
   strm >> len;                          // reads length
   str = new char[len+1];
   strm >> str;                          // reads string
}
void THIS::storer(OIOout& strm) const    // opposite direction
{
   BASE::storer(strm);                   // write base class data
   strm << len << str;                   // store length and string
}
```
158

```
String S1="string1";     // define and initialize
String S2("string2");    // alternative construction
S1[7]= '2';              // index checked access
cout << S1 << "\n"       // prints "string1"
     << S2 << "\n";      // prints "string2"
S2[9]= '1';              // runtime error
```
159

16.4 Frequently Used Classes

In this section we list useful classes that are provided both by NIHCL and STL. The classes mentioned here can also be found in Smalltalk.

Strings are frequently used structures, and string manipulations on character pointers in C++ as well as C are error prone, since explicit requests and releases of memory are required. NIHCL provides handy classes for dynamic strings including access and manipulation.[7] As in Smalltalk, these classes are called String and SubString. The methods available for objects of the class String are, for example, concatenation, comparison of strings, the selection of one character of a given string, methods for determining the length of a string, etc. The class SubString supports some manipulation of parts of a string. For example, a constructor is defined for declaring a substring of a specified length of a known object of the class String. Some applications are shown in Listing 159. Individual characters can be accessed by an overloaded index operator. Allocation and release of the memory for the strings is managed automatically during construction and destruction.

NIHCL provides classes for the access and manipulation of the date and time. As in Smalltalk, the classes are called Date and Time. In these classes, the complexity of calendars is encapsulated. In application programs Time and Date, objects provide arithmetical manipulations of this data. The programmer can handle these objects as if they were ordinary numbers. For instance, the date can be compared with another one or you can add some days and will get the new resulting date. Some applications are shown in Listing 160.

Numerical data in C++ is represented as in C as standard predefined data type. No object-oriented programming is possible with these data types. NIHCL defines the classes Integer

---

[7]Compare Listing 89 and Exercise 10.a on page 114.

```
Date bdpa(9,"April",59);      // create date object
Date bdho(10,"August",67) ;
int year= bdho.year();        // select the year
Time t(bdho,                  // date
       8,                     // hour
       12,                    // minute
       0);                    // second
cout << bdho - bdpa << "\n";  // difference
```

and `Float` which can be accessed as *objects*. Thereby, they can for example be stored in object streams. Arithmetic methods are available, operation is, however, slow in comparison to standard data types.

The STL library, which we will inspect in more detail in Sect. 16.7, also provides such commonly used application classes. Strings as well as complex numbers are defined there as templates. Their implementation is more efficient and renounces the use of inheritance. The complex number class of STL can be used for numeric problems without loss of efficiency. Our implementation of complex numbers in Chapter 13 is compatible with the definition in STL.

16.5 Collection Classes

Common examples for frequently used data structures are linked lists, stacks, or sets. In NIHCL the general super-class `Collection` holds instances of NIHCL classes as described in the previous sections. The methods of the abstract class `Collection` are functions for comparing instances of the `Collection` class, adding objects, removing objects, converting containers, the "element of" relation or a function for determining the cardinality of an object. The polymorphic implementation guarantees that the code is useful for a wide range of applications.

Derived classes are the already mentioned classes `Set`, `Stack`, and `LinkedList` with their customary meanings. A subclass `Bag` can contain multiple occurrences of one object, or several objects which are equal. The classes `OrderedCltn` and `SeqCltn` are used to store arbitrary objects which are either sorted by a compare function (which has to be defined for the object to be added) or by the temporal order in which they are added to the `SeqCltn`. Elements of collections can be arbitrary NIHCL objects; a method `hash` and a predicate `isEqual` has to be provided for those collections that compare for equality; comparison has to be implemented for ordered collections. A concept of *iterator* classes allows one to step thru a collection element by element in an ordinary while-loop.

In addition to the high degree of reusability of the polymorphic container classes, they also allow the definition of recursive data structures. For example, the elements of a set can also be sets and so on. Most of the problems concerning the use of container classes are due to the fact that container classes hold pointers to objects and do not represent the objects explicitly, i.e. they hold no explicit copy of objects, only references. Therefore, the programmer should take care and pay attention to correct memory management. In particular, we must be very careful about the lifetime of the objects which are parts of containers.

```
Set s;                       // define an empty set
OrderedCltn o;               // objects will be sorted
String s1="Carola";          // define and initialize
String s2("Jonathan");       // other initialization
String s3= "Joachim";        // s3 and s4 will be
String s4= "Joachim";        // equal, but not the same
String s5("Corinna");        // other initialization
s.add(s1);                   // add several strings
s.add(s2);                   // to the set s
s.add(s3);                   // here comes joe
s.add(s4);                   // will have no effect
s.remove(s1);                // remove element
o.add(s3);                   // now add strings
o.add(s2);                   // to the ordered
o.add(s1);                   // collection
o.add(s4);                   // joe will go in twice (s3,s4)!
cout << "s:" << s << endl;   // print contents of s
cout << "o:" << o << endl;   // print contents of o
DO(s,String,elem)            // LOOP macro contains type
   cout << *elem << endl;    // print each element
OD                           // LOOP macro end
```

161

Some applications of sets and collections are shown in Listing 161. Elements can be added to and removed from collections. When an element is added to a set, the existing objects are compared for *equality* with the new object. The contents of the set s will be "Jonathan" and "Joachim" when it is printed. The collection o will contain "Joachim", "Jonathan", "Carola", and "Joachim". Collection management is further enhanced by the use of a hashing function (hash).

An attempt to remove an element which is not in the collection is an error and will raise an exception.[8] NIHCL also provides macros for iteration over all elements in a collection in a loop as shown in Listing 161. The concept behind this are so-called iterators which are hidden in NIHCL; in STL, we will see them explicitely.

Listing 81 (p. 105) showed a simple class declaration of an "association" data type between a string and an integer. NIHCL provides a more elaborate version of associations using a key-object and a value-object. The String class is often used for the key and an arbitrary Object as value. For example the key can be an English word and the value object is a list of all possible German translations of this word. A collection of these associations is called a Dictionary, if every key occurs only once. The class name Dictionary is obvious with respect to the above example. An application is shown in Listing 162. NIHCL collections may contain any object derived from Object. Even within one set, each element may have a different type. This implies that the general manipulation functions can operate only on objects. For example, the dictionary look-up using the method atKey in Listing 162 returns an object. The programmer, of course, will know that the object pointer returned will be a String; the compiler, however, cannot know this semantical information. A conversion of this object pointer to a String pointer is thus required, which is a conversion *downwards* in the class hierarchy. This was hidden in the DO...OD loop in Listing 161. Such casts require

---

[8]NIHCL has its own class for exception handling since at the time of its writing, exceptions (Sect. 4.8) were not part of the C++ language.

16.6 Memory Allocation

```
Dictionary d;                        // define object
String word1("time");                // some string object
String word2("date");                // another string
d.addAssoc(word1,word2);             // add to dictionary
Object * op = d.atKey(word1);        // retrieve information
cout << d << " " << *op << endl;     // print d and op
```
162

```
Set s;                               // empty set
for (int i = 0 ; i < 10 ; ++i ) {
   Integer j(i);                     // create temporary object
   s.add(j);                         // add it to set
}                                    // object will be deleted here
cout << s;                           // Chaos !
```
163

special care and may cause problems especially when multiple inheritance is used. We will come back to this problem in Sect. 16.9.

Multiple occurrences of the same object in a collection will be recognized upon write and only one copy will be stored. This will also be recognized when a collection is being read in. Using this mechanism, object *references* can be stored and restored.

The core of STL (Sect. 16.7) also provides collections which are again efficiently coded by templates. The basic definitions include a so-called `vector`[9] (for 1-d arrays), `list` (for lists linked backward and forward), `queue` (for first in, first out), `set` (for sets which include each element only once), `stack` (for first in, last out), and `map` (for key value pairs, similar to the NIHCL class `Dictionary`). In contrast to NIHCL, these definitions are not related by inheritance. Instead, they only have syntactically identical interfaces, so they can be exchanged easily in an implementation (Sect. 16.7).

16.6 Memory Allocation

In order to work efficiently with NIHCL, it is necessary to know about some internal features with respect to memory management. In particular this refers to input and output as well as to collections.

Objects to be put into a container class have to be allocated either dynamically, or they will be lost after they go out of scope. Collections only keep *references* to the objects inside. Listing 163 gives an example of a incorrect allocation strategy. The set should technically be empty but it will probably have references to objects that no longer exist when it is output to `cout`. The `Integer j` is local to the loop and will be destroyed when the loop is finished.

Another pitfall is the required cooperation of

- copy constructor, (`THIS::THIS(const THIS&)`)
- assignment operator, (`THIS::operator= (const THIS&)()`)

---

[9] STL vectors are not vectors in the mathematical sense, as they can change their size dynamically; they are rather containers similar to the class `Collection` in NIHCL.

```
template <class T> void Matrix<T>::operator= (const Matrix& m)
{                     // simple version, should check sizes and x = x;
    int j, xs = m.xsize, i, ys = m.ysize;
    for (i = 0; i < ys; ++i)
      for (j = 0; j < xs; ++j)
        (*this)[i][j] = m[i][j]; // index checked!
}
```
164

```
template <class T> Matrix<T>::Matrix(const Matrix& m)
{
    int j, xs = m.xsize, i, ys = m.ysize;
    T * array = new T[x*y];        // vector of size x*y
    matrix = new T*[y];            // generate matrix of T's
    for (i = 0; i < ys; ++i)
       matrix[i] = & (array[i*x]); // fill in vector pointers
    Matrix::operator= (m);         // use assignment operator
}
```
165

- object's copy method (THIS::deepenShallowCopy()).

If member allocation is done incorrectly in these functions, assignment, passing as parameter to functions, etc. may on the one hand result in "tangling references", i.e., memory which is still allocated but can no longer be accessed by a pointer; this is called a *memory leak*. On the other hand, failure in allocation can also result in disastrous effects when an object frees memory which is still referenced and required in another object.

Listing 164 and Listing 165 show an implementation for the matrix template declared in Listing 107. Instead of the slow safe assignment (index checked), one should first check whether the matrix sizes match and then assign without index checking. The special case of assigning an object to itself has to be considered if in the operator the memory is freed, reallocated, and then assigned. Listing 166 shows an application.

The implementation of the method deepenShallowCopy() for classes derived from NIHCL-object is described in [Gor90; p. 127–134]. The purpose of this method is to ask an object to provide a complete copy of itself. In a *deep copy* all referenced objects have to be copied as well. The method deepenShallowCopy() is called for all member objects and pointers recursively. What is missing in [Gor90; p. 127–134] is the case of objects having pointers to data as members that do not point to an NIHCL-object but must be copied. An example of how to implement this is shown in Listing 167.

A call to shallowCopy makes a copy using the copy constructor. It returns an object pointer which can be disposed via delete. This implies that copy constructor, destructor, assignment operator and copy method have to be compatible. Especially for real-time programs it is crucial that all memory allocated will be deleted by the destructor. The following rules serve as a general guideline for an allocation strategy, no matter whether NIHCL is used or not:

```
Matrix<int> A(10,10);    // 10x10 integers
Matrix<int> B(A);        // copy constructor
Matrix<int> C = A;       // also copy constructor
B = A;                   // assignment operator
```
166

```
class A : public Object {          // artificial example
    unsigned int n;                // number of elements
    int* field;                    // field[0...n-1]
  public:
    void deepenShallowCopy();
};

void A::deepenShallowCopy()
{
  int* orig = this->field;                  // save original data
  this->field = new int[this->n];           // reallocate
  for (unsigned int i=0; i<this->n; i++)    // for each element
    this->field[i] = orig[i];               // replace new by old
}
```
167

```
String& String::operator= (const String &s)
{
    delete str;                              // release allocated memory
    str = new char [strlen(s.str) + 1];      // reallocate
    strcpy(str,s.str);                       // copy to new memory
    len = s.len;
    return *this;
}
```
168

- Every constructor *copies* its arguments. If the argument is a pointer, the constructor creates a copy of what the pointer references. In particular, the copy constructor makes copies of all data referenced by pointers.
- The assignment operator releases its allocated memory and then also copies the data of its operand. It also checks whether an object is assigned to itself.
- The destructor releases the memory allocated by the constructor.

This strategy has been previously applied in Listing 90. The natural extension for the assignment operator is shown in Listing 168 for our new class `String`.

The next two guidelines refer to classes derived from NIHCL objects:

- Since `deepCopy` calls `shallowCopy` which in turn uses the copy constructor, the function `deepenShallowCopy` will be empty in most cases.
- Use the same allocation strategy as NIHCL for collections: Leave the allocation and disposal to the application programmer. Only the classes using collections will have to implement the function `deepenShallowCopy`.

16.7 Standard Template Library

The Standard Template Library (STL,[Mus96]), which is now part of the standard C++ distribution, satisfies similar needs as NIHCL for general collection classes, as already outlined in Sect. 16.5. STL also provides a class `string` and some other useful classes; the complex number class of STL has already been mentioned in Chapter 10.1. A similar idea for `Matrix` classes as introduced in Sect. 11.2 is described for STL in [Str97] using so-called *slices*.

```
class Option;            // defined later
class Parser {
 private:
    char ** argv;        // used to save arguments
    static vector<Option*> ol; // list of options
 public:
    static void add(Option*);
    Parser(char** HelpText, int argc, char ** argv);
};

class Option {           // Command line option
    friend class Parser; // allow Parser to access internals
 private:
    char * tag;          // option identifier
    char * hlp;          // explanation
    int   nargs;         // expected number of values
    vector<char*> vals;  // values from command line
    short is_set;        // set, if option is present on command line
 public:
    Option(char * t, char * h, int na = 0);
    operator const char * () { return tag; }
    int isSet()        const { return is_set; }
    char * arg(int i) { return vals[i]; }  // note the operator []
};
```

Listing 169

As indicated by the name STL, templates are used instead of a hierarchy of classes. The authors claim that this design is fastest, i.e., more runtime efficient than the exhaustive use of virtual functions. Syntactically similar template interfaces are provided for implementations with different runtime characteristics; these interfaces are not related to each other by inheritance. For example, adding an element to a linked list with constant runtime uses the same syntax as adding to an indexed pointer array which in turn has constant access time.[10] Elements of a set must all be of the same type. A new template instantiation is required for each type of elements. In contrast to NIHCL, STL currently provides no general concept for storing and retrieving collection objects.

The implementation of STL separates *algorithms*, *iterators*, and *data representation*, which we will introduce by examples: We proceed to implement a powerful command line parser which uses STL data representation and iterators. Algorithms in STL allow for various manipulations of containers, e.g. sorting the contents of a vector. We will see examples later in Sect. 17.2.

The functions used so far for parsing command line arguments (Sect. 5.9) were not too sophisticated. Naturally, we want to provide a command line parser as a properly encapsulated class. Such a concept is proposed in Listing 169. A parser class will be used to read and analyze command line parameters. In the Parser class we maintain a list of all instantiated Option objects. Conversely, all Option objects require the definition of the parser class. This circular dependency is solved by an empty (forward) class declaration. Also note the local definition for the list of options OptionList.[11]

In the implementation in Listing 170 we initialize the static variables and demonstrate how the linked list can be filled. The Parser object compares the arguments on the command line with

---
[10] In ERNEST [Nie90b] we implemented similar ideas in C using the C macro pre-processor. The application programmer's interface was simple, the internal implementation rather messy.
[11] The ideas and original implementation are due to M. Harbeck and R. Beß.

16.7 Standard Template Library

```
vector<Option*> Parser::ol;                // static class member
Option::Option(char * t, char * h, int na)
{
    tag = t;                               // set tag
    hlp = h;                               // store help text
    nargs = na;                            // store number of arguments
    Parser::add(this);                     // add to global option list
}

void Parser::add(Option* o)    // add option to global list
{
    ol.push_back(o);
}

Parser::Parser(char** HelpText, int ac, char ** av)
{
    argv = av;                             // save state
    while (*++av != NULL) {
      vector<Option*>::iterator            // example of iterator
              vi = ol.begin();
      while (vi != ol.end()) {             // loop over option list
        if (strcmp(**vi,1+(*av)) == 0) {   // skip '-' in option string
          for (int i = 0; i < (*vi)->nargs; ++i)
            (*vi)->vals.push_back(*++av);  // save args
        }
      }
    }
}
```

the tags found in the option objects and fills in the value pointers with the appropriate strings from the command line. Note that the pointer provided by the iterator `vi` will be converted to a `Option*` in the loop; in the function call to `strcmp` we apply the conversion operator to `const char *` for the first argument.

In the implementation of the class `Parser` we access private parts of `Option` directly; this is possible, as we declare `Parser` as a `friend` of the class `Option`. This language feature of C++ grants access to private parts of the class without any restrictions; this permission is given only to those classes or functions which are declared as friends. Friends should generally be declared only rarely, since they disturb modularity and data abstraction. In this example, however, friends can be used; the dependencies are clear and both classes can be in the same module. So this is, in effect, a useful application of the friend concept. In general, we recommend that classes related as "`friends`" are declared in the same header file, and that this feature is well documented.

The further implementation is left as Exercise 24.d. An application is shown in Listing 171.[12] We put a much more elaborated version of this concept on the `ftp` site listed in Appendix B.3, including default arguments, distinction between options and arguments, abbreviations, etc.

---

[12] Two constant strings are concatenated when there is nothing than spaces in between them, even when they are on separate lines.

```
#include <fstream.h>          /* interface for STL file streams */
static char rcsid[] = "$ Id:$";       // will be filled in by rcs
static char * HelpText [] = {         // Help text
  "This program demonstrates the use of " // no comma ! (see explanation)
  "commmand line parsing ",               // ... continued
  rcsid,                                  // include rcs info here
  NULL                                    // terminate text
};
main(int argc, char  **argv)
{
   Option inp  ("input",  "input file", 1);  // input file option
   Option outp ("output", "output file", 1); // output file option
   Option verb ("verbose", "flag");          // should we talk about actions?
   Option size ("size", "lines columns", 2); // should we talk about actions?
   Parser p(HelpText,argc,argv);             // command line interpretation

   if (verb.isSet()) cout << "Reading file" << endl;

   ifstream in(inp.arg(0));
   int i = atoi(size.arg(1));
   // etc.
}
```

171

```
class Zoom : public Motor {
   // variables referring to the device and to
   // associated objects for camera control
public:
   int operator= (int pos);      // set stepper motor
   int operator++ ();            // increase zoom position
   int operator<< (int speed);   // continuous change with speed
   int operator() ();            // get stepper motor position
   operator int();               // cast operator: get position
};
```

172

16.8   Advanced C++ Features

The C++ features described so far are those language constructs that are used in most of the programs that we know. More sophisticated syntax is supported by the language. We only briefly mention some advanced features that might be interesting for complex systems and refer to [Str97].

Overloading of many operators is possible in addition to the ones we introduced in the text. For operators which can be either prefix or postfix, a special syntax for declaration was provided. We briefly give some examples which can be used in active vision. For active vision we often need motor controlled devices, such as pan-tilt-units or stereo cameras with motor lenses (cf. Sect. 8.8). Programming of motor control is often tedious work when it comes to hardware protocols. It can be facilitated when motors, joints of a device, axes, lenses, etc. are encapsulated as classes and access is provided by simple operators. Assigning an integer to a stepper motor object can then move the device to the desired position. The implementation is sketched in Listing 172; it has to be decided carefully whether the use of operators does not make the program hard to read and understand. The advantage is that no method names have to be typed and that nested expressions can be easier to read.

16.8 Advanced C++ Features

```
template <class T> T swap(T&,T&);      // declaration
template <class T> T swap(T& a,T& b)   // definition
{
    T c = a;                           // save
    a = b;                             // swap first
    return (b = c);                    // return result of second swap
}

int main()
{
    int a = 0, b = 1;
    double c = 0, d = 1;
    double e = swap(c,d);              // will generate function for double swap
    return swap(a,b);                  // function for integers
}
```
173

```
namespace ExtLib {
    int v;
    double x;
}
namespace MyLib {
    int i,j;
    int f();
}
namespace YourLib {
    int m,l;
    using ExtLib::v;
}
int MyLib::f() { return MyLib::i; }
void fct()
{
    using MyLib::j;            // use variable declared in MyLib
    using MyLib::f;            // N.B.: f, not f()
    using namespace YourLib;   // include complete namespace
    m = f() + j;               // YourLib::m = MyLib::f() + MyLib::j;
    m += v;                    // ExtLib::v via MyLib
}
```
174

Function templates are perhaps similar to the class templates introduced in Sect. 11.2. A simple example is shown in Listing 173. When calling such a function, the template argument does not have to be specified!

The concept of namespaces was introduced, which helps to reduce name conflicts for global names. Simultaneously, it resolves the multiple use of the keyword 'static' which was used in C and older C++ programs to indicate that the name of a global varibale should not be visible outside the module. In Listing 174 we see how a namespace is declared which contains some definitions and declarations; using the scope operator, these variables can be accessed. The syntax of namespaces is thus very similar to classes. The keyword `using` is used to make all declarations visible without the need of a scope operator. Parts of a namespace can also be included into another namespace.

Dynamic type information (*rtti*, runtime type information) is available for each class which has virtual methods. This can replace the ideas we showed in Sect. 16.2. Casting is made more secure using an extended syntax which makes use of this new information. A new operator `typeid` can be used to check the type of an object, which returns an object of a class

```
struct A { virtual ~A(); A(); };
struct B : public A { virtual ~B(); B(); };
int fct(const B* bc)
{
  B   * b = const_cast<B*>(bc);
  A   * a = dynamic_cast<B*>(b);
  int * i = reinterpret_cast<int*>(0x0123);
}
```
`175`

`type_info` which is also defined in STL. New secure type conversion and casting can make use of this type information. Similar to the `static_cast` introduced in Sect. 2.6, three other cast operators are provided:

- When using classes and inheritance, a `dynamic_cast` can be used to convert from a pointer to a base class to a pointer to a derived class. The validity of this cast is checked during run time and an exception occurs, if the conversion is incorrect.
- The `reinterpret_cast` can be used to convert from one type to another which is not related, e.g. from an integer to a pointer, as it is required in low-level interfaces.
- The `const_cast` can be used to convert constant values to quantities which have not be declared as `const`.

Examples are shown in Listing 175.

We conclude this section by a list of other C++ features, which are not used in the reminder of the book. It might, however, be useful to know that such mechanisms exist when building up a system for image or speech analysis in C++.

One example are pointers to members or pointers to member functions, which have a weird syntax, but are occasionally useful. Another possibility is to define storage management by overloading the operators `new` and `delete`. Function and variable declarations can be more specific when the new keywords `mutable`, `volatile`, and `explicit` are used. Their semantics can be found in the manuals.

Many extra rules are required when multiple inheritance is used in a programming system. Scoping rules, access regulations, etc. have to be carefully inspected before one decides to use this kind of design.

16.9 Templates vs. Inheritance

The beauty of object–oriented programming is strongly connected with inheritance and code reuse of abstract function definitions. Template definitions as well as the concept of genericity are historically more related to the ideas of Ada. However, this beauty is sometimes difficult to realize in C++.

Although the operations on a NIHCL collection can be mostly implemented in an abstract way, a type conversion by a cast is often required. To continue with Listing 162, the conversion of pointers can be done as in Listing 176: either we use a dynamic cast, or we use a macro

16.9 Templates vs. Inheritance

```
String s6 = * dynamic_cast<String*>(op);
String s7 = *String::castdown(d.atKey(word1));
DO(d, LookupKey, l)
   cout << l->key() << " -> " << l->value() << endl;
OD
```
176

provided by NIHCL. The example also shows how an iteration over a NIHCL dictionary is done; the elements of the object d are of the NIHCL type `LookupKey`. The DO macro creates an iterator and casts the elements down to the type of the elements (here of type `LookupKey`). The static function `castdown` can be used to convert to another object type.[13]

[Str97] proposes to encapsulate such general container classes by templates. These problems do not occur in STL containers, since these containers are typed and the iterators return a pointer to the given type. The STL authors also argue that classes in an inheritance tree are usually overloaded with functions which, in a particular application, are not used at all.

Templates are hard to implement but often easy to use once they are implemented. Even new versions still vary in the strategy for template instantiation. Since templates can not be completely syntax-checked when they are provided by the programmer, it may be that, during template instantiation, an incorrect use may give you a *compiler error* in a piece of code which is not written by you! This may of course puzzle at least the inexperienced programmer.

We found that the use of virtual functions adds very little runtime overhead (cf. Sect. 17.8) if used wisely. A wrong decision for a hash function, however, may dramatically reduce efficiency of NIHCL. Concrete comparisons of virtual functions and direct function calls will be outlined in Sect. 17.8.

This book is mainly dedicated to the application of object–oriented programming to pattern recognition and signal processing. It is not our goal to judge which design of general purpose classes is better suited, templates or inheritance. Often, the right choice might be a mixture of both:

- The requirement of a common file interface for segmentation results is in any case simplified by NIHCL.
- Matrix objects are efficiently implemented as templates.
- Collections which are not stored on files are efficiently handled by STL. Collections for which external storage is desired, can nicely be implemented in NIHCL.
- Data to be included in collections of NIHCL has to be taken from objects which are derived of the class `Object`. Data to be stored in STL collections can be of any kind; it may even be an object from NIHCL. Thus, if a new data type is planned to be included in NIHCL collections, it has to be derived from class `Object`.

---

[13] In Listing 221 we will provide dummy definitions for all the classes that are used in this chapter and that are not defined elsewhere in the book.

Exercises

16.a Implement the class `Image` using the class `Class` for runtime information about the objects.

16.b Extend the classes that we have implemented so far with respect to input and output facilities using streams.

16.c Implement a `String` and `SubString` class compatible with Listing 89. Carefully apply the allocation guidelines listed in Sect. 16.6.

16.d Implement a `Date` and `Time` class compatible with what you saw in Listing 160.

16.e Extend the option classes to contain default values for the values.
Hint: try for example the following syntax
`Option size("size","lines colums",2,"256 512");`
where the last string contains the default values for the two values that are expected on the command line.

Part III
Pattern Analysis

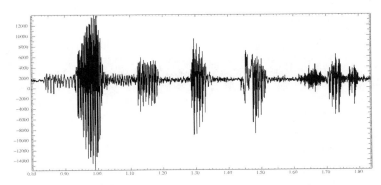

Sound signal: "This is a picture" spoken by D. Paulus

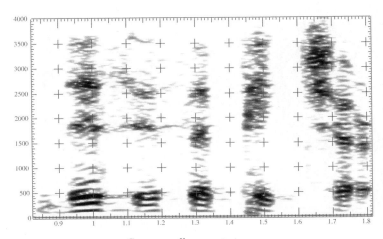

Corresponding spectrogram

In this part of the book we will describe a system for pattern classification. We will show several applications of spectral features and applied statistics.

Chapter 17

Filtering and Smoothing Signals

Filters and operators used for smoothing signals are fundamental parts of the pre-processing stage. Filters, in general, can be designed for two different domains: the frequency and the spatial domain. In Sect. 13.9 we already showed how the Fourier transform can be used to filter a signal in the spectral domain. In the following sections we will filter images in the spatial domain, rather than using the spectral domain.

In chapter 12 we implemented some algorithms for generating noisy signals. Noise in images or other signals used for pattern recognition purposes is an undesirable effect and has to be reduced or eliminated, as far as possible. The reduction of noise can be realized by the smoothing of patterns. Many different approaches for smoothing and filtering signals can be found in the literature. The following sections will briefly introduce some basic algorithms which are useful for images as well as speech. We describe the more complicated case of two-dimensional signals; the simpler version of one-dimensional signals can easily be derived from the examples.

Beside the elimination of noise, digital filters are also used for emphasizing interesting parts of an image, such as regions or edges. For getting higher continuity in digital signals, smoothing operators are used.

In the first chapter we introduced and discussed the problems of how digital images can be computed out of analog signals. The quantization of intensity values induces noise effects which can be measured by the signal to noise ratio (Eq. 7.41). The following sections describe filters which reduce noise and smooth an image. One section is dedicated to the problem of how to magnify an image to double its size using linear reconstruction techniques.

At the end of this chapter, we start implementing our hierarchy of image operator classes.

17.1 Linear Filters

A filter is called *linear* if it can be expressed by the convolution of a signal f with a mask h (cf. (15.7)), and the filtering operation is a linear transform from signals to signals. For speech signals represented as vectors, the mask is a 1-D vector. As images are represented as matrices, the mask is a small 2-D array often also called a window. In the following we will discuss

Figure 17.1: Mean-filter (left) and Gaussian-filter on square subimage (right) of Figure 1.3 (right)

some elementary linear filters; another, more complicated linear filter, which mathematically characterizes human speech production, is introduced in Sect. 21.7.

Mean-filtering is a very simple and obvious linear smoothing technique. A current pixel gray-level or value in a time-ordered signal is set to the mean of neighboring sample data. In image processing applications the neighborhood is usually defined by a square 3×3 or 5×5 mask. For time ordered signals the mean is computed using some predecessors or successors of the current position. For an $n \times n$ *mean-filter*, the matrix of size $n \times n$ to convolve with is:

$$\frac{1}{n^2} \begin{pmatrix} 1 & 1 & \ldots & 1 \\ 1 & 1 & \ldots & 1 \\ \vdots & \vdots & \ddots & \vdots \\ 1 & 1 & \ldots & 1 \end{pmatrix}. \tag{17.1}$$

It should be mentioned that this filter smears the signal values. Images will blur and edge detection is made more difficult as a result of its use. The detection of homogeneous regions, however, is simplified if this filtering operation is used. In practice, mean-filters are easily implemented and the runtime depends on the image size and grows linearly in proportion to the window size, if convolution is used. The runtime of an efficient implementation, however, is approximately independent of the size of a given neighborhood. In the so-called sliding sum algorithm we first compute the n means of the columns in the window and store them. We then compute and store the sum of these stored means and divide it by the number of colums to get the value for the filtered image. When advancing by one pixel horizontally, we add the column mean of the new column appearing under the mask to the sum and subtract the column mean of the column which no longer is under the mask. When the next vertical position has to be computed, the stored values of the column means are updated similarly, adding the value of one new pixel and subtracting the oldest one.

Each gray-level in the defined neighborhood is weighted with the same value in the case of the mean-filter (cf. Eq. (17.1)). It is a reasonable assumption that increasing the distance should imply a decrease in weights. In the case of *Gaussian-filters* these weights are defined using the Gaussian density function (cf. Sect. 7.2). A digitized version for a 3 × 3 neighborhood[1] is, for example,

$$\frac{1}{16}\begin{pmatrix} 1 & 2 & 1 \\ 2 & 4 & 2 \\ 1 & 2 & 1 \end{pmatrix}. \tag{17.2}$$

Of course, this filter is linear as well. Figure 17.1 shows examples for images filtered by mean and Gaussian filters. Again, a more efficient implementation than using a convolution is possible, as the filter is *separable*, i.e. it can be computed as the combination of two independent convolutions in the horizontal and vertical direction.

Filters that eliminate rough changes in intensity values and smooth the original signal, remove high frequencies. For that reason, these filters are called *low-pass filters*, i.e. high frequencies in the spectrum will be reduced or completely suppressed.

17.2 Rank Order Operations

The general algorithms for rank order operations first require the definition of a neighborhood of the current pixel. Here we use masks of square shape; in general, arbitrary neighborhoods are possible. All gray-levels of the n neighboring pixels $f_1, f_2, \ldots, f_n$ are ordered using the „≤"–relation of real numbers. If the new pixel value is the gray-level of the pixel $f_{\lfloor n/2 \rfloor}$ in the middle of this ordering, we get the so-called *median-filter*.

If we take the minimum f_1 of these ordered values, we get the *erosion-filter*. Dilatation is the filter which results from the maximum value f_n. In general, filters which use ordered sequences of its neighboring signal values (such as the examples in Figure 17.2) are elements of the class of *morphological operations*. One more such operation is the morphological edge detector $f_n - f_1$. Morphological operations provide very important tools for computer vision and image analysis. There exists a theoretical framework for morphological operations and their use in high-level computer vision, which cannot be introduced here. For interested readers, we strongly recommend [Ser88].

The rank order operations are fairly easy to implement. The runtime of these algorithms depends linearly on the image size and on the window size.

The edge preserving character of the median-filter justifies its popularity. If a high signal-to-noise ratio is given, it is recommended to give median-filters priority over other filters (cf. for example [Mac81]). A lot of research is being done to weight the advantages and disadvantages of this non-linear filter [Bov87, Chi83]. In [Yam81] it is shown that in images with the presence of convex or concave ramp edges and impulsive noise, median filtering will improve edge detection results.

In [Luo94] the median-filter is extended to a corner preserving filter operation called the *smoothed median filter*. The basic idea of this algorithm is a graduated application of median filtering. The 5 × 5 mask is divided into four differing stripes (see Figure 17.3). For each

---
[1] Assuming square pixels.

Figure 17.2: Median-filter (left), erosion (middle), and dilation (right)

Figure 17.3: Four elliptic masks (1–4) where the median is separately applied (left); result of smoothed-median filtering (right)

subset of included pixels (1–4) the classical median is computed. The final pixel value of the center of the 5×5 mask is computed by the median of the four resulting values of the prior median operations. It can be shown that the described smoothed median filter also suppresses Gaussian noise.

A color vector median, as proposed in [Smo99], is implemented in Listing 178 using STL vector templates. We enclose the definitions into an unnamed namespace, so they will be local to this module. The required definitions for sorting and inserting into the STL container are shown in in Listing 177. Note that the STL `vector` is first filled by values (which are pointers here) and later sorted using a simple routine for comparison. The `sort` function is taken from the collection of algorithms in STL (Sect. 16.7). This implementation also shows how pixel at the image borders can be treated in a mask operation nicely.

Results are shown in Figure 17.4; whereas no new colors are created for the color vector median, the application of a median to each channel separately may create artifacts.

17.3 Edge Preserving Filters

In the so-called *edge preserving smoothing* algorithm, the selection of pixels for averaging is done by the use of a special technique based on statistical principles. The algorithm suggested in [Nag79] uses nine different 5×5 masks for each pixel P; three of them are shown in Figure 17.5. The pixels in the environment of P with a distinguishing mark are used for the

17.3 Edge Preserving Filters

```
namespace { // unnamed
struct RGBpix {                     // auxiliary data structure
   byte r,g,b;                      // pixel
   double l;                        // color vector length
   inline void set(int r0, int g0, int b0);
};

static bool less_RGBpix(const RGBpix* p1, const RGBpix* p2)
   { return p1->l < p2->l; }        // compare two pixels

inline void RGBpix::set(int r0, int g0, int b0)
{
   r = r0; g = g0; b = b0;          // store r g b
   l = sqrt(r*r + g*g + b*b);       // compute length
}
} // end namespace
```
177

```
#include <algorithm>    /* definitions for sort */
void ColorMedian (const ColorImage& in, ColorImage & out,
         int xs, int ys, int mxsize, int mysize)
{
   int pxh = (mxsize-1)/2, pyh = (mysize-1)/2;

   for (int i = 0; i < ys; ++i) {
     for (int j = 0; j < xs ; ++j) {
        int cnt = 0;
        RGBpix f[mxsize*mysize];    /* mask */
        vector<RGBpix*> f1;         /* STL */
        for (int k = max(0,i-pyh); k < min(ys,i+pyh); ++k) {
           for (int l = max(0,j-pxh); l < min(xs,j+pxh); ++l) {
              f[cnt].set(in.r[0][k][l], in.g[0][k][l], in.b[0][k][l]);
              f1.push_back(f+cnt);  /* insert pointer */
              ++cnt;
           }
        }
        sort(f1.begin(),f1.end(),less_RGBpix); /* sort pointers */
        out.r[0][i][j]=f1[cnt/2]->r;    // select median from
        out.g[0][i][j]=f1[cnt/2]->g;    // the vectors
        out.b[0][i][j]=f1[cnt/2]->b;    // as output
     }
   }
}
```
178

following computations. The symmetrical use of 17.5 (a) and (b) results in eight different masks. Each of these masks include seven points for the calculation of the new gray-level. The contrast mask (c) includes nine elements for the following computations. For each mask we compute the variance (7.9). The mask with the lowest variance is selected. The central pixel P gets the mean value of all points marked in this mask. An example of the result of this filter is shown in 17.6.

The filter of *K Nearest Neighbor Averaging* [Dav78] is an additional edge preserving filter which can be used iteratively. Let P be a pixel from an array with N points. Take K points out of this array which are closest to the gray-value of the image point P, including P itself. Assign the mean of these points to the pixel P. With a growing value of K, this filter converges to the mean-filter, the reduction of noise grows and the complete image blurs.

Figure 17.4: Noise added to test image Figure 11.3 (left), color vector median (center), median applied to each color channel individually (right)

Figure 17.5: Masks for edge preserving smoothing

It is suggested to use $N = 9$ and $K = 6$ [Dav78]. In this case you take eight neighbors of P and determine the five nearest gray-levels. The mean of the gray-levels of P and the five additional points is assigned to the new intensity of P.

In [Brü90] it is shown that this filter is very powerful. The computation time and the result of smoothing depends on the number of iterations. The runtime increases linearly with the image size. From previous experience it is known that three iterations yield satisfiable results.

Figure 17.6 illustrates three different results of this filtering operation with varying K values.

Another iteratively applicable filter is suggested in [Pra80] and is called *Conditional Average Filter*. In a 5×5 mask around the central pixel P we compute the mean of all pixels whose difference in the gray-level with the intensity of P is lower or equal to a given threshold θ. The gray-level of P is assigned to this value. The problem of this algorithm is obviously the selection of the threshold θ which is picture dependent. In [Brü90], the threshold θ is computed by $\theta = \alpha \cdot G_{\max}$, where $\alpha \in [0, 1]$ and $G_{\max}$ is the maximum gray-level of the image. The best results were made choosing $\alpha = 0.1$. The advantage of conditional averaging is that edges, where the change in gray-levels exceeds θ, are not blurred. Regions, where gray-levels differ with a difference lower or equal to θ, are smoothed. In practice, this filter eliminates weak edges. Therefore, even an adaptive selection of the threshold should be used with caution.

Figure 17.6: Edge Preserving Filtering (left); K–nearest neighbor filtering with $K = 2, 9$ (middle, right)

Figure 17.7: Conditional average for different thresholds ($\theta = 100, 150, 200$)

Compare the images shown in Figure 17.7, which are computed using different thresholds. Herein, various levels of the smoothing property are illustrated.

The sorting of gray-levels is not necessary, therefore the runtime of conditional average filters is in general lower than the one in Sect. 17.3.

17.4 Elimination of Noisy Image Rows

Most commercial CCD cameras do not record image line by line, but sample first the odd and then the even lines. If we have moving objects in the scene we can observe the so called *interlace effect*. Assume the sampling of each line takes t_s ms time. When we start at time t at the first line of the image, the record of the second line will be $n\,t_s$ ms later, where $2n$ represents the number of lines of the CCD chip. A moving object can change its position in $n\,t_s$ ms, and the odd and even image rows are shifted. This shift can be computed analytically, if the technical data of the CCD chip and the speed of the moving object are known. In practice, there is nothing known a priori about the moving object. Therefore, we have to find another – more convenient – approach to remove interlace effects. In practice, it is sometimes sufficient to cancel rows with even numbers and to double each odd numbered row although this violates the sampling theorem.

If rows of the image do not include the moving object we have no interlace and therefore nothing to change. One possible approach to locate and remove interlace effects in the image is with the use of statistical methods. Based on the experience that the transition of one row

Figure 17.8: Examples for magnifications of an image

to its successor does not change gray-level dramatically, using a correlation coefficient we can decide whether one row is corrupted by interlacing or some other kind of noise. If the test is positive, we have to reduce this disturbance.

Let $f_{i,j}$ ($0 \leq i < M$, and $0 \leq j < N$) be the gray-levels of the given image. We compare the covariance $\sigma_{r,r+1}$ of two successive rows r and $r+1$

$$\sigma_{r,r+1} = \frac{1}{N} \sum_{k=0}^{N-1} (f_{r,k} - \mu_r)(f_{r+1,k} - \mu_{r+1}) \quad , \tag{17.3}$$

where μ_r and μ_{r+1} are the means of gray-levels of the current rows. The correlation coefficient

$$\rho_{r,r+1} = \frac{\sigma_{r,r+1}}{\sqrt{\sigma_{r,r}\sigma_{r+1,r+1}}} \tag{17.4}$$

yields the following decision rule for two rows: If $|\rho_{r,r+1}| > \theta$, where θ is a threshold value, we will do no changes. Otherwise, we say both rows are not similar, consequently we have to smooth the transition from row r to $r+1$. This can be done by copying r to $r+1$ or by averaging two rows.

17.5 Resizing an Image

Often it is required to change the size of an image (cf. Figure 17.8). Image resizing requires filter applications. For size reduction we have to apply a low-pass filter in order to fulfill the sampling theorem. First we show a simple method for image magnification based on linear reconstruction, i.e. the gray-levels of new pixels are linear combinations of gray-levels of neighboring image points.

To get double size of the image we successively decompose the image into 2×2 squares

$$\begin{array}{cc} f_{i,j} & f_{i,j+1} \\ f_{i+1,j} & f_{i+1,j+1} \end{array}$$

and compute the gray-levels of five additional points $a, b, c, d,$ and e using linear interpolation between the gray-levels. For that purpose, two gray-levels are connected by a straight line, and the missing value results from the function value of the straight line at the required image point. If the considered point is in the middle of two points, a simple mean computation of gray-levels allows the estimation of the missing value. For instance, if the gray-level of a in

$$\begin{array}{ccc} f_{i,j} & a & f_{i,j+1} \\ b & c & d \\ f_{i+1,j} & e & f_{i+1,j+1} \end{array}$$

has to be computed, we get

$$a = \frac{f_{i,j} + f_{i,j+1}}{2} \quad . \tag{17.5}$$

The value of c can be computed by an interpolation of b and d. The implementation is left as Exercise 17.f.

The theoretically correct method for resizing uses the Fourier transform. As a result of the sampling theorem we can reconstruct the image from its spectrum. The algorithm for resizing an image of size $M \times N$ to an image of size $m \times n$ is simple:

1. Compute the Fourier transform of the input image of size $M \times N$.
2. Resize the resulting complex matrix to size $m \times n$
   - if $M > m$, discard the rows greater than m
   - if $N > n$, discard the columns greater than n
   - if $M < m$, add new zero-filled rows to get n rows
   - if $N < n$, add new zero-filled columns to get n columns
3. Do an inverse DFT of the new complex matrix of size $m \times n$ to get an image of size $m \times n$.

This algorithm includes all that is done, including downsampling and low-pass filtering! An inverse FFT cannot be used in step 3, as the resulting size $m \times n$ is not a square matrix in general.

17.6 Resolution Hierarchies

The runtime behavior of many algorithms, such as filtering, edge detection, or region segmentation, depends on the size of the processed image. For some applications one does not need maximal image resolution. In active vision, for instance, one of the main principles is selectivity in resolutin of the algorithms. This can lead to a lower computation time needed, for example, in real-time image processing. Another example is some edge detection algorithm that first searches for edges on a low resolution image, and then takes these edges as an initial edge estimation for another search at a higher resolution. In this way, a more precise result can be obtained, stepwise.

The representation of an image at several resolutions leads to *image pyramids* (which look like the pyramid in Figure 17.8, although it is computed differently). An image pyramid is a series of images $f_k(i,j)$, where $0 < k < n$, and $0 \leq i,j < 2^n$. Herein, n is given by the size of the original image. The pyramid is created by a bottom up approach. Formally, the image $f_k(i,j)$ is computed from $f_{k+1}(i,j)$ by applying

$$f_k(i,j) = \text{reduce}\,(f_{k+1}(i,j)) \quad . \tag{17.6}$$

Herein, the function reduce($\cdot$) is called the *generating function*. For each reduced image both the resolution and the sample density are decreased. One simple form of the function reduce($\cdot$) is defined by

$$\text{reduce}(f_{k+1}(i,j)) = \sum_{m=a}^{b}\sum_{n=c}^{d} w(m,n) f_{k+1}(2i+m, 2j+n) \quad , \tag{17.7}$$

where $w(m,n) \in \mathbb{R}$ is a weighting function and a,b,c,d are integers. A simple version of $w(m,n)$ and the integral constants is given by $w(m,n) = \frac{1}{4}, a = c = 0$, and $b = d = 1$. In this case, the pyramid is generated by an averaging process.

There exist many variations in the way that the next lower resolution can be computed. One possible approach is to use another weighting function or another type of function reduce($\cdot$), for example, a local maximum, minimum or morphological function.

One special case of a pyramid is the so called *Gaussian pyramid* [Bur83]:

$$a = c = -2, b = d = 2, w(m,n) = \hat{w}(m)\hat{w}(n) \tag{17.8}$$

with

$$\hat{w}(0) = \alpha \tag{17.9}$$

$$\hat{w}(-1) = \hat{w}(1) = \frac{1}{4} \tag{17.10}$$

$$\hat{w}(-2) = \hat{w}(2) = \frac{1}{4} - \frac{\alpha}{2} \quad . \tag{17.11}$$

The Gaussian pyramid results in a sequence of images. Each computed image represents a low-pass filtered copy of its predecessor in the given hierarchy. In [Bur83] it is shown that the Gaussian pyramid construction generates images with a band limit one octave lower than their predecessors. Thus, the pre-conditions of the sampling theorem are valid and the computationally expensive DFT as in Sect. 17.5 can be avoided in this special case. The implementation is left as Exercise 17.g.

17.7 Geometric Distortions

We now interest ourselves in another feature of C++ classes which can simplify the interfaces for image operations. We use a low-level image operation as an example of an object–oriented implementation of operators.

A typical pre-processing step is the inversion of geometric distortions of an input image (arrow 5 in Figure 24.2). Examples may be found in [Nie90a]. An ideal (undistorted) image $s(x,y)$ is observed as $f(u,v)$, whereby the coordinates are distorted by

$$u = \Phi_1(x,y), \quad v = \Phi_2(x,y) \quad . \tag{17.12}$$

The ideal image can be computed by

$$s(x,y) = f(\Phi_1(x,y), \Phi_2(x,y)) \quad . \tag{17.13}$$

The distortion functions Φ_1, Φ_2 are usually taken from a parametric family of functions. Typical classes are polynomial, affine, or projective transformations. Φ_1 and Φ_2 may belong to the same class and differ only in the parameters. For example, Φ_1 and Φ_2 may be affine transforms $u = a_{11} x + a_{12} y + a_{13}$ and $v = a_{21} x + a_{22} y + a_{23}$.

It is convenient, if we can code (17.13) directly into the programming language:

$$\texttt{s[i][j] = f[Phi1(i,j)][Phi2(i,j)];} \tag{17.14}$$

The problem of reconstructing the ideal image is inherently independent of the actual distortion functions. A change in these functions should not affect the algorithm directly.

Using conventional programming languages, geometric distortions can be implemented as functions. The implementation of (17.13), for instance, will call the distortion functions via function pointers (Sect. 6.8).

Now, imagine that Φ_1 and Φ_2 belong to the same class of parametric functions, e.g., 2–D affine distortions, and differ only in their coefficients. The major problem then is to combine the function pointers with their parameter sets without duplicating code.

One might attach the parameters as a vector argument to the functions:

$$\texttt{f[Phi1(i,j,a1)][Phi2(i,j,a2)];} \tag{17.15}$$

However, the number of parameters for the different transformation classes are different (e.g., three parameters for the affine, six for the projective transformation). We can also find examples where the parameters differ not only in number but also in type.

17.8 Polymorphic Image Processing

Section 17.7 showed how mathematicians write down algorithms using functional syntax. The functions Φ_1 and Φ_2 in (17.13), implemented as `Phi1` and `Phi2` in (17.15) exhibit *polymorphic* behavior. Nothing is being said about the type of these functions at this point. At the time of the actual computation, they may be either affine transformations, polynomials or perspective transformations; it may as well be the case that both functions are affine transformations with different parameter sets.

```
struct Dist {       // abstract class          // abstract interface
    virtual float operator() (int,int);        // apply distortion function
};
struct PolyDist: public Dist {                 // polynomial distortion
    virtual float operator()(int,int);         // apply distortion function
};
class AffineDist : public PolyDist {
    double a,b,c;                // coefficients for the affine transformation
  public:
    AffineDist(int,int,int);     // set a,b,c
    virtual float operator()(int,int);
};

float AffineDist::operator() (int x, int y)
{
    return int(a * x + b * y + c);
}
```
179

```
void correct(Dist& const Phi1, Dist& const Phi2,
             GrayLevelImage& s, GrayLevelImage& const f)
{
  for(int i = 0; i < s.SizeY(); ++i)           // all lines
    for(int j = 0; j < s.SizeX(); ++j)         // all columns
      s[i][j] = f[int(Phi1(i,j))][int(Phi2(i,j))];  // use distortion objects
}
```
180

This kind of semantics can be expressed by the syntax of object-oriented programming languages. It greatly simplifies programming and enables safe extensibility. If another programmer has to add radial distortions to the above mentioned transformations, the basic idea (and of course, the formula (17.13)) would not change. Neither would the (object-oriented) program.

The great advantage of polymorphic functions over conventional function pointers will now be outlined. An abstract super-class provides the general interface to geometric distortions. Special classes inherit the interface and redefine the details.

Listing 179 is a simplified piece of C++ code for the declaration of three classes. The class `Dist` defines the abstract interface which is inherited by the derived classes for polynomial and affine distortion. The virtual constant operator declares an object interface in *functional syntax*. The `operator()` can be used to address objects like function calls without the need for specifying a method name. Using the code fragment, a geometric correction mapping function can be written without actually knowing which kind of transformation will be applied. Distorted image f, corrected image object s, and the two transformation objects `Phi1` and `Phi2` are passed to the function as arguments (Listing 180).

Of course, a complete algorithm will have to take care of re-sampling, interpolation, and filtering, etc. An idea similar to (17.5) can be used to interpolate pixels at positions (x,y) in a discrete image f_{ij}, with $x, y \in \mathbb{R}$. Using the notation introduced in Figure 17.9 we inspect the closest neighbors on the discrete grid which are denoted by f_{ur}, f_{ul}, f_{lr}, and f_{ll} in the figure. In the so-called *bilinear* interpolation, we compute a new gray value by

$$f_{\text{ux}} = f_{\text{ul}} + (f_{\text{ur}} - f_{\text{ul}})(x - \lfloor x \rfloor) \qquad (17.16)$$

$$f_{\text{lx}} = f_{\text{ll}} + (f_{\text{lr}} - f_{\text{ll}})(x - \lfloor x \rfloor) \qquad (17.17)$$

17.8 Polymorphic Image Processing

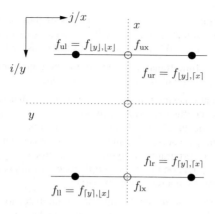

Figure 17.9: Bilinear interpolation

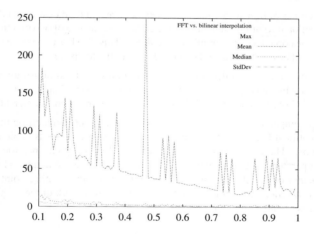

Figure 17.10: Comparison of scaling methods. Maximum, mean, median, and variance of difference image computed from Figure 1.3 in full resolution and scaled down copy. Scaling was done from 10% to 99%.

$$f(x,y) = f_{\text{ux}} + (f_{\text{lx}} - f_{\text{ux}})(y - \lfloor y \rfloor) \qquad (17.18)$$

The complete implementation is left as Exercise 17.h and Exercise 17.i. We considered just four pixels to estimate the new gray-level. There exist many other strategies; some of them are compared in [Leh99]. The differences between images scaled by bi-linear interpolation and by FFT may be considerable. Figure 17.10 shows the maximum, mean, and median differences between images scaled with the two methods.

The classes declare a hierarchy of *operations*; instances of these classes (objects) represent the actual (mathematical) parametric function with a fixed set of parameters. For example, an affine transformation $u = 1.1\,x + 0.9\,y$ will be an object of class `AffineDist`.

Two distortion objects for affine transformations *share* the code for the computation. They differ in the coefficients (a, b, c) which are bound to the object.

A conventional implementation using function pointers would either have to use a complicated mechanism for linking the coefficients to the computation, or duplicate code in order to provide two functions `Phi1` and `Phi2`, which are textually identical, except for the coefficients of the polynomial. This may be acceptable in this (simple) case; but in general, this will decrease the maintainability of programs: in typical image processing programs, *many* simple functions are used; code duplication in several simple functions imposes the same problems on maintainability as duplications in a few complex parts.

For example, if at a later stage, someone decides that radial distortions are required, the function `correct` in the previous source code fragment will *not* have to be modified. A new class for radial distortions redefining the `operator()(int,int)` will simply be derived from the abstract base class.

An arbitrary number of transformation-objects can be created (and destroyed) during runtime. If, in the conventional solution using duplicated code, three instead of two functions are needed, the code has to be copied again, compiled, linked, etc. This also has to be done if templates are used, i.e., one further function has to be expanded from the template.

Sometimes people argue that object-oriented programming adds administrational overhead to the programs thereby causing a slow down in execution speed. This is not always the case, especially not in C++. Efficient image class access was described in Chapter 11.

For example, a comparison of the execution times for a geometric distortion in an implementation in conventional C and the C++ implementation showed *no* measurable differences for affine distortions. The times were measured with `inline` virtual operators and `inline` image access operators. The conventional program used indirect function calls (via function pointer arguments) or direct function calls. In either case, the floating point arithmetic required for the evaluation of the transformation — i.e., the *real* work of the programs — by far exceeded the access and calling mechanisms.

17.9 Image Operator Hierarchy

In this section we illustrate a top down design of a program for image segmentation. The classes introduced in Part II are used for data representation. Operator classes (Sect. 17.8) are declared for image segmentation, and the actual implementation of these operators will be described in the following.

Using the function call operator as introduced in Sect. 17.8, we implement a hierarchy of operator classes that declares an interface even for future extensions by inheritance.

17.9 Image Operator Hierarchy

```
class IP_OP : public Object { };        // general image operator class
struct Filter: public IP_OP {           // abstract class for filters
   virtual void operator() (const GrayLevelImage&,GrayLevelImage&) = 0;
};
struct LowPass : public Filter {};      // abstract low-pass filter
struct EdgeDet: public IP_OP {          // abstract class for edge detection
   virtual void operator() (const GrayLevelImage&,EdgeImage&) = 0;
};
```
`181`

```
class Mean: public LowPass {            // mean filter as a special case
   int xs, ys;                          // size of the filter mask
  public:
   Mean(int sizeh, int sizev) : xs(sizeh/2), ys(sizev/2) {}
   virtual void operator() (const GrayLevelImage&,GrayLevelImage&) ;
};
class GaussFilter: public LowPass {     // gauss filter as a special case
   double sigma;                        // parameters of the gaussian
   double * mask;                       // filter mask
  public:
   GaussFilter (double s);
   virtual void operator() (const GrayLevelImage&,GrayLevelImage&) ;
};
```
`182`

Listing 182 extends Listing 181 and declares the interface to filter operations that transform one gray-level image into another. A simple implementation of a mean filter that also works at the border of images is given in Listing 183.

Note, that we do not declare the `operator()` to be `const`, since in future (derived) classes we might want to record temporary values inside the class during computation of the operation. This is possible only for a non-constant function. A `virtual operator()` is different from `operator() const`, i.e., the declaration will *hide* the inherited virtual function. This would most likely be a source of errors, or at least cause confusion for the programmers.

```
void Mean::operator() (const GrayLevelImage& in, GrayLevelImage& out)
{
   for (int i = 0 ; i < in.SizeY(); ++i)         // all image lines
      for (int j = 0 ; j < in.SizeX(); ++j) {    // all image columns
         int r = 0, c = 0;                       // temporary values
         for (int k = -1* ys ; k <= ys ; ++k) {  // all mask lines
            for (int l = -1 * xs ; l <= xs; ++l) {  // all mask columns
               if ((i + k < 0) || (i + k >= in.SizeY()) ||  // works also
                   (j + l < 0) || (j + l >= in.SizeX()))    // at borders
                  continue;                      // use only valid indices
               ++c; r += in[i+k][j+l]; }         // sum up and count
         }
         out [i][j] = r / c; // store mean in output;  c always >= 1 !
      }
}
```
`183`

Exercises

17.a Verify by experiments the characteristics of introduced filter operations – like the suppression of Gaussian noise by the use of smoothed median filtering using noise added to synthetic and natural images (Chapter 12).

17.b Use the tools of Sect. 12.5 to visualize the difference of two images f and g. (Hint: display $(f - g) + (g - f)$ and implement the difference of two pixels in such a way that negative values will be set to zero.)

17.c The idea of smoothed median filtering is a subsequent application of the median filter to different sets of pixels. Use this idea to develop other hybrid filters using types other than median operations. Which object–oriented programming techniques provide useful tools for realizing this kind of *polymorphism*? Do as many experiments as you like and formalize the observed results of your filters.

17.d Implement a class hierarchy for filters as declared in Listing 182.

17.e Show that the total number of pixels M of a Gaussian pyramid is bounded by $M < \frac{4}{3}N^2$, where the first image has a resolution of $N \times N$ and a decreasing factor of two per stage.

17.f Implement a function `doubleSize` which magnifies the input image using the techniques sketched in this chapter. Discuss different strategies for the computation of the non-unique gray-level c.

Use your program and magnify an arbitrary image iteratively. Which effects are observable? Is it possible that images shown in Figure 17.8 are computed using the above method?

17.g For this exercise an image pyramid class for images has to be implemented. Start with an abstract base class, which contains methods for computing a weighting function, a generating function, and methods to select special resolutions of the pyramid elements. Take into consideration that several image types are possible, for example, binary images, gray-level images or edge images. Derive a concrete class and then implement the special form of a Gaussian pyramid for a `GrayLevelImage`.

17.h The following essential parts are missing in Listing 179:

- the parameters for the polynomial mapping,
- constructors (setting the parameters),
- definition of the virtual functions (basically straightforward).

Complete the example!

17.i Extend Listing 180 to handle interpolation using (17.18).

17.j Write a program to resize an image using the DFT or bi-linear interpolation.

17.k The plot in Figure 17.10 has been created as follows: The program of exercise-name 17.j has been called in a loop of a script. The two output images for each scale have been compared by the program of Exercise 12.g. The output image of this comparison has been processed by the program of Exercise 11.h which prints the requested values. These printouts have been recorded in a file and parsed later on to create a command file for `gnuplot`.

Using script tools, as mentioned in Sect. A.6, Sect. A.8, Sect. A.7, Sect. A.9, combine your programs in the same fashion!

Chapter 18
Histogram Algorithms

Histograms were already introduced in Chapter 7. In the following sections we will define several useful image pre-processing steps using histograms. Each algorithm can easily be implemented and tested using a class *Histogram*. In addition to standard methods working on gray-level images, we also introduce two algorithms for color image based on histograms.

18.1 Discriminant Analysis Threshold

Histograms are conventionally used for computing a binary image $[b_{i,j}]_{1 \leq i \leq N, 1 \leq j \leq M}$ from a given gray-level image $[f_{i,j}]_{1 \leq i \leq N, 1 \leq j \leq M}$. Binary images reduce input data and they are often applied for separating an object from its background. The *binarization* is usually done by a threshold operation which is defined by

$$b_{i,j} = \begin{cases} 0 & \text{, if } f_{i,j} \leq \theta \\ 1 & \text{, otherwise} \end{cases} \quad (18.1)$$

A suitable value θ for binarization can be found by creating a gray-level histogram. If the background and the observed object have considerably different gray-levels, then both regions can be separated by looking at relative frequencies in the histogram. This distinguishing of an object from its background produces what is known as a *bi-modal histogram*: the gray-levels for object and background pixels will have the highest relative frequencies, other gray-levels will be weighted by lower probabilities. The threshold that divides up the pixels into object and background image points is assumed to be the minimum that lies between the maxima found in the histogram. Figure 18.1 shows two examples of binarization. The threshold was computed using the minimum between the two maxima of gray-levels in the (smoothed) bi-modal histogram.

The technique based on bi-modal histograms is not applicable generally, because foreground and background usually have more than just the two extrema in the histogram. Other methods are required for the computation of the threshold. A promising approach to solve this problem is to use some statistical information about the gray-levels and formalizing an optimization problem for the separation of two classes, i.e. object and background pixels.

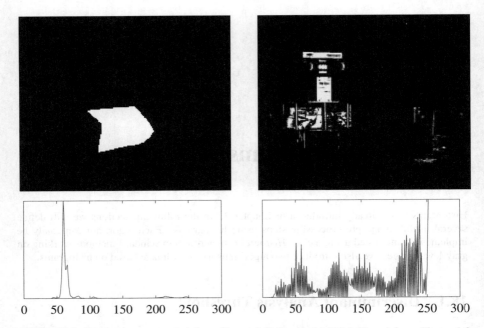

Figure 18.1: Binary image created from Figure 1.2 (threshold 120 left) and from Figure 1.2 (threshold 249 right) with bi-modal histogram analysis. The plots show the gray-level histograms of the input gray-level images.

As in the above case a threshold θ has to be computed. We define the values of admissible gray-levels by $g_1, g_2, \ldots, g_L$. The discrete probability for each gray-level in a given image can be easily determined by a gray-level histogram. Let $f_{i,j}$ be the gray-level at the image point (i,j). The probability p_ν that the image point (i,j) has the gray-level g_ν is the relative frequency

$$p(f_{i,j} = g_\nu) = p_\nu := \frac{|\text{image points with gray-level } g_\nu|}{|\text{image points}|} \quad . \tag{18.2}$$

The bipartition of all gray-levels is done using a threshold $\theta = g_l$, where $l \in \{1, 2, \ldots, L\}$. Let $^l\Omega_1$ and $^l\Omega_2$ be the disjoint sets of gray-levels induced by a given threshold value g_l, i.e.

$$^l\Omega_1 = \{f_{i,j} \,;\, f_{i,j} \leq g_l\} \quad \text{and} \quad ^l\Omega_2 = \{f_{i,j} \,;\, f_{i,j} > g_l\} \quad . \tag{18.3}$$

Using this notation, the probability that an image point lies in one of the above classes is

$$p(^l\Omega_1) = \sum_{\nu=1}^{l} p_\nu \quad \text{and} \quad p(^l\Omega_2) = 1 - p(^l\Omega_1) \quad . \tag{18.4}$$

The threshold θ is expected to satisfy the following properties:

18.1 Discriminant Analysis Threshold

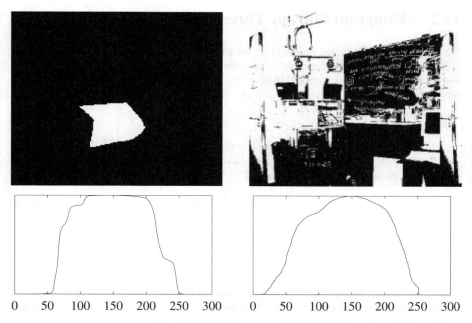

Figure 18.2: Binary image created from Figure 1.2 (threshold 141 left) and from Figure 1.2 (threshold 149 right) with discriminant analysis. The plots show the value of J_l (eqn. 18.5).

1. Neither $p(^l\Omega_1)$ nor $p(^l\Omega_2)$ should be equal to zero, and
2. the absolute difference of means for the gray-levels appearing in Ω_1 and Ω_2 should be maximized.

A criterion which takes into account these requirements is the objective function

$$J_l = p(^l\Omega_1)\, p(^l\Omega_2) \cdot \left(\sum_{\nu=1}^{l} \frac{p_\nu g_\nu}{p(^l\Omega_1)} - \sum_{\nu=l+1}^{L} \frac{p_\nu g_\nu}{p(^l\Omega_2)} \right)^2 , \qquad (18.5)$$

which has to be maximized with respect to the gray-level index l:

$$l' = \operatorname*{argmax}_{l} J_l . \qquad (18.6)$$

Thus, the computation of $\theta = g_l$ using the introduced *discriminant analysis* is bound by L evaluations of J_l. An example for a binary image computed using the threshold computed by (18.6) is shown in Figure 18.2. More details concerning this technique can be found in [Nie83].

18.2 Histogram Entropy Thresholding

We now define an alternative algorithm for threshold determination using the entropy concept (cf. Sect. 7.8). Let θ be the threshold value g_l for a bipartition of the gray-levels as in (18.3), and let us assume that this threshold induces two distributions for the following sets of formal random variables

$$A_l = \left\{ \frac{p_1}{\sum_{\nu=1}^{l} p_\nu}, \frac{p_2}{\sum_{\nu=1}^{l} p_\nu}, \ldots, \frac{p_l}{\sum_{\nu=1}^{l} p_\nu} \right\}, \quad (18.7)$$

$$B_l = \left\{ \frac{p_{l+1}}{1 - \sum_{\nu=1}^{l} p_\nu}, \frac{p_{l+2}}{1 - \sum_{\nu=1}^{l} p_\nu}, \ldots, \frac{p_L}{1 - \sum_{\nu=1}^{l} p_\nu} \right\}. \quad (18.8)$$

For each set, the entropy can be computed as

$$H(A_l) = -\sum_{\mu=1}^{l} \frac{p_\mu}{\sum_{\nu=1}^{l} p_\nu} \log \frac{p_\mu}{\sum_{\nu=1}^{l} p_\nu} \quad (18.9)$$

and

$$H(B_l) = -\sum_{\mu=l+1}^{L} \frac{p_\mu}{1 - \sum_{\nu=1}^{l} p_\nu} \log \frac{p_\mu}{1 - \sum_{\nu=1}^{l} p_\nu}. \quad (18.10)$$

The optimal threshold for binarization results from the entropy maximization of the complete image, i.e. the sum of the entropy of the distributions A_l and B_l. The index of the discriminating gray-level $g_l = \theta$ is computed, solving the optimization task

$$l' = \underset{l}{\mathrm{argmax}} \ (H(A_l) + H(B_l)). \quad (18.11)$$

Here again, the complexity for computing the required threshold θ is bounded by the number of gray-levels L. An application of this threshold for binarization is visualized in Figure 18.3.

18.3 Multi-Thresholding

If more than one object is superimposed on a homogeneous background such that the gray-level histogram has multiple maxima, the histogram is multimodal. The image should be decomposed into regions with different gray-levels. Each separate object and the background get uniform, but different gray-levels.

A straightforward approach for the computation of the set of thresholds can be done by the optimization of the following multivariate function, which is an obvious generalization of the entropy method of the previous section:

$$\Psi(l_1, l_2, \ldots, l_k) = \log \left(\sum_{\nu=1}^{l_1} p_\nu \right) + \log \left(\sum_{\nu=l_1+1}^{l_2} p_\nu \right) + \ldots + \log \left(\sum_{\nu=l_k+1}^{L} p_\nu \right)$$

$$- \frac{\sum_{\nu=1}^{l_1} p_\nu \log p_\nu}{\sum_{\nu=1}^{l_1} p_\nu} - \frac{\sum_{\nu=l_1+1}^{l_2} p_\nu \log p_\nu}{\sum_{\nu=l_1+1}^{l_2} p_\nu} - \ldots - \frac{\sum_{\nu=l_k+1}^{L} p_\nu \log p_\nu}{\sum_{\nu=l_k+1}^{L} p_\nu} \quad (18.12)$$

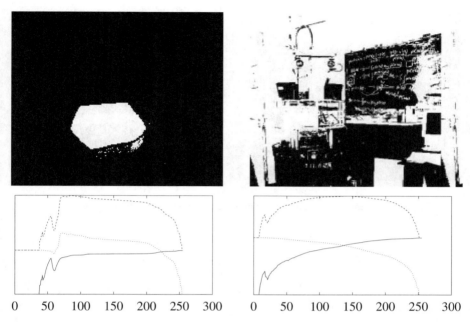

Figure 18.3: Binary image created from Figure 1.2 (threshold 85 left) and from Figure 1.2 (threshold 139 right) with entropy analysis. The plots show the values for $H(A_l)$ and $H(B_l)$ (eqn. 18.9) as well as the sum $H(A_l) + H(B_l)$.

where the number k of different gray-levels must be known a priori. We simply sum up the entropies of the partition and maximize this sum. The set of thresholds is computed by solving the following discrete optimization problem:

$$(l'_1, l'_2, \ldots, l'_k) = \underset{(l_1, l_2, \ldots, l_k)}{\mathrm{argmax}}\ \Psi(l_1, l_2, \ldots, l_k) \quad . \tag{18.13}$$

A simple and non-sophisticated implementation will do a recursive maximization of objective function (18.12) with respect to the unknown parameters $l_1, l_2, \ldots, l_k$. Figure 18.4 shows examples for multi-thresholding.

18.4 Global Histogram Equalization

Normally, the distribution of range values is a priori unknown. One possible way to get information about the underlying statistics of the gray-levels of an image is the computation of the relative frequency of possible values in the observed sample. Histograms render possible graphical representations of these frequencies. The discrete distribution of these quantities is shown in an empirical distribution by adding the relative frequencies successively from left

Figure 18.4: Images created from Figure 1.2 using multi-thresholding ($k = 5, 15$)

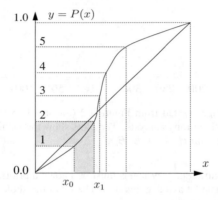

Figure 18.5: Linearization of discrete distributions

to right. Figure 7.1 already a histogram of gray-levels and the associated discrete empirical distribution for the image on p. 3.

The transformation of histograms is quite easy. A frequently used technique in the pre-processing phase of image analysis systems is gray-level scaling using histograms and the associated discrete distributions. The discrete or continuous distribution is adapted to a special distribution – for example, uniform distribution – with the help of a distortion function. For this, the y–axis is divided up into equidistant intervals and reflected onto the x–axis. In Figure 18.5 all gray-levels in the interval $[x_0, x_1[$ are mapped to the new value 2. In Figure 18.6 the result of the described linearization is shown, including the gray-level image, the distribution, and the resulting histogram. The distribution is not exactly linear due to quantization, but the differences in the gray-level frequencies are considerable compared to Figure 7.1.

Practically established transformations based on histograms are the linear or logarithmic representation of speech signals with eight bits, which are given with twelve bits. In image process-

18.5 Local Histogram Equalization

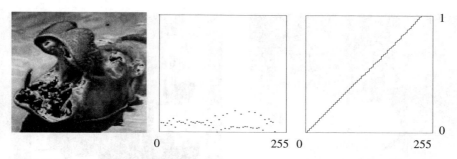

Figure 18.6: Results of linearization on image shown on p. 3 using 64 intervals, frequencies, and cummulative histogram of gray-levels.

ing, the distortion of gray-levels is used e.g. to raise the contrast of a picture. A higher contrast of the image causes the visual impression that the image is more suitable for automatic processing. Indeed, the histogram linearization does not increase the information of an image. If programs work well on linearized images but yield no or bad results for the original images, it shows that the implementation depends on hard encoded thresholds that expect higher contrasts. Well implemented and robust image processing operators usually do not show such dependencies.

18.5 Local Histogram Equalization

The principle of local histogram linearization is to use a window of size $M \times M$ instead of the complete image. The transformation of the central pixel in the window is found by equalizing the histogram of the local window. The discrete density function p_ν is defined by the relative frequencies of each gray-level g_ν in the mask. The discrete distribution function is known to be

$$P(g_l) \;=\; \sum_{\nu=1}^{l} p_\nu \;. \tag{18.14}$$

Due to the small window size, the histogram equalization transformation τ over the given window, which maps gray-levels to gray-levels, is now approximated by

$$\tau(f_{i,j}) \;=\; \lfloor g_{\max} P(f_{i,j}) \rfloor \tag{18.15}$$

for the central pixel at the point (i,j). Herein $g_{\max}$ is the maximal gray-level of the considered window. After this transform the gray-levels of the considered window are uniformly distributed over elements of $\{1, 2, \ldots, g_{\max}\}$. This result is based on the fact that the random variable $x = P(f)$ is uniformly distributed, where $P(f)$ denotes an arbitrary cumulative distribution for gray-levels f. This is true, because the cumulative density $P_x(x)$ of the random variable $x \in [0,1]$ is monotonic and thus holds

$$P_x(x) \;=\; p(P(f) \leq x) = p(f \leq P^{-1}(x)) = P(P^{-1}(x)) = x \;. \tag{18.16}$$

In Figure 18.7 you can find an example of local histogram equalization.

Figure 18.7: Result of local histogram equalization on Figure 1.2 (left) and Figure 1.2 (right) with window size 5×5

18.6 Look-up Table Transformation

The transformation of gray-levels via histograms is often used as a pre-processing step. Another transform of gray-levels g can be defined by a function $\tau(g) \in \{0, 1, \ldots, 255\}$, for instance, a univariate polynomial.

Two functions $\tau_1(g)$ and $\tau_2(g)$ in Figure 18.8 describe the assignment of each gray-level of the original image (g–axis) to the new value. The distortion in this example is based on a polygon or a third order polynomial

$$\tau(g) = \sum_{i=0}^{3} \lambda_i \, g^i \qquad (18.17)$$

which is determined by four points $(0, a), (b, c), (d, e)$, and $(255, f)$.

The computation of the coefficients can be done by solving the system of linear equations:

$$\begin{aligned} a &= \lambda_0, & (18.18) \\ c &= \lambda_0 + \lambda_1 b + \lambda_2 b^2 + \lambda_3 b^3, & (18.19) \\ e &= \lambda_0 + \lambda_1 d + \lambda_2 d^2 + \lambda_3 d^3, \text{ and} & (18.20) \\ f &= \lambda_0 + 255\lambda_1 + 255^2\lambda_2 + 255^3\lambda_3. & (18.21) \end{aligned}$$

A solution of the parameters is given in Appendix C.1. An application of this technique is shown in Figure 18.9.

The look-up table transform introduced can be defined by arbitrary functions and is, of course, not restricted to polynomials. An exponential mapping of the intensity is used in color imaging; this transformation is called *gamma correction*. This mapping reverses the non-linear sensitivity of the human eye to intensity. For computer vision purposes, it is often convenient to invert this mapping which is built-in to many cameras, in order to get a linear response.

18.7 Histogram Classes

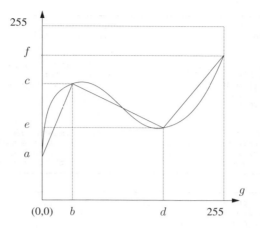

Figure 18.8: Correction of gray-levels

Figure 18.9: Result of a look-up table transform with polyline ($a = 50, b = 70, c = 90, d = 144, e = 200, f = 100$) on Figure 1.2 (left) and Figure 1.2 (right)

18.7 Histogram Classes

The previous sections show that there are a lot of operations on histograms which can naturally be implemented as a class `Histogram`. The concrete representation and computation of histograms is hidden from its users. A suitable header file for this class is given below (Listing 184). The internal representation of a histogram is based on a vector of integers, i.e. `Vector<int>`. The index represents the current gray-level and the associated entry the number of occurrences in the given image.

```
class Histogram {                           // class for 1-D histograms
  Vector<int> bins;                         // absolute frequencies
  long nelem;                               // number of entries
 public:
  Histogram(int);                           // number of bins
  Histogram(const Histogram &);             // copy constructor
  double operator[] (int i) const;          // relative frequency of occurrence i
  void addto(int i, int v = 1);             // advance bin i to a value v
  long at(int i) const;                     // return bin i
};
int bimodal_threshold(const Histogram&);    // minimum between two maxima
int least_square_threshold(const Histogram&); // least square method
int max_entropy_threshold(const Histogram&);  // entropy method
void smooth(Histogram&);                    // smooth the histogram
```
184

```
double Histogram::operator[] (int i) const {return bins[i]/(1.0*nelem); }
void Histogram::addto(int i, int v) { nelem +=v; bins[i] += v; }
Histogram::Histogram(int nb) : bins(nb) { nelem = 0; }
```
185

The detailed implementation of each method is easily done by applying the explanations given so far. One example is shown in Listing 185. Extending the ideas of Sect. 17.9 we create an interface to a class hierarchy for binarization in Listing 186.

18.8 Color Quantization

Histogram equalization was used to create images with linear distribution of gray-levels. A somewhat similar principle is used in the so called *median cut algorithm* for color images [Hec82]. The general aim here is the reduction of the number of possible color vectors (e.g. in RGB). For example, one wants to represent an image with 256 colors instead of the maximally possible 2^{24} color combinations. The basic idea is that each of the coded color values should occur with approximately the same frequency in the new image.

The procedure is as follows: initially, all colors of a color look-up table are combined in a so called *box*. This box is then recursively partitioned until the desired number of boxes (each representing a new color) is reached. For that purpose, inside each box we choose one of the three coordinate directions for which the color values vary the most, i.e., for which the difference of the minimal and maximal value or the statistical variance is maximal. The vectors in the box are sorted in ascending order for this coordinate. The median of this list is used to split the box into two new boxes which again are subject to the same procedure. Therein, all color vectors inside a box are represented by their mean vector. This is a special case of a

```
class Binarize : public IP_OP {
public:
    virtual int operator() (const Histogram &, GrayLevelImage &) = 0;
};
```
186

Figure 18.10: Median cut algorithm applied to the image in Figure 11.3 left with 128, 64, and 8 output colors

so called *vector quantization* which encodes a cluster of vectors by one representative vector (cf. Sect. 22.2).

An example of this algorithm on a color image (here printed as gray-level image) is shown in Figure 18.10.[1] Alternative color quantization algorithms use simple modifications of standard vector quantization methods that are widely used in speech processing and coding [Fuk90]. Another highly efficient algorithm for color quantization, which applies similar statistical criteria for clustering, can be found, for instance, in [Wu91]; herein the reduction of color is optimized through a linear search process.

18.9 Histogram Back-Projection

Another algorithm primarily used with color histograms is the so called *histogram back-projection algorithm* [Swa91]. This algorithm can localize a known object in a scene based on its color appearance. For that purpose we need histograms which are represented by a sequence of relative frequencies for color values. Since the color spaces are large, we define so called *bins* which combine several possible color values. For instance, in the histogram $H = [H_k]_{k=1...K}$ H_k represents the probability to observe a color value of the k-th bin. We are free to choose an appropriate value for the number of bins K. For example, we can split the usual RGB color space from 2^{24} possible values into $K = 512$ bins of size $8 \times 8 \times 8$.

For the object o to be localized, we first need an image from which we compute the histogram $T = [T_k]_{k=1...K}$. Then we try to find this object in the scene s for which we again compute a histogram R. The algorithm uses the following definitions:

---

[1] Of course, the images are printed here as gray-level images. On the slides (Sect. B.5) you can see them in full color!

Given: image histogram $T = [T_k]_{k=1...K}$ of an object,
Wanted: object position (i_t, j_t)
Compute color histogram $H = [H_k]_{k=1...K}$ of given image
FOR each bin $k \in \{1, \ldots, K\}$
$\quad R_k = \min\{\frac{T_k}{H_k}, 1\}$ (compute ratio histogram $R = [R_k]_{k=1...K}$)
FOR all positions (i, j) in the image
$\quad A_{i,j} := R_{h(\boldsymbol{f}_{i,j})}$, where $\boldsymbol{f}_{i,j}$ denotes the color vector at position (i, j)
$B := D_r \star A$, where $\star$ denotes convolution
$(i_t, j_t) := \mathrm{argmax}_{i,j}(B_{i,j})$

Figure 18.11: Histogram back-projection algorithm

- ratio histogram $R = [R_k]_{k=1...K}$ with $R_k := \min\{\frac{T_k}{H_k}, 1\}$
- $h(c)$ maps each color vector c to a color-bin in the histogram
- a mask $D_r = [1]_{1 \leq i,j < r}$ representing the size of the object, or some other mask D_r describing the shape of the object at size r

The algorithm is shown in Figure 18.11. This simple and fast idea can be similarly applied to 2–D or 3–D histograms in various color spaces or components, such as RGB, UV, or H. Examples are shown in Figure 18.12: the interest map on the bottom right is inverted so that black points correspond to positions where it is very likely to find the desired object.

Figure 18.12 shows an example object on the top, a scene on the bottom left and the back-projection in the UV color space on the bottom right. The red part of the object is clearly visible.

Exercises

18.a Implement a complete class `Histogram`. The methods should include all algorithms described so far, i.e. smoothing, global histogram linearization, and local histogram equalization.

18.b Write utilities for the visualization of histograms and the discrete distribution function of gray-levels.

18.c Prove that (18.5) is equivalent to

$$J_l = \frac{p(^l\Omega_1)\sum_{\nu=1}^{L} g_\nu p_\nu - \sum_{\nu=1}^{l} g_\nu p_\nu}{p(^l\Omega_1)(1 - p(^l\Omega_1))}. \quad (18.22)$$

18.d Generalize the least square threshold technique (Sect. 18.1) for solving the multi-threshold problem (Sect. 18.3).

18.e Show that the multi-threshold computation is bounded by $\binom{L+k-1}{k}$ evaluations of $\Psi(l_1, l_2, \ldots, l_k)$.

18.f Extend Exercise 15.c such that you use histogram equalization to transform the edge strength to 256 gray-levels.

18.9 Histogram Back-Projection

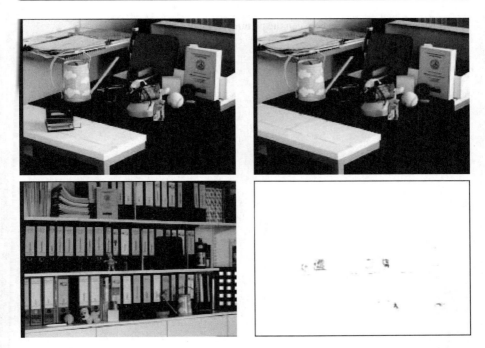

Figure 18.12: Histogram back-projection examples: red object to be found results from difference of the two images on the top, scene (bottom left), back-projection (bottom right) shows red objects

18.g Do you think it is useful to apply global histogram equalization for the binarization of images? Why?

18.h Why is the function in Figure 18.6 (right) not exactly linear?

18.i Often, matrices of floating point elements are created during image processing, e.g. when the power spectrum is computed. The problem arises, of how to visualize these values as gray levels.
The idea of histogram linerarization (Sect. 18.4) is that each gray level in the displayed image has (approximately) the same number of occurences. The same is true for the color quantization algorithm (Sect. 18.8).
A simple algorithm for displaying floating point numbers is the following:

(a) Sort all values in the matrix in ascending order creating a linear list.

(b) Split that list into n parts of equal length, where n is the number of desired gray-levels.

(c) Determine the borders of the intervals defined by those n parts.

(d) Remap your input image to n gray-levels using those intervals.

Find an efficient implementation of this idea.

18.j Find ten differences between the pictures in Figure 18.10!

Chapter 19
Edges and Lines

Various principles for pre-processing methods which create edge images from gray-level images could be seen in Chapter 15. As already outlined in Sect. 15.1, further algorithms for edge detection and line segmentation exist. Some of them will be introduced in this chapter. Especially some line detection algorithms which are based on connecting edge elements will be discussed. The optimal line detector for a given edge image depends upon the image data and on the subsequent processing steps. There is, in general, no way of defining an universally optimal method for line segmentation. Which type of segmentation algorithm has to be used depends on the given application. Under certain assumptions, however, an optimal detector can be defined (Sect. 19.9).

19.1 More Edge Detectors

The masks in Sect. 15.3 and 15.8 were used to compute discrete derivatives of bivariate intensity functions by the convolution of image functions and masks.

Another approach to edge detection is the application of several edge masks which represent typical shapes or directions of edges; a convolution of the image function with these masks will yield a large response if an edge of the expected form and direction is present at the actual position in the image. Figure 19.1 shows four elementary masks of size 3×3 which define the *Robinson operator* [Rob77]. For every pixel of the image, all four masks are applied; the greatest response is used as the edge strength. The four masks represent edge directions of 0, 45, 90, and 135 degrees. The sign of the response can be used to extend the directions to the range 180...360 degrees. Figure 19.2 shows one result of this operator. The orientation image has only the values $0, 18, 36, 54, \ldots 144$.

Another operator, which also allows the computation of edge strength and edge orientation, is introduced in [Nev80]. It uses six masks of size 5×5 which detect twelve orientations; three masks are shown in Figure 19.3, the others result from a rotation by 90 degrees and from a mirrored version of the masks. The relatively large masks will smooth the image implicitly; the operator is thus less sensitive to small changes in the image intensities than, for example, the

1	2	1		2	1	0		0	-1	-2		1	0	-1
0	0	0		1	0	-1		1	0	-1		2	0	-2
-1	-2	-1		0	-1	-2		2	1	0		1	0	-1

Figure 19.1: Mask definition for the Robinson operator.

Figure 19.2: Robinson operator on Figure 1.2: strength and orientation

Robinson-operator. The result of the Nevatia/Babu operator is shown in Figure 19.4. Further operators of this type are, for example, by Prewitt [Pre70] and Ritter [Rit86].

Another type of edge detection algorithms uses parametric models for edges instead of mask operators, which compute discrete derivatives. The image intensity function is compared to the model function and the parameters are tuned to an optimal fit according to an error criterion. The classical algorithm of this type was published by Hückel in [Hue73]. Such methods are, however, computationally expensive and used only for special applications.

Several other ideas for edge detection have been published and tested. Indeed, many applications take advantage of edge detectors which operate in the frequency domain using the

100	100	100	100	100		100	100	100	100	100		100	100	100	-32	-100
100	100	100	100	100		100	100	100	78	-32		100	100	92	-78	-100
0	0	0	0	0		100	92	0	-92	-100		100	100	0	-100	-100
-100	-100	-100	-100	-100		32	-78	-100	-100	-100		100	78	-92	-100	-100
-100	-100	-100	-100	-100		-100	-100	-100	-100	-100		100	32	-100	-100	-100

0°　　　　　　　　　　　　　30°　　　　　　　　　　　　　60°

Figure 19.3: Mask definition according to Nevatia and Babu

Figure 19.4: Nevatia/Babu operator on Figure 1.2: strength and orientation

2–D Fourier transform. High frequencies correspond to sharp edges in the spatial domain. In general, edges can be found using a high-pass filter [Ros82]. A detailed discussion of these algorithms is out of the scope of this book.

Statistical classification principles can also be used for edge detection (e.g., in [Har88]). So-called *multi scale algorithms* use different spatial resolutions for edge detection (e.g., [Mar80]).

19.2 Edge Thinning

Due to the presence of noise in an image, most edge detectors will erroneously indicate a possible edge at many points. In addition, edges in the images are normally neither ideal step edges (Figure 15.1) nor roof edges (i.e., edge profiles looking like the roof of a house) but instead are blurred or disturbed due to sensor and quantization noise. Edge operators will thus find many false edges in the neighborhood of a real edge. Therefore, real edges appear smeared. Edge operators like the Sobel operator (Sect. 15.3) will create two edges in the edge image — even for an ideal step edge in the intensity image.

In order to facilitate the connection of edge points to lines, it is useful to eliminate some edge points after edge detection. Three algorithms will be presented in the following. They transform an edge image into a new edge image. The actual position (i, j) in the edge image will be called the point P. We compute the following values which can be directly mapped to the members in the class Edge and EdgeImage:

- $f(P)$ the gray-value at point P,
- $s(P)$ the edge strength at point P,
- $r(P)$ the edge orientation at point P, and
- $S_{\max} = \max_P s(P)$ the maximal edge strength in the image.

The simplest method for reduction of weak edge elements is to use a global threshold. All edges with strength below the threshold will be removed, i.e., their edge strength will be set to

 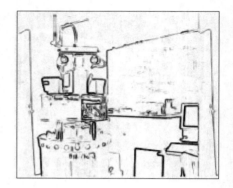

Figure 19.5: Thresholded image of Figure 19.4 On the left: threshold of 10 %, on the right: threshold of 20% (images inverted)

zero. Usually, this method is too simple. Thresholds have to be chosen differently for every image in order to get reasonably good results. A slightly better technique is to use a threshold relative to maximum edge strength in the image:

$$s'(P) := \begin{cases} s(P) & , \quad \text{if } s(P) > \gamma \cdot S_{\max} \\ 0 & , \quad \text{otherwise} \end{cases} \quad (19.1)$$

The parameter γ can be set globally for an image. Since this method uses the maximal edge strength, it can be applied to an edge image no matter which edge operator was used to create it.[1] The result of this operation is shown in Figure 19.5.

The algorithms for **Non–Maxima Suppression** (NMS) use the local context of an edge position for edge thinning. Preferably those edge points are taken into consideration that are close to the edge gradient, i.e., in an orthogonal direction to the edge orientation. If these neighbors have the same orientation as the actual point, they will most likely belong to the same edge in the intensity image. The goal is now to select the *best* among these points and to suppress others. An edge point is simply removed if its strength is smaller than those of its neighbors having the same orientation.

A two-phase implementation is proposed in [Nev80]: the edge image is scanned, and an internal label image is created of the same size. For every edge element P the neighbors N_L and N_R (Figure 19.6) are located. The following conditions are tested, where S_{th} is an appropriate lower threshold for the edge strength and 30° delimits the maximum difference in angle of the orientation:

- $s(P) \geq s(N_L)$ and $s(P) \geq s(N_R)$,
- $(|r(P) - r(N_L)| \bmod 180°) < 30°$, and $(|r(P) - r(N_R)| \bmod 180°) < 30°$, and
- $s(P) > S_{\text{th}}$.

---

[1] Remember, the edge strength in an edge image is not normalized. Different operators will have completely different ranges of the edge strength!

9.2 Edge Thinning

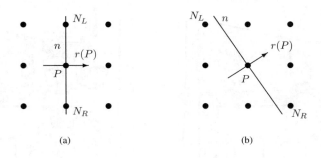

Figure 19.6: Edge thinning according to Nevatia/Babu

Figure 19.7: NMS image Figure 19.4 Left: threshold 10%, right: threshold 20% (images inverted for visualization)

If all three conditions are true, P is marked in a label image of the same size as the input image, and N_L and N_R are marked as *excluded*.

The label image is then scanned; a new edge image is created; all edge elements marked in the label image that are not simultaneously excluded will be included in the output image. The result of NMS is shown in Figure 19.7.

The **Non-Maxima Absorption** (NMA) is also an iterative edge thinning method. Rather than eliminating some edge elements — as in the previous methods — the idea here is to shift edge strength from the smaller edge elements to the bigger ones. The basic ground rules are:

- if the edge strength in P is the biggest of the three, then $\alpha \cdot (s(N_L) + s(N_R))$ of the strength of its neighbors is added to the strength of P;
- if the edge strength in P is the smallest of the three, then it will be reduced by $2 \cdot \alpha \cdot s(P)$;

Figure 19.8: NMA image Figure 19.4. Left: threshold 10%, right: threshold 20%

is_closed	if start is equal to end
is_start	starts a line
is_end	ends a line
is_edge	is an edge (no matter whether strength is high)
is_vertex	several lines meet here

Table 19.1: Flags for structure edge

- if P has one neighbor P^+ with a larger strength, and another one P^- with a smaller strength value, then the strength of P will be reduced by $\alpha \cdot s(P^+)$ and increased by $\alpha \cdot s(P^-)$.

This will be done only if the orientations are similar. A difference in edge orientation of ≤ 30 degrees turns out to be a feasible value. The result of this method is shown in Figure 19.8.

In our first version of an implementation for the class Edge in (Listing 196) some bits of the storage were unused. In Table 19.1 we list several flag values which can be associated with an edge element and which can be stored in the remaining storage space of an Edge object.

These new features will be used in next sections. Listing 187 shows how they are incorporated in the class for edges (Listing 146). Special care has to be taken for the external representation of edge objects. The order of bit fields is machine dependent; thus, the value of all may not be used for external storage.[2]

A simple implementation of the Sobel operator (Sect. 15.3) and the Prewitt operator (Sect. 19.1) using this edge class is declared in Listing 188 and implemented in Listing 189. As already mentioned in Sect. 15.2, a simplified version of the arctan function could be used in the auxiliary function geto in Listing 189. The maximum possible value for the edge strength computed by this operator is included as a static variable in the class and can be used to set the corresponding value in the edge image (Sect. 15.6).

---

[2]That means that the method storeOn for the class EdgeImage has to code the flags into an integer value using bit operations

9.2 Edge Thinning

```
struct Edge_V1 {
   static const int ONUM;          // constants in class-scope
   static const float odunit, orunit;
   union {                         // anonymous union
     unsigned int all;
     struct {
       unsigned int f_strength : 16;
       unsigned int f_orient   :  8;
       unsigned int is_closed  :  1; // see table
       unsigned int is_start   :  1; // see table
       unsigned int is_end     :  1; // see table
       unsigned int is_edge    :  1; // see table
       unsigned int is_vertex  :  1; // see table
       unsigned int successor  :  3; // used later
     } fields ;
   };
   Edge_V1() { all = 0; }    // clear
   // etc.
};
#if defined(EDGE_VERS) && (EDGE_VERS == 1)
typedef class Edge_V1 Edge;
#endif
```

```
struct Sobel: public EdgeDet {   // Sobel operator as a special case
   static const int maxStrength;  //  = 2040;
   virtual void operator() (const GrayLevelImage&,EdgeImage&) ;
};
struct Prewitt : public EdgeDet {  // Prewitt edge operator
   static const int maxStrength;   //  = 1020;
   virtual void operator() (const GrayLevelImage&,EdgeImage&) ;
};
```

```
namespace { // unnamed namepace
const int Edge_V1::ONUM = 144;         // discretization for angle
const int Sobel::maxStrength = 2040;   // maximum value for 0 - 255 edge

static int geto(int fx, int fy)        // get orientation from x and y
{
 return (((fx==0) && (fy==0)) ? Edge_V1::ONUM+1 :
         int((M_PI+ atan2(fy,fx)) / Edge_V1::ONUM));
}

void Sobel::operator() (const GrayLevelImage& in,EdgeImage& out)
{
  out.Max(Sobel::maxStrength);                          // set max strength
  for (int i = 1 ; i < in.SizeY()-1; ++i) {             // rows
    for (int j = 1 ; j < in.SizeX()-1; ++j) {           // columns
      int fx= -in[i-1][j-1] - 2*in[i][j-1] - in[i+1][j-1]   // horizontal
            + in[i-1][j+1] + 2*in[i][j+1] + in[i+1][j+1];   //
      int fy= -in[i-1][j-1] - 2*in[i-1][j] - in[i-1][j+1]   // vertical
            + in[i+1][j-1] + 2*in[i+1][j] + in[i+1][j+1];
      out[i][j].fields.f_strength = int(fabs(fx) + fabs(fy)); // convert
      out[i][j].fields.f_orient   = geto(fy,fx);              // gradient
    }                                                         // to angle
  }                                                           // and strength
};
} // end unnamed namespace
```

19.3 Line Detection

After edge detection with one of the various edge operators, edge elements may still be isolated or scattered in space. In order to detect continuous lines, these edge elements have to be connected and gaps have to be closed. Groups of edge elements are connected to lines.

The chain code representation introduced now is a common representation for lines and very close to the pixel raster data. This representation uses the start point of a line and a sequence of numbers from the interval 0 ... 7 which indicate the next point in the line, called *links*. This is exemplified in Figure 19.9. The information about the intensity of a line along a chain code is lost.[3]

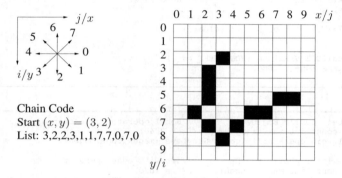

Figure 19.9: Definition of the directions in a chain code and example for a line represented by a chain code

For simple line detection based on edge images, we now compute three additional values for each element of the edge image:

- We number all the lines found in the image. The first number is a label for the line that the edge element belongs to. A temporary label field is needed for this purpose (a matrix of integers).
- The second value is a chain code number pointing from the actual edge element to the potential successor. The edge class was already extended for that reason (Sect. 19.2).
- The flag field in the edge class will contain information about features of the edge as indicated in Table 19.1.

The so-called *local connectivity analysis* can be used to connect edge elements to lines. The neighborhood of an edge element is searched for potential line elements.

Nevatia and Babu [Nev80] propose a parallel and a sequential component for the algorithm. In the parallel part (Figure 19.11), we inspect a 8–neighborhood of each edge point. As shown in Figure 19.10, three points N_1, N_2 and N_3 will be used, which are closest to the inspected edge

---
[3] We will, however, record the mean intensity difference — the so called contrast — along the line in an attribute of the base class HipposObj.(Sect. 24.2).

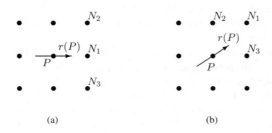

Figure 19.10: Neighborhood for line following [Nev80].

direction $r(P)$ of the actual point P. The successor of P is selected from these points based on the most similar edge direction $r(P)$. If more than one point have similar directions, the one with the highest edge strength will be chosen. If all three neighbors show similar directions and strengths, the point closest to the edge direction — in Figure 19.10 this is always called N_1 — of pixel P is chosen. This direction is recorded as a chain code in the field `successor`.

In the next (serial) step, all marked edge points will be grouped to lines (Figure 19.12). The image is scanned line by line to find potential start points for lines. If the edge strength at the actual position exceeds a given threshold and if the actual point does not yet belong to another line, it is marked as a start point of a new line; a new line label is created. Using the successor field, the line is then tracked through the image until the path reaches a position with an edge strength that is too low, or a position that belongs to another line already. All these points are marked with the same line label. The lines, represented as chain code objects, have to be somehow stored in a data structure. We will discuss this in Sect. 24.3. Since this algorithm tries to connect *all* edge points to lines, it is essential to apply line thinning before line tracking.

19.4 Hysteresis Thresholds

The use of larger contexts for edge localization may enhance the recognition, but also increases the computational complexity of the problem. Instead of considering small neighborhoods for edge detection, the whole context along the line can be important for line detection.

Two thresholds for the edge strength are used in the so-called *hysteresis algorithm*: an upper threshold θ_o and a lower threshold θ_l. These parameters are coupled by a factor β according to

$$\theta_l = \beta \theta_o \quad . \tag{19.2}$$

Good results can be obtained with β in the range of 0.3 to 0.5. Experimental evaluation in [Brü90] showed that the choice of β is not critical for the result. A default value of $\beta = 0.33$ is reasonable.

After an edge thinning step, all those positions in the edge image which have an edge strength higher than θ_o are chosen as candidates for a start of a line. Each start point is tracked in

	Search for edge point P_{act} which does not belong to any segment.			
	Assign to P_{act}: new number *SegNum* and label "has no predecessor".			
	IF	P_{act} has a successor $c(P_{act})$		
	THEN	Choose point P_N which is successor of P_{act} reachable by $c(P_{act})$.		
	ELSE	**Try to jump over gaps of one pixel** (Sect. 19.5)		
		Compute potential successors $N_i \in \{N_1, N_2, N_3\}$ of P_{act}, and for all N_i the potential successors N_{i1}, N_{i2} and N_{i3} (Figure 19.10).		
		Search for the first point N_{ij}, where $i, j \in \{1, 2, 3\}$ and: $(|r(N_i) - r(P_{act})| \bmod 180°) < 30$ degrees $\wedge$ $(|r(N_{ij}) - r(N_i)| \bmod 180°) < 30$ degrees $\wedge$ chain code element $c(N_{ij})$ (i.e., there exists a successor of N_{ij}).		
		IF	N_{ij} is found (i.e., closing of gaps succeeded)	
		THEN	Connect (P_{act}) and N_i. Let next point P_N be N_{ij}.	
		ELSE	No successor P_N of P_{act} is found (end of segment).	
	IF	Successor P_N of P_{act} is found		
	THEN	IF	P_N has already a segment number S_N	
		THEN	IF	S_N is equal to *SegNum*
			THEN	P_{act} is labeled by "end cycle". Label P_N "start cycle".
			End of segment is reached.	
		ELSE	P_N gets actual segment number *SegNum*.	
			Let P_N be the new actual point P_{act}.	
	UNTIL End of segment is reached..			
UNTIL Each edge point has a segment number (i.e., all image points are traversed).				
Label segments with new numbers (Figure 19.12).				

Figure 19.11: Parallel part of line following algorithm according to [Nev80].

both directions — along the edge orientation and in the opposite direction. Candidates for successors are selected as illustrated in Figure 19.10.

In order to be accepted as a line element, a candidate has to fulfill three conditions:

- the edge strength has to be greater than the lower threshold θ_l,
- the orientation in the actual position P must be similar to the candidate's orientation, and
- the candidate may not be a member of another line.

If more than one candidate fulfill all three conditions, the one with the highest edge strength is chosen. This can happen in only two cases. In the first case, these candidates belong to the same line and have not been eliminated by the edge thinning phase. Such points should not be used as members of other lines: their edge strength is reduced to a value below the upper limit θ_o. In the second case, candidates belong to different lines, their edge strength should be high enough to allow further inclusion into another line. Therefore it will be set to $\theta_l(1 + \epsilon)$, where $\epsilon = 0.01$. This is illustrated in Figure 19.13–19.15.

New number for each segment:
Let new segment number *NewSegNum* = 0.
FOR All points P_a with the label "has no predecessor" or "start cycle"
Increment *NewSegNum*.
Choose successor of P_a as next point P_N reachable by $c(P_a)$.
Set the segment number of P_N to *NewSegNum*.
Let P_N be the new actual point P_a.
UNTIL There exists no successor of P_a (i.e., $c(P_a)$ has no value) $\vee$ P_a is labeled by "end cycle").

Figure 19.12: Serial part of line following algorithm according to [Nev80] cont.

Search for one edge point P without a segment number, where the edge strength $s(P)$ is greater than the upper threshold θ_o. Call this point P_{act} and assign to this point the not yet used segment number *SegNum*.
Search forward
Set the actual point P_{act} to the start point P.
Search backward
UNTIL All edge points are processed (i.e., traverse the whole image).

Figure 19.13: Line following with the hysteresis algorithm (1) [Brü90]

19.5 Closing of Gaps

After the lines have been followed as outlined above, an attempt can be made to close small gaps which result from errors or noise in the edge image. The goal of this step is to combine lines which are separated by few (here: up to two) pixels.

For each line found in the image, the end is inspected and the points shown in Figure 19.16 are searched for possible start or end points of another line. The positions will be visited in the order given by the numbers. The points are shown for an edge orientation of $r(P) = 0°$ in Figure 19.16 (a) and for $r(P) = 45°$ in Figure 19.16 (b). Similar neighbor masks can be used for other directions.

Usually, small segments are discarded in a final processing step, e.g., all those chain codes shorter than three pixels.

19.6 Zero-Crossings in Laplace Images

The Laplace operator (Sect. 15.8) will generate an edge image with zero-crossings corresponding to lines in the intensity image. These have to be located. Since we have to deal with images, zero-crossings of a two-dimensional function have to be found.

Search forward		
	Compute possible successors $N_i \in \{N_1, N_2, N_3\}$ of P_{act} of the direction $r(P_{act})$ (Figure 19.10).	
	Compute successor N_i, where: $s(N_i) > \theta_l \quad \wedge \quad (\|r(N_i) - r(P_{act})\| \mod° 180) < 30$ degrees $\wedge \quad \{N_i$ has no segment number $\vee \; N_i = P$ (= start point of the segment)$\}$.	
IF	Successor N_i was found	
THEN	IF	One point is P (start point of the line)
	THEN	A cyclic period is found. Connect P_{act} and P. The start and end of the segment is reached.
	ELSE	Let N be the candidate with maximum $s(N_i)$. Connect N and P_{act}. Let N be the actual point P_{act}. Let N be the temporary end point P_e.
	Reduce the set of non-processed candidates $s(N_i)$ to $\theta_l + \epsilon$.	
ELSE	End of segment is reached.	
UNTIL	End of segment is reached.	

Figure 19.14: Line following with the hysteresis algorithm (2) [Brü90]

Search backward		
	Determine potential predecessors $V_i \in \{V_1, V_2, V_3\}$ of P_{act} with the orientation $r(P_{act}) + 180$ degrees according to Figure 19.10.	
	Compute the predecessor V_i, where: $s(V_i) > \theta_l \quad \wedge \quad (\|r(V_i) - r(P_{act})\| \mod 180°) < 30$ degrees $\wedge \quad \{V_i$ has no segment number $\vee \; V_i = P_e$ (= end point of the segment)$\}$.	
IF	Predecessor V_i is found	
THEN	IF	One of the candidates is P_e (end point of the line)
	THEN	Cyclic period is found. Connect P and P_{act}. The start point of the segment is reached.
	ELSE	Let V be the candidate with maximum $s(V_i)$. Connect V and P_{act}. Let V be the actual point P_{act}.
	Reduce the set of non-processed points $s(V_i)$ to $\theta_l + \epsilon$.	
ELSE	Start of the segment is reached.	
UNTIL	Start of the segment is reached.	

Figure 19.15: Line following with the hysteresis algorithm (3) [Brü90]

Figure 19.17 shows a diagonal edge with some noise and the corresponding response of the operator (using Figure 15.11, left). One simple algorithm is to locate horizontal and vertical zero-crossings and to mark these points as edges. A heuristic search for tracking these points and generating lines is described in [Mar76].

Another method is to search the neighborhood of a pixel for zero crossings of the same direction (either negative to positive, or vice versa) and connect these points by a chain coded line.

We can also trace the borders of areas in the Laplace image that are defined by the property that they contain only negative values or only positive values. An algorithm for this idea will be introduced in Sect. 20.5.

19.7 Hough Transform

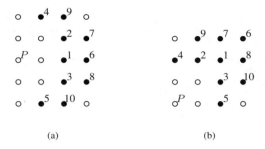

Figure 19.16: Points that will be inspected for gap closing.

```
Input
0    0    0    0    0    0    0
0    0    0    255  255  255  0
0    0    2    255  255  0    0
0    0    255  255  0    0    0
0    254  255  255  10   0    0
0    255  255  0    0    10   0
0    0    0    0    0    0    0
```

```
Output
.      .     .     .     .     .     .
.      0    -257   510   255   765   .
.     -2    -502   253   510  -510   .
.    -509    508   255  -520    0    .
.     506     1    500  -215   -20   .
.     511    510  -510   -20    40   .
.      .     .     .     .     .     .
```

Figure 19.17: Image and Laplacian image

19.7 Hough Transform

The application of the *Hough transform* [Hou62] is one example of an algorithm that generates straight line segments without intermediate chain code representation [Bal82]. The very general idea behind the Hough transform is to express features in a parameterized form; we will use this idea below in the special case where the features to be detected are straight lines which will be computed directly from the edge image. The signal, associated with parameters, is transformed to the *parameter space*. If a feature, for instance, is uniquely defined by a parameter vector, the feature is mapped to a point in the parameter space, and a set of features is mapped to a set of points in the parameter space. The parameter space is sampled and quantized

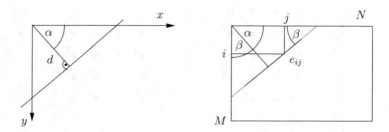

Figure 19.18: A straight line and its parameters d and α of the accumulator array

```
inline int dist(int dmax, int y, int x, int o)
{
   extern int sin_tab[], cos_tab[];   // values of sine and cosine functions
   return dmax + (int)(x*sin_tab[o]+y*cos_tab[o]);   // add offset to sin/cos!
}

/* will work only with latest version of edges*/
void hough(Edge_V1** E, int sizex, int sizey)
{
   const int M = int(1+sqrt(sizex*sizex+sizey*sizey));
   const int N = Edge_V1::ONUM;
   Matrix<int> A(N, 2 * M); A = 0;            // accumulator
   for(int i = sizey-1; i >= 0; --i)
      for(int j = sizex-1; j >= 0; --j) {
         Edge_V1* e = & E[i][j];
         int alpha = int(e->fields.f_orient + (360.0 / N * 90)) % N; // general !
         if (e->fields.f_orient < Edge_V1::ONUM)
            A[dist(M,i,j,e->fields.f_orient)][alpha] += e->fields.f_strength;
      }
}
```

190

and called an *accumulator array*. Occurrences of features are recorded in the accumulator, i.e., all features indicating an object at a certain position increment the value at the corresponding parameter *position* in the parameter space. Local maxima in the accumulator are used as an indication of high frequency of this feature in the image.

This rather theoretical idea can be applied to the detection of straight lines.[4] The lines are expressed in a two-dimensional parameter space by their orientation α and the distance d of the line to the origin (see Figure 19.18 (left)). This representation is preferred to the common description as $y = ax + b$ which parametrizes the line by (a, b), since the values for (α, d) are in a finite range for images of a known size, whereas a is infinite for lines parallel to the y axis.

Assume an input edge image $\boldsymbol{E} = [e_{ij}]_{i=1...M, j=1...N}$ of size $M \times N$. A temporary integer array called the *accumulator* $\boldsymbol{A}$ of dimension $2\sqrt{M^2 + N^2} \times 144$ — this is twice the maximum distance of a line in the image to the origin times the quantized orientation — is initialized to zero.

---

[4] A nice implementation can be found in
http://www.lut.fi/dep/tite/XHoughtool/xhoughtool.html.

9.7 Hough Transform

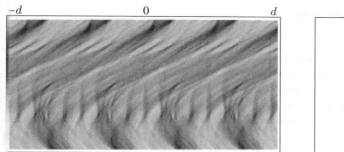

Figure 19.19: Hough accumulator (left) and result of straight line detection with the Hough-Transform of Figure 11.2

For each edge element e_{ij} in the edge image we calculate the parameters of a line that possibly passes through this point $P = (i, j)$. The parameter α is computed from $90° - \beta$, where β is the line orientation $r(P)$. From geometrical considerations, which can be derived from Figure 19.18 (right), the distance d turns out to be $d = i \cos\beta + j \sin\beta$. Since this can result in a negative value for d, we add the maximal value for d to shift the range to positive values and use an accumulator array of the required size.

The two values α and d are used as indices in the accumulator $A[\alpha][d]$ which is incremented by the edge strength $s(P)$. Maximal values in the accumulator are then used as an indication of a straight line in the input image. Listing 190 shows the core of the transform algorithm in C++. Since the angle `alpha` is an integer in the range 0...144, we can use a table for the sine and cosine computations to speed up computation. Listing 190 also shows how the implementation can be kept independent of the quantization for the angle (see the line for the computation of `alpha`).

Some problems in the implementation are the difficulty to find maxima in the accumulator and the fact that non-connected straight lines in the input image create *one* value resp. cluster in the accumulator. After such a maximum has been found, the *edge image* has to be inspected, and the start and end of one or more lines have to be found. A simple method for maxima detection in the Hough accumulator has been proposed in [vdH94]: sequentially, maxima are localized in the accumulator; if the value found exceeds a given threshold, it is recorded and the neighbors in parameter space are cancelled out. This is repeated, until no more new maxima can be found.

An example for lines detected with the Hough transform is shown in Figure 19.19. This result was created with a slightly different implementation where the accumulator was incremented by one for all possible edge directions at those positions exceeding a certain edge threshold.

19.8 Circle Detection

The idea of the Hough transform can be used to detect objects which can be described as parametric curves with more than two parameters. Some restrictions have to be imposed on the parameter space in order to reduce the effort for searching in the accumulator. This way, circles or ellipses [Bal82, Hor93] can be detected.

For the detection of a single circle in an image, we can avoid computationally expansive search in a three-dimensional (x_c, y_c, r) accumulator array which would be induced by the parametric circle description

$$(x - x_c)^2 + (y - y_c)^2 = r^2 \quad . \tag{19.3}$$

In a two-step procedure we proceed as follows: we first search for the centers of possible circles using a Hough transform; then we search for the circle itself in the edge image, where we use the estimated centers and inspect circles with increasing radius around them. The detection of the center is based on the following relation which uses a line representation as $y = ax + b$:

For all straight lines $g_i : y = a_i x + b_i$ which intersect in one point $x = (x_c, y_c)^\mathrm{T}$ we can associate points (a_i, b_i) in a Hough space. These points are all elements of one line in the Hough space.

To prove this, we notice that all lines g_i, $i = 1, \ldots, N$, fulfill the condition

$$y = a_i(x - x_c) + y_c = a_i x + (y_c - a_i x_c) \quad .$$

The associated points for the lines g_i in the Hough space are $(a_i, y_c - a_i x_c)$. These points lie on the line $b_i = -a_i x_c + y_c$ in the Hough space.[5]

The idea now is, to compute the radii of circles in an image which are of the same direction as the gray-level gradient on the circle. For a digital image and for the edge detectors described so far, the direction of the gradient will, however, be not very accurate, i.e., the lines will not intersect in one point. This situation is sketched in Figure 19.20 (left) where some gradient vectors for a crudely digitized circle are drawn. The points in Hough space corresponding to these lines will consequently not lie on one line as sketched in Figure 19.20 (right).

For the line in the Hough space $b = -x_c a + y_c$ which will be used to localize the center of the circle $(x_c, y_c)^\mathrm{T}$, we have to solve a system of linear equations $b_i = -x_c a_i + y_c$ which result from the computations for the gradients in the circle image. Depending on the number of equations used and also the image noise, this system of equations will probably not be solvable. Instead, we follow an elementary algebraic approach and use the *pseudo-inverse matrix* of the linear system of equations above. The minimization of the mean square error for the computation of prediction coefficients can be interpreted in a geometrical manner. We rewrite the system of N equations in the form $b = A\,x$ as

$$b = \begin{pmatrix} -a_1 & 1 \\ -a_2 & 1 \\ \ldots & 1 \\ -a_N & 1 \end{pmatrix} \begin{pmatrix} x_c \\ y_c \end{pmatrix} \quad . \tag{19.4}$$

---

[5]This relation reveals the duality principle for this line representation as $y = a_i x + b_i$, where a point in Hough space corresponds to a line in the image, and vice versa.

19.8 Circle Detection

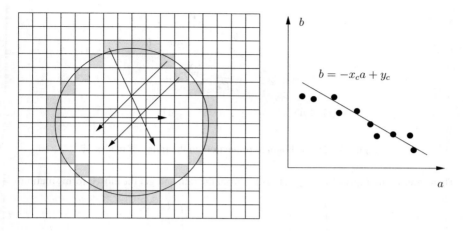

Figure 19.20: Detection of a circle's center with Hough transform

The matrix A defines a linear mapping from $\mathbb{R}^2$ to $\mathbb{R}^N$. More general, we can use this approach to solve any system of linear equations for M unknowns based on N observations; $A \in \mathbb{R}^{N \times M}$ then defines a mapping from $\mathbb{R}^M$ to $\mathbb{R}^N$. If there exists no vector $x = (x_1, x_2, \ldots, x_M)^T$ which satisfies equation (19.4), we conclude that the vector $b = (b_1, b_2, \ldots, b_N)^T$ of sample data is not an element of the range of matrix A. The range

$$\operatorname{im}(A) \;=\; \{v \mid v = Aw, \quad w \in \mathbb{R}^M\} \;\subseteq\; \mathbb{R}^N \tag{19.5}$$

is a sub-vector space of $\mathbb{R}^N$. The minimization of the mean square error is thus equivalent to solving the system of linear equations

$$A x \;=\; P b \;, \tag{19.6}$$

where $P b$ is the orthogonal projection of b onto the sub-space defined by the range of matrix A (Figure 19.21). The orthogonal projection coincides with

$$(A x - b) A v \;=\; 0 \tag{19.7}$$

for all $v \in \mathbb{R}^M$, which is equivalent to

$$(A^T A x - A^T b) v \;=\; 0 \;. \tag{19.8}$$

Since (19.8) has to be valid for *all* vectors v in the domain of matrix A, we conclude that the best parameter vector x with respect to criterion (19.4) can be computed by

$$A^T A x - A^T b = 0 \;. \tag{19.9}$$

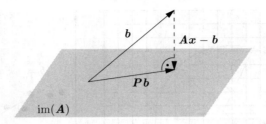

Figure 19.21: Orthogonal projection on the range of matrix A

Therefore, we multiply (19.9) by $\left(A^{\mathrm{T}}A\right)^{-1}$ from the left, and get the closed form solution

$$\begin{pmatrix} x_1 \\ x_2 \\ x_3 \\ \vdots \\ x_M \end{pmatrix} = \left(A^{\mathrm{T}}A\right)^{-1} A^{\mathrm{T}} \begin{pmatrix} b_1 \\ b_2 \\ b_3 \\ \vdots \\ b_M \end{pmatrix} . \quad (19.10)$$

The matrix $A^+ = \left(A^{\mathrm{T}}A\right)^{-1} A^{\mathrm{T}}$ is the *pseudo-inverse* of A.[6]

From a numerical point of view, the computation of the pseudo-inverse using (19.10) is extremely sensitive. For that reason, it is advantageous to use the highly robust *singular value decomposition* instead [Gol97].

The singular value decomposition (SVD) of a matrix $A \in \mathbb{R}^{m \times n}$ computes matrices $U \in \mathbb{R}^{m \times m}$, $\Sigma \in \mathbb{R}^{m \times n}$ and $V \in \mathbb{R}^{n \times n}$ such that

$$A = U \Sigma V^{\mathrm{T}} , \quad (19.11)$$

where U and V are orthogonal matrices and Σ is a diagonal matrix. The non-negative diagonal elements σ_i ($i = 1, 2, \ldots, \min(m, n)$) of Σ are called *singular values* and hold: $\sigma_1 \geq \sigma_2 \geq \ldots \geq \sigma_{\min(m,n)} \geq 0$. Singular values are the square roots of the positive eigenvalues of A. Knowing the singular value decomposition of A the pseudo-inverse is now given by:

$$(A^{\mathrm{T}}A)^{-1} A^{\mathrm{T}} = V \Sigma^+ U^{\mathrm{T}} ,$$

where

$$\Sigma^+ = \begin{pmatrix} 1/\sigma_1 & 0 & \cdots & 0 & 0 & \cdots & 0 \\ 0 & 1/\sigma_2 & \cdots & 0 & 0 & \cdots & 0 \\ \vdots & \vdots & \ddots & \vdots & \vdots & \ddots & 0 \\ 0 & 0 & \cdots & 1/\sigma_r & 0 & \vdots & 0 \\ \vdots & \vdots & \vdots & \vdots & \vdots & \ddots & \vdots \\ 0 & 0 & \cdots & 0 & 0 & \ddots & 0 \end{pmatrix} . \quad (19.12)$$

---

[6]See also Exercise 19.h.

Figure 19.22: Canny operator on Figure 1.2: strength and orientation

Herein σ_r denotes the smallest nonzero singular value.

To conclude our search for circles in the image, we estimate a line from a set of approximatively co-linear points in the accumulator and thereby get the position of the circle's center. We then test various radii around this center and try to optimize the fit of the circle using a criterion which takes into account the edge strength on the circle and the size of the circle. One such choice is to sum up the edge strength on the circle for all those points which have an edge orientation close to the tangent and to divide the sum by the radius. The maximal response is used to determine the final circle.

19.9 Optimal Line Detection

Canny introduced an algorithm for line detection in [Can86] which optimizes the following criteria for the detection lines based on step edges (cf. Figure 15.1) in images:

- *detection,*
- *localization*, and
- *uniqueness.*

This algorithm combines Gaussian-filtering, edge detection, edge thinning, and line detection into an optimal solution for a given type of edge. A complete mathematical description of this idea would be beyond the scope of this book, see [Can86] for details. One principal result of this work is the fact that we cannot maximize these criteria simultaneously. The better the detection is, the worse the localization will be. Resulting lines are shown in Figure 19.23.

Various implementations of this operator can be found in public domain software (cf. Sect. B.3). In most cases a shell has to be built around these routines in order to incorporate them into the object–oriented framework. A result of the Canny edge detection is shown in Figure 19.22.

Although Canny showed the principally optimal solution for edge detection (under certain assumptions), the research still continues. The Deriche-Filter [Der91] and the *operator of Shen*

Figure 19.23: Result of line detection using the algorithm of Sect. 19.4 on Figure 19.22 (left), and on Figure 19.4 (right)

and Castan [She86, She88] also use Gaussian-filters and combined edge detection; the major advantage in comparison to the Canny operator is a more efficient implementation.

Exercises

19.a Which discrete values for the orientation (Sect. 4.5) will be appropriate for the masks in Sect. 19.1?
19.b Estimate minimal, maximal, and *normal* edge strength for the various edge operators.
19.c Implement a fast and machine independent storage routine for the edge elements (Listing 187).
19.d Convert an edge image to a gray-level image using the edge strength. Normalize it to 256 gray-values using histogram equalization.
19.e Implement a class `StrLineSeg` for straight line segments. Derive it from the class `LineRep2D`.
19.f Get public domain versions of various edge detectors and adapt them to your object–oriented system. Use external C functions (Sect. 6.4) and encapsulate the functions without modifying them (if possible).
19.g Prove the correctness of distance computation in Listing 190!
19.h For the matrix A in (19.4), prove that

$$(A^T A)^{-1} = \frac{1}{N \sum_{i=1}^{N} a_i^2 - (\sum_{i=1}^{N} a_i)^2} \begin{pmatrix} N & \sum_{i=1}^{N} a_i \\ \sum_{i=1}^{N} a_i & \sum_{i=1}^{N} a_i^2 \end{pmatrix} . \quad (19.13)$$

19.i We could try to localize a circle in an image by just computing the mean of all intersections of lines shown in Figure 19.20 (left). Why is the Hough transform more robust?

Chapter 20
Image Segmentation

In the first stage of segmentation which we reached in Chapter 19, we used images and transform them into other images. The next step in segmentation (in the sense of Figure 8.4) is to detect geometric objects in a representation close to pixel data. One suitable and often used representation for lines is the *chain code*; the basic idea was already introduced in Sect. 19.3 and in Figure 19.9. In this chapter we describe some additional methods on chain codes. Some of the described algorithms are suggested in [Fre80, Zam91].

20.1 Chain Code Class

For the implementation of a class for chain codes (Sect. 19.3), we first introduce an auxiliary class `ChainSeq` (Listing 191) to represent sequences of links. This class will be usable only by the class `Chain` (Listing 194) which is a `friend` of the class `ChainSeq`. As in Sect. 16.7, friends are used here wisely; the auxiliary class cannot be used from a class other than `Chain`, as all its constructors are private. The class `ChainSeq` interfaces the chain code class to STL (Sect. 16.7).

```
class ChainSeq {
private:                        // no public part
    friend class Chain;         // defined later, grant access to internals
    // data
    vector<byte> seq;           // actual chains  (STL)
#ifdef COMPACT_CHAIN             /* see text */
    unsigned int l;             // number of links
#endif

    // methods
    ~ChainSeq();                // destructor
    ChainSeq();                 // default constructor
    ChainSeq(const ChainSeq&);  // copy constructor
    void append(byte);          // appends to the sequence seq
    int length() const;         // geometric line length
    byte   at(int i) const;     // read access
    void put_at(int, byte);     // write
};
```

```
int  ChainSeq::length()  const
#ifdef COMPACT_CHAIN
    { return 1; }
#else
    { return seq.size(); }
#endif

byte ChainSeq::at(int i) const
#ifdef COMPACT_CHAIN
    { /* left as an exercise */ }
#else
  #ifdef DEBUG
    { return seq.at(i); }      // safe read access
  #else
    { return seq[i]; }         // read access
  #endif
#endif
void ChainSeq::put_at(int i, byte b)
#ifdef COMPACT_CHAIN
    { /* left as an exercise */ }
#else
    { seq[i] = b; } // write
#endif
void ChainSeq::append(byte b)
#ifdef COMPACT_CHAIN
    { /* left as an exercise */ }
#else
    { seq.push_back(b); }
#endif
```
192

Listing 192 shows the implementation of some of the auxiliary methods for chains. The method `at` on a vector object checks the range of the index. In principle, we could pack two chain elements into one byte inside this class to save storage; only the methods in Listing 192 have to be changed for this and the number of chains will have to be recorded in the `ChainSeq` class explicitly, rather than implicitly by the length of the vector: this value is included in the conditional compilation based on the symbol COMPACT_CHAIN in Listing 191. As this idea requires additional operations, no such packing is done in practice in order to save execution time and the implementation is left as Exercise 20.f. The method `ChainSeq::append` appends a byte to the sequence.

20.2 Edges

Chain codes are a special case of a representation for lines. Other representations exist. We introduce an abstract base class for line representations in Listing 193. It contains the general interface for lines including access to start and end, predicates for closed lines, etc., and it separates these representations from those for regions. This class utilizes the class `PointXY` (Listing 87, Exercise 10.b).

As described in Chapter 19, edges have to be connected in edge images and chain codes can be extracted from an edge image. It is a useful extension for edges to add a possible successor to an edge element that points to any of its eight neighbors. This can naturally be done with a chain code, i.e., with the enumeration inside the class `Chain` (Listing 195).

20.2 Edges

```
class LineRep : public Represent {   // class for line representations
  private:
    DECLARE_MEMBERS(LineRep)          // required by NIHCL
    PointXY start;                    // only member
  public:
    LineRep();                        // default constructor
    LineRep(const PointXY&);          // set point
    LineRep(const LineRep&);          // copy constructor
    virtual PointXY End() const;      // must be part of derived class
    const PointXY& Start() const;     // reference to member
    int isClosed() const ;            // e.g., { return start == End(); }
    virtual double length() const;    // return length
};
```
[193]

```
class Chain : public LineRep {
  private:
    DECLARE_MEMBERS(Chain)
    ChainSeq chain;
  public:
    enum ChainDir { east = 0, se = 1, south = 2, sw = 3,
        west = 4, nw = 5, north = 6, ne = 7};
    static const int DefaultLen; // default chunk length for chain
    ~Chain();
    Chain();
    Chain(PointXY &, int = Chain::DefaultLen);
    Chain(const Chain &);
    int number() const { return chain.length(); }  // current length
    void append(byte b)   { chain.append(b); }     // extend
    void append(const Chain&);                     // concatenate
    inline byte operator[] (int) const;            // direct access to links
    virtual double length() const;                 // return length
};
inline byte Chain::operator[] (int i) const {return chain.at(i); }
```
[194]

Since we made the definition of the chain direction public, we can use it in an extended edge class (Listing 196, cf. Listing 146). With each element we store the flags that indicate whether we consider it part of an edge, part of a closed line, start or end of a line, etc. We use an enumeration data type in class scope for the symbolic description of these features. The constant class variable Edge_V1::ONUM will have to be initialized as 144 in Listing 195.[1] It is also useful if the implementation of chain codes has a method for joining two chain codes (method append(const Chain&) in Listing 194).

---

[1] Of course, we do not derive the class Edge from Object since it would then have a virtual function table and edge images would at least double in size!

```
DEFINE_CLASS(Chain,LineRep,0)                // NIHCL functions
const int Chain::DefaultLen = 8;             // static member initialization
Chain::Chain() : chain() {}                  // default constructor
Chain::Chain(PointXY & p, int l) : LineRep(p), chain() {}
Chain::Chain(const Chain &c)    : LineRep(c.Start()), chain(c.chain) {}
```
[195]

```
struct Edge_V2 {                         // incomplete new version
   static const int ONUM;                // will be defined as 144
   enum edge_type { start = 0, end = 1, closed = 2 };
   unsigned int     strength  : 16;
   unsigned int     orient    :  8;
   edge_type        features  :  5;      // for later extension
   Chain::ChainDir  succ      :  3;      // use Chain definition
};
#if defined(EDGE_VERS) && (EDGE_VERS == 2)
typedef struct Edge_V2 Edge;  // V2 not fully compatible with V0, V1!!
#endif
```

$M - m$	m	new direction
0	—	no change
1	—	no change
2	odd	$m+1, m+1$
2	even	$m+1$
3	odd	$m+1$
3	even	$m+2$
4	—	delete m and M
5	odd	$m-1$
5	even	$m-2$
6	odd	$m-1, m-1$
6	even	$m-1$
7	—	no change

Table 20.1: Rules for smoothing chain codes

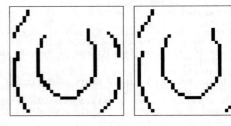

Figure 20.1: Original chain code (left) and smoothed line (right).

20.3 Chain Code Algorithms

A variety of chain code algorithms exist that can be integrated into the chain code class. In the following we show how we can smooth a chain coded line, compute its length, compute the area enclosed by a closed chain coded line, compute intersections of a chain code with another or with itself, etc.

Chain codes created by line detection algorithms are often twisted, disturbed by noise, and have indentations. We need a method in the class for chain codes that *smoothes* lines represented as chain codes, and still preserves as much information as possible.

Let S_1 and S_2 be two subsequent directions in the given chain code. In Table 20.1 (from [Zam91; p. 21]) rules are summarized which can be used for smoothing chain codes. For that purpose, we define $m = \min(S_1, S_2)$ and $M = \max(S_1, S_2)$. The arithmetic, i.e., addition, is done modulo 8. The smoothing procedure has to be repeated until there is no change in the chain code. Figure 20.1 shows an example.

A slightly more complex smoothing algorithm is proposed in [Hu97]; the iterative algorithm eliminates repetitive small variations while an error measure computed with respect to the original curve is below a given threshold.

20.3 Chain Code Algorithms

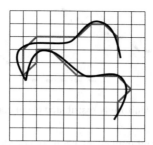

Figure 20.2: Illustration of a line, the rotation of the line (40°) and the corresponding chain codes

A line can have *intersections with itself*. For example, the digit 8 is written with one intersected line. We have to extend the class for chain codes by a method which computes the set of intersections of one chain code.

A method for the determination of *intersections of two chains* is also required. For that purpose, we determine the bounding rectangle for each chain. Obviously, any intersections of both chains will lie in the common area of these two bounding rectangles. If there exist no intersections, the two chains are disjunctive. For the intersection areas of the bounding boxes we proceed recursively as follows: we discard the portions of the chain codes lying outside, and for the remaining parts we compute the bounding rectangles, again. This process is repeated until all intersections are found or it is established that no intersection exists.

It is often useful to provide geometric objects with methods for *geometric transformations*. In this section we inspect rotations and translations for chain codes. The translation is trivial; only the starting point has to be moved. For that reason, it is useful to provide point objects with an additional method which translates the point for this purpose (cf. Listing 87). Even the rotation by multiples of 45° or 90° is fairly easy. The directions can be modified using modulo summation. Arbitrary rotations, however, will cause distortions. The chain must be treated as a curve and thus rotated, re-quantized as well as re-coded considering the underlying image lattice (cf. Figure 20.2). Let the center of rotation be the starting point of the actual chain. A simple implementation proceeds as follows:

1. Rotate each element of the image grid belonging to the given line using the induced rotation matrix (use a modified version of the method already discussed in Sect. 12.6 for that purpose!).
2. Compute the difference in horizontal and vertical direction taking into account the rotation angle for each of the eight chain code directions.
3. Move along the chain and compute the new sequence of directions by the minimization of distances induced by the floating point and discrete coordinates.

Due to the fact that chain codes have only eight discrete directions, straight lines in the image have to be approximated by these discrete steps. The process of drawing straight lines characterized by two points, i.e., the start and the end point, was already an exercise (Exercise 12.c).

Figure 20.3: Uniformly distributed chain code directions

We can now use this function and implement a constructor for a chain code of a straight line, where the start and end points are given arguments. Furthermore, a boolean function has to be implemented which returns true if a given chain code *represents a straight line* and false otherwise. The decision criteria for a straight line are specified as follows:

(a) The whole chain code includes only two different directions, S_1 and S_2, where the following constraint has to be valid: $|S_1 - S_2| \equiv 1 \bmod 8$.

(b) The direction which is less often element of the chain code always has the other direction as predecessor and successor in the sequence of directions.

(c) S_1 and S_2 must be *homogeneously distributed* over the complete chain code.

The conditions (a) and (b) are easily checked. The homogeneity can be computed using the following recursive procedure: let the direction, which is more often part of the chain code, be denoted by S. We compute from the given chain code a new formal chain code where the directions are the number of directly subsequent elements of the direction S. We check for this formal chain code conditions (a), (b), (c) until convergence.

In a statistical framework, the term *homogeneously distributed* indicates uniformly distributed directions, i.e., $p(S_1) = p(S_2) = 1/2$. Figure 20.3 shows that this constraint is not sufficient to define straight line elements. The changes in directions of subsequent chain elements are also assumed to be uniformly distributed. We need a method which tests hypotheses on distributions and give some measure for reliability.

The χ^2–*test* allows deciding to which extent you can believe hypotheses for observed relative frequencies. Let us assume we have n random variables $X_1, \ldots X_n$, where $X_i \in \{1, \ldots, k\}$, and let $p_1, p_2, \ldots, p_k$ denote the discrete probabilities over the domain $\{1, 2, \ldots, k\}$, i.e., these probabilities define a histogram. Our hypothesis is that

$$p(X_j = i) = p_i \; , \tag{20.1}$$

where $j \in \{1, 2, \ldots, n\}$ and $i \in \{1, 2, \ldots, k\}$. The basic random variable related to the test is the so-called *Pearson statistic* T of order n which is defined for n observations by

$$T_n = \sum_{i=1}^{k} \frac{(N^{(i)} - np_i)^2}{np_i} \; ; \tag{20.2}$$

herein $N^{(i)}$ denotes the number of observed random variables X_j that satisfy $X_j = i$. We define α to be the so called *level* of the test, and compute the probability $p(T \geq s)$ for which

20.3 Chain Code Algorithms

```
double Chain::length() const            // return length
{
    int a=0, b=0;                       // two counters
    for (int i = chain.length() -1; i >= 0; --i)   // iterate along chain
        if (chain.seq[i] & 0x01) ++a; else ++b;    // check even/odd link
    return M_SQRT2 * a + b;             // compute length
}
```
197

we demand that $p(T \geq s) \leq \alpha$. The value

$$t(\alpha) = \operatorname*{argmin}_{s} \{p(T \geq s) \leq \alpha; s\} \qquad (20.3)$$

is the basic measure of the test. We accept the hypothesis, if the experimental value T_n holds $T_n \leq t(\alpha)$, otherwise it is rejected. The discrete probability $p(T \geq s)$ is defined by a χ^2–distribution with $k-1$ degrees of freedom [And58]. For an infinite number of observations we have

$$\lim_{n \to \infty} p(T_n \geq s) = \frac{1}{2^{k/2}\Gamma(k/2)} \int_0^s y^{(k-1)/2} \exp(y/2) \, dy \quad . \qquad (20.4)$$

The Gamma-function is defined by

$$\Gamma(x) = \int_0^\infty \exp(-t) \, t^{x-1} \, dt \quad . \qquad (20.5)$$

This distribution is used to approximate $p(T_n \geq s)$ for a given set of observations. The implementation of the χ^2–test requires the distribution (20.4) for various k. The code for the χ^2–test and the required probability distribution can be found in look-up tables [Bro85] or in [Pre92].[2]

The *length* of a chain coded line can be computed using the simple formula

$$l = a + b \cdot \sqrt{2} \quad , \qquad (20.6)$$

where a is the number of even– and b the number of odd-valued links in the given chain corresponding to the 4–neighborhood and the 8–neighborhood in Sect. 20.4. An implementation of the method `length` which was declared in Listing 194, is shown in Listing 197. This definition is too simple in real applications: think, for example, of a chain code $[(0,0)020202020202]$; more effort has to be put into the implementation of the method `length()` to treat such special cases correctly. Some problems of twisted chain codes can be solved by smoothing techniques described in the previous section.

The *area* enclosed by a closed chain code can simply be computed. The basic idea is to sum up all the y values along the one side of the contour, i.e., to integrate over the x–axis, and to subtract the integral of the opposite side. (Figure 20.4). This will result in the number of pixels inside the area; in addition, we count diagonal contour elements as only half a pixel. We assume two tables which can be added to the class chain as static members; one is called x_next and one is called y_next. These tables are of size eight and contain the differences for the x and the y coordinate for a given link (e.g., x_next[3]=-1 and y_next[3]=1). The algorithm is shown in Figure 20.5.

---
[2] cf. http://cfatab.harvard.edu/nr/bookc.html

Figure 20.4: Area of closed chain code. The thick bars are subtracted from the thin bars.

Procedure `chain::area`;		
Auxiliary variables: A = 0; ypos = StartPoint.y(); A = 0		
FOR i = first TO last link		
	IF	`x_next[act[i]]=-1`
	THEN	`A -= ypos + ypos + y_next[act[i]];`
	ELSE	IF `x_next[act[i]]=1`
		THEN `A += ypos + ypos + y_next[act[i]];`
	`ypos += y_next[act[i]]`	
return A/2.0		

Figure 20.5: Structogram for computation of area from a closed chain code

For the classification of objects based on lines, like e.g. classification based on shapes, it is often necessary to *match chain codes*. Of course, the lines will not fit exactly, when real images are used. Therefore, we need a similarity measure for chain codes. For that purpose compute the absolute area A included by two lines. We assume that the area equals to the number of enclosed pixels and the start and end points of each chain code are connected by virtual lines. Let l_1 and l_2 be the length of both lines. A measure for difference is defined by

$$d = 2A/(l_1 + l_2) \quad . \tag{20.7}$$

Using the length computed in (20.6) we can easily implement this measure.

20.4 Neighborhood

Rectangular or quadratic tessellation of digital images and the definition of different types of chain codes induce the problem of how to define a neighborhood of a pixel and the directions of the chain code. A pixel (i, j) is usually considered closer to $(i + 1, j)$ than to $(i + 1, j + 1)$. Two alternatives can be chosen for those pixels which are assumed to be directly adjacent to (i, j):

- *4–connectivity*, for which the four pixels

$$\{(i+1, j), (i-1, j), (i, j+1), (i, j-1)\} \tag{20.8}$$

20.5 Contours in Binary Images

Figure 20.6: Neighborhood of a pixel: 4–connectivity (left) and 8–connectivity (right)

are used, and

- *8–connectivity*, for which eight pixels are used, namely the 4–connected pixels and the set

$$\{(i-1, j-1), (i+1, j-1), (i-1, j+1), (i+1, j+1)\} \quad . \tag{20.9}$$

The neighborhood definitions are visualized in Figure 20.6. Both versions have advantages and disadvantages, when sets of similar pixels are searched in segmentation that should result in a connected region. Imagine, for example, a chess board; if we define that each of the eight neighbors of a pixel is adjacent to it, all white fields are connected — as well as all black fields.

In the next section we need this notion of a neighborhood to trace lines.

20.5 Contours in Binary Images

In [Nie74] a simple algorithm for contour tracking in binary images is presented which will create a chain coded line. Assuming that the object is white and the background is black, the following rules are used to create a line around an object:

1. after three consecutive turns in the same direction, turn in the other direction and ignore the following rules
2. turn left if you are on a white pixel
3. turn right if you are on a black pixel

The foreground (white) is regarded as 4–connected here. The background is 8–connected. An example is shown in Figure 20.7. Binary regions which can be used for this algorithm can simply be computed by the threshold algorithms of Chapter 18.

Using this algorithm, we can complete line detection using the Laplace operator. We apply the operator and create an image which has three values as in Figure 15.12: the image will be 0 for negative results, it will be 128 wherever the operator results in 0, and will be 255 for the positive case. We can now detect lines when we trace the borders of these regions. The results will, however, be satisfying only if some extra filtering is done on the input image.

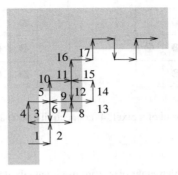

Figure 20.7: Contour following algorithm

20.6 Polygon Representation

A data reduction of chain code representations results from a polygonal approximation of lines by using straight line segments. A polygon is a line represented by a sequence of straight line segments. The computation of the needed straight line segments can be formalized as an optimization problem: the approximation error should be below a given threshold; whereas, the number of line segments should be as minimal as possible. This principle was proposed in [Ram72]. Some algorithms for the conversion of chain codes to polygons are proposed in [Hu97].

For the judgment of the quality of the approximation a distance measure between straight lines and a chain code element is needed. One suitable measure was defined in Sect. 136. In the current case, we have the constraint that both the chain code and the polygonal approximation begin and end it dentical points.

A more sophisticated solution of this problem is the so called *split algorithm*. The basic idea of this approach is due to a recursive division of the line segment into smaller segments. The decomposition of one segment stops, if the linear segment approximates the curved segment with an appropriate error. An example for polygonal approximations of line segments was already shown in Figure 20.8.

The segments of a polygon can be characterized by a sequence of points. An example of segmentation of a gray-level image into a set of polygons (a segmentation object) is shown in Figure 20.8. Polygon may be computed from a line segmentation in chain codes (cf. Sect. 20.6). A simple algorithm for polygonal approximation is left as Exercise 24.f. Some more algorithms will be outlined in Sect. 20.6.

Polygons — like chain codes — are derived from the line representation class. A basic declaration is given in Listing 198. The sequential collection (`OrderedCltn`) of NIHCL is used

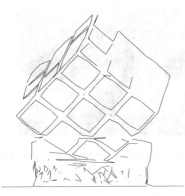 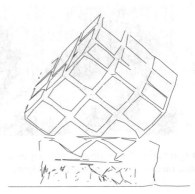

Figure 20.8: Polygon-approximation of a chain code segmented from the red channel (left) and Sobel on color image (right) of Figure 11.2 (left).

```
class Polygon : public LineRep {
 private:
    OrderedCltn points;           // sequence of points excluding start
 public:
    virtual double length() const; // read length (inherited)
    // ...
};
```

to store the sequence of points. For more runtime efficiency, this could be changed to an STL object without change to the user interface.[3]

20.7 Region Segmentation

In the previous chapters we described how images can be segmented into lines and various other features related to lines. An alternative to this approach is to segment the image into regions which are similar with respect to a similarity measure. The classical approach is the split-and-merge procedure for regions [Hor74] which creates a set of regions. A modern algorithm called CSC is described in [Pri93].

Similarly to a class for the representation of lines, a class for region representation has to be created which can be specialized to well-known representation schemes, such as quadtrees. Figure 20.9 (left) shows a color image[4] and a segmentation into regions based on color information (right). Since the algorithm uses a quadtree, only a rectangular subimage is segmented.

---

[3] If not implemented carefully, such changes may, however, severely interfere with input/output functions and external data formats, since the type of an object and version information is stored along with each object!

[4] printed as gray-scale image

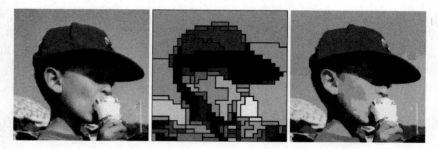

Figure 20.9: Color image (left) segmented into regions represented by contours; result of split and merge (center) and of CSC (right)

The result of region segmentation has to be stored somehow. One option is to store the contours as chain codes (Figure 20.9 (middle)). As we will see in the next section, points can also be the results of segmentation algorithms. We still lack a data structure or class which serves as a container for arbitrary segmentation results. In [Pau92b] it was shown that the so-called segmentation object, which we will see in Listing 215, has all the required methods for storing arbitrary segmentation results, including regions and points.

20.8 Point Segmentation

The simplest result from segmentation is a set of points. They can be either detect directly, as shown in the following, or they can be derived from the structure of lines. Interesting points can be, for example, the intersection of lines.

A well-known method to find interesting points in an image is due to Moravec and is thus called the *Moravec interest* operator. He extended his own method in [Mor96]; for each pixel in the input image, he uses a local window

$$\boldsymbol{W}_{ij} = [w_{ij,\mu\nu}]_{\mu,\nu=0,\ldots,7} = \left[f_{a,b}\right]_{a=i,\ldots,i+7, b=j,\ldots,j+7} \quad (20.10)$$

The following features are computed from these windows:

$$m_{\text{xx}\,ij} = \sum_{\mu=0}^{6}\sum_{\nu=0}^{6} (w_{ij,\mu\nu} - w_{ij,\mu\nu+1})^2 \quad (20.11)$$

$$m_{\text{yy}\,ij} = \sum_{\mu=0}^{6}\sum_{\nu=0}^{6} (w_{ij,\mu\nu} - w_{ij,\mu+1\nu})^2 \quad (20.12)$$

$$m_{\text{xy}\,ij} = \sum_{\mu=0}^{6}\sum_{\nu=0}^{6} (w_{ij,\mu\nu} - w_{ij,\mu+1\nu+1})^2 \quad (20.13)$$

$$m_{\text{yx}\,ij} = \sum_{\mu=0}^{6}\sum_{\nu=0}^{6} (w_{ij,\mu+1\nu} - w_{ij,\mu\nu+1})^2 \quad (20.14)$$

The operator now is

$$H_{ij} = \min\left\{m_{xx_{ij}}, m_{xy_{ij}}, m_{yx_{ij}}, m_{yy_{ij}}\right\} \quad . \tag{20.15}$$

The application of this operator on an image results in an interest map which is subsequently filtered by a Laplace-operator. The intrest map denotes the importance of a pixel for the subsequent processing steps. It can be derived from the Image class as just another type of images.

20.9 Image Analysis

One important part of image analysis is to localize objects in an image. In this section we give a simplistic recipe of how to compose an object recognition system using the modules described so far.

Recipe: *Build your (simplistic) image analysis system (object recognition)*:

1. filter the image to reduce noise (Chapter 17)
2. segment the image into points, lines, regions, etc. and store result in a segmentation object
3. hypothesize some objects in the scene using knowledge about the objects.
4. verify them matching your segmentation results with knowledge about objects
5. repeat, until sufficiently many objects are found
6. optionally: new action (see below)

To give an example of how step 3 can be done, we consider the problem of finding cubes in a blocks world. If we guess a pose and an orientation of a cube, we can create an image from it using the methods described in Sect. 12.6. The following verification step will test whether the predicted lines can be found in the real image.

For a better pose estimation, it is useful to have 3–D information. Some ideas are given in Sect. 24.2. Knowledge about the scenes is required in step 3. We will finally outline some ideas in Sect. 23.9.

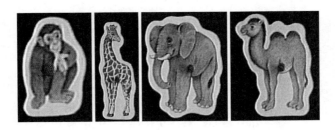

Figure 20.10: Toy Animals

Exercises

20.a Implement the contour tracking algorithm described in Sect. 20.5. Represent the resulting line as a chain code.

20.b Images of animals such as shown in Figure 20.10 should be recognized and distinguished in gray-level images. Assume a homogeneous black background and let $\Omega_1, \Omega_2, \Omega_3$ and Ω_4 be the associated pattern classes.

    (a) Binarize the images using a threshold detection algorithm.

    (b) Compute the closed contour-line for each object from a given gray-level image using the algorithm in Sect. 20.5.

    (c) Write programs for the determination of features like the area, length of the contour, or moments using the algorithm in Sect. 136.

We will later continue with this problem in Exercise 22.c.

20.c Give a proof that the algorithm in Sect. 20.3 terminates after a finite number of iterations. Write a program for the visualization of chain codes, i.e., generate a synthetic image that shows the (set of) chain codes. Describe the smoothing effects!

20.d Implement a boolean function for Sect. 20.3 and check whether your straight lines generated in Exercise 12.c fulfill this criterion.

20.e Implement the similarity measure of Sect. 136 as a method in your class. Test this distance function using several examples and discuss your results.

20.f Extend Listing 191 and Listing 192 so that two chain links are stored in one byte in the class `ChainSeq` when the macro COMPACT_CHAIN is defined.

Chapter 21

Spatial and Spectral Features

The goal of pattern analysis, in general, is to transform signals into symbolic descriptions [Dud73, Nie90a]. For simple classification problems this corresponds to the computation of a class number for an observed signal (cf. Figure 8.1). Since the amount of data is too high if images or speech signals are used directly, the signals are transformed into lower dimensional vectors, so called *features*. Features retain all the information needed for pattern recognition. For image and speech recognition, it is necessary to have a set of features that are, for example, appropriate for the subsequent classification of objects, single words, or the identification of speakers. The following sections introduce several types of features which can be applied to solve selected classification problems in the fields of image and speech processing.

21.1 Different Types of Features

A variety of parameters can be used to represent digital signals. You can take, for instance, differences between gray-levels or the waveform of speech signals. Features like the zero crossing rate, the energy of the signal or first derivatives (average slopes) might be computed [Nie90a, Rab88]. In particular, for speech recognition applications it has proven to be advantageous that features are not computed in the spatial domain,[1] but in the frequency domain of the signal (cf. Chapter 13). Features of the frequency domain show some characteristics; like the fundamental frequency or the perceptual equivalent, the pitch, that are not directly evident in spatial data. Features of the frequency domain often provide a higher discriminating power [Dud73].

The task of the system and the classification strategy influence the choice of useful features. If we have to implement a speaker independent speech recognition system, features have to be used which are significant for words and which can be detected within speech signals produced by arbitrary speakers [ST95]. In contrast, identification of speakers requires features that characterize the speaker [Fal95]; herein, the recognition of spoken words is of minor interest. The same holds for topic spotting applications [War97], where the system has to recognize the topic of utterances and not the sequence of words. Similar decisions have to be made for image

---

[1]In speech processing the spatial domain is usually called temporal domain. Here we simply use "spatial domain" for both cases, image and speech processing.

analysis. The identification of people based on their video images, for example, requires features that are invariant with respect to movements of their faces, i.e., invariant under geometric transformations and distortions. In contrast, for gripping objects and pose/orientation estimation we need features that include information about the object's position and orientation in the world coordinate system.

It should be obvious that speech and image features of the mentioned examples will differ from each other extremely. Until now, there exists no unified mathematical framework that allows the (efficient) computation of features from an arbitrary signal, which are optimal with respect to a pre-defined recognition task. In general, in pattern recognition theory it is distinguished between heuristic and analytical methods for the computation of features [Nie83]. Heuristic methods apply well-known mathematical methods for signal to feature transforms, like the Fourier transform (cf. Chapter 13) or orthographic projections into sub-spaces (cf. Sect. 19.8). Experience and the computed recognition rates justify their use. Analytically computed features usually result from problem specific derivations. The given pattern recognition problem is formalized as an optimization task based on a well-defined objective function. For instance, features are computed by maximization of the recognition rate for a given classifier [Nie83].

The following sections will give an introduction to the computation of heuristic features like the short time Fourier transform. Methods for the calculation of spatial and frequency features for speech signals and images are discussed. The treatment of analytical techniques for feature extraction and selection methods to get the best elements for a set of features are left out here; these methods are much more difficult than heuristic methods. For interested readers, we recommend e.g. [Nie83, Rip96, The89].

21.2 Frames and Blocks

The computation of only one feature for a given signal seems difficult and inadequate. One and the same spoken word might have varying duration or an utterance is a sequence of completely different words. Multiple object scenes show an unknown number of objects, and therefore feature vectors of constant dimensions cannot be expected. These simple examples make clear that the decomposition of signals into smaller units is essential. The subdivision here, however, is done in a systematic way, i.e., in contrast to those methods introduced in Chapter 15, no explicit segmentation will be done. Without considering any knowledge about the spoken words or the objects shown in a scene, sensor signals are divided up into short intervals of equal length or size.

In the case of speech signals, these intervals are called *frames* or *windows*. The length of frames has to be large enough to keep characteristic information about the speech signal, which is necessary for solving the recognition problem successfully. It is expected that the frequencies of the digital time signal does not vary too much within the chosen frame, i.e., the frame should be relatively small. The length of the window should at least include two periods of the glottis (cf. Figure 21.13). In fact, the frame size depends on the application and the system design should adjust the balance between resolution in time and in frequency. In general, short frames induce high resolutions in time, but low resolution in frequencies. For increasing window size, the resolution in time decreases and the frequency resolution increases. In speech

21.2 Frames and Blocks

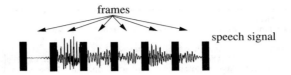

Figure 21.1: Decomposition of speech signals into frames

recognition, for instance, the windows have an average duration of 10–20 ms and they may overlap [Nie90a, ST95]. For topic spotting, however, frame sizes of 80 ms haven proven to be more appropriate [War97], since this corresponds to the average duration of phonemes.

Also images can be partitioned into smaller subimages or *blocks* which usually have quadratic size; commonly used window sizes are 3×3 or 5×5 [Bal82]. The partitioning of images is not as common as for speech signals. Nevertheless, there exist some low– and high-level vision applications that make use of window functions. For instance, JPEG image coding (cf. Chapter 11) requires a partition into blocks of size 8×8. For high-level vision, the use of blocks is mainly restricted to the computation and use of resolution hierarchies (Sect. 17.6). Further examples are stereo or object tracking algorithms that are based on block matching techniques, where blocks correspond to subimages [Pos90].

Mathematically, the decomposition of a sequence $[f_t]_{t \geq 0}$ of sample data into frames is done by multiplying the original signal with a window function w_τ. The components of the new signal $[f_t^{(\tau)}]_{t \geq 0}$ are defined by[2]

$$f_t^{(\tau)} = w_{\tau-t} f_t \ . \qquad (21.1)$$

There exist different types of window functions that are applied in practice. The easiest one is the rectangle window function given by

$$w_\tau = \begin{cases} 1 & , \quad \text{if } \tau \in \{0, 1, \ldots, M-1\} \\ 0 & , \quad \text{otherwise} \end{cases} \ . \qquad (21.2)$$

The parameter M controls the window size. More often used functions are the Hamming window

$$w_\tau = \begin{cases} \frac{27}{50} - \frac{23}{50} \cos\left(\frac{2\pi\tau}{M-1}\right) & , \quad \text{if } \tau \in \{0, 1, \ldots, M-1\} \\ 0 & , \quad \text{otherwise} \end{cases} \qquad (21.3)$$

and the Hann window

$$w_\tau = \begin{cases} \frac{1}{2} - \frac{1}{2} \cos\left(\frac{2\pi\tau}{M-1}\right) & , \quad \text{if } \tau \in \{0, 1, \ldots, M-1\} \\ 0 & , \quad \text{otherwise} \end{cases} \ . \qquad (21.4)$$

The introduced window functions allow the transformation of speech signals into single frames of length M. For the implementation we apply the same idea as in the case of the hierarchy

---

[2] In the following we denote all windowed quantities by a superscript (τ).

```
#include <math.h>
class SpeechWin {   // abstract class for speech windowing functions
protected:
    int width;      // width of the window
public:             // frames are computed with function call operator
    virtual SpeechFrame operator() (SpeechSignal &, Time &) = 0;
};
class RectangularWin : public SpeechWin {
 public :
    virtual SpeechFrame operator() (SpeechSignal &, Time &);
    RectangularWin(int w) { width = w; }
};
class HammingWin : public SpeechWin {
 Vector<float> cosTab;
 public :
    HammingWin(int w) : cosTab(w) {
        width = w;
        for (int i = 0; i < w; ++i) // initialize internal table once
            cosTab[i] = 27.0/50 - 23.0/50 * cos(2 * M_PI * i / (w - 1));
    }
    virtual SpeechFrame operator() (SpeechSignal &, Time &);
};
```

199

of filter operations in Sect. 17.9. A general class `SpeechWin` provides the abstract interface; derived classes for the window functions have an internal table for efficient computation of speech frames to form a speech signal (Listing 199). Both the Hamming and the Hann weighting window functions attach smaller weights to samples at the right and left sides of windows. This reduces noise effects in the computed feature sequences [ST95].

21.3   Spatial Features

Spatial features result from the sample values without transforming the signal into the frequency domain or other domains. The algorithms for feature detection work on the quantized signal directly. In the following we will consider some selected sets of spatial features, which are appropriate for solving simple classification tasks.

Let $[f_t]_{t \geq 0}$ be a discrete speech signal. The speech signal is decomposed into a sequence of frames. For each frame, several spatial features can be computed:

- the zero-crossing rate,
- the autocorrelation,
- the sequence of average slopes for zero-crossings,
- the short time energy.

Dependent on the utterance, the zero-crossing rate of speech signals varies. Vowels like the "a" show a lower frequency of zero-crossings than the the spoken letter "s" (Figure 21.2). Thus, the zero-crossing rate seems to be an appropriate feature for discriminating voiced and unvoiced. The zero-crossing frequency threshold for the classification of voiceless and voiced signals is 1000 Hz for male and 1500 Hz for female speakers. Many systems also apply the

21.3 Spatial Features

Figure 21.2: Speech signals corresponding to the utterances "a" (upper) and "s" (lower)

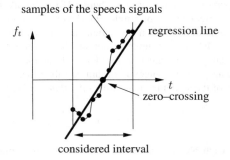

Figure 21.3: Linear regression to compute average slopes

autocorrelation

$$c_\nu^{(\tau)} = \sum_{t=-\infty}^{+\infty} f_t^{(\tau)} f_{t+\nu}^{(\tau)} \tag{21.5}$$

to identify voiced and voiceless parts [ST95].

Another appropriate feature, which is associated with zero-crossings, is the average slope of the speech signal at those points where the speech signal intersects the time axis. The computation of slopes for a given neighborhood is usually done by linear regression introduced in Sect. 19.8. The principle of slope computation is illustrated in Figure 21.3.

For many applications in speech recognition, the system records signals all the time, but the recognition module should only start working if somebody speaks to the system. The classification of speech and silence is required for that reason, and it can be done by using the short time energy. The energy of the complete signal is defined by

$$E = \sum_{t=-\infty}^{+\infty} f_t^2 \;, \tag{21.6}$$

but usually frames are considered instead of the complete utterance. For single frames we get the *short time energy* by

$$E^{(\tau)} = \sum_{t=0}^{M-1} \left(f_t^{(\tau)}\right)^2 = \sum_{t=0}^{M-1} w_{\tau-t}^2 f_t^2 \quad . \tag{21.7}$$

By the definition of a proper threshold θ, speech and silence can be classified using a simple threshold operation similar to (18.1) for computing binary images. In practice, it is suggested to use a threshold of 5 dB.[3]

Binary images are often the first step towards spatial features for computer vision purposes. Many classification systems in image processing apply features like the area of objects or the length of boundary lines which are computed using binary images. Another type of feature is the ratio of black and white pixels or simply the threshold for binarization, which is usually computed using operations on histograms (Chapter 18). Not only the threshold for binarization, but also the relative frequencies of single gray-levels, the number of maxima or the shape in general are features derived from histograms and used for solving many problems of practical relevance [Jäh93]. Averaging techniques based on gray-level images are especially useful for solving simple classification problems. Examples for averaging methods are the computation of means μ and variances σ^2 of sample values in a frame (cf. Sect. 7.2). A measure for the smoothness of the signal is the *relative smoothness* which is defined by

$$s = 1 - \frac{1}{1+\sigma^2} \tag{21.8}$$

and computed for each block considered. The relative smoothness allows, for instance, the classification of textures (cf. Chapter 12). The value of s vanishes for blocks of constant intensity, and it is close to one for rough textures with varying gray-levels.

The mean and variance are powerful features for the classification of objects, where no rigorous changes in gray-levels of the test images and illumination conditions occur. Features computed by averaging techniques are approximately invariant with respect to 2–D rotations and translations of objects.[4] Other features for texture identification are the gray-level matrix, or other statistical measure, which characterize the distribution of gray-levels [Nie90a]. Other spatial features are based on edge images instead of gray-level or binary images. Features are defined by the major edge direction, the average edge strength, the variance of edge strength or the zero-crossing rate using the second derivatives computed by the Laplace mask (cf. Chapter 15).

21.4 Short Time Fourier Analysis

The computation of the energy (21.6) or the Fourier transform for complete signals is not useful, because changes of the spectrum within the signal include a high degree of information.

---

[3]This threshold, of course, depends on your recording device and varies.
[4]From a theoretical point of view this is not correct, but in practice averaged features show sufficient invariance with respect to different types of transforms.

21.4 Short Time Fourier Analysis

Figure 21.4: Speech signal of the utterance: "this is one word"

Therefore, the integrand of the signal's Fourier transform is weighted by window functions that were introduced in Sect. 21.2. Instead of transforming the complete signal, we compute the Fourier transform frame by frame. In order to use the FFT (Sect. 13.4), it is useful and advantageous to have a frame length M that is a power of two (e.g., M=256 samples).

The discrete Fourier transform of this weighted signal is

$$F_\nu^{(\tau)} = \sum_{t=0}^{M-1} f_t^{(\tau)} \exp\left(\frac{-2\pi i \nu t}{M}\right) = \sum_{t=0}^{M-1} w_{\tau-t} f_t \exp\left(\frac{-2\pi i \nu t}{M}\right) . \quad (21.9)$$

Since the window function fades out most of the signal, this transform is called the *short time Fourier transform*.

The computation of the short time Fourier transform proceeds as follows: the speech signal is transformed into a sequence of frames. For each frame the discrete Fourier transform yields a sequence of Fourier coefficients $[F_\nu^{(\tau)}]_{\nu \geq 0}$, where $F_\nu^{(\tau)} \in \mathbb{C}$. These coefficients or subsets of these coefficients can be used as features. Instead of using these coefficients directly, the absolute values of these complex numbers are used. This is advantageous, because we are more familiar with real than with complex numbers; the main reason, however, is due to the fact that absolute values are invariant with respect to translations of the signal. The phase of the signal does not influence these features, because due to the shifting property of Fourier transforms, the translation corresponds to a multiplication by $\exp\left(-2\pi i \nu m / M\right)$, and we know that $|\exp\left(-2\pi i \nu m / M\right)| = 1$ such that:

$$\left|F_\nu^{(\tau)} \exp\left(\frac{-2\pi i \nu m}{M}\right)\right| = |F_\nu^{(\tau)}| . \quad (21.10)$$

The absolute values $[|F_\nu^{(\tau)}|]_{\nu \geq 0}$, for instance, are called the *power spectrum* of the speech signal, which provides appropriate features for speech processing. Figures 21.5, 21.6, and 21.7 show examples of *logarithmic spectra* $[\log |F_\nu^{(\tau)}|]_{\nu \geq 0}$ with different window functions and varying frame size corresponding to the speech signal of the utterance "this is one word" (Figure 21.4). Each frame of the speech signal can be associated with a spectrum. An utterance thus induces a sequence of spectra, like those shown so far.

There is a way from sound back to images. Image generation and visualization methods can be applied for the construction of *spectrograms*. Spectrograms allow the illustration of all frames' spectra in a single image. For each pixel in the image, the row is determined by the frequency $|F_\nu|$ (or its logarithm), the column is determined by the time. The intensity or color values are related to the the real values $|F_\nu|$ or $\log |F_\nu|$ of the related frequency in the sound signal.

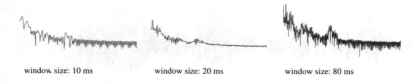

window size: 10 ms   window size: 20 ms   window size: 80 ms

Figure 21.5: Logarithmic spectrum using rectangular windows of varying size

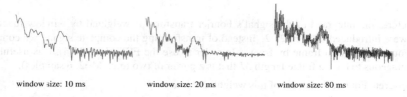

window size: 10 ms   window size: 20 ms   window size: 80 ms

Figure 21.6: Logarithmic spectrum using Hamming windows of varying size

For that reason, a mapping has to be defined which assigns real values to discrete pixel values. The frequency analysis of each individual frame in the speech signal is done using the short time Fourier transform, and defines one column of the synthetic image. For simplicity, we compute the absolute values of Fourier coefficients from sample values and scale the resulting floating point numbers to 256 gray values or colors. These 256 values now correspond to a column in the image. An example of a spectrogram corresponding to the complete utterance of Figure 21.4 is shown in Figure 21.8. Spectrograms are distinguished with respect to the chosen frame size. *Narrow band* spectrograms resolve harmonics and blur temporal details, and *wide band* spectrograms resolve temporal details, but loose line frequency details. The terms "narrow" and "wide" refer to the resolution in frequency, i.e. a narrow band spectogram can be computed by a large window w_τ, and a wide band spectogram will need a small window. Figure 21.8 shows an example of a narrow band spectrogram, and illustrates the wide band spectrogram of the same utterance.[5]

The idea of the short time Fourier transform can also be applied to image processing. The image is decomposed into blocks, and the Fourier transform can be done on each block separately.

---

[5]There is a nice URL where you can find information on "Seeing with your ears": http://home.pi.net/%7Emeijerpb/javoice.htm

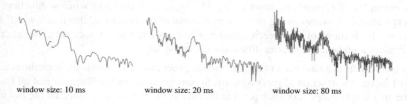

window size: 10 ms   window size: 20 ms   window size: 80 ms

Figure 21.7: Logarithmic spectrum using Hann windows of varying size

21.4 Short Time Fourier Analysis

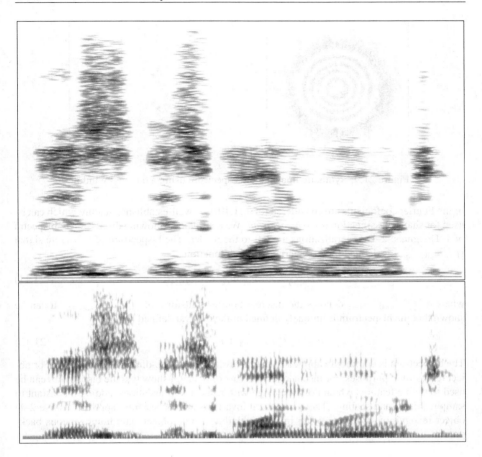

Figure 21.8: Narrow band (top) and wide band (bottom) spectrogram of the utterance: "this is one word"

Figure 21.9 (left) shows an example of a synthetic interferogram; such pictures result, for instance, from the superposition of a holographic image with its optical image [Ost91]. For the analysis of this image, it is useful to compute the Fourier transform for each 64×64 window. The absolute values of the result are visualized in Figure 21.9 (right). For JPEG, 8×8 subimages are converted to the spectral domain by the discrete cosine-transform (Sect. 13.2), and then processed further.[6]

It is well-known that you can get the information about the shape of a signal using primarily relative phases. Obviously, the absolute phases cannot be responsible for shapes, since shapes change with translations. The absolute phase, however, is eliminated, whenever the magnitudes

---
[6]Thanks to Torsten Merz for providing the images.

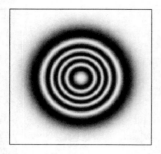 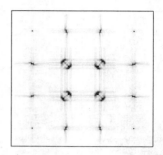

Figure 21.9: Synthetic image and its spectrum using a 64×64 window

of the Fourier coefficients are considered (cf. (21.10)). A well-established feature which can be used for shape classification is the *bispectrum*. We restrict the following discussion to bispectra of 1–D signals; 2–D generalizations are left to the reader. The bispectrum of a discrete signal $[f_t^{(\tau)}]_{t=0,\ldots,M-1}$ is defined by the bivariate discrete function

$$B_{\nu_1,\nu_2}^{(\tau)} = F_{\nu_1}^{(\tau)} F_{\nu_2}^{(\tau)} F_{-\nu_1-\nu_2}^{(\tau)} , \qquad (21.11)$$

wherein $[F_\nu^{(\tau)}]_{\nu=0,\ldots,M-1}$ denotes the discrete Fourier transform of $[f_t^{(\tau)}]_{\tau=0,\ldots,M-1}$. It can be shown that the bispectrum is uniquely defined in the interval defined by

$$0 \leq \nu_1 \leq \nu_2 \leq \nu_1 + \nu_2 \leq 1 . \qquad (21.12)$$

The bispectrum is commonly applied to define invariants for one-dimensional signals. For object recognition purposes, for instance, the authors of [Cha92] show that the bispectrum can be used to define features which do not change with respect to translations, adding a constant to sample values, and scaling. These bispectral invariants are successfully applied to solve 2–D object recognition problems using images including single objects and homogeneous background.

21.5 Cepstral Features

Another fundamental spectral feature for speech processing applications is the so-called *cepstrum*. The components $c_\nu^{(\tau)}$ of the complex cepstrum $\boldsymbol{c}^{(\tau)} = (c_0^{(\tau)}, c_1^{(\tau)}, \ldots, c_{M-1}^{(\tau)})^\mathrm{T}$ are defined by

$$c_\nu^{(\tau)} = \frac{1}{M} \sum_{\nu'=0}^{M-1} (\log F_{\nu'}^{(\tau)}) \exp\left(\frac{2\pi i \nu \nu'}{M}\right) ; \qquad (21.13)$$

these features are usually applied for the classification of phonemes. The sequence of computational steps is shown in Figure 21.10. Due to the fact that the Fourier transform produces complex results, it is necessary to compute the complex logarithm, which is defined by

$$\log z = \log |z| + i \arg(z) , \qquad (21.14)$$

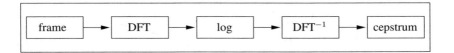

Figure 21.10: Computation of cepstral features

where $z = \text{re}(z) + i\,\text{im}(z)$, $\arg(z) = \text{im}(z)/\text{re}(z)$, and $\text{re}(z), \text{im}(z) \in \mathbb{R}$ (cf. Listing 120 on p. 145). The real valued (and more practical) cepstrum $^r c_\nu^{(\tau)}$ uses the absolute values instead of complex numbers and is thus defined by

$$^r c_\nu^{(\tau)} = \frac{1}{M} \sum_{\nu'=0}^{M-1} (\log|F_{\nu'}^{(\tau)}|) \exp\left(\frac{2\pi i \nu \nu'}{M}\right) \quad ; \qquad (21.15)$$

obviously it avoids the evaluation of the complex logarithm. Due to the fact that the magnitudes of the Fourier coefficients are both real valued and symmetric (!), the computation of the cepstrum can be done by applying the so-called cosine-transform to $\log|F_{\nu'}^{(\tau)}|$, $\nu' = 0 \ldots M/2 - 1$, and we get the features:

$$^r c_\nu^{(\tau)} = \frac{s(\nu)}{\sqrt{M}} \sum_{\nu'=0}^{M/2-1} \log|F_{\nu'}^{(\tau)}| \cos \frac{\nu \pi (2\nu' + 1)}{M} \quad , \qquad (21.16)$$

where

$$s(\nu) = \begin{cases} \sqrt{2} & , \text{ if } \nu = 0 \\ 2 & , \text{ otherwise} \end{cases} \qquad (21.17)$$

A closer look at the definition of the cepstrum shows that the cepstrum is indeed a spectral analysis of the spectrum. The mathematical modeling of Fant's source filter theory [ST95] allows a systematical derivation of the spectrum and is omitted here. In fact, cepstral features allow the decomposition of the signal into independent components concerning stimulation and impulse response of the human vocal tract. A low-passed filtered cepstrum eliminates the excitation, whereas the characteristics of resonances remain in the features. A more detailed and deeper discussion of different spectral and cepstral features, and their use for speech recognition applications can be found in [Hua90, Nie90a]. Nevertheless, the following sections summarize some further important features applied in pattern recognition, omitting physiological and mathematical details.

21.6 Mel Spectral and Cepstral Features

Many researchers in the field of physiology and speech processing have tried to determine the type of frequency analysis performed by the human ear. Speech signals are received by humans as pressure variations. The real frequencies are mapped to activities of the basilar membrane. Empirical studies have shown that this mapping is a non-linear frequency transform. Indeed,

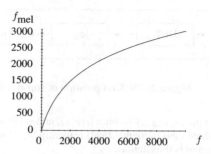

Figure 21.11: Mel scale

the human ear resolves frequencies in different ways: the higher the frequency of speech signals, the lower the resolution. This empirical result has lead to the definition of scales for frequencies based on human perception capabilities. The dependency of human resolution and real frequencies was determined by experiments, where humans had to listen to sound of varying frequencies. They had to describe the change in perception, like high frequency, half as high frequency etc. Using these empirical data, the linear frequency axis (f) is converted into a *Mel scale* (f_{mel}) applying the transform [Fan73] (Figure 21.11)

$$f_{\text{mel}} = 2595 \log\left(1 + \frac{f}{700\,\text{Hz}}\right) . \tag{21.18}$$

With respect to this observation, we have to consider modified definitions of the originally introduced spectrum and cepstrum. The *Mel spectrum* results in a weighted version of the original spectrum. The basic idea is to define discrete filters $[h_t^{(k)}]_{t\geq 0}$, $k = \{0, 1, \ldots, K-1\}$, which operate on the discrete signal $[f_t^{(\tau)}]_{t\geq 0}$. Examples of three different triangular discrete filters are illustrated in Figure 21.12. The resulting signal $[g_t^{(k,\tau)}]_{t\geq 0}$ is defined by

$$g_t^{(k,\tau)} = \sum_\mu f_\mu^{(\tau)} h_{t-\mu}^{(k)} . \tag{21.19}$$

Obviously, the operation in (21.19) is a discrete convolution of $[f_t^{(\tau)}]_{t\geq 0}$ and $[h_t^{(k)}]_{t\geq 0}$. Therefore, the Fourier transforms $F_\nu^{(\tau)}$, $G_\nu^{(\tau,k)}$, and $H_\nu^{(k)}$ satisfy (convolution theorem, cf. Sect. 13.3)

$$G_\nu^{(\tau,k)} = F_\nu^{(\tau)} H_\nu^{(k)} . \tag{21.20}$$

Using this equation, the Mel spectrum is simply defined by

$$\text{MFC}^{(\tau,k)} = \sum_{\nu=0}^{M-1} (H_\nu^{(k)})^2 (F_\nu^{(\tau)})^2 , \tag{21.21}$$

and the *Mel cepstrum* is analogously

$$\text{MFCC}_\nu^{(\tau)} = \sum_{k=0}^{K-1} \log |\text{MFC}^{(\tau,k)}| \cos \frac{\nu\,\pi(2k+3)}{2K} . \tag{21.22}$$

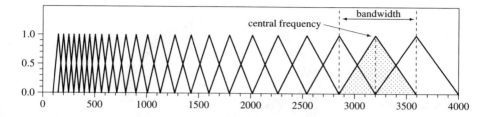

Figure 21.12: Triangular filters for 25 frequency groups (from [ST95; p. 55])

The 25 linear filters, which are commonly used for computing Mel spectra and Mel cepstra, are based on seven triangle shaped functions with $f_1 = 150$ Hz, $f_2 = 200$ Hz, $f_3 = 250$ Hz, ..., $f_7 = 450$ Hz. The width of each triangle is 100 Hz. Furthermore, each octave between 500 Hz and 4000 Hz[7] includes six filters, where the filters start and end at the frequencies of their neighbors [ST95].

21.7 Linear Predictive Coding

Speech recognition algorithms apply combinations of spatial, spectral, and cepstral features, to construct features, and to improve the recognition results. The crucial point of speech recognition algorithms and the associated features is that researchers look for suitable mathematical models. These models should consider both the speech production and the speech perception of human beings, because for pattern analysis it is useful to know about the principles of speech generation and about speech reception. In this sense, speech analysis is more complex than computer vision, which simulates only the human *sensor* (the eye, Figure 1.8). The human sensor — the ear — was already shown in Figure 1.4, and the perception as well as the resolution of frequencies was empirically studied, and is modeled with the Mel scale. In Figure 21.13, we see the anatomy of the human speech generation system. All speech signals are produced by air streaming from the lungs through the *vocal tract* including the throat and mouth. Consequently, the characteristics of the vocal tract influence speech signals. The average length of the adult male vocal tract is 17 cm, and the diameter varies up to 2.5 cm. If voiced speech is produced, the vocal folds are caused to vibrate. The vibration frequency is the so-called *pitch frequency*. The pitch frequency of an adult speaker is in the range of 50 to 500 Hz. Children or women have higher pitch frequencies than male speakers, because the vocal folds are shorter. In a physical sense, the vocal tract forms a tube that is characterized by its resonances, the so-called *formants*. Since humans show differences in the structure of the vocal tract (length, diameter, resonance, etc.), the influence of the tube on the speech signal is not significant for recognition purposes and should be eliminated. Linear predictive coding (LPC) provides a complete model for speech production, and it analyzes the speech signal such that the characteristic effects of the vocal tract and its formants can be separated from the excitation.

---

[7] i.e., 500 Hz — 1000 Hz, 1000 Hz — 2000 Hz, and 2000 Hz — 4000 Hz

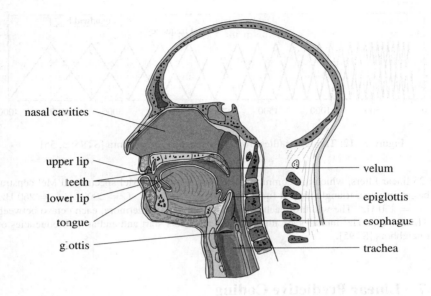

Figure 21.13: Speech production: the vocal tract

The process of removing the formants is called *inverse filtering*, whereas the remaining signal is called the *residue*.

Without introducing mathematical details and results from signal theory, the basic idea of LPC is that each discrete value f_t of the speech signal $[f_t]_{t\geq 0}$ has to be represented by a linear combination

$$f_t = \sum_{\mu=1}^{M} a_\mu f_{t-\mu} \qquad (21.23)$$

of M predecessors $f_{t-1}, f_{t-2}, \ldots, f_{t-M}$. For all samples f_t, $t_0 \leq t \leq t_1$, of a given frame, this linear combination (21.23) can be transformed into an equivalent matrix equation

$$\begin{pmatrix} \hat{f}_{t_0} \\ \hat{f}_{t_0+1} \\ \hat{f}_{t_0+2} \\ \vdots \\ \hat{f}_{t_1} \end{pmatrix} = \underbrace{\begin{pmatrix} f_{t_0-1} & f_{t_0-2} & \cdots & f_{t_0-M} \\ f_{t_0} & f_{t_0-1} & \cdots & f_{t_0-M+1} \\ f_{t_0+1} & f_{t_0} & \cdots & f_{t_0-M+2} \\ \vdots & \vdots & \vdots & \vdots \\ f_{t_1-1} & f_{t_1-2} & \cdots & f_{t_1-M} \end{pmatrix}}_{M \in \mathbb{R}^{(t_1-t_0) \times M}} \begin{pmatrix} a_1 \\ a_2 \\ a_3 \\ \vdots \\ a_M \end{pmatrix} . \qquad (21.24)$$

Generally, there will exist no solution $\boldsymbol{a} = (a_1, a_2, \ldots, a_M)^{\mathrm{T}}$ for the system of equations, $\boldsymbol{f} = \boldsymbol{M}\boldsymbol{a}$. For that reason, we search for parameters $\boldsymbol{a}$ which minimize an error measure

21.7 Linear Predictive Coding

between the real values f_t and their approximations $\hat{f}_t$ defined by the sum in (21.23). Here we take the mean square error. The predictor coefficients $a_\mu \in \mathbb{R}$ of the linear combination (21.23) are computed by minimizing the parameterized mean square error ϵ (which is a M-variate function of the vector $\boldsymbol{a}$). This error is a measure of the differences between the real values f_t and its predictions $\hat{f}_t$, i.e., we search for the global minimum of the multivariate function

$$\epsilon = \sum_{t=t_0}^{t_1}(f_t - \hat{f}_t)^2 = \sum_{t=t_0}^{t_1}\left(f_t - \sum_{\mu=1}^{M} a_\mu f_{t-\mu}\right)^2. \quad (21.25)$$

The optimization of (21.25) can be done using the gradient and the zero-crossings of the gradient vector with respect to the variables $a_1, a_2, \ldots, a_M$. The partial derivatives are

$$\frac{\partial \epsilon}{\partial a_\nu} = -2 \cdot \sum_{t=t_0}^{t_1}\left(f_t - \sum_{\mu=1}^{M} a_\mu f_{t-\mu}\right) \cdot f_{t-\nu}, \quad (21.26)$$

for $1 \leq \nu \leq M$, and we get M linear equations

$$\sum_{\mu=1}^{M} a_\mu \sum_{t=t_0}^{t_1} f_{t-\mu} f_{t-\nu} = -\sum_{t=t_0}^{t_1} f_t f_{t-\nu}, \quad (21.27)$$

wherein the computation of the autocorrelation (cf. (21.5)) is required. A recursive and efficient way to solve this system of linear equations is due to Levinson (cf. [Nie83; p. 99]), but this method will not be introduced here. Instead, we use the pseudo-inverse matrix, which was already introduced in Sect. 19.8, and get

$$\begin{pmatrix} a_1 \\ a_2 \\ a_3 \\ \vdots \\ a_M \end{pmatrix} = \boldsymbol{M}^+ \begin{pmatrix} f_{t_0} \\ f_{t_0+1} \\ f_{t_0+2} \\ \vdots \\ f_{t_1} \end{pmatrix}, \quad (21.28)$$

where $\boldsymbol{M}^+ = \left(\boldsymbol{M}^T \boldsymbol{M}\right)^{-1} \boldsymbol{M}^T$ is the pseudo-inverse of $\boldsymbol{M}$.

One common problem associated with linear prediction is the question of how many predecessors of f_t should be considered in the linear combination. Experimental evaluations have shown that the sampling frequency, measured in kHz, plus 4 or 5 is an appropriate number of prediction coefficients ([Nie83], p. 100). This general rule allows an appropriate computation of residues.

The practical use of LPC coefficients is multifarious. They are used for speech encoding, speech synthesis, and speech recognition. Of course, for different speech signals we get different prediction coefficients. The vector of LPC coefficients can thus serve as a feature vector for discriminating signals of different classes. In addition to the coefficient vector $\boldsymbol{a}$, usually the mean-square error (21.25) is also used as a component of the feature vector [Nie83, Nie90a].

The discussion so far is restricted to one-dimensional signals. Of course, linear prediction is also applied for image processing, especially for texture modeling [Mao92]. A suitable

Figure 21.14: Logarithmic model spectrum using Hamming windows (duration 10 ms) and 20, 30 and 40 prediction coefficients

neighborhood $[f_{i,j}]_{n_0 \leq i \leq n_1, m_0 \leq j \leq m_1}$ is chosen and gray-levels of the image are expressed by linear combinations of their neighbors, i.e.,

$$f_{i,j} = \sum_{\substack{\mu=n_0 \\ i \neq \mu}}^{n_1} \sum_{\substack{\nu=m_0 \\ j \neq \nu}}^{m_1} a_{\mu,\nu} f_{i-\mu, j-\nu} \quad . \quad (21.29)$$

The computation of the coefficient matrix $(a_{\mu,\nu})_{\mu,\nu}$ is done analogously to the one-dimensional case. We have to minimize the mean square error of the prediction:

$$\epsilon = \sum_{i,j} (f_{i,j} - \hat{f}_{i,j})^2 \quad . \quad (21.30)$$

The resulting matrix of coefficients can be used as image features and can be applied for the comparison or classification of textures or images.

21.8 Model Spectrum and Cepstrum

Most speech recognition system use two types of cepstral features. On the one hard DFT cepstral features are applied as introduced in Sect. 21.5 and Sect. 21.6, where the Fourier transform is directly operating on the speech signal. The LPC coefficients a can be used to compute the *model spectrum* (or *LPC spectrum*), which is the discrete Fourier transform of the computed prediction coefficients a.

The model spectrum is a smoothed version of the Fourier transform of the original signal. The maxima of the model spectrum indicate the formants and are discriminating features for vowels ([Nie83], p. 108). Figure 21.14 shows the model spectrum using a varying number of prediction coefficients. The smoothing property is illustrated in Figure 21.15. Cepstral coefficients corresponding to the LPC coefficients are widely used in speech recognition.

The model spectrum can be used to compute the *model cepstrum*. For that purpose, the magnitude of Fourier coefficients related to the model spectrum are the input components of a discrete Fourier transform. A nice theoretical result shows that the model cepstrum can be computed without an explicit Fourier transform. The required recursive formulas are omitted and can be found in [ST95]. In general, the cepstral features resulting from LPC coefficients represent the characteristics of the vocal tract and excitation separately. The advantages of the model cepstrum are that higher order coefficients encode the excitation coefficients, whereas the lower ones include the characteristic properties of the vocal tract.

21.9 Implementation Issues

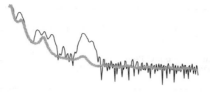

Figure 21.15: Logarithmic spectrum and logarithmic model spectrum (20 prediction coefficients) using Hamming windows (duration 10 ms)

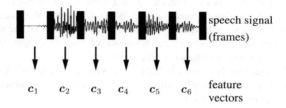

Figure 21.16: Decomposition of speech signals into frames, and the associated sequence of features

21.9 Implementation Issues

The computation of the pseudo-inverse in Sect. 21.7 requires matrix inversion and multiplication. All these operations were already introduced and implemented in our template class for matrices. Thus, the computation of LPC coefficients is easy and straightforward.

The regression line in Figure 21.3 could as well be computed using the pseudo-inverse. A more efficient and easier solution was shown in Exercise 19.h.

This chapter treats many features and methods to compute them. A very general view of speech classification is shown in Figure 21.16. The features denoted by c_i vary greatly between applications: they may be sequences of scalars, sequences of vectors, sequences of feature sequences, matrices, sets of matrices and others. With respect to implementation issues, classifiers should work with arbitrary features. They should be independent from the concrete representation as much as possible. For that reason, we define an abstract class for features to be used for classification purposes (Listing 200). As we will see in Chapter 22, it is most useful to have a distance function in order to compare two features; this is implemented in Listing 200 as a pure virtual operator. For the implementation of a classification we will now have to derive our own class for features from this abstract base class; in this derived class we can have any combination of the numeric feature values which were introduced in this chapter. Our derived class will have to define a distance function that is dependent on the particular classifier and on the application.

For statistical classification it is often useful to convert a feature to a random variable. We also provide a conversion for this purpose and outline how this can be declared in Listing 200.

```
#include "Object.h"
class RandomVariable : public Object {} ;  // to be refined later
class Feature : public Object {
 public :
   virtual double operator- (const Feature&) const = 0;  // distance function
   virtual operator RandomVariable () const = 0;
};
```

Exercises

21.a Typical features of a speech signal are the zero-crossings and the slopes of the univariate function at those points. Write a program that computes all zero-crossings of a given speech signal. Implement the calculation of the slope for a zero-crossing. For that purpose define a neighborhood of discrete sample values and use the pseudo-inverse for determination of the slope.

21.b Use the signals created in Sect. 12.1. Overlay them with noise created in Sect. 12.3 using a tool as described in Sect. 12.1. Create an image object of appropriate size and compute the spectrum.

21.c A one-dimensional signal is defined by

t	0	1	2	3	4	5
f_t	2	6	1	−4	−3	0

Compute the coefficients a_1 and a_2 of the linear prediction and use the result for the determination of f_6.

21.d Implement a function which computes the LPC prediction coefficients for each sample of a given frame of the speech signal. Use the Gauss elimination procedure for solving the occurring system of linear equations. Now apply your algorithm for speech encoding and send the resynthetisized signal to your soundcard.

Chapter 22

Numerical Pattern Classification

As outlined in Sect. 8.1 numerical pattern classification deals with the problem of assigning feature vectors c to a class Ω_κ taken from a set of discrete categorical variables $\Omega = \{\Omega_1, \Omega_2, \ldots, \Omega_K\}$. The features are computed from sensor data like images or speech signals. Since these signals are usually corrupted by noise, the features are regarded as probabilistic quantities. We postulate that signals can be associated with features that allow classification, i.e., features of different classes should be different and separated from each other. Features belonging to the same class are expected to occupy a compact area of the feature space [Nie90a].

Let us assume that the numerical feature c is a d–dimensional real-valued vector. A classifier is mathematically defined by the discrete mapping

$$\zeta : \begin{cases} \mathbb{R}^d & \to & \{1, 2, \ldots, K\} \\ c & \mapsto & \kappa \end{cases} \qquad (22.1)$$

which assigns a class index κ, i.e., a discrete value, to a feature vector c. The assignment ζ is the so-called *decision function*.[1]

In speech recognition, for instance, this function might map a speech signal to a single word of a given lexicon or to a sentence with its semantics. Other examples, where it is not important to understand *what* is said, are the identification of languages or speakers. The classifier maps the associated features to a language class or a person's name.

Special types of classification problems, which are widely applied in computer vision, were already discussed in Sect. 18.1: The computation of binary images requires the classification of each pixel. We have to decide for each pixel, whether it is part of the background or of the object. In this case, the features are gray-level values and the decision rule is defined by a simple threshold operation. The multi-thresholding algorithm (cf. Sect. 18.3) applies another classifier which maps pixels to more than two classes. The classification rule for binarization was easily derived from fairly elementary arguments using histograms and expected properties of relative frequencies; the classification of speech or image signals, in general, requires more complicated and sophisticated decision rules. More common and far more complicated computer vision applications of classifiers than simple pre-processing operations are, for example, the identification and localization of objects shown in an image of a scene.

---
[1] In the following text we use *decision function* and *decision rule* for ζ.

Several numerical classifiers are introduced and discussed in the following sections. The reader will get a brief and illustrative introduction to classification theory and a proper insight into various classifiers without extensive mathematical expositions. For detailed theoretical considerations, we strongly recommend [Bis95, Nie83, Rip96].

22.1 General Notes on Classifiers

Before we start with various definitions of the decision function ζ, we have to explain some basic concepts of classification theory.

In Figure 8.1 we introduced the common structure of simple pattern classification systems, where the classification module requires the definition of an appropriate decision function ζ. The classification rule depends on the problem domain. A general decision procedure that solves all classification problems within the given feature space seems impossible. The construction of classifiers basically uses observable data and takes experience and domain knowledge (not necessarily of experts) into consideration. Using these sources of information, a general decision rule is computed which also allows the classification of features which were *not* part of the sample data. The process of constructing a decision rule using a set of samples is usually called the *learning* or *training*. In pattern recognition theory we make a distinction between two different types of learning: if the classes of sample elements are known, we call it *supervised learning*; otherwise, the learning stage is called *unsupervised*. Both learning strategies can be used to create a classifier automatically, i.e., without manual support. The training of classifiers based on unlabeled feature vectors is incomparably harder than the supervised case of learning [Rip96]. The classification of previously unobserved features is called the generalization property of classifiers.

A common problem is the judgement of classifiers and the development of measures for the quality of classifiers. Obvious and often applied criteria are the probability of misclassification or the concrete recognition rate for predefined sample sets. Standard test beds and benchmark data for pattern recognition are, for instance, the U.S. Postal Service database [Vap96], the Computer Vision Test Images,[2] the ECVnet Benchmarking[3] or the speech data of the North American Business Corpus. In general, the optimality of classifiers depends on the chosen criteria. If, for example, a classifier provides the lowest probability for misclassification but the computational complexity prohibits its practical use, we will not denote this decision procedure to be optimal for real world applications. Nevertheless, classifiers are often judged by the costs produced by their decision rule. Correct, false, and rejected classifications may lead to different costs. The expected costs of a decision function might be considered as an appropriate measure for the implemented classifier. A classifier, for instance, that decides whether a person is allowed to enter a high security zone, will have lower costs if an authorized person is rejected, as opposed to allowing access to an unauthorized person. Nevertheless, in the following we define the best classifier by the minimization of the error probability. It can be shown that this classifier is equal to the classifier using a cost function that weighs correct decisions by zero and misclassifications by one. The error probability p_B of this optimal classifier is the

---
[2]cf. http://www.cs.cmu.edu/~cil/v-images.html
[3]cf. http://peipa.essex.ac.uk/benchmark

```
struct Sample : public Object { // auxiliary class
  int classnumber;               // ordered pair for labeled
  Feature * feature;             // sample
};

class Classifier : public Object {
  int number_of_classes; // dimension
  bool has_reject_class; // if true, classes range from 0...number_of_classes
  bool trained;          // if true, classifier is ready to do classification
  public:
  virtual int classify(const Feature & f) const = 0;
  virtual void train(const Bag&);  // supply training 'set'
};
```

Listing 201

so-called *Bayesian error probability*. The major problem is the computation of a decision rule that results in an optimal classifier.

Different types of decision rules result in classifiers with various properties. It is interesting from a theoretical point of view to compare different classifiers with respect to several characteristics. In particular, the relationship between the considered and the optimal classifier is of highest importance. Another significant property of classifiers is the consistency of their decision rules. A discrimination rule is called *consistent* if an increase of the sample data size implies that the expected error of the given classifier converges against the Bayesian error p_B.

22.2 Design of Classifiers

The design of classifiers is based on the fundamental assumption that feature vectors of the same class have a small distance with respect to a suitably defined distance function. This measure might be a geometric distance function (e.g., the Euclidean distance), some probability measure (e.g., a posteriori probability) or others. The very general structure of a classifier in C++ is shown in Listing 201. A function which gets a reference to a feature computes the class number; this function is a pure virtual function of the abstract class `Classifier`. Various ideas for the implementation of this function are considered in the following sections.

Training a classifier can be defined by a method `train` which accepts a `Bag` as an argument, i.e., an unsorted collection of samples where each sample may occur several times. The class `Sample` is derived from `Object`, so objects of this class can be added to the `Bag`.[4] For supervised learning, this collection will consist of pairs that associate a feature with a class number. We introduce an auxiliary class for this purpose. For unsupervised learning, however, this training set will consist of unlabeled features only, and the classifier clusters the sample into classes. The derived classes will have to define the learning procedures which are defined by the method `train(Bag&)`.

A decision rule induces a partition of the feature space. Each subset is associated with a class. This partition is automatically computed in the case of threshold operations (cf. Sect. 18.3). The same holds for the quantization of signals, where a continuous signal is mapped to a discrete value. Methods that compute a partition of a vector space without knowing the class

---

[4]Only NIHCL-objects are allowed as elements of collections, cf. Sect. 16.5.

assignments of learning samples are called *vector quantization methods*. Surprisingly, for real-valued scalar features, there exist closed form solutions for quantization. These computations are based on certain residual functions that have to be minimized to define the optimal partition. For higher dimensional feature vectors, however, no analytical solution is available [Nie83]. The existing algorithms for vector quantization are basically iterative search techniques. A simple example of vector quantization was already discussed in Sect. 18.8, where the number of different color vectors was reduced. In this case, features were three-dimensional color vectors.

Classifiers can use discriminating functions or rely on probabilistic properties of sample data, as we will show in the following sections.

22.3 Linear Discriminants

The discussion of linear discriminants is first restricted to two classes, i.e., we deal only with binary classes Ω_1 and Ω_2. This simplifies the understanding of linear classifiers, and allows an easier and clearer insight into basic concepts.

Linear functions can be used to define hyperplanes. The idea of linear discriminants is to split the feature space by such a hyperplane into two half-spaces. Each of these half-spaces represents the area of a single class.

For a formal definition, we set $c = (c_1, c_2, \ldots, c_d)^T \in \mathbb{R}^d$ to be the observed, d-dimensional feature vector. A linear discriminant classifier applies the decision rule

$$\zeta(c) = \begin{cases} 1, & \text{if } q(c) > 0 \\ 2, & \text{otherwise} \end{cases}, \tag{22.2}$$

with a *splitting function*

$$q(c) = q_0 + \sum_{i=1}^{d} q_i c_i = q_0 + (q_1, q_2, \ldots, q_d) \cdot (c_1, c_2, \ldots, c_d)^T, \tag{22.3}$$

and $q_i \in \mathbb{R}$. This decision rule is easily implemented and the computational complexity of the decision process is linear in d.

Figures 22.1 and 22.2 illustrate linear discriminants for one- and two-dimensional feature vectors. Boxes are samples belonging to one class, circles to the other. In the 1–D case, (22.2) defines a single point in the feature space, the *splitting point*. The linear function $q(c)$ reduces here to $q(c) = q_0 + q_1 c_1$. This classifier corresponds to the decision rule applied for binarization (18.6), where we computed a threshold $\theta = -q_0/q_1$, $q_1 > 0$, for discrimination. Remarkably, the threshold was computed unsupervised, i.e., without knowing the assignment of gray-levels to background and foreground. In case of 2–D feature vectors, the classifier is defined by (22.2), where $d = 2$, and the induced partition of the feature space is characterized by a single 2–D line (cf. Figure 22.2), the *splitting line*. It should be clear that misclassification can occur, whereas the optimal classifier in this case will define a splitting curve which is not necessarily linear, such that the number of misclassifications is minimal. The given 2–D example shows two misclassifications.

22.3 Linear Discriminants

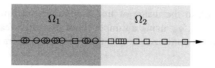

Figure 22.1: Two classes in a one-dimensional feature space

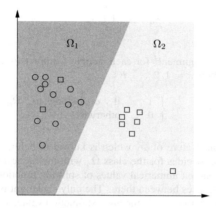

Figure 22.2: Two classes in a two-dimensional feature space

If the set of features includes n sample vectors, the computation of the optimal linear classifier corresponds to a discrete optimization problem. Given d–dimensional real-valued features, it can be shown that the exhaustive search over all possible linear classifiers is bounded by the total number of $2\binom{n}{d}$ different linear discriminants (Exercise 22.e).

Now we extend the decision rule (22.2) such that multiple class problems can be treated. For that purpose, we introduce two linear functions $q_1(c)$ and $q_2(c)$, one for each class Ω_1 and Ω_2, where $q_\lambda(c) = q_{\lambda,0} + \sum_{i=1}^{d} q_{\lambda,i} c_i$. Let the splitting function be defined by $\tilde{q}_1(c) := q_1(c) - q_2(c)$. For a given feature vector c we decide for class Ω_1, if $\tilde{q}_1(c) > 0$, i.e., in this case we have $q_1(c) > q_2(c)$. Analogously, we can define $\tilde{q}_2(c) := q_2(c) - q_1(c)$, and we decide for Ω_2, if $\tilde{q}_2(c) > 0$ resp. $q_2(c) > q_1(c)$. This observation motivates the following definition for the multiple class decision rule of linear classifiers:

$$\zeta(c) = \operatorname*{argmax}_{\lambda} \tilde{q}_\lambda(c) = \operatorname*{argmax}_{\lambda} \left(\tilde{q}_{\lambda,0} + \sum_{i=1}^{d} \tilde{q}_{\lambda,i} c_i \right) , \qquad (22.4)$$

where $\tilde{q}_\lambda$ denotes the *splitting polynomial* of class Ω_λ which is defined by the $(d+1)$–dimensional vector $\tilde{\boldsymbol{q}}_\lambda^T = (\tilde{q}_{\lambda,0}, \tilde{q}_{\lambda,1}, \ldots, \tilde{q}_{\lambda,d},)$. Thus, we associate with each class Ω_λ a linear function, and decide for the class with the highest function value for a given feature vector c. Unfortunately, the geometric interpretation and visualization of splitting functions for $\lambda > 2$ is not as obvious as for $\lambda = 1, 2$ [Sch77], i.e., the polynomial does *not* separate the samples geometrically.

The major problem related to the usage of linear splitting functions is the computation of coefficient vectors $q_1, q_2, \ldots, q_K$ using a sample set of classified feature vectors. In fact, this problem can be reduced to an optimization task that leads to a system of equations linear in the unknowns.

Let $\omega_\kappa = \{{}^1 c_\kappa, {}^2 c_\kappa, \ldots, {}^{N_\kappa} c_\kappa\}$ be the set of sample data assigned to class Ω_κ, i.e., we observe N_κ samples for classes Ω_κ, $\kappa = 1, 2, \ldots, K$. The complete set of samples is

$$\omega = \bigcup_{\kappa=1}^{K} \omega_\kappa \quad . \tag{22.5}$$

Since we know the class assignment[5] for each sample feature $c \in \omega \subset \mathbb{R}^d$ we can define *indicator functions* χ_κ, where $\kappa = 1, 2, \ldots, K$:

$$\chi_\kappa(c) = \begin{cases} 1, & \text{if } c \text{ belongs to } \Omega_\kappa \\ 0, & \text{otherwise} \end{cases} \tag{22.6}$$

Let ${}^j c_\lambda$ be the j-th sample feature of ω_λ which is known to belong to class Ω_λ. Since the classifier defined by (22.2) decides for the class Ω_κ with the highest function value $q_\kappa({}^j c_\lambda)$, the decision does not depend on numerical values of splitting functions evaluated for a given feature vector but on differences between them. The only constraint is that the linear splitting function of the correct class will result in the highest function value. Without loss of generality we expect the function value to be *one* for the correct class, and *zero* otherwise. Due to the fact that we know the class assignment of each sample feature in ω, we use the indicator function defined in (22.6) as the *ideal splitting function*. For each d–dimensional feature vector ${}^j c_\lambda = ({}^j c_{\lambda,1}, {}^j c_{\lambda,2}, \ldots, {}^j c_{\lambda,d})^\mathrm{T}$ ($\lambda = 1, 2, \ldots, K$, and $j = 1, 2, \ldots, N_\lambda$) of the training set we get K equations ($\kappa = 1, 2, \ldots, K$):

$$q_\kappa({}^j c_\lambda) = q_{\kappa,0} + \sum_{i=1}^{d} q_{\kappa,i} {}^j c_{\lambda,i} = \chi_\kappa({}^j c_\lambda) \quad , \tag{22.7}$$

which are *linear* in the coefficients of splitting functions. This system of linear equations can be written in matrix notation. For that purpose, we define extended features by ${}^j \tilde{c}_\lambda = (1, {}^j c_{\lambda,1}, {}^j c_{\lambda,2}, \ldots, {}^j c_{\lambda,d})^\mathrm{T}$ by just adding the component 1. This trick allows us to introduce the a matrix $A \in \mathbb{R}^{D \times K(d+1)}$ which is shown below in (22.12) where

$$D = K \cdot \sum_{\kappa=1}^{K} N_\kappa \quad . \tag{22.8}$$

Furthermore we set the vector $x \in \mathbb{R}^{K(d+1)}$ to

$$x = (q_{1,0}, q_{1,1}, \ldots, q_{1,d}, q_{2,0}, q_{2,1}, \ldots, q_{2,d}, \ldots, q_{K,0}, q_{K,1}, \ldots, q_{K,d})^\mathrm{T} \tag{22.9}$$

and finally introduce the binary vector $b \in \mathbb{R}^D$ which is shown below in (22.12).

---
[5] which is unique; one feature is assigned to exactly *one* class

22.3 Linear Discriminants

Using the above notation, the computation of linear splitting functions now corresponds to solving the system of linear equations:

$$\boldsymbol{A}\boldsymbol{x} = \boldsymbol{b} \ . \tag{22.10}$$

For real data, the probability that the vector $\boldsymbol{b}$ is not in the range of the matrix $\boldsymbol{A}$, is one. Therefore, we compute the solution $\boldsymbol{x}$ which minimizes the residual $\|\boldsymbol{A}\boldsymbol{x} - \boldsymbol{b}\|$. The coefficients $\boldsymbol{x}$ of the linear splitting functions are thus given by

$$\boldsymbol{x} = (\boldsymbol{A}^\mathrm{T}\boldsymbol{A})^{-1}\boldsymbol{A}^\mathrm{T}\boldsymbol{b} \ . \tag{22.11}$$

The pseudo-inverse is usually computed using SVD (cf. Sect. 19.8).

$$\boldsymbol{A} = \begin{pmatrix} {}^1\tilde{\boldsymbol{c}}_1{}^\mathrm{T} & \boldsymbol{0}^\mathrm{T} & \cdots & \boldsymbol{0}^\mathrm{T} \\ \boldsymbol{0}^\mathrm{T} & {}^1\tilde{\boldsymbol{c}}_1{}^\mathrm{T} & & \boldsymbol{0}^\mathrm{T} \\ \vdots & & \ddots & \vdots \\ \boldsymbol{0}^\mathrm{T} & \cdots & \boldsymbol{0}^\mathrm{T} & {}^1\tilde{\boldsymbol{c}}_1{}^\mathrm{T} \\ {}^2\tilde{\boldsymbol{c}}_1{}^\mathrm{T} & \boldsymbol{0}^\mathrm{T} & \cdots & \boldsymbol{0}^\mathrm{T} \\ \boldsymbol{0}^\mathrm{T} & {}^2\tilde{\boldsymbol{c}}_1{}^\mathrm{T} & & \boldsymbol{0}^\mathrm{T} \\ \vdots & & \ddots & \vdots \\ \boldsymbol{0}^\mathrm{T} & \cdots & \boldsymbol{0}^\mathrm{T} & {}^2\tilde{\boldsymbol{c}}_1{}^\mathrm{T} \\ \vdots & & & \vdots \\ {}^{N_1}\tilde{\boldsymbol{c}}_1{}^\mathrm{T} & \boldsymbol{0}^\mathrm{T} & \cdots & \boldsymbol{0}^\mathrm{T} \\ \boldsymbol{0}^\mathrm{T} & {}^{N_1}\tilde{\boldsymbol{c}}_1{}^\mathrm{T} & & \boldsymbol{0}^\mathrm{T} \\ \vdots & & \ddots & \vdots \\ \boldsymbol{0}^\mathrm{T} & \cdots & \boldsymbol{0}^\mathrm{T} & {}^{N_1}\tilde{\boldsymbol{c}}_1{}^\mathrm{T} \\ \vdots & \vdots & \vdots & \vdots \\ {}^1\tilde{\boldsymbol{c}}_K{}^\mathrm{T} & \boldsymbol{0}^\mathrm{T} & \cdots & \boldsymbol{0}^\mathrm{T} \\ \boldsymbol{0}^\mathrm{T} & {}^1\tilde{\boldsymbol{c}}_K{}^\mathrm{T} & & \boldsymbol{0}^\mathrm{T} \\ \vdots & & \ddots & \vdots \\ \boldsymbol{0}^\mathrm{T} & \cdots & \boldsymbol{0}^\mathrm{T} & {}^1\tilde{\boldsymbol{c}}_K{}^\mathrm{T} \\ \vdots & & & \vdots \\ {}^{N_K}\tilde{\boldsymbol{c}}_1{}^\mathrm{T} & \boldsymbol{0}^\mathrm{T} & \cdots & \boldsymbol{0}^\mathrm{T} \\ \boldsymbol{0}^\mathrm{T} & {}^{N_K}\tilde{\boldsymbol{c}}_1{}^\mathrm{T} & & \boldsymbol{0}^\mathrm{T} \\ \vdots & & \ddots & \vdots \\ \boldsymbol{0}^\mathrm{T} & \cdots & \boldsymbol{0}^\mathrm{T} & {}^{N_K}\tilde{\boldsymbol{c}}_1{}^\mathrm{T} \end{pmatrix} \quad \boldsymbol{b} = \begin{pmatrix} \chi_1({}^1\boldsymbol{c}_1) \\ \chi_2({}^1\boldsymbol{c}_1) \\ \vdots \\ \chi_K({}^1\boldsymbol{c}_1) \\ \chi_1({}^2\boldsymbol{c}_1) \\ \chi_2({}^2\boldsymbol{c}_1) \\ \vdots \\ \chi_K({}^2\boldsymbol{c}_1) \\ \vdots \\ \chi_1({}^{N_K}\boldsymbol{c}_K) \\ \chi_2({}^{N_K}\boldsymbol{c}_K) \\ \vdots \\ \chi_K({}^{N_K}\boldsymbol{c}_K) \end{pmatrix}$$

$$(22.12)$$

22.4 Polynomial Classifiers

An obvious generalization of linear discriminant classifiers is possible, if multivariate polynomials of higher degrees are used instead of linear functions. A multivariate polynomial

$$q_\lambda(c) = \sum_{i_1,i_2,\ldots,i_d=1}^{m} q_{\lambda,i_1,i_2,\ldots,i_d}\, c_1^{i_1} c_2^{i_2} \cdot \ldots \cdot c_d^{i_d} \quad , \tag{22.13}$$

is attached to each class Ω_λ, and the decision rule (22.4) remains unchanged.

Polynomial classifiers, in general, show several degrees of freedom: the degree m of the multivariate polynomial and the coefficients $q_{\lambda,i_1,i_2,\ldots,i_d} \in \mathbb{R}$. It is a highly non-trivial problem to optimize these parameters regarding the recognition rate. The degree of discriminating polynomials is a priori bounded by the number of free coefficients, the problem of over-fitting, and the available training data which is used for the computation of these unknown parameters. Usually, the training data consists of a set of feature vectors $\{c_1, c_2, \ldots, c_N\}$. The classes of these features might be known or unknown (supervised and unsupervised learning). In Sect. 18.1 we have already discussed methods for the estimation of the splitting point for image binarization, and we have seen that this is — even for this restricted classification task — a hard problem. Without considering the mathematical details, the computation of the coefficients and determination of discriminating polynomials can be solved, for instance, by linear programming methods, like the simplex algorithm (cf. [Sch77]), stochastic approximation, or in some cases even by closed form solutions [Nie83]. The introduction and discussion of the required mathematical framework is not in the scope of this book. We recommend [Nie83, Sch77] for more details. Nevertheless, the general implementation of a classifier in an object–oriented framework can provide possible extension slots for such ideas, as we show in the following sections.

In the next section, we choose density functions and discrete probability mass functions instead of polynomials for discrimination. In contrast to polynomials, we already know (partially) how to compute free parameters of statistical measures: In Chapter 7 we have discussed the calculation of relative frequencies and maximum likelihood methods to estimate parameters of probability density functions.

22.5 Bayesian Classifiers

In most practical applications, pattern classes have different a priori probabilities. Words of a language, for example, have different prior probabilities. In an arbitrary text, an auxiliary verb like "is" appears more probably than the word "Hefeweizen". If we have to classify a gastric ulcer in an image with respect to malignity, we know that benign ulcers have higher prior probabilities. This prior knowledge, of course, should influence decision finding, and an appropriate way of doing so is the usage of a probabilistic framework. We can describe feature vectors statistically if we already know that they are computed for patterns of a certain class; the probabilistic properties usually vary among the different classes. More formally, the probabilistic characterization of classes requires both the a priori probability $p(\Omega_\kappa)$ and the probability density function $p(c|\Omega_\kappa)$ of each class $\Omega_\kappa \in \Omega$.

22.5 Bayesian Classifiers

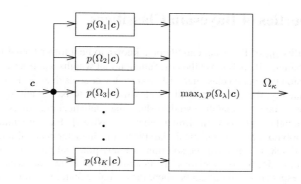

Figure 22.3: The principle of the Bayesian classifier

The value $p(\Omega_\kappa)$ denotes the probability to observe the class Ω_κ without taking the observed feature vector into consideration. If, for instance, all classes appear with the same probability, we have $p(\Omega_\kappa) = p(\Omega_\lambda)$ for $\kappa, \lambda \in \{1, 2, \ldots, K\}$.

The class-specific density $p(c|\Omega_\kappa)$ is a measure for the probability to observe feature vector c if the pattern class Ω_κ is present. This density might be, for instance, a Gaussian density function or, in the case of discrete features, a histogram. The a posteriori probability

$$p(\Omega_\kappa|c) = \frac{p(\Omega_\kappa)\,p(c|\Omega_\kappa)}{p(c)} = \frac{p(\Omega_\kappa)\,p(c|\Omega_\kappa)}{\sum_{\lambda=1}^{K} p(\Omega_\lambda)\,p(c|\Omega_\lambda)} \quad . \tag{22.14}$$

summarizes the probability that the class Ω_κ is present, if the feature vector c is observed. This discrete measure is the basic component of the Bayesian classifier and its decision rule.

For an observed feature vector c, the Bayesian classifier chooses the class with the highest a posteriori probability, i.e., the class index is computed by solving the optimization problem

$$\zeta(c) = \operatorname*{argmax}_{\lambda} p(\Omega_\lambda|c) = \operatorname*{argmax}_{\lambda} p(\Omega_\lambda)\,p(c|\Omega_\lambda) \quad . \tag{22.15}$$

The principle of Bayesian classifiers is illustrated in Figure 22.3. The second part of this equation holds, since the class index for the maximum of the a posteriori probability does not depend on the scaling factor $1/p(c)$. Thus the result of the optimization is independent of the denominator $p(c)$.

The above equation also shows that, in the case of uniformly distributed classes ($p(\Omega_\kappa) = p(\Omega_\lambda)$ for all classes), the Bayesian decision rule (22.15) reduces to the maximum likelihood decision, i.e.,

$$\begin{aligned}\zeta(c) &= \operatorname*{argmax}_{\lambda} p(\Omega_\lambda|c) = \operatorname*{argmax}_{\lambda} p(\Omega_\lambda)\,p(c|\Omega_\lambda) \\ &= \operatorname*{argmax}_{\lambda} p(c|\Omega_\lambda) \quad .\end{aligned} \tag{22.16}$$

22.6 Properties of Bayesian Classifiers

The error probability p_B of Bayesian classifiers is known to be a lower bound for misclassifications of all classifiers. If we choose the cost function that weighs a correct decision by zero and a wrong decision by one, no classifier will produce lower costs than the Bayesian classifier [Nie83]. Consequently, the design goal of all classifiers has to be the approximation of the Bayesian classifier. Many comparative studies show that statistical classifiers can be approximated by polynomial classifiers with similar reliability [Nie83]. Experimental comparisons, for example, of polynomial and statistical classifiers for character recognition show similar recognition rates [Nie83]. Thus, for the solution of many practical problems, reliable classifiers exist that do not depend on statistics. Non-statistical classifiers are usually applied for practical reasons, especially in those cases where the available feature vectors are not normally distributed and the parametric density is unknown. This already points out the most important task concerning Bayesian classifiers: the determination of statistical properties of pattern classes and of associated feature vectors.

The a priori probabilities $p(\Omega_\kappa)$, $1 \leq \kappa \leq K$, are easily computed via relative frequencies and classified sample data. If the sample data is not classified, incomplete data estimation techniques are required [Tan96] which can deal with this unsupervised learning problem.

The modeling of probability density functions of features is more difficult. Depending on their representation, we distinguish between parametric and non-parametric statistical classifiers in pattern recognition theory. We will not introduce these types of classifiers theoretically, but show the difference in two examples.

A non-parametric classifier applies discrete probabilities for decision finding. We have already introduced histograms. In general, histograms characterize discrete probabilities, which can be applied for statistical classification directly. Histograms for the probabilistic modeling of features and a priori probabilities can be estimated using discrete observations (cf. Chapter 7). Figure 22.4 shows the a priori probabilities (left) and the class specific probabilities of features (middle, right) for two classes. If a scalar feature $c \in \{1, 2, \ldots, 13\}$ has to be assigned to

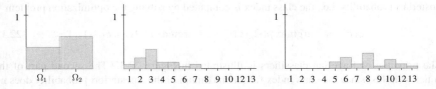

Figure 22.4: A priori probabilities (left), probabilities of scalar discrete features corresponding to class Ω_1 (middle), and class Ω_2 (right)

a class, the a priori probability $p(\Omega_\kappa)$ results from the left histogram, and the probabilities $p(c|\Omega_\kappa)$ for each class are computed using the middle histogram for Ω_1 and the right one for Ω_2.

If the features underlie a parametric distribution, parametric densities instead of histograms can be used for classification. We consider the most commonly used parametric density con-

22.6 Properties of Bayesian Classifiers

```
class Density : public Object {          // abstract interface
 public:                                  // all data to be defined in
  Density(void);                          // derived classes
  virtual ~Density(void);
  virtual double probability(const RandomVariable& X) const = 0;
  virtual double log_probability(const RandomVariable& X) const;
};
```
202

```
class Gauss : public Density {
  Vector<double> Mu;            // mean vector
  Matrix<double> Cov;           // covariance matrix
  Matrix<double> InverseCov;    // inverse covariance matrix
  double          Det;          // determinant
 public:
  Gauss(void);
  Gauss(int order);
  Gauss(const Gauss & g);
  Gauss(const Vector<double> & mu, const Matrix<double> & cov);
  virtual ~Gauss(void);
  const Vector<double> & mean(void) const;
  const Matrix<double> & covariance(void) const;
  const Matrix<double> & inverse_covariance(void) const;
  double determinant(void) const;              // compute determinant
  void estimateParameters(const Bag & trs);    // training 'set'
  virtual double probability(const RandomVariable & X) const;
  virtual double log_probability(const RandomVariable & X) const;
};
```
203

cerning statistical classification: the Gaussian probability density function (cf. Sect. 7.2). If d–dimensional feature vectors of a class are normally distributed, each class $\Omega_\kappa \in \Omega$ and its corresponding features can be characterized by the multivariate Gaussian density function

$$p(\boldsymbol{c}|\Omega_\kappa) = \frac{1}{\sqrt{|\det\, 2\pi \boldsymbol{\Sigma}_\kappa|}} \; \exp\left(-\frac{(\boldsymbol{c} - \boldsymbol{\mu}_\kappa)^\mathrm{T} \boldsymbol{\Sigma}_\kappa^{-1}(\boldsymbol{c} - \boldsymbol{\mu}_\kappa)}{2}\right) \quad . \tag{22.17}$$

The parameters of this probability density, the mean vector $\boldsymbol{\mu}_\kappa$ and the covariance matrix $\boldsymbol{\Sigma}_\kappa$, can be estimated applying the maximum likelihood method discussed in Chapter 7, presupposing that classes of sample data are known. If the training samples are not classified, again incomplete data estimation algorithms have to be applied [Red84]. As a consequence, it is not the histograms that have to be stored, but the parameters of the densities, i.e., $\boldsymbol{\mu}_\kappa$ and $\boldsymbol{\Sigma}_\kappa$. This shows the low storage requirements of parametric Bayesian classifiers.

A density function is a mathematical function satisfying several properties (cf. Chapter 7). For this reason, we introduce an abstract class `Density` for probability density functions, which is shown in Listing 202. This class includes pure virtual functions for the evaluation of densities for given random variables. The derived class for Gaussian densities provide a concrete implementation of these pure virtual methods (cf. Listing 203) and also provides parameter estimation from a set of samples, where the samples are again provided in a class `Bag`.

22.7 From Bayesian to Geometric Classifiers

By specialization, the Bayesian classifier which uses normally distributed features can be reduced to a simple classifier. In this special classifier, decision making depends on Euclidean distances only.

Let us consider two classes Ω_1 and Ω_2. The discrete prior probabilities $p(\Omega_1)$ and $p(\Omega_2)$ as well as the Gaussian densities $p(c|\Omega_1)$ and $p(c|\Omega_2)$ are assumed to be known. In this situation the Bayesian classifier decides for class Ω_1 if

$$p(\Omega_1)p(c|\Omega_1) > p(\Omega_2)p(c|\Omega_2) \ . \tag{22.18}$$

Now we specialize this decision rule by setting

$$\Sigma_1 = \Sigma_2 = \Sigma \ ; \tag{22.19}$$

taking the logarithm of both sides in (22.18), we get

$$\log p(\Omega_1) + \mu_1^T \Sigma^{-1} c - \frac{1}{2} \mu_1^T \Sigma^{-1} \mu_1 > \log p(\Omega_2) + \mu_2^T \Sigma^{-1} c - \frac{1}{2} \mu_2^T \Sigma^{-1} \mu_2. \tag{22.20}$$

This decision rule proves the following important result: both splitting functions are linear in the components of the feature vector, and thus the Bayesian classifier reduces to a *linear splitting function* if the features are normally distributed and have the same covariance matrix. The coefficients of the polynomials are defined by functions of prior probabilities, of the mean vectors, and of the covariance matrix. For practical applications, this observation has an important consequence. For d–dimensional feature vectors, the linear splitting functions require the estimation of $K(d+1)$ parameters in the presence of K pattern classes. In contrast, the use of normal distributions expects the computation of $d(d+1)/2 + K(d+1)$ parameters. Therefore, for high-dimensional feature vectors and small values of K, the learning of linear splitting function parameters might lead to more robust estimates.

A further specialization results from uniform priors:

$$p(\Omega_1) = p(\Omega_2) \ . \tag{22.21}$$

Using this constraint we obtain the discriminant

$$\mu_1^T \Sigma^{-1} c - \frac{1}{2} \mu_1^T \Sigma^{-1} \mu_1 > \mu_2^T \Sigma^{-1} c - \frac{1}{2} \mu_2^T \Sigma^{-1} \mu_2 \tag{22.22}$$

which is a simplified version of the widely used *Mahalanobis* distance defined by

$$(c - \mu_1)^T \Sigma^{-1} (c - \mu_1) < (c - \mu_2)^T \Sigma^{-1} (c - \mu_2) \ . \tag{22.23}$$

For implementation purposes, of course, we prefer (22.22) to (22.23) because these splitting functions are linear in the components of c.

If we additionally assume that the covariance matrix Σ is the identity matrix, the classification is based on the inequality

$$(c - \mu_1)^T (c - \mu_1) < (c - \mu_2)^T (c - \mu_2) \ . \tag{22.24}$$

22.8 Nearest Neighbor Classifier

This decision rule compares the quadratic Euclidean distances

$$||c - \mu_1||^2 < ||c - \mu_2||^2 , \qquad (22.25)$$

between feature and mean vectors, i.e., class centers.

The final specialization has shown that statistical classifiers lead to a simple distance measure for restricted statistical assumptions. The minimum distance classifier with respect to class dependent mean vectors is optimal if the feature vectors used are normally distributed with covariance matrices Σ that are equal to the identity matrix.

Classifiers based on parametric densities show the disadvantage that a parametric distribution of used feature vectors must be known. This causes some problems, especially for features that are not normally distributed. In general, there exist three possibilities to verify a density assumption:

1. the distribution of features is known by construction,
2. the hypothesized parametric density is proven by statistical tests or
3. the recognition rate of the resulting classifier suggests the correctness.

The use of the Euclidean distance to a reference vector — the mean vector of each class — motivates the introduction of nearest neighbor classifiers. Instead of computing mean vectors for each class and using a distance measure to mean vectors for discrimination, we utilize all observed feature vectors of the training set as a reference. The resulting classifier is the nearest neighbor classifier.

22.8 Nearest Neighbor Classifier

The nearest neighbor classifier requires a set of classified sample data, i.e., for each element c_i of $C = \{c_1, c_2, \ldots, c_n\}$ the class number $\zeta(c_i)$ is known. For a new feature vector, the class that points to the reference vector with the closest distance to the new vector is chosen. Thus, the decision rule is defined by

$$\zeta(c) = \operatorname*{argmin}_{\zeta(c_i)} \{||c - c_i|| \mid i = 1, 2, \ldots, n\} . \qquad (22.26)$$

This simple decision rule shows several degrees of freedom: the number of reference vectors and the choice of the distance measure. The distance function is not predefined, and the performance of the classifier will depend on the chosen metric. Two possible distance measures are the Euclidean distance or the city block metric. If the number of reference vectors is n, the complexity of the suggested nearest neighbor classifier is linear in n and thus bounded by $\mathcal{O}(n)$.

The nearest neighbor decision rule is very simple and used for many applications. Without any knowledge about pattern recognition or decision theory, the most obvious classifier applies the nearest neighbor decision rule. Depending on the training data, the nearest neighbor classifier induces a partition of the feature space. Every feature of the feature space is assigned to the

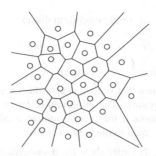

Figure 22.5: Voronoi diagram with 27 two-dimensional reference vectors

class of the closest training feature. The set of points whose nearest neighbor is c_i is called the Voronoi cell of c_i. Figure 22.5 shows the set of Voronoi cells induced by 27 two-dimensional feature vectors. Obviously, these cells result in a partition of the feature space, the Voronoi partition. The theory shows that the nearest neighbor classifier yields a suitable approximation of the distribution of features if no concrete density functions are available [Fuk90].

The success of this classifier strongly depends on the chosen reference patterns. It is a theoretically proven and well-known result that the nearest neighbor classifier is consistent and the error probability p_{NN} satisfies the following fundamental inequality

$$p_B \leq p_{NN} \leq 2 p_B \quad , \tag{22.27}$$

presupposing that an infinite sample set is available. In addition to experimental tests that prove the reliability of classifiers, this relation to the optimal Bayesian classifier justifies the practical use of nearest neighbor classifiers.

There exist various modifications of the nearest neighbor classifier. An obvious extension can be done by introduction of the k–nearest neighbor decision rule, which we already applied in the case of edge thinning (Sect. 19.2). Instead of looking for the closest reference vector, we decide for that class, which is the class of the majority of the k nearest neighbors. The probability of misclassifications for the k–nearest neighbor classifier converges to the Bayesian error probability with increasing training data. Compared to the nearest neighbor classifier, the suggested modification, in general, leads to more reliable decisions.

The computational complexity and the storage requirements of nearest neighbor classifiers are influenced by the size of reference data sets. Storing n reference vectors and applying the k–nearest neighbor decision rule, classification time is bounded by $\mathcal{O}(k\,n)$, if naive comparisons are done. The time complexity can be decreased to $\mathcal{O}(k\,\log n)$ if an approximated version of the nearest neighbor classifier is used [Ary94]. This classifier returns the nearest neighbor with a relative error margin. The more reference patterns that are available, the higher are the storage requirements and the number of comparisons needed for decision finding. However, less reference patterns induce a lower recognition rate.

22.9 Implementation of Classifiers

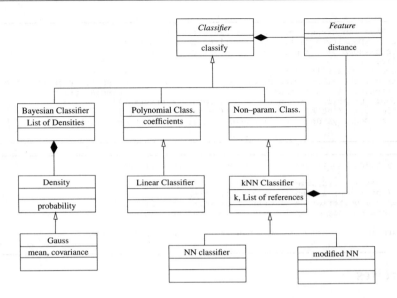

Figure 22.6: Class hierarchy for classifiers and features

22.9 Implementation of Classifiers

The implementation of classifiers, which we give in the following, is restricted to the explicit encoding of decision rules and the management of reference patterns, density functions or discriminating functions. The decision rule depends on the features used and the chosen classifier. Since the distance measure for the nearest neighbor classifier, for instance, can be any metric (Euclidean distance measure, city block metric or others), an implementation should leave the choice of the actual measure. This is the reason why we declared the virtual `operator-` in Listing 200.

Figure 22.6 suggests a class hierarchy for different types of classifiers. An abstract base class provides the pure virtual function `classify` (cf. Listing 201), which assigns features (objects of the class `Feature`) to classes. The derived classes implement the concrete decision rule of selected classifiers. For example, the maximum a posteriori decision is programmed for Bayesian classifiers, or the nearest neighbor classification rule is implemented if no density functions or parametric discriminating functions are available.

Assume that objects of a class `Density` defined in Listing 202 are defined and represent the density functions associated with each class. Concrete classes might be a Gaussian density as in Figure 22.6 or any other probability density function like a Poisson distribution. If the class definition of Bayesian classifiers provides a method for evaluating a posteriori probabilities, the Bayesian classifier is implemented as shown in Listing 204 and Listing 205. More density classes will be shown in Chapter 23.

```
class Bayesian_Classifier : public Classifier {
  Vector<Density*> densities;    // list of class densities
  Vector<double>   a_priori;     // a priori probabilities
public:
  Bayesian_Classifier(int k);                        // k classes
  virtual int classify(const Feature & f) const;     // classification interface
  virtual void train(const Bag&);                    // Bayesian training
  double prior(int k) const        { return a_priori[k]; }
  void   prior(int k, double d)    { a_priori[k] = d; }
  const Density& dens(int k) const { return *(densities[k]); }
};
```

```
int Bayesian_Classifier::classify(const Feature & f) const
{
  int index = -1; double max  = 0;
  for (int i = 0; i< densities.SizeX(); i++) {
    double a_posteriori = prior(i) * dens(i).probability(f);
    if (max < a_posteriori) { max  = a_posteriori; index = i; }
  }
  return index+1;   // classes range from 1 to number_of_classes
}
```

Exercises

22.a   Determine a threshold θ such that the optimal classifier will apply the decision rule

$$\zeta(\mathbf{c}) \;=\; \begin{cases} 2 & ,\text{ if } p(\mathbf{c}\mid\Omega_1)/p(\mathbf{c}\mid\Omega_2) > \theta \\ 1 & ,\text{ otherwise} \end{cases} \qquad (22.28)$$

for the discrimination of two classes.

22.b   Let the set of 2–D vectors $\left\{(2,3)^{\mathrm{T}},(3,3)^{\mathrm{T}},(1,2)^{\mathrm{T}},(1,6)^{\mathrm{T}},(5,5)^{\mathrm{T}},(5,1)^{\mathrm{T}}\right\}$ represent the reference data for a nearest neighbor classifier. Implement a graphical tool that computes the Voronoi diagram! Compute the areas for class Ω_1 and Ω_2 if the following bipartition is valid:

$$\begin{aligned} \text{features assigned to } \Omega_1 \;&:\; \left\{(2,3)^{\mathrm{T}},(3,3)^{\mathrm{T}},(1,2)^{\mathrm{T}},\right\} \\ \text{features assigned to } \Omega_2 \;&:\; \left\{(1,6)^{\mathrm{T}},(5,5)^{\mathrm{T}},(5,1)^{\mathrm{T}},(1,2)^{\mathrm{T}}\right\} \end{aligned}$$

22.c   We now proceed with the animal recognition problem in Exercise 20.b. We define for each object a reference pattern r_λ and classify an observed object characterized by f using the decision rule

$$\kappa \;=\; \min_\lambda \|r_\lambda - f\|, \qquad (22.29)$$

where κ is the computed class number and $\|.\|$ denotes the Euclidean distance of vectors.

Capture a sufficiently large sample of images such as the ones shown in Figure 20.10 and test your classifier.

22.d   Extend the class hierarchy shown in Figure 22.6 for histograms.

22.e   Show that the number of linear classifiers for d–dimensional real-valued features is bounded by $2\binom{n}{d}$.

Chapter 23

Speech Recognition

Speaker-independent recognition, analysis, and understanding of spoken language is much more complicated than the classification of simple patterns such as isolated printed characters in an image. With each simple pattern a feature vector of known dimension can be computed, and decision rules introduced in Chapter 22 can be applied to solve the classification task.

As it was already shown, speech signals are decomposed into frames. Thus, each speech signal is associated with a *sequence* of feature vectors. The number of sequence elements depends on the duration of the utterance and varies for each signal. Obviously, the simple application of the Bayesian classifier or the nearest neighbor decision rule, as defined for single feature vectors in (22.14), is not possible.

Extensions of these decision procedures are required, even for the implementation of a single word recognition system.

In this chapter we introduce algorithms for solving the classification problem in the presence of feature sets and feature sequences of varying cardinality. In the first part we motivate classification in speech recognition, discuss several problems we have to deal with, and introduce the mathematical notation. We explain the dynamic time warping (DTW) algorithm for the comparison of feature sequences with missing correspondences of single features. Motivated by some disadvantages of DTW, a basic statistical technique for the classification of speech signals using mixtures of densities and Hidden-Markov-Models (HMM) is explained, considering both automatic training and classification algorithms. This chapter concludes with a discussion of different types of Hidden-Markov-Models and remarks on an object–oriented implementation.

23.1 Classification of Speech Signals

Speech signals can induce several types of classification problems with increasing complexity. Generally, we distinguish between single word recognition, recognition of a sequence of words, and speech understanding, where the word sequence and its meaning are required [Jel98, Nie90a, ST95]. Here the discussion is restricted to single word recognition problems.

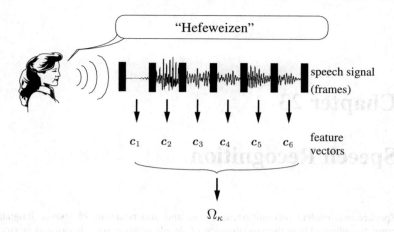

Figure 23.1: Single word recognition (according to [You96])

For that purpose, each speech signal is transformed into a sequence of feature vectors (cf. Chapter 21).

Each of the K words known to the system is denoted by a class Ω_κ. The decision rule ζ maps a feature sequence to a class index κ of class Ω_κ, i.e.,

$$\zeta : [c_k]_{k=1,2,\ldots,m} \mapsto \kappa \quad . \tag{23.1}$$

Figure 23.1 shows the general structure of a single word recognition system: the utterance is decomposed into frames, features are computed, and the recognition has to be done using the resulting sequence of features. Independent of the speaker and the duration of an utterance, the classification of this speech signal should be possible, although speech signals differ considerably between speakers (Figure 23.2). The energy of the speech signal as well as the chosen microphone should not influence the class decision. Thus, the classifiers have to deal with variations both in the feature vectors' values and in the number of features. These observations suggest the use of statistical methods for recognition. The following sections introduce statistical principles for modeling. Starting with dynamic time warping and geometrically based methods, we introduce a general, unified, and new statistical framework, which will later be applied to image analysis as well (Sect. 24.8).

23.2 Dynamic Time Warping

The classification of speech signals can be done by the comparison of input signals with prototypes of different pattern classes. If a distance measure suitable for the comparison of sequences is available, the nearest neighbor decision rule can be applied. We decide for that class which nearest reference pattern it belongs to (nearest neighbor classifier, Sect. 22.8). For

23.2 Dynamic Time Warping

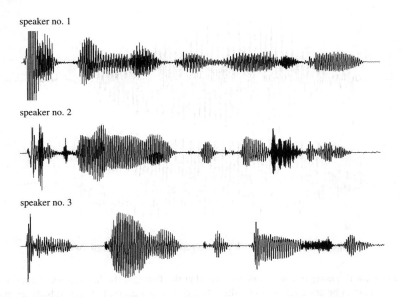

Figure 23.2: The utterance "pattern recognition" of three different speakers

classification purposes, we can use sample values, spectral features, cepstral features, zero-crossings of the speech signal, LPC coefficients or sequences of any other types of features [Nie83], as they were introduced in Chapter 21. An easy way to obtain a similarity measure for time signals is through the computation of the features' distances along corresponding time and accumulation. This simple distance measure is practically prohibited [Nie83]: depending on the speed of speaking, speech signals can be stretched or compressed, and the induced distortion of the speech signal is supposed to be non-linear. Vowels, like the "o" of the word "word" can be stretched in different manner, whereas the duration of "d" is approximately constant. Figure 23.3 shows two speech signals for the word "word" with different durations. This example shows that a non-linear mapping ζ_λ from the feature sequence $[c_k]_{k=1,2,...,m}$ resulting from the speech signal to the prototype sequence of class Ω_λ, i.e., $[c_{\lambda,l}]_{l=1,2,...,n_\lambda}$, is required. The *assignment function* ζ_λ relates the observed and reference features. The accuracy of the complete distance between reference pattern and the observed signal significantly increases through the use of a non-linear mapping ζ_λ, which minimizes the effects of stretching and compressing. The non-linear mapping has to be computed during the classification stage and — unfortunately — increases the complexity of classification.

The distance measure is thus characterized by two fundamental components:

1. the (non-linear) assignment function ζ_λ for the reference and the observed pattern or feature sequence, and

2. the distance measure for a single pair of corresponding features.

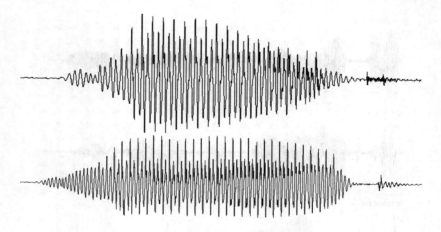

Figure 23.3: Two speech signals representing the word "word"

Constraints for the assignment function ζ_λ are that the first and the last feature values of both sequences have to be assigned to each other. The correspondence of observed features and the reference pattern starts from left to right, and ends with the assignment of the last feature c_m of the observation. The index of the reference sequence in the t-th step of this assignment procedure is defined by $i(t)$ and the corresponding index of the other sequence is $j(t)$. Thus, a pair $(i(t), j(t))$ denotes the correspondence of $c_{\lambda,i(t)}$ and $c_{j(t)}$. The resulting sequence of completely matched pairs is denoted by the sequence of corresponding indices

$$S = [(i(1), j(1)), (i(2), j(2)), \ldots, (i(m), j(m))] \quad . \tag{23.2}$$

The assignment of features can be illustrated by a graph, and the computation of the best assignment corresponds to a graph search problem. The pair $(i(t), j(t))$ defines a node of a graph. The path ${}^tS = ((i(1), j(1)), (i(2), j(2)), \ldots, (i(t), j(t)))$ defines a sequence of vertices and edges of this graph. The weight of the path is the sum of single distances of corresponding features. Figure 23.4 shows a graph and the path associated with the assignment

$$S = [(1, 1), (1, 2), (1, 3), (2, 4), (3, 5), (4, 6), \ldots, (13, 19)] \quad . \tag{23.3}$$

If the constraints for the assignment of the first and last features are considered, the total number of possible assignments is $11^{17} = 505447028499293771$. A first reduction of assignments is enforced by the constraint of monotonically increasing indices, i.e., for all t we have

$$i(t) \leq i(t+1) \quad \text{and} \quad j(t) \leq j(t+1) \quad . \tag{23.4}$$

Using this inequality, we have *only* $\binom{11+17-1}{17} = 13123110$ paths to check for the minimum distance.[1] The complexity of this search procedure further can be reduced. For that reason, we take a closer look at the distance measure and its properties.

[1] Prove this!

23.2 Dynamic Time Warping

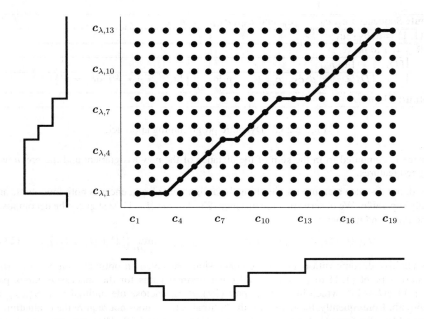

Figure 23.4: Assignment of features: a graph search problem

The optimization problem is the minimization of the accumulated distance D_λ for the matching of observed and reference sequences, i.e.,

$$D_\lambda = \min_S \sum_{t=1}^{m} d(c_{\lambda,i(t)}, c_{j(t)}) \quad , \tag{23.5}$$

where $d(c_{\lambda,i(t)}, c_{j(t)})$ denotes a suitable distance measure, like, for example, the Euclidean distance. The minimization runs over all possible assignments (i.e., paths of the graph) between the observation and the reference. If all combinations without any constraints are considered, the complexity of this optimization is bounded by $\mathcal{O}(n_\lambda^m)$; the monotonicity constraint (23.4) for indices reduces the complexity to $\mathcal{O}\left(\binom{n_\lambda+m-1}{m}\right)$.

An efficient algorithm for the computation of the optimal sequence S^* of index pairs, which minimizes the distance D_λ, results from the application of the *dynamic programming* technique [Big89]. Dynamic programming is well-known in discrete mathematics and indeed supports efficiency in computing the non-linear mapping between two sequences of features that we are looking for. The basic idea is a recursive decomposition of the given optimization problem. The use of a recursive procedure is possible, if *Bellman's principle of optimality* is valid [Bel67]. This principle states that all sub-paths of the optimal path are already paths with minimal distances. Distance measures which satisfy the optimality principle are usually monotonic and locally separable. A distance measure is called *monotonic*, if the distance increases monotonically with the number of assignments. The distance is defined to be *locally separable*, if the

Input: Sequences $c_1, c_2, \ldots, c_m$ and $c_{\lambda,1}, c_{\lambda,2}, \ldots, c_{\lambda,n_\lambda}$
$D_\lambda(1,1) = a(c_{\lambda,1}, c_1)$
FOR $j = 1$ to m
FOR $i = 1$ to n_λ
$D_\lambda(i,j) = d(c_{\lambda,i}, c_j) + \min_{i' \leq i, j' \in \{j-1,j\}} \{D_\lambda(i',j'); \ i \neq i' \text{ or } j \neq j'\}$
Output: $D_\lambda(n_\lambda, m)$

Figure 23.5: Dynamic programming approach

distance is computed from the sum of the distance of the new assignment and the previously assigned features.

Indeed, our distance measure for weighing the assignment of sequences is both monotonic and locally separable. We observe that the distance (23.5) of the $(t+1)$-st step can be decomposed in the following manner:

$$^{t+1}D_\lambda(i(t+1), j(t+1)) = d(c_{\lambda,i(t+1)}, c_{j(t+1)}) + \min_{i(t),j(t)} \left\{ {}^t D_\lambda(i(t), j(t)) \right\} . \quad (23.6)$$

This additive decomposition allows the conclusion that given an optimal path $S^*_{i(t),j(t)}$ from the staring point $(1,1)$ to $(i(t), j(t))$, all other optimal paths for the successive index pair $(i(t+1), j(t+1))$, which include the pair $(i(t), j(t))$, enclose the optimal path $S^*_{i(t),j(t)}$ as a sub-path. Consequently, the search for the optimal path S^* does not require the evaluation of all possible paths from $(1,1)$ to $(i(t+1), j(t+1))$ including $(i(t), j(t))$, but only one. Using this observation, the combinatorial search space is drastically reduced and only the best assignments for a subsequence ending up in a special pair $(i(t), j(t))$ have to be stored. Figure 23.5 shows the principle of the assignment procedure that computes the minimum distance between the observed and the reference sequence. The complexity is obviously bounded by $\mathcal{O}(mn_\lambda^2)$. The description also shows that the name "dynamic programming" is rather misleading, and it is better considered as a recursive optimization method.

In speech recognition applications the set of corresponding indices is usually restricted to special types of index pairs. For single word recognition, for instance, the constraint

$$(i(t), j(t)) \in \left\{ \begin{array}{l} (i(t-1), j(t-1)+1), \\ (i(t-1)+1, j(t-1)+1), \\ (i(t-1)+1, j(t-1)), \end{array} \right\} \quad (23.7)$$

defines a suitable reduction of admissible indices, if prototype and spoken word do not differ too much in duration. If this neighborhood function (23.7) is used in Figure 23.5, then the complexity of the dynamic time programming approach reduces to $\mathcal{O}(mn_\lambda)$ and no recursion is required. This modified algorithm is called *dynamic time warping*, and widely used in (simple) speech recognition applications, e.g. word recognition. A simple implementation is given

If minimum distances D_λ, $\lambda = 1, 2, \ldots, K$, are computed between a given speech signal and the reference signals of classes Ω_λ, $1 \leq \lambda \leq K$, the classification can be done applying the nearest neighbor decision rule (Sect. 22.8); we decide for that class which shows the minimum distance, i.e.,

$$\zeta([c_k]_{1 \leq k \leq m}) = \kappa = \arg\min_\lambda D_\lambda . \quad (23.8)$$

23.2 Dynamic Time Warping

An object–oriented implementation of the dynamic time warping algorithm should be as general as possible. The theoretical discussion motivates several basic requirements for an implementation of the dynamic programming approach:

- Without neglecting the generality of dynamic programming, the above discussion was restricted to the comparison of feature vectors. Of course, the dynamic programming approach also works for sequences of arbitrary features. The classifier has to be implemented for general sequences of features. The features have to belong to the class Feature which was already introduced in Chapter 21.
- The dynamic programming algorithm requires a distance measure for the comparison of single features. It should not be restricted to the Euclidean distance measure. The concrete implementation of the distance measure is not required for the implementation of the algorithm shown in Figure 23.5. If the distance function is a virtual function, dynamic linkage cares for the right implementation dependent on the chosen features.
- It is expected that the dynamic programming module can be extended to use restrictions for the considered neighborhood, for instance, defined by (23.7).

Dynamic programming approaches are not only restricted to speech recognition, but have many applications in pattern recognition [Moo79, Wat85] and operation research [Big89]. Prospective examples for image processing applications are line following algorithms [Bal82] or the classification of contours [Bal82]. A generalization of dynamic programming algorithms for one-dimensional sequences to two-dimensional arrays can be found in [Wat85]. However, there are still many open research problems related to the mathematical properties of extensions of dynamic programming to higher dimensions.

All in all, dynamic programming is a powerful tool for the classification of patterns, especially speech signals [Nie90a]. The success of complex speech recognition systems, however, is not based on this technique. Statistical methods applying several types of stochastic automata are more established for recognition purposes. The advantages of statistical approaches for solving classification problems are numerous:

1. Statistical approaches can deal with uncertainties in a natural manner.
2. The classifier is trainable (cf. Sect. 7.3); a sufficient set of training samples is used to adopt the free parameters by mathematical estimation techniques.
3. Prior knowledge can be explicitly modeled (cf. Sect. 22.5).
4. The application of the maximum a posteriori decision rule (cf. Sect. 22.5) leads to an optimal classification system with respect to the probability of misclassifications.

The design of statistical classifiers, in general, requires the solution of several problems: an appropriate statistical model for pattern classes has to be defined (*structure of models*), and the parameters of these models have to be estimated using a set of training samples (*parameter estimation*). The following sections omit structural learning techniques (see e.g. [Von98]) and restrict discussions to simpler problems related to the estimation of parameters. The topology of the model is supposed to be known [McL96, Tan96]. We introduce mixtures and Hidden-Markov-Models as well as related parameter estimation algorithms based on the dynamic programming approach discussed in this section. These models form the fundamental concepts of most modern speech recognition, analysis, and dialog systems [Jel98, Nie90a, ST95].

23.3 Mixture Densities

The dynamic programming approach requires both the computation of an appropriate reference sequence (prototype) and the definition of a distance measure for comparing single features. The most challenging problem is the automatic construction of reference patterns based on a set of sample data. Instead of one single reference utterance, some kind of *mean feature sequence* has to be computed, i.e., we implicitly incorporate statistical information. In a general probabilistic framework, however, the distance measure is induced by a probability density functions. For that reason, we associate with each feature $c_{\lambda,l}$ of the reference sequence $[c_{\lambda,l}]_{l=1,2,\ldots,n_\lambda}$ a parametric density function, i.e., $p(c|a_{\lambda,l})$. For instance, this could be a Gaussian density where the parameter $a_{\lambda,l}$ includes the mean vector $\mu_{\lambda,l}$ and the covariance matrix $K_{\lambda,l}$ of the considered reference vector $c_{\lambda,l}$. The reference is thus related to a sequence of probability density functions, i.e., $[p(c|a_{\lambda,l})]_{l=1,2,\ldots,n_\lambda}$. The densities are identified by their parameters $[a_{\lambda,l}]_{l=1,2,\ldots,n_\lambda}$.

Using the sequence of densities for classification instead of features and the Euclidean distance, for example, this concept allows the definition of prototypes that take the probabilistic behavior of features into consideration. The length n_λ of prototype sequences, however, remains constant and cannot be varied (up to now). If the densities (i.e., parameters $a_{\lambda,l}$) are known, the algorithm sketched in Figure 23.5 can be applied for statistical classification purposes with minor changes:

The distance $d(c_{\lambda,i(t)}, c_{j(t)})$ used in (23.5) is simply substituted by the conditional probability density $p(c_{j(t)}|a_{\lambda,i(t)})$, but instead of the sum we use the product, and the minimization moves to a maximization, i.e.,

$$P_\lambda = \max_S \prod_{t=1}^{m} p(c_{j(t)}|a_{\lambda,i(t)}) \;, \qquad (23.9)$$

where S is defined by (23.2). Figure 23.6 illustrates the major changes concerning geometric and probabilistic methods for pattern classification. Herein, however, we still need an explicit mapping of observed and prototype features.

We can now show in several steps how the concepts of mixture densities are related to optimal classification. If the prior probabilities $p(\Omega_1), p(\Omega_2), \ldots, p(\Omega_K)$ of pattern classes are known, the dynamic programming approach combined with the probabilistic modeling of single features allows the implementation of a Bayesian classifier that applies the maximum a posteriori decision rule:

$$\begin{aligned}\zeta([c_k]_{k=1,2,\ldots,m}) &= \operatorname*{argmax}_\lambda p(\Omega_\lambda|[c_k]_{k=1,2,\ldots,m}) \\ &= \operatorname*{argmax}_\lambda p(\Omega_\lambda) p([c_k]_{k=1,2,\ldots,m}|[a_{\lambda,l}]_{l=1,2,\ldots,n_\lambda}) \;, \qquad (23.10)\end{aligned}$$

where the fundamental difference between P_λ and $p([c_k]_{k=1,2,\ldots,m}|[a_{\lambda,l}]_{l=1,2,\ldots,n_\lambda})$ is that the second does not include the *optimal* assignment. Neither the concrete mathematical structure of the probability density function $p([c_k]_{k=1,2,\ldots,m}|[a_{\lambda,l}]_{l=1,2,\ldots,n_\lambda})$, nor the automatic computation of the involved parameters are obvious, yet. The generation of each reference pattern, which is required for the dynamic time warping approach, can be done using one sample or by averaging

23.3 Mixture Densities

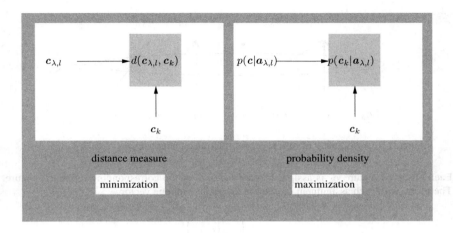

Figure 23.6: From geometric distance measures to density functions

techniques based on a set of training patterns. For that purpose, the mean vectors of observed features are computed, wherein the assignment of features can also be done by the introduced dynamic time warping approach.

If statistical models are used, the parameters $a_{\lambda,l}$, $l = 1, 2, \ldots, n_\lambda$ have to be estimated, which include more statistical information on features than mean vectors. Usually, the assignment between observed features and reference densities is unknown and non-available for parameter estimation. Of course, we can compute the *most probable* assignment using dynamic programming, but if any errors occur within the assignment process, the estimated parameters are influenced. From a theoretical point of view, the statistical modeling of the assignment function would be nice. We recall that marginals allow the elimination of random variables: If, for instance, the density function $p(\boldsymbol{X}, \boldsymbol{Y})$ is known, we get the density function $p(\boldsymbol{X})$ computing the marginal

$$p(\boldsymbol{X}) = \int p(\boldsymbol{X}, \boldsymbol{Y}) \, d\boldsymbol{Y} \quad , \tag{23.11}$$

i.e., we just integrate out the latent random variable $\boldsymbol{Y}$ of this density. Thus, a statistical modeling of the assignment function allows the elimination of the unknown correspondence of reference and observed features by marginalization.

The statistical modeling of assignments is straightforward, if we consider the assignment ζ_λ as a discrete function, defined by

$$\zeta_\lambda : \left\{ \begin{array}{ccc} \{c_1, c_2, \ldots, c_m\} & \to & \{1, 2, \ldots, n_\lambda\} \\ c_k & \mapsto & l_k \end{array} \right. . \tag{23.12}$$

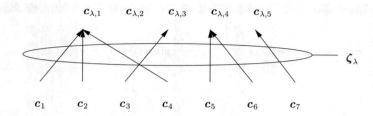

Figure 23.7: Assignment of observed and reference features $\boldsymbol{\zeta}_\lambda = (1, 1, 3, 1, 4, 4, 5)^{\mathrm{T}}$.

Each observed feature c_k is assigned to the index l_k of the corresponding reference feature. Therefore, with each assignment ζ_λ, we can associate a unique vector

$$\boldsymbol{\zeta}_\lambda = \begin{pmatrix} \zeta_\lambda(c_1) \\ \zeta_\lambda(c_2) \\ \vdots \\ \zeta_\lambda(c_m) \end{pmatrix}, \qquad (23.13)$$

which is the so-called *assignment vector*. This vector can be considered as a *random vector* related to a probability mass function $p(\boldsymbol{\zeta}_\lambda)$ that holds

$$\sum_{\boldsymbol{\zeta}_\lambda} p(\boldsymbol{\zeta}_\lambda) = 1 \ . \qquad (23.14)$$

Figure 23.7 shows an example of the assignment vector. This vector can be used to get the density for an observed sequence of features by the following marginal:

$$\begin{aligned} p([\boldsymbol{c}_k]_{k=1,2,\ldots,m} | [\boldsymbol{a}_{\lambda,l}]_{l=1,2,\ldots,n_\lambda}) &= \sum_{\boldsymbol{\zeta}_\lambda} p([\boldsymbol{c}_k]_{k=1,2,\ldots,m}, \boldsymbol{\zeta}_\lambda | [\boldsymbol{a}_{\lambda,l}]_{l=1,2,\ldots,n_\lambda}) \\ &= \sum_{\boldsymbol{\zeta}_\lambda} p(\boldsymbol{\zeta}_\lambda) \, p([\boldsymbol{c}_k]_{k=1,2,\ldots,m} | \boldsymbol{\zeta}_\lambda, [\boldsymbol{a}_{\lambda,l}]_{l=1,2,\ldots,n_\lambda}) \ . \end{aligned} \qquad (23.15)$$

For a known assignment vector $\boldsymbol{\zeta}_\lambda$ we make use of definition (23.12) and the product density in (23.9) for a given assignment. Thus, we obtain the factorization

$$p([\boldsymbol{c}_k]_{k=1,2,\ldots,m} | \boldsymbol{\zeta}_\lambda, [\boldsymbol{a}_{\lambda,l}]_{l=1,2,\ldots,n_\lambda}) = \prod_{k=1}^m p(\boldsymbol{c}_k | \boldsymbol{a}_{\lambda,\zeta_\lambda(c_k)}) \ , \qquad (23.16)$$

and therefore

$$p([\boldsymbol{c}_k]_{k=1,2,\ldots,m} | [\boldsymbol{a}_{\lambda,l}]_{l=1,2,\ldots,n_\lambda}) = \sum_{\boldsymbol{\zeta}_\lambda} p(\boldsymbol{\zeta}_\lambda) \prod_{k=1}^m p(\boldsymbol{c}_k | \boldsymbol{a}_{\lambda,\zeta_\lambda(c_k)}) \ . \qquad (23.17)$$

The evaluation of this sum requires at least $\mathcal{O}(mn_\lambda^m)$ multiplications and additions. There is no obvious advantage compared to a direct search for an optimal assignment. If we introduce, however, independency assumptions, the complexity can be reduced drastically.

23.3 Mixture Densities

Figure 23.8: The handwritten word *minimum*

Let us assume statistically independent assignments, i.e., all components of the random vector $\boldsymbol{\zeta}_\lambda$ are pairwise statistically independent, then we obtain the factorization

$$p(\boldsymbol{\zeta}_\lambda) \;=\; \prod_{k=1}^{m} p(\zeta_\lambda(\boldsymbol{c}_k) = l_k) \tag{23.18}$$

for the discrete probability of the assignment vector. It is little tricky to show[2] that the multiple sum in (23.17) reduces to a product of single sums:

$$p([\boldsymbol{c}_k]_{k=1,2,\ldots,m} \mid [\boldsymbol{a}_{\lambda,l}]_{l=1,2,\ldots,n_\lambda}) \;=\; \prod_{k=1}^{N_m} \sum_{l=1}^{n_\lambda} p(\zeta_\lambda(\boldsymbol{c}_k) = l)\, p(\boldsymbol{c}_k \mid \boldsymbol{a}_{\lambda,l}) \;. \tag{23.19}$$

The density function for an observation is a product of m *mixture densities*. Mixture densities have already been introduced in Sect. 7.7. This fundamental result shows that statistically independent assignments reduce the original exponential complexity of the original marginal density evaluations (23.17) to $\mathcal{O}(mn_\lambda)$.

To summarize the sequence of conclusions and facts we have seen so far in this section, we now know how to use dynamic programming ideas to derive and implement a Bayesian approach for the classification of feature sequences.

The efficiency of density evaluation crucially depends on the independency assumption. Assignments are considered independent of each other. In many applications, however, the consideration of context leads to essential improvements in classification results. Standard examples are speech recognition in general or — concerning image processing applications — the recognition of handwritten characters. Figure 23.8 shows the handwritten word *minimum*. The classification of single letters is difficult even for the human being. Nobody can decide which part of the word represents "m", "n" or "i". Only the consideration of context allows the correct recognition of this word.

This simple example shows that context is useful and sometimes necessary for classification. For that reason, we will give up the assumption of statistically independent assignments as stated in this section, and introduce dependent assignments of bounded order. Generally we will conclude the (expected) ground rule: *the higher the dependencies, the higher the complexity of involved algorithms*. There is a remarkable trade-off between recognition rates, dependency assumptions, and computational complexities.

---

[2]cf. Appendix C.3

23.4 Hidden-Markov-Models

One established stochastic modeling approach for speech recognition purposes which considers context are *Hidden-Markov-Models* (HMMs) [Bau67, Rab88]. HMMs are an extension of finite automata with respect to stochastic transitions and probabilistic output generation. HMMs, however, also result from (23.17) directly, if some specializations in (23.15) or if some generalizations in (23.19) are considered; if we assume first order dependencies of assignments, the discrete probability for assignments is factorized to

$$p(\boldsymbol{\zeta}_\lambda) = p(\zeta_\lambda(\boldsymbol{c}_1) = l_1) \prod_{k=2}^{N_m} p(\zeta_\lambda(\boldsymbol{c}_k) = l_k | \zeta_\lambda(\boldsymbol{c}_{k-1}) = l_{k-1}) \quad . \tag{23.20}$$

An obvious way of computing $p([\boldsymbol{c}_k]_{k=1,2,\ldots,m}|[\boldsymbol{a}_{\lambda,l}]_{l=1,2,\ldots,n_\lambda})$ is the use of the marginal density over all possible assignments, i.e., we obtain the probability density function

$$p([\boldsymbol{c}_k]_{k=1,2,\ldots,m}|[\boldsymbol{a}_{\lambda,l}]_{l=1,2,\ldots,n_\lambda}) = \sum_{\boldsymbol{\zeta}_\lambda} p(\boldsymbol{\zeta}_\lambda) \prod_{k=1}^{m} p(\boldsymbol{c}_k | \boldsymbol{a}_{\lambda,\zeta_\lambda(\boldsymbol{c}_k)}) \quad . \tag{23.21}$$

If we consider (23.20), then the marginal (23.21) is

$$p([\boldsymbol{c}_k]_{k=1,2,\ldots,m}|[\boldsymbol{a}_{\lambda,l}]_{l=1,2,\ldots,n_\lambda})$$
$$= \sum_{l_1=1}^{n_\lambda} \cdots \sum_{l_m=1}^{n_\lambda} p(\zeta_\lambda(\boldsymbol{c}_1)=l_1) \prod_{k=2}^{N_m} p(\zeta_\lambda(\boldsymbol{c}_k)=l_k|\zeta_\lambda(\boldsymbol{c}_{k-1})=l_{k-1}) \prod_{k=1}^{m} p(\boldsymbol{c}_k|\boldsymbol{a}_{\lambda,l_k}) \tag{23.22}$$

where we sum over all m–dimensional assignment vectors $(l_1, l_2, \ldots, l_m)^T$, $l_k = 1, 2, \ldots, n_\lambda$. The evaluation of (23.22) requires an exponentially bounded number of summations and multiplications. In case of mutually independent assignments, this complexity was reduced to $\mathcal{O}(mn_\lambda)$. In fact, a smart re-organization of summations and products also leads to an efficient evaluation algorithm of polynomial complexity for first order dependencies. For that purpose, we define the *forward variable*

$$\alpha_{t,l_t} = p([\boldsymbol{c}_k]_{k=1,2,\ldots,t}, \zeta_\lambda(\boldsymbol{c}_t) = l_t \mid [\boldsymbol{a}_{\lambda,l}]_{l=1,2,\ldots,n_\lambda}) \tag{23.23}$$

to be the probability density of observing the first t features $\boldsymbol{c}_1, \boldsymbol{c}_2, \ldots, \boldsymbol{c}_t$, where the t–th feature is assigned to $\boldsymbol{c}_{\lambda,l_t}$ resp. its associated density $p(\boldsymbol{c}|\boldsymbol{a}_{\lambda,l_t})$. Using the forward variable, we can recursively define

$$\alpha_{t+1,l_{t+1}} = \left(\sum_{l_t=1}^{n_\lambda} \alpha_{t,l_t} \, p(\zeta_\lambda(\boldsymbol{c}_{t+1}) = l_{t+1} | \zeta_\lambda(\boldsymbol{c}_t) = l_t) \right) p(\boldsymbol{c}_{t+1}|\boldsymbol{a}_{\lambda,l_{t+1}}) \tag{23.24}$$

to assign the $(t+1)$–st feature to the l_{t+1}–th density. Since this probability does not depend on the assignment of the t–th feature, we use the marginal over all assignments. The value of the forward variables $\alpha_{1,1}, \alpha_{1,2}, \ldots, \alpha_{1,n_\lambda}$ for the first feature is obviously

$$\alpha_{1,l_1} = p(\zeta_\lambda(\boldsymbol{c}_1) = l_1) \, p(\boldsymbol{c}_1|\boldsymbol{a}_{\lambda,l_1}) \quad , \tag{23.25}$$

23.4 Hidden-Markov-Models

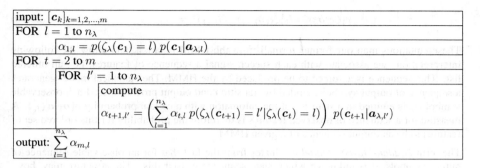

Figure 23.9: Forward algorithm

such that we finally get the marginal

$$p([c_k]_{k=1,2,\ldots,m}|[a_{\lambda,l}]_{l=1,2,\ldots,n_\lambda}) = \sum_{l_m=1}^{n_\lambda} \alpha_{m,l_m} \quad . \tag{23.26}$$

The evaluation of (23.26) is bounded by $\mathcal{O}(mn_\lambda^2)$. Figure 23.9 summarizes the suggested iterative evaluation of marginals. This algorithm is widely used in the literature; it is the so-called *forward algorithm*.

By a further specialization of (23.22), we can reduce the introduced formalism to the standard Hidden-Markov modeling scheme. A Hidden-Markov-Model associated with a pattern class Ω_λ is characterized by:

- a set of states $S = \{S_1, S_2, \ldots, S_{n_\lambda}\}$,
- initial state distribution $\pi_1, \pi_2, \ldots, \pi_{n_\lambda}$,
- transition probabilities a_{l_{k-1},l_k} which denote the discrete probability to change from state $S_{l_{k-1}}$ to S_{l_k},
- output symbols o_k, and
- output density functions $p(o|a_{\lambda,l})$, $l = 1, 2, \ldots, n_\lambda$.

Using this definition, we conclude

$$0 \leq \pi_l, a_{l_{k-1},l_k} \leq 1 \quad , \tag{23.27}$$

and

$$\sum_{l=1}^{n_\lambda} \pi_l = 1 \quad \text{and} \quad \sum_{l_k=1}^{n_\lambda} a_{l_{k-1},l_k} = 1 \quad . \tag{23.28}$$

We now denote the observed features $[c_k]_{k=1,2,\ldots,m}$ by $[o_k]_{k=1,2,\ldots,m}$, and set for all k

$$p(\zeta_\lambda(o_k) = l) = \pi_l \quad , \quad \text{and} \tag{23.29}$$

$$p(\zeta_\lambda(o_k) = l_k | \zeta_\lambda(o_{k-1}) = l_{k-1}) = a_{l_{k-1}, l_k} \quad . \tag{23.30}$$

These equations map our former formalism to the HMM notation, and allow the following interpretation we associate with each speech signal a sequence of features, i.e., an ordered list. This sequence is assumed to be produced by the HMM. The statistical model generates a sequence of output symbols, guided by transition and output probabilities. Each observable symbol o_k is emitted in a state S_{l_k} of the automaton with a certain probability $p(o_k|a_{\lambda,l_k})$. A measure for a sequence of observed features is therefore the probability for this ordered set of features to be an output sequence of a given HMM.

The term *Hidden-Markov-Model* originates from the fact that for an observable sequence of output symbols, it is unknown which state sequence caused this. The structure may, however, be known, e.g., the number of states is defined and some transitions might be impossible ($a_{l_{k-1}, l_k} = 0$). The gray box in Figure 23.10 shows one example of a HMM with three states. The emission probabilities are omitted in the figure.

During the training phase of an HMM, the initial state distribution, the transition probabilities, and the output density functions (or their parameters) have to be estimated. There exist various techniques for computing statistical parameters from a set of observable training samples. In the case of HMM, we compute the parameters such that for all observed learning sequences the likelihood function is maximized. This parameter estimation procedure has to be unsupervised, because it is not known which state sequences have generated the observable output symbols (Figure 23.10). Thus, we have to use parameter estimation techniques that can deal with such a type of incomplete data (cf. Sect. 23.6). A direct ML estimation seems unfeasable due to the high dimensionality of the parameter space.

Some training algorithms and applications of HMMs require an algorithm that computes the most probable state sequence for a sequence of observations. The optimal state sequence for an observation O is generated by the Viterbi algorithm [Rab88] which is closely related to the forward-algorithm. We just replace the sum of the marginal by the maximization operator.

We define the highest probability for a partial path ending up in state S_i:

$$\delta_{t,i} = \max_{s_1, s_2, \ldots, s_{t-1}} P(s_1, s_2, \ldots, s_t = S_i, o_1, o_2, \ldots, o_t | \lambda_l) \quad . \tag{23.31}$$

A recursive computation of the measure can be done based on the following observation: the highest probability of being in the state S_j after $t + 1$ steps only depends on the transition probabilities a_{ij}, ($1 \leq i \leq N$), and the probabilities for paths through the model of length t. By multiplying the output probability of the $t + 1$ observation we get:

$$\delta_{t+1,j} = \max_i \{\delta_{t,i} a_{i,j}\} \cdot b_j(o_{t+1}) \quad . \tag{23.32}$$

These considerations show that the principle of optimality is valid and the dynamic programming technique can be applied to solve this problem. The above described optimization task is similar to (23.5) and (23.6).

Since we are looking for a path that maximizes (23.32) we have to store the actual state of each step. For that purpose we define the array $\Phi_{t,i}$ for tracing back the optimal path in the Viterbi algorithm:

23.4 Hidden-Markov-Models

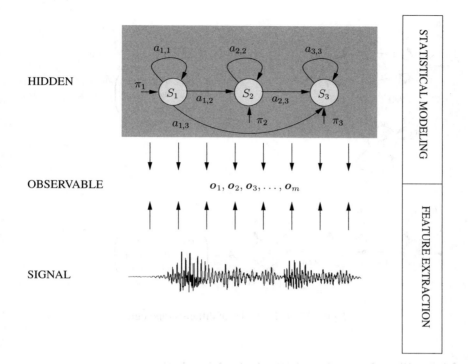

Figure 23.10: The hidden statistical processes and an observable feature sequence for parameter estimation

1. Initialization: for $1 \leq i \leq N$:

$$\delta_{1i} = \pi_i b_i(\boldsymbol{o}_1)$$
$$\Phi_{1i} = 0$$

2. Compute recursively: for $2 \leq t \leq T$ and $1 \leq j \leq N$:

$$\delta_{t,j} = \max_{1 \leq i \leq N} \{\delta_{t-1,i} a_{i,j}\} b_j(\boldsymbol{o}_t)$$
$$\Phi_{t,j} = \arg \max_{1 \leq i \leq N} \{\delta_{t-1,i} a_{i,j}\}$$

3. Terminate:

$$P^* = \max_{1 \leq i \leq N} \{\delta_{Ti}\}$$
$$s_T^* = \arg \max_{1 \leq i \leq N} \{\delta_{Ti}\}$$

4. Computation of the optimal path: for $t = T-1, T-2, \ldots, 1$:

$$s_t^* = \Phi_{t+1, s_{t+1}^*}.$$

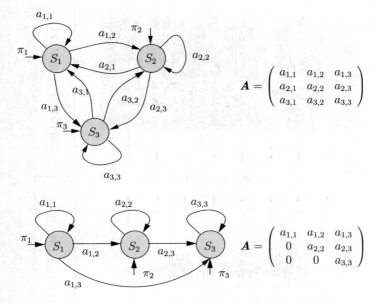

Figure 23.11: Examples of different topologies

23.5 Topological and Statistical Variations

Before we start with the discussion of parameter estimation techniques and the computation of training formulas, we discuss different types of HMMs. HMMs, in general, can be classified with respect to their *topological structure* (graph of the automaton), and the *statistical properties* of their transition and output probability functions.

Ergodic and *left-right-HMMs* are the most important topologies for pattern recognition applications. An HMM is called *ergodic*, if the graph of the stochastic automaton is complete, i.e., for all transitions a_{l_{k-1},l_k}, $(1 \leq l_{k-1}, l_k \leq n_\lambda)$, we have the constraint $a_{l_{k-1},l_k} \neq 0$. Analogously, the *left-right-HMMs* are characterized by the transition probabilities $a_{l_{k-1},l_k} = 0$ for $l_{k-1} \leq l_k$. This type of Hidden-Markov-Models is mostly used in speech recognition systems. Figure 23.11 shows an example of an ergodic and a left-right-HMM with the corresponding transition matrices. Again, output probabilities are omitted in the illustration.

Not only the graphical structure of HMMs allows the introduction of different types. Also the statistical properties of Markov-models induce the definition of various models. An HMM is called *discrete*, if the emission probabilities of all states are discrete and we observe discrete random variables. In those cases, the emission probabilities can be represented using relative frequencies, i.e., histograms. The training of discrete HMMs corresponds therefore to the estimation of discrete input, transition, and output probabilities.

In case of continuous emission density functions, we call the resulting HMM *continuous*. For example, the parametric Gaussian density function (7.6) can be used for modeling the output densities.

There exist various other types of Hidden-Markov-Models which are successfully applied to speech recognition applications: stationary and non-stationary HMMs [Hor96, He91], semi-continuous HMMs (SCHMM, [Jel98, ST95]), feature transform HMMs (FTHMM, [Sch95]) or generalized HMMs [Hor96].

So far we have introduced statistical modeling schemes for discrete assignments. The complexity of density evaluations for observed feature sequences was reduced by considering independencies. We got mixtures of densities for pairwise independent assignments, and Hidden-Markov-Models for dependencies of first order. The related evaluation algorithms are bounded by $\mathcal{O}(mn_\lambda)$ for products of mixtures, and $\mathcal{O}(mn_\lambda^2)$ for HMMs using the forward-algorithm.

By increasing the dependencies to g–th order, it can be shown that the complexity of these generalized Hidden-Markov-Models is bounded by $\mathcal{O}(mn_\lambda^{g+1})$ using a generalized version of the forward-algorithm. A detailed derivation of generalized HMMs and related algorithms is omitted here and can be found in [Hor96].

In the following, we consider the involved parameter estimation techniques which are required for automatic training purposes.

23.6 Incomplete Data Estimation

Modeling schemes including statistical properties of features should be generated of a set including representative training samples. The manual and painstaking construction of stochastic models should be avoided and computers should learn the appearance of features in speech signals automatically. The ultimate goal is that different speakers provide sample data, and the recognition system learns the patterns presented on its own — without any manual support. Therefore, the available training set should be sufficient for generalizations. The software should be able to classify patterns which are not elements of the training set.

We consider the parameter estimation problems related to statistical models introduced in previous sections. It was already mentioned that the main problems are the incompleteness of available training data, and the infeasibility of a direct maximum likelihood estimation due to the high dimension of the search space. The basic idea of the *Expectation Maximization algorithm* (EM-algorithm) [Dem77, McL96] is the augmentation of the observable data with latent data to simplify the parameter estimation algorithm. In most applications this technique reduces complicated, high-dimensional optimization problems to a series of independent simpler maximizations. In an informal and colloquial manner we describe the available information for parameter estimation by the difference

observed information = complete information − missing information .

This simple equation induces the *missing information principle*, since there exists a one-to-one translation into a statistical framework. Let us assume that the observable random variables are denoted by X and the missing random variables are Y. If the associated densities are parameterized with respect to B, we have (cf. (7.32))

$$p(X, Y|B) = p(X|B)\, p(Y|X, B) \quad , \tag{23.33}$$

and therefore we get the fraction

$$p(X|B) = \frac{p(X, Y|B)}{p(Y|X, B)} \quad . \tag{23.34}$$

Taking the logarithm on both sides, we obtain an information theoretic formalization of the above difference

$$(-\log p(X|B)) = (-\log p(X, Y|B)) - (-\log p(Y|X, B)) \quad , \tag{23.35}$$

because due to definition (7.38) in Sect. 7.8, we have

$$I(X|B) = -\log p(X|B) \tag{23.36}$$
$$I(X, Y|B) = -\log p(X, Y|B) \quad , \text{ and} \tag{23.37}$$
$$I(Y|X, B) = -\log p(Y|X, B) \tag{23.38}$$

— the *observed*, the *complete*, and the *missing information*.

Equation (23.35) leads to an iterative method for incomplete data estimation. Let us assume $\widehat{B}^{(i)}$ and $\widehat{B}^{(i+1)}$ are estimates of the parameter B of the i–th and $(i+1)$–st iterations. We consider (23.35) in the $(i+1)$–st iteration, multiply both sides by $p(Y|X, \widehat{B}^{(i)})$, and integrate out the missing component Y. These operations lead to the *key-equation* of the EM-algorithm [Dem77]

$$L(\widehat{B}^{(i+1)}|\widehat{B}^{(i)}) = Q(\widehat{B}^{(i+1)}|\widehat{B}^{(i)}) - H(\widehat{B}^{(i+1)}|\widehat{B}^{(i)}) \quad , \tag{23.39}$$

where

$$L(\widehat{B}^{(i+1)}|\widehat{B}^{(i)}) = \int p(Y|X, \widehat{B}^{(i)}) \log p(X|\widehat{B}^{(i+1)})\, dY \quad , \tag{23.40}$$

$$Q(\widehat{B}^{(i+1)}|\widehat{B}^{(i)}) = \int p(Y|X, \widehat{B}^{(i)}) \log p(X, Y|\widehat{B}^{(i+1)})\, dY \quad , \tag{23.41}$$

and

$$H(\widehat{B}^{(i+1)}|\widehat{B}^{(i)}) = \int p(Y|X, \widehat{B}^{(i)}) \log p(Y|X, \widehat{B}^{(i+1)})\, dY \quad . \tag{23.42}$$

For the left side of the key-equation (23.39), we obtain

$$\int p(Y|X, \widehat{B}^{(i)}) \log p(X|\widehat{B}^{(i+1)})\, dY =$$
$$= \int \left(\log p(X|\widehat{B}^{(i+1)})\right) p(Y|X, \widehat{B}^{(i)})\, dY$$
$$= \log p(X|\widehat{B}^{(i+1)}) \underbrace{\int p(Y|X, \widehat{B}^{(i)})\, dY}_{=1} = \log p(X|\widehat{B}^{(i+1)}) \; ; \tag{23.43}$$

23.7 Learning from Multiple Observations

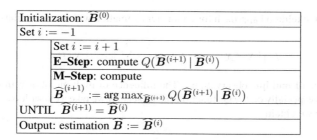

Figure 23.12: EM-algorithm

this is exactly the log-likelihood function.

Changes in the parameter set $\widehat{B}^{(i+1)}$ induce a decrease in $H(\widehat{B}^{(i+1)}|\widehat{B}^{(i)})$, thus an increase of the *Kullback-Leibler statistics* $Q(\widehat{B}^{(i+1)}|\widehat{B}^{(i)})$ causes a reduction of the *conditional entropy* $H(\widehat{B}^{(i+1)}|\widehat{B}^{(i)})$. Indeed, the following inequality holds for the introduced H–function (cf. Appendix C.4):

$$H(\widehat{B}^{(i+1)}|\widehat{B}^{(i)}) \leq H(\widehat{B}^{(i)}|\widehat{B}^{(i)}) \quad . \tag{23.44}$$

This result shows that a maximum likelihood estimation can be *simulated* by an iterative maximization of the Kullback-Leibler-statistics $Q(\widehat{B}^{(i+1)}|\widehat{B}^{(i)})$, which is also called the Q–function. The final success of the EM iterations crucially depends on the initial estimate $\widehat{B}^{(0)}$, because the EM-algorithm is a local optimization technique and provides a linear convergence behavior [Wu83]. The previously mentioned advantage of EM iterations instead of a straightforward ML estimation is that in most applications dealing with missing data, the search space splits into independent lower dimensional sub-spaces. Furthermore, due to its iterative nature the storage requirements remain constant. An impressive application of the introduced parameter estimation technique will be discussed in the following subsection.

23.7 Learning from Multiple Observations

Sample data for mixtures and HMMs are usually sequences of features. Let us assume, we have N training sequences that are denoted by

$$\{{}^\varrho C \; ; \; \varrho = 1, 2, \ldots, N\} = \{[{}^\varrho c_k]_{k=1,2,\ldots,{}^\varrho m} \; ; \; \varrho = 1, 2, \ldots, N\} \quad , \tag{23.45}$$

where ${}^\varrho m$ denotes the number of sequence elements of the ϱ–th observation. Due to the fact that the assignment function ζ_λ, which maps observed features to reference elements, is not part of the training set, we have to deal with an incomplete data estimation problem. The estimation of mixture and HMM parameters has to be done by applying the EM-algorithm. However, the EM–algorithm described so far is based on a single observation sequence, i.e., $X = [c_k]_{k=1,2,\ldots,m}$ instead of the training set

$$\{{}^\varrho X \; ; \; \varrho = 1, 2, \ldots, N\} = \{{}^\varrho C \; ; \; \varrho = 1, 2, \ldots, N\} \quad . \tag{23.46}$$

The maximum likelihood approach for parameter estimation will maximize the objective function

$$L(\{{}^1\boldsymbol{X},{}^2\boldsymbol{X},\ldots,{}^N\boldsymbol{X}\},\boldsymbol{B}) = \sum_{\varrho=1}^{N} \log p({}^\varrho\boldsymbol{X}|\boldsymbol{B}) \tag{23.47}$$

in the presence of multiple observations. The influence of multiple observations on the EM-algorithm and especially on the Q–function can be seen, if we take a closer look at its definition. Using (23.41) we obtain

$$Q(\widehat{\boldsymbol{B}}^{(i+1)}|\widehat{\boldsymbol{B}}^{(i)}) = \int \prod_{\rho=1}^{N} p({}^\rho\boldsymbol{Y}|{}^\rho\boldsymbol{X},\widehat{\boldsymbol{B}}^{(i)}) \sum_{\varrho=1}^{N} \log p({}^\varrho\boldsymbol{X},{}^\varrho\boldsymbol{Y}|\widehat{\boldsymbol{B}}^{(i+1)}) d^1\boldsymbol{Y} d^2\boldsymbol{Y} \ldots d^N\boldsymbol{Y}$$

$$= \sum_{\varrho=1}^{N} \int \prod_{\rho=1}^{N} p({}^\rho\boldsymbol{Y}|{}^\rho\boldsymbol{X},\widehat{\boldsymbol{B}}^{(i)}) \log p({}^\varrho\boldsymbol{X},{}^\varrho\boldsymbol{Y}|\widehat{\boldsymbol{B}}^{(i+1)}) d^1\boldsymbol{Y} d^2\boldsymbol{Y} \ldots d^N\boldsymbol{Y}$$

$$= \sum_{\varrho=1}^{N} \underbrace{\prod_{\substack{\rho=1 \\ \rho\neq\varrho}}^{N} \int p({}^\rho\boldsymbol{Y}|{}^\rho\boldsymbol{X},\widehat{\boldsymbol{B}}^{(i)}) d^\rho\boldsymbol{Y}}_{=1} \underbrace{\int p({}^\varrho\boldsymbol{Y}|{}^\varrho\boldsymbol{X},\widehat{\boldsymbol{B}}^{(i)}) \log p({}^\varrho\boldsymbol{X},{}^\varrho\boldsymbol{Y}|\widehat{\boldsymbol{B}}^{(i+1)}) d^\varrho\boldsymbol{Y}}_{={}^\varrho Q(\widehat{\boldsymbol{B}}^{(i+1)}|\widehat{\boldsymbol{B}}^{(i)})}$$

$$= \sum_{\varrho=1}^{N} {}^\varrho Q(\widehat{\boldsymbol{B}}^{(i+1)}|\widehat{\boldsymbol{B}}^{(i)}) \quad,$$

where ${}^\varrho Q(\widehat{\boldsymbol{B}}^{(i+1)}|\widehat{\boldsymbol{B}}^{(i)})$ denotes the Kullback-Leibler-statistics corresponding to ${}^\varrho\boldsymbol{X}$. This result shows that in case of multiple observations, EM iterations have to maximize the sum of single Q–functions ${}^\varrho Q(\widehat{\boldsymbol{B}}^{(i+1)}|\widehat{\boldsymbol{B}}^{(i)})$ associated with single elements of the sample data, and provides the necessary mathematical tools for the computation of iterative estimation algorithms. We can explicitly derive formulas which allow the estimation of statistical parameters of mixtures and HMMs. It is a hard computation to get these formulas. For that reason, we will only show one detailed example. Other re-estimation formulas — usually without derivations, but sufficient for implementation purposes — can be found in standard speech recognition literature.

We restrict the discussion to the estimation of discrete assignment probabilities $p(\zeta_\lambda)$. In fact, without any independency assumptions, exponentially many parameters have to be estimated. The application of the missing information principle requires the identification of the observable and hidden parts, which are denoted by ${}^\varrho\boldsymbol{X}$ and ${}^\varrho\boldsymbol{Y}$. The observable random variables are N feature sequences, i.e.,

$${}^\varrho\boldsymbol{X} = [{}^\varrho c_k]_{k=1,2,\ldots,{}^\varrho m} \quad, \tag{23.48}$$

and the hidden part is characterized by the assignment function ζ_λ, which is considered to be a random vector. The densities $p({}^\varrho\boldsymbol{X},{}^\varrho\boldsymbol{Y}|\boldsymbol{B})$ and $p({}^\varrho\boldsymbol{Y}|{}^\varrho\boldsymbol{X},\boldsymbol{B})$ required for the computation of the Q–function are therefore:

$$p([{}^\varrho c_k]_{k=1,2,\ldots,{}^\varrho m}, {}^\varrho\zeta_\lambda|\boldsymbol{B}_\lambda) = p({}^\varrho\zeta_\lambda) \prod_{k=1}^{{}^\varrho m} p({}^\varrho c_k|a_{\lambda,{}^\varrho\zeta_\lambda({}^\varrho c_k)}) \quad. \tag{23.49}$$

Using the identity

$$p({}^\varrho\boldsymbol{Y}|{}^\varrho\boldsymbol{X},\boldsymbol{B}) = \frac{p({}^\varrho\boldsymbol{X},{}^\varrho\boldsymbol{Y}|\boldsymbol{B})}{p({}^\varrho\boldsymbol{X}|\boldsymbol{B})} = \frac{p({}^\varrho\boldsymbol{X},{}^\varrho\boldsymbol{Y}|\boldsymbol{B})}{\int p({}^\varrho\boldsymbol{X},{}^\varrho\boldsymbol{Y}|\boldsymbol{B}) d^\varrho\boldsymbol{Y}} \quad, \tag{23.50}$$

23.7 Learning from Multiple Observations

we get

$$p(^{\varrho}\boldsymbol{\zeta}_\lambda | [^{\varrho}\boldsymbol{c}_k]_{k=1,2,\ldots,^{\varrho}m}, \boldsymbol{B}_\lambda) = \frac{p([^{\varrho}\boldsymbol{c}_k]_{k=1,2,\ldots,^{\varrho}m}, ^{\varrho}\boldsymbol{\zeta}_\lambda | \boldsymbol{B}_\lambda)}{\sum_{^{\varrho}\boldsymbol{\zeta}_\lambda} p([^{\varrho}\boldsymbol{c}_k]_{k=1,2,\ldots,^{\varrho}m}, ^{\varrho}\boldsymbol{\zeta}_\lambda | \boldsymbol{B}_\lambda)}$$

$$= \frac{p(^{\varrho}\boldsymbol{\zeta}_\lambda) \prod_{k=1}^{^{\varrho}m} p(^{\varrho}\boldsymbol{c}_k | \boldsymbol{a}_{\lambda,^{\varrho}\zeta_\lambda(^{\varrho}c_k)})}{\sum_{^{\varrho}\boldsymbol{\zeta}_\lambda} p(^{\varrho}\boldsymbol{\zeta}_\lambda) \prod_{k=1}^{^{\varrho}m} p(^{\varrho}\boldsymbol{c}_k | \boldsymbol{a}_{\lambda,^{\varrho}\zeta_\lambda(^{\varrho}c_k)})} . \qquad (23.51)$$

The required Q-function thus is

$$Q(\widehat{\boldsymbol{B}}_\lambda^{(i+1)} | \widehat{\boldsymbol{B}}_\lambda^{(i)}) = \sum_{\varrho=1}^{N} {}^{\varrho}Q(\widehat{\boldsymbol{B}}_\lambda^{(i+1)} | \widehat{\boldsymbol{B}}_\lambda^{(i)})$$

$$= \sum_{\varrho=1}^{N} \sum_{^{\varrho}\boldsymbol{\zeta}_\lambda} p(^{\varrho}\boldsymbol{\zeta}_\lambda | [^{\varrho}\boldsymbol{c}_k]_{k=1,2,\ldots,^{\varrho}m}, \widehat{\boldsymbol{B}}_\lambda^{(i)}) \log p([^{\varrho}\boldsymbol{c}_k]_{k=1,2,\ldots,^{\varrho}m}, ^{\varrho}\boldsymbol{\zeta}_\lambda | \widehat{\boldsymbol{B}}_\lambda^{(i+1)}) \qquad (23.52)$$

$$= \sum_{\varrho=1}^{N} \sum_{^{\varrho}\boldsymbol{\zeta}_\lambda} \frac{\widehat{p}^{(i)}(^{\varrho}\boldsymbol{\zeta}_\lambda) \prod_{k=1}^{^{\varrho}m} p(^{\varrho}\boldsymbol{c}_k | \widehat{\boldsymbol{a}}_{\lambda,^{\varrho}\zeta_\lambda(^{\varrho}c_k)}^{(i)})}{\sum_{^{\varrho}\boldsymbol{\zeta}_\lambda} \widehat{p}^{(i)}(^{\varrho}\boldsymbol{\zeta}_\lambda) \prod_{k=1}^{^{\varrho}m} p(^{\varrho}\boldsymbol{c}_k | \widehat{\boldsymbol{a}}_{\lambda,^{\varrho}\zeta_\lambda(^{\varrho}c_k)}^{(i)})} \log \left(\widehat{p}^{(i+1)}(^{\varrho}\boldsymbol{\zeta}_\lambda) \prod_{k=1}^{^{\varrho}m} p(^{\varrho}\boldsymbol{c}_k | \widehat{\boldsymbol{a}}_{\lambda,^{\varrho}\zeta_\lambda(^{\varrho}c_k)}^{(i+1)}) \right)$$

Since the arguments of the logarithm in (23.52) are products, we obtain

$$\log \left(\widehat{p}^{(i+1)}(^{\varrho}\boldsymbol{\zeta}_\lambda) \prod_{k=1}^{^{\varrho}m} p(^{\varrho}\boldsymbol{c}_k | \widehat{\boldsymbol{a}}_{\lambda,^{\varrho}\zeta_\lambda(^{\varrho}c_k)}^{(i+1)}) \right) =$$

$$= \log \widehat{p}^{(i+1)}(^{\varrho}\boldsymbol{\zeta}_\lambda) + \sum_{k=1}^{^{\varrho}m} \log p(^{\varrho}\boldsymbol{c}_k | \widehat{\boldsymbol{a}}_{\lambda,^{\varrho}\zeta_\lambda(^{\varrho}c_k)}^{(i+1)}) \qquad (23.53)$$

The maximization of the Q-function (23.52) with respect to $p(\boldsymbol{\zeta}_\lambda)$ has to be done such that the constraint $\sum_{\boldsymbol{\zeta}_\lambda} p(\boldsymbol{\zeta}_\lambda) = 1$ holds. Usually the optimization of continuous functions is based on the computation of partial derivatives and their zero-crossings. According to Appendix (C.5) Lagrange multipliers are appropriate for considering constraints on the required parameters. For an arbitrary but fixed assignment $\boldsymbol{\zeta}_\lambda$ we get the following closed-form re-estimation formula using the partial derivative and the result of the example in Appendix (C.5):

$$p^{(i+1)}(\boldsymbol{\zeta}_\lambda) = \frac{\sum_{\varrho=1}^{N} \frac{\widehat{p}^{(i)}(\boldsymbol{\zeta}_\lambda) \prod_{k=1}^{^{\varrho}m} p(^{\varrho}\boldsymbol{c}_k | \widehat{\boldsymbol{a}}_{\lambda,\zeta_\lambda(^{\varrho}c_k)}^{(i)})}{\sum_{^{\varrho}\boldsymbol{\zeta}_\lambda} \widehat{p}^{(i)}(^{\varrho}\boldsymbol{\zeta}_\lambda) \prod_{k=1}^{^{\varrho}m} p(^{\varrho}\boldsymbol{c}_k | \widehat{\boldsymbol{a}}_{\lambda,^{\varrho}\zeta_\lambda(^{\varrho}c_k)}^{(i)})}}{\sum_{\varrho=1}^{N} \sum_{^{\varrho}\boldsymbol{\zeta}_\lambda} \frac{\widehat{p}^{(i)}(^{\varrho}\boldsymbol{\zeta}_\lambda) \prod_{k=1}^{^{\varrho}m} p(^{\varrho}\boldsymbol{c}_k | \widehat{\boldsymbol{a}}_{\lambda,^{\varrho}\zeta_\lambda(^{\varrho}c_k)}^{(i)})}{\sum_{^{\varrho}\boldsymbol{\zeta}_\lambda} \widehat{p}^{(i)}(^{\varrho}\boldsymbol{\zeta}_\lambda) \prod_{k=1}^{^{\varrho}m} p(^{\varrho}\boldsymbol{c}_k | \widehat{\boldsymbol{a}}_{\lambda,^{\varrho}\zeta_\lambda(^{\varrho}c_k)}^{(i)})}} . \qquad (23.54)$$

At first sight, this formula seems quite complicated. The numerator includes the "probability" to observe the assignment ζ_λ given the sequences of observations. The denominator denotes the probability to observe the feature sequence for *any* and *unknown* assignment. In fact this intuitive principle holds also for the estimation of probabilities related to pairwise independent assignments, and the input and transition probabilities of Hidden-Markov-Models.

Assignments induce a random vector. Let $(l_1, l_2, \ldots, l_m)^\mathrm{T}$ be such a random vector. Statistical independent assignments allow the following factorization

$$p((l_1, l_2, \ldots, l_m)^\mathrm{T}) = \prod_{k=1}^{m} p(l_k) \quad . \tag{23.55}$$

Since $l_k = 1, 2, \ldots, n_\lambda$, the parameters that have to be estimated are: $p(1), p(2), \ldots, p(n_\lambda)$. For this special case, formula (23.54) reduces to:

$$\widehat{p}^{(i+1)}(l) = \frac{\text{expected number of assignments to a feature } c_{\lambda,l}}{\text{number of features}} \quad .$$

In case of HMMs, assignments show dependencies of first order. The parameters are $p(1)$, $p(2), \ldots, p(n_\lambda)$, and $p(l'|l'')$ where $l', l'' = 1, 2, \ldots, n_\lambda$. The EM-algorithm leads to the famous Baum-Welch formulas, which are

$$\widehat{p}^{(i+1)}(l) = \frac{\text{expected number of assigning the first feature to } c_{\lambda,l}}{\text{number of features}}$$

and

$$\widehat{p}^{(i+1)}(l'|l'') = \frac{\text{expected number of assigning a feature to } c_{\lambda,l''} \text{ and its successor to } c_{\lambda,l'}}{\text{expected number of assigning a feature to } c_{\lambda,l''}}$$

These estimation formulas show a remarkable property that is important with respect to an object–oriented implementation: the concrete representation of features' densities $p(c|a_{\lambda,l})$ is not required. Only a function that allows the evaluation of these densities for a given feature is necessary. For the computation of the parameters $a_{\lambda,l}$, however, we need the knowledge of the parametric densities $p(c|a_{\lambda,l})$. If, for instance, normally distributed features are assumed, the estimation of $a_{\lambda,l}$ corresponds to the computation of the mean vector and the covariance matrix. These formulas are omitted here. We recommend [Hua90] for further explanations.

23.8 Hidden-Markov-Model Classes

Single density functions, mixture densities, Hidden-Markov-Models, and its generalization are probability density functions from an abstract point of view. For all statistical models, we need inference algorithms that allow the efficient computation of density values for given observations. Furthermore, parameter estimation algorithms are required, and we have to consider

23.8 Hidden-Markov-Model Classes

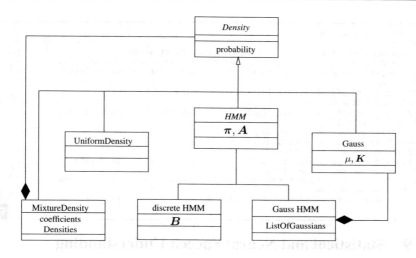

Figure 23.13: Class hierarchy for density functions

different types of density functions, like ergodic or left-right HMMs, mixtures of Gaussians, mixtures of discrete probabilities, etc. The algorithms should be implemented as generally as possible. For instance, the estimation of transition probabilities of HMMs can be implemented without specifying the output density functions. The use of virtual functions allows such implementations.

The suggested class hierarchy for statistical models is shown in Figure 23.13. We define an abstract base class `Density` including the pure virtual function `probability` which evaluates the probability density function for a given observation. Therein an observation is an instance of the class `RandomVariable`. Histograms, Gaussian densities, Hidden-Markov-Models as well as mixtures of densities are density functions and therefore derived classes. In Chapter 22 we have already discussed the code of base class `Density` and the derived density class `Gaussian` (cf. Listing 203). An HMM, for instance, is defined by the initial probabilities, the transition probabilities, and a vector of output densities — one density for each state. These state densities can be Gaussians, histograms, mixtures or any other type of densities, even HMMs. This required recursive structure is provided by the suggested class hierarchy. Each class derived from the base class `Density` can be used within the density vector of the internal representation of HMMs.

In addition to classes for statistics, the implementation uses the class `SeqCltn` from NIHCL to represent sequences of output symbols in the Baum-Welch training method. As in the case of the class `Bag` in Sect. 22.2 this implies that these symbols are objects in the sense of NIHCL.

```
class HMM : public Density {
public:
  Vector<double>   H_Pi;   // initial probability of states
  Matrix<double>   H_A;    // matrix including transition probabilities
  Vector<Density>  H_P;    // ordered set of densities (class Density!)
  HMM(void);
  HMM(int NumberOfStates); // initialize Vectors and Matrices
  HMM(const HMM & g);
  HMM(const Vector<Density>&, const Vector<double>&, Matrix<double>&);
  virtual ~HMM(void);
  const Vector<double> & pi(void) const;
  const Matrix<double> & A(void) const;
  const Density &        P(void) const;
  virtual double probability(const RandomVariable & feature) const;
  // forward-backward algorithm
  void state_sequence(const RandomVariable & feat, SeqCltn & seq) const;
  // Viterbi algorithm
  void BaumWelchTraining(const SeqCltn & obs); // for discrete prob.
};
```

[206]

23.9 Statistical and Neural Speech Understanding

Instead of statistical classification, many people prefer to use artificial neural networks (ANNs) for classification, e.g. in [Has94]. The relation between both approaches is described in [Che91].

Like statistical models such as HMMs, ANNs can be trained based on learning data and their behavior will then be verified using test data. The design of ANNs is usually done with an ANN–simulator, such as SNNS.[3] A terse description of ANNs for pattern understanding is given in [Nie90a; p. 199–205]. Of course, implementations in C++ for ANNs exist, e.g. [Wel94], and can be applied for pattern recognition purposes.

As for image analysis, we now give a recipe for a speech understanding system.

Recipe: *Build your (simplistic) speech understanding system*:

1. filter the signal to reduce noise (Chapter 17)
2. divide signals into frames (Sect. 23.1)
3. compute spectral features (Chapter 21)
4. hypothesize words using HMM (Sect. 23.4) or ANN (Sect. 23.9)
5. constrain word sequences by linguistic knowledge
6. repeat, until utterance is interpreted
7. optionally: new "action" (see below)

The "action" here may be a dialogue step, such as asking a question or confirming some fact. This feedback is similar to active vision for image analysis.

---

[3] Available from http://www.uni-stuttgart.de.

Exercises

23.a Can you tell which speech signal in Figure 23.2 shows an Austrian accent?
23.b Discuss basic similarities and the differences between the dynamic programming approach, the product of mixtures, and the forward-algorithm.
23.c Apply the ideas of the forward-algorithm and dynamic programming to find an algorithm that computes the most probable sequence of HMM states for a given observation. Show that this algorithm — which is the well-known *Viterbi algorithm* [Nie90a] — is bounded by $\mathcal{O}(mn_\lambda^2)$. Compare your result with the algorithm you get, if statistically independent assignments are considered.
23.d Use the class hierarchy of Figure 22.6, and adapt your implementation of DTW such that you can use the class for nearest neighbor classifiers.
23.e Define a class for discrete Hidden-Markov-Models. Which member variables are needed? Implement methods for learning the parameters of a Hidden-Markov-Model given a set of observation sequences. Use the cited literature and define methods for computing the probability that a given HMM has generated an observed sequence of features.
23.f Implement the dynamic time warping algorithm using different types of neighborhoods and distance measures. A basic implementation is shown in Listing 207.

```c
#include <stdio.h>                          // Tiny (D)ynamic (P)rogramming
                                            // 1999 (D)ietrich (P)aulus
int pred[][2] = {{-1,0},{-1,-1},{0,-1}};
double vx[]   = { 1, 3, 2, 4, 6, 10, 9, 12, 14, 22, 24, 27};
double vy[]   = { 3, 2, 2, 6, 6, 9, 17, 20, 25};
const int ps = sizeof(pred)/(sizeof(int)*2); // algorithm independent
const int xs = sizeof(vy)/sizeof(double);    // of test data sizes
const int ys = sizeof(vx)/sizeof(double);    // and predec. list
static struct DPE {                 // matrix for search management
    int prev;                       // index into list of predecessors
    double cost;                    // minimal cost up to here
    DPE() { cost = 10e6; }          // initialize
} dpmat[ys][xs];                    // initialized with large numbers

inline double abs(double d)          { return d > 0 ? d : -d ; }
inline double Cost(int x, int y) { return abs(vx[y] - vy[x]); }

main()
{
    dpmat[0][0].cost = Cost(0,0);               // hook to start up with
    for (int i = 0; i < ys; ++i )               // for each element in ...
      for (int j = 0; j < xs; ++j )             // ...the search matrix
        for (int k = 0; k < ps; ++k ) {         // all predecessors
            int px = j + pred[k][0],
                py = i + pred[k][1];
            if ((px < 0)  || (py < 0)) continue;  // skip borders
            double c=dpmat[py][px].cost+Cost(j,i);
            if (c < dpmat[i][j].cost) {          // better path found
                dpmat[i][j].cost = c;            // record its costs
                dpmat[i][j].prev = k;            // keep track or path
            }
        }
}
```

Chapter 24

An Image Analysis System

In this chapter we introduce the design of the image analysis system ANIMALS (AN IMage AnaLysis System, [Pau92b]) composed of classes that we introduced in the previous chapters. We provide a uniform interface for segmentation data and present a top level program for image segmentation.

24.1 Design of PUMA and ANIMALS

In Chapter 8, image segmentation was described and presented as a series of steps from the image signal to an initial symbolic description (Sect. 8.6, Figure 8.4). Every step has its own typical algorithms. The implementation of these algorithms as separate processes introduces the problem of how to connect the results. Figuratively speaking, some algorithms skip over a step in Figure 8.4, some introduce intermediate data structures and require other processes before the next step can be reached. Thru this approach, the image segmentation problem can be seen as one of data flow analysis.

A very general view of this data flow is shown in Figure 24.1, where the following units can be identified. We have seen various *image* types such as gray-level images, color images, and edge images. Among several alternatives, algorithms suitable for the task of the vision system have to be chosen in the *segmentation* as well as in the *analysis* stage; the results have to be connected in a way that will eventually lead to the *symbolic description*. The dotted lines represent the feedback in a closed control loop for active vision (Sect. 8.8), where an *action* is expected rather than a description. The data structure containing results of segmentation will be called a *segmentation object*. This information can also be used for *classification* of an image, if image analysis is not the required task; in this case, the descritpion is simply the class label. Models and model generation, which are also shown will be discussed in Sect. 24.9.

We now introduce a software system that executes and links these stages of image acquisition, processing, and analysis.

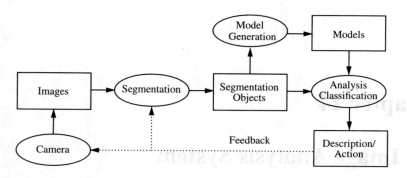

Figure 24.1: Data flow in an image analysis system

Program development and experiments in the field of pattern recognition are costly and time consuming. For simplifying this process, the programming environment PUMA[1] was designed and developed [Pau92b]. PUMA is machine-independent; consequently, experiments and programs can be implemented without considering special hardware constraints. Special mechanisms — like the automatic generation of documentation — support the implementation of the software engineering principles discussed in Chapter 3. The system is used as a pool for common functions, classes, and programs for image and speech analysis.

PUMA includes ANIMALS (**AN IM**age **A**na**L**ysis **S**ystem). The implemented classes for data representation are named „HIPPOS" (**HI**erarchy of **P**icture **P**rocessing **O**bject**S**), from now on written with Greek letters ἵππος (pronounce as: „hippos") [Pau92b], which we will present in Sect. 24.2. In ANIMALS we define common command line interfaces using an extended version of the command line classes introduced in Sect. 16.7. Each major image processing or segmentation algorithm is available as a program; several such programs have been proposed in the previous chapters, e.g. in Exercise 11.h, 15.f, 12.a, 12.b, 12.g, 12.h, 12.a, 12.b, 12.g, 12.h, 17.j, 17.k, 19.d, 20.f, and in Figure 24.1. Different programs doing similar things look similar to the user. ANIMALS collects the algorithms, ἵππος manages the data representation.

The ANIMALS system is designed in an object–oriented way according to the data flow in Figure 24.1. Data and algorithms for image processing are organized into hierarchies. Image analysis is mainly seen as a problem of transforming information between different levels of abstraction. Naturally, the transformations are implemented as separate processes.

Figure 24.2 shows the various paths from images to line segments [Pau92c]. At level A, images are created; at level B, images are transformed; at C, edge images are transformed; at D, segmentation objects are processed. The major data classes appearing in this scheme are intensity images, edge images, chain codes, lines, and segmentation objects. Edge detection leads from intensity images (gray or color) to edge images (arrow 8). The reverse direction (arrow 9) is used for the visualization of edge images (e.g., Figure 15.9). Line detection (Chapter 19) leads from edge images to segmentation objects containing chain codes (arrow 11). Visualization

---

[1]**P**rogrammier-**U**mgebung für die **M**uster–**A**nalyse — in English: a programming environment for pattern analysis

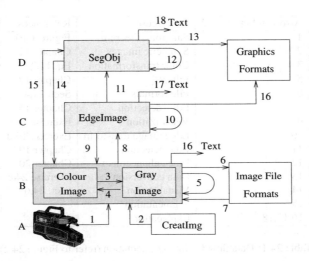

Figure 24.2: Data flow for line-based image segmentation. The arrows indicate processes that transform from one representation to another (cmp. Figure 8.4); they are explained in the text and in Table 24.1.

of segmentation objects can be done using raster images (arrow 14) or after conversion to a graphics format (arrow 13). Intensity images can be segmented directly and be transformed to segmentation objects (arrow 15); one example, not elaborated in this book, is to apply the Hough transform not on the edge image, but on the intensity image. Often, textual descriptions of the objects are desired (arrows 16–18).[2]

The above transitions from one block to another can be implemented as functions, processes or operator classes.

Implementation as well as data storage of a program should be machine-independent. As we will show in Sect. 24.4, all external representations of objects is done via XDR which is a binary, machine-independent format. The interfaces between different processing stages can thus be reduced to the objects passed from one process to another. Since the representation is machine-independent, the processes can run on different architectures.

24.2 Hierarchy of Picture Processing Objects

The object–oriented programming system ἵππος for image analysis was introduced in [Pau92a, Pau92b, Pau92c]. In this chapter we outline the ἵππος-system in general. We describe the concepts of lines, their representations as classes, and the implementation in C++ in detail. The classes described in this book and in the appendix are only a trimmed down subset of the corresponding classes in the ἵππος system, with a reduced number of classes and much fewer

---

[2]Textual description of images are not covered in this volume.

Arrow in Figure 24.2	Description	References
1	Sampling theorem	Figure 1.10
2	Synthetic images	Chapter 12
3,4	Color transformation	Eq. 11.2
5	Filters	Chapter 17
6,7	File formats	Sect. 11.4
8	Edge detection	Chapter 15
9	Visualization	Exercise 15.c
10	Edge image transform	Exercise 19.d
11	Line detection	Chapter 19
12	Line enhancement	Chapter 20
13	Data conversion	Exercise 24.c
14	Visualization	Sect. 24.6
15	Segmentation	—
16,17,18	Explanation	—

Table 24.1: Data flow for line segmentation (refer to Figure 24.2)

```
#include <exception> /* STL exceptions */
class PUMAException : public exception {
protected:
    char * s; // store error message
public:
    PUMAException();
    PUMAException(char *);
    const char * msg() const { return s; }
};
```
208

methods. Algorithms and programs using these smaller classes can be compiled and run with very few changes in the complete system for 2–D segmentation.

The complete system consists of a large class tree with the top node class HipposObj (Figure 24.3) which is directly derived from the NIHCL-class Object (Sect. 16.2). All classes required for image segmentation are derived from this class; they inherit the basic functionality for image processing. Some other classes in ἵππος are derived from other branches of the NIHCL-tree. This is done for concepts that are not directly related to image processing. Template classes for matrices are defined and derived in a matrix-subtree. The classes above the dotted line are NIHCL-classes (cf. Figure 16.1); the classes below belong to ἵππος. On the left we show the superclasses for representation of data, on the right we depict the classes which extend NIHCL for data storage with XDR (Sect. 24.4). Matrix classes obtain input and output facilities simultaneously with the efficient data structure described in Listing 107 by a combination of multiple inheritance and a template base class. The classes OIOxdrin and OIOxdrout extend the notion of a binary stream implemented in NIHCL by the idea of machine-independent data representation. We also implement exception handlers for these classes which are conveniently derived from the STL exception templates as shown in Listing 208.

24.2 Hierarchy of Picture Processing Objects

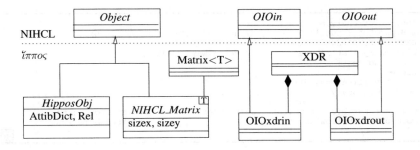

Figure 24.3: Interface of NIHCL and ἵππος

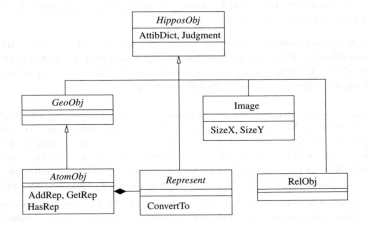

Figure 24.4: Top of image processing class hierarchy

The ἵππος tree is dedicated to the *representation* of data that is computed during image segmentation. The representation is general enough to include all known segmentation algorithms. These classes are collected in a subtree under the abstract class `HipposObj`. Its basic purpose is to bundle all the derived classes for image processing and analysis and to provide the basic functionality of every object of this application area (Figure 24.4). All image types are derived from the abstract `Image` class. The representation subtree contains classes for the results of various line-based or region-based algorithms. Geometric objects provide a more abstract interface to these representations (Sect. 24.2). Relational objects `RelObj` will be needed in Sect. 24.3.

Three major features can be found in all imaging objects:

- Image processing objects usually reflect some sort of visual information. They can commonly be displayed on an appropriate graphics display.

```
#include "Dictionary.h"
class HipposObj : public Object { // abstract class, no public part
    DECLARE_MEMBERS(HipposObj)
    Dictionary * attributes;           // not always != NULL
    float judgment;
protected:
    HipposObj(float r=0.0);
    const Dictionary & Attributes() const;
    float            Judgment() const;
    void setAttrib(const char *, const Object *);   // add to Dictionary
    void deepenShallowCopy();                        // required here
};
```

Listing 209

- In order to specify a problem independent control strategy for knowledge based image analysis (Sect. 8.5), it is essential that every segmented object is attached with a judgment or quality measure (Sect.8.6).

- In addition to compiled-in members, image processing objects often have varying additional information that may be useful in one application but not required in another. An example is the mean contrast along a segmented line that may be computed by a line finding algorithm but ignored in the following steps.

These features are translated to C++ in a straightforward way. The varying information on attributes is stored in an NIHCL-Dictionary with keys restricted to strings. The judgment is a floating point value that is inherited by every object in the hierarchy. A basic implementation of this class is shown in Listing 209. As recommended in Sect. 16.6, we require that an object set as an attribute has to be allocated by the user. Consequently, this class will need a function deepenShallowCopy that will replace the attribute dictionary by a deep copy of itself.

Images were introduced by a class hierarchy in chapter 11; these classes are now integrated in the image processing hierarchy. Several classes for images are derived from a common abstract base class Image in ἵππος. Representations for so-called stereo images, range images, color images, gray-level images, binary images, edge images, etc. are provided together with the appropriate operations. Subimages, as described in Sect. 11.7, are available for any image class. Stereo images are a pair of intensity images that result from a setup where one scene is seen thru two lenses, such as humans do with their two eyes. Technically, two cameras with similar viewing direction are used. From the difference of the two images, an estimate of the three-dimensional structure of the scene can be computed. The two images constituting the stereo image may be either gray-level or color images. The single stereo image introduced in Sect. 12.7 used a trick to provide the visual system with the illusion of a three-dimensional scene.

Pixels are naturally stored in matrix objects. A matrix class hierarchy was created for parametric matrix classes. Matrix templates with numeric elements declare mathematical operations like addition, multiplication, transposition, etc. Other matrices — e. g. those containing edge elements — provide only basic access and input-output functions. Since these matrix classes do not directly refer to image processing, they are not derived from the HipposObj. Thereby they are available to speech processing or any other non-image processing purposes without linkage of the ἵππος class library.

24.2 Hierarchy of Picture Processing Objects

```
class Image_V1 : public HipposObj {   // extend as outlined in the text
    int x,y;                          // private data
  public:
    Image_V1 (int xs,int ys) : x(xs), y(ys) {}  // set size info
    int SizeY() const { return y; }             // read size y
    int SizeX() const { return x; }             // read size x
};
#if defined(IMAGE_VERS) && (IMAGE_VERS == 1)
typedef class Image_V1 Image;
#endif
```
210

```
class GrayLevelImage_V2 : public Image {
    DECLARE_MEMBERS(GrayLevelImage_V2)
    Matrix<byte> img;                 // image data
  public:
    GrayLevelImage_V2(int x,int y) : Image(x,y), img(x,y) { };
    byte* operator[] (int i) {return img[i];}
    const byte* operator[] (int i) const {return img[i];}
};
#if defined(GLI_VERS) && (GLI_VERS == 2)
typedef class GrayLevelImage_V2 GrayLevelImage;
#endif
```
211

The abstract class Image in Listing 210. can contain additional textual and numeric descriptions, such as the camera used and its parameters (lens, focus, aperture, exposure time, etc.). similar to the first version in Listing 140. A re-definition for a gray-level image is given in Listing 211.

The purpose of the class GeoObj is to collect geometric objects such as lines or points. Several representations of one line in an image (or in a scene) may even exist simultaneously. For example, a chain code may be approximated by several polygons with different approximation errors. These representations are stored in an object of class AtomLine. The same holds for regions that may have several representations. An AtomLine and an AtomRegion are derived from the class GeoObj which bundles the subtree for geometric objects. The class AtomObj is introduced which separates compound objects (e.g., a collection of lines forming a rectangle) from those which contain only one instance of a given type. Compound objects are called *segmentation objects* and will be introduced in Sect. 24.3. The class hierarchy of these classes is shown in Figure 24.5.

Basic implementations of geometric objects and atomic objects are given in Listing 212, 213, and 214. In Listing 212 we define the abstract base class for this part of the hierarchy. Atomic objects are derived from class GeoObj; this class is abstract as well (Listing 213). The method getRep will return a representation of a class indicated by the argument. If a representation is requested that is not currently stored in the set of representations, a conversion method in the class Represent is used to produce such a representation (cf. Figure 24.4).[3]

---

[3] In the small system introduced in this book, this feature, as well as the whole class Represent is not further elaborated.

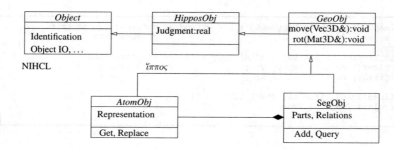

Figure 24.5: Hierarchy for geometric objects and segmentation objects

```
class GeoObj : public HipposObj {   // geometric objects
    DECLARE_MEMBERS(GeoObj)         // NIHCL functions
    Set represent;                  // set of representations
protected:                          // abstract, no public parts
    GeoObj();                       // only default constructor here
};
```

24.3 Segmentation Objects

It is very important to represent intermediate results of image segmentation in a common format which can be used by many segmentation programs. Generally, a so-called *segmentation object* consists of a set of parts and the relations between those parts. In most applications, these parts are geometric objects that cannot be further split, i.e., they are atomic objects. Occasionally, segmentation objects may be recursive and include other segmentation objects, i.e., compound objects.

Segmentation results are represented in a common interface class called SegObj (Figure 24.5). Listing 215 shows a basic implementation. This class is also derived from the class GeoObj and provides compound segmentation data. Parts may be added that are of the class GeoObj, i.e., either atomic objects or geometric objects. Since sets of objects of NIHCL are used, efficient functions for comparing objects have to be provided for geometric objects. Also, the function deepenShallowCopy has to be implemented to create copies of a segmentation object. As outlined in Sect. 16.6, this implies that the copy constructor creates a shallow copy of the member objects parts and rels. The same principle holds for the class AtomObj.

```
class AtomObj : public GeoObj {
    DECLARE_MEMBERS(AtomObj)
    Set representations;                            // will never be empty
protected:
    AtomObj();                                      // derived class will fill
    virtual addRep(const Represent&) = 0;           // the set!
    Represent * getRep(const Class&);               // get a particular representation
    bool hasRep(const Class&) const;                // check for a representation
    void deepenShallowCopy();                       // since Sets are used internally
};
```

24.3 Segmentation Objects

```
class AtomLine : public AtomObj {
    DECLARE_MEMBERS(AtomLine)            // NIHCL functions
  public:
    AtomLine();
    AtomLine(const Represent&);
    virtual addRep(const Represent&);    // will add a line representation
};
```
214

```
#include "Set.h"
class SegObj : public GeoObj {
    DECLARE_MEMBERS(SegObj)
    Set parts;                           // set of GeoObj (!)
    Set rels;                            // set of RelObjs
  public:
    SegObj();                            // will have empty sets
    void add(const GeoObj &s);           // add element to set
    void deepenShallowCopy();            // since Sets are used internally
    // etc.
};
```
215

The very powerful SegObj class is the central class of the ἵππος system. Since segmentation objects may contain other segmentation objects, special care has to be taken that no circular list of references will be created. The implementation of the method add guarantees that parts may only be included in the object if this will not create an inconsistent (i.e., cyclic) *part-of* relation. Further restrictions improve the safety of this representation scheme.

Several features not shown in Listing 215 are implemented in ἵππος. Parts of segmentation objects may be related in various ways to each other. For example, lines may be marked as parallel. Such relations between objects are represented by relations in the mathematical sense that we also provided as classes (see RelObj in Figure 24.3). These relational features are stored in the set rels. Vertices (see for example Figure 8.3) are special segmentation objects defined by the intersection of at least two lines.

The input to line detection algorithms is an edge image (EdgeImage); the output is a set of lines that are represented by a segmentation object. Different line detection algorithms create different line representations. The most basic result is a segmentation object (SegObj) consisting of lines represented as chain codes (Chain). Some algorithms (e.g., the Hough transform, Sect. 19.7) will compute straight line segments without going through the chain code representation. Extending Listing 181 we can define an object for line segmentation in Listing 216

```
class LineDet : public IP_OP {          // Line detection algorithm
    double threshold;                    // some parameter
  public:
    virtual void operator() (const EdgeImage&, SegObj&) = 0;
};
```
216

```
main(int argc, char **argv)
{
  HipposObj * o = NULL;
  try {
    OIOxdrin If(*++argv);                          // open input file
    o = HipposObj::readFrom(If);                   // read arbitrary object
  } catch (PUMAException pe) {                     // error reading image
      fprintf(stderr,"Error %s\n", pe.msg());      // print
      exit(1);                                     // and stop program
  }
  try {
    OIOxdrout of(*++argv);                         // open output file
    o->storeOn(of);                                // store it
  } catch (PUMAException pe) {                     // Error writing image
      fprintf(stderr,"Error %s\n", pe.msg());      // print
      exit(1);                                     // and stop program
  }
}
```
217

For the implmentation of the Hough transform (Sect. 19.7), we use an edge image (EdgeImage) as input and create a segmentation object (SegObj) as output containing straight lines (that have to be represented as objects; in ἵππος this is done in a class StrLineSeg[4]).

24.4 External Representation

The NIHCL-system introduces streams for persistent objects (i.e., permanent storage of objects, Sect. 16.3). In ἵππος this concept was extended to machine-independent binary storage using XDR (eXternal Data Representation, [XDR88]), which is available on almost any computer via the SUN network file system (nfs). A class XDR was introduced for this purpose. This enables a portable and highly efficient data transfer between different computer architectures. All NIHCL-objects can be stored and retrieved from XDR–streams using their storeOn and readFrom methods of the derived streams. No changes are required for NIHCL.

This is a nice example of the power of virtual functions. Existing class libraries can be extended by inheritance and existing functionality can be overwritten with new virtual functions. A new class OIOxdrout is derived from the NIHCL-class OIOout. The overloaded virtual functions put declared for the NIHCL-class (Sect. 16.3) are redefined and mapped directly to the xdr functions. The method OIOxdrout::put(int i), for example, uses the xdr_int function. This derivation scheme is shown in Figure 24.3 on the right.

Without any modification or re-compilation of the code, NIHCL-objects can now be stored to OIOxdrout–streams. The method storeOn(OIOout&) will be used for this purpose. The same holds for the new class OIOxdrin which is derived from the NIHCL-class OIOin.

Listing 217 provides a good example of object–oriented programming. The main program just reads an object, which can be any class derived from HipposObj, and stores it using the virtual function storeOn. When a new class is added to the image processing hierarchy, this program will just have to be linked again in order to know about the new possible objects and

---

[4] The implementation was left as an exercise (19.e).

their display methods. As opening and closing of the files is part of object construction and desctruction, error handling can only be done using exceptions.

In an evolving programming environment, changes in classes are common. Often this requires a change, e.g., an addition, in the external representation. It is unacceptable that old external data would then have to be discarded as a result of this change. One possibility is to provide conversion routines which convert old data to the new format. A more elegant way is to extend the routines for storage and reading to handle different versions. This way, new programs will both write new data formats as well as recognize and decode old formats during read operations. Old programs will of course not be able to read the new format. Normally, old programs will either have to be re-compiled or simply re-linked, depending on the extent of the changes made. These mechanisms were incorporated into the class XDR without any changes to the underlying NIHCL mechanisms.[5]

In any modular programming system it is highly recommended that function calls will have no side effects. With respect to input and output to files, this means that no function should open a stream and write data to it, unless this is the only purpose of this function. Listing 217 also shows how we recommend file input and output for image processing applications: the streams are opened and closed in the main program; file names are clearly visible to the programmer and the functions called will do the computation without further input and output. This also shows that all files will be closed properly. In most of the cases, such a structure is possible for imaging programs. This structure is consistent with the recommendation in Sect. 10.9, that memory allocation and memory release should be done in the same function, wherever possible, i.e, `new` and `delete` should occur as pairs in the source code.

24.5 Graphical User Interfaces

Providing a comfortable and intuitive user interface with graphical tools for image analysis is a complicated matter. Graphical user interfaces (GUI's) are more useful for program development and for teaching. In industrial applications, in particular in real-time applications, this is less important. Real-time image analysis and active vision usually has to be performed without continuous user interaction. In ANIMALS, we can use the X11 tool that automatically creates an interface to `tcl/tk` [Ous94]. One big advantage is that all programms appear with a uniform interface. A graphical shell is put around the program that is used for argument processing in a text window and may display input and results in separate windows.[6] We will discuss the basic idea using a typical image segmentation program.

Listing 218 shows the static declarations for the main module. We use pointers to operator objects that can vary upon the actual command line arguments. The classes LowPass,

---

[5]It is, however, not possible to deal with all kinds of changes in a class. For example, changes in the inheritance scheme cannot be easily masked out. Also, since the type and the version of a member variable are stored along with the data, changing the type of a member may also be difficult, i.e., programs for data conversion are sometimes required.

[6]We put the source code for argument processing into the public domain (cf. Appendix B); using a tcl/tk script, a GUI can be created automatically from the output of these argument objects.

```
#define GLI_VERS 2                  // will only work with newest version
#include "ipop.h"
static char * inp, *outp;           // strings
static LowPass * filter = NULL;     // filter object
static EdgeDet * edgdet = NULL;     // edge detection object
static LineDet * lindet = NULL;     // line detection object
```
218

```
static char rcsid[] = "RCSINFO";
static char * HelpText [] = {
  "This program demonstrates the use of " // no comma: concatenate strings
  "commmand line parsing for an",
  "image processing system",
  rcsid,
  NULL                              // terminate text
};
main(int argc, char **argv)
{
  Option inp  ("input",  "input file",  1);  // input file option
  Option outp ("output", "output file", 1);  // output file option
  Option verb ("verbose", "flag");           // should we talk about actions?
  Parser p(HelpText,argc,argv);              // command line interpretation
  if (verb.isSet())
    cout << "Reading file" << endl;
  OIOxdrin  f_in(inp);                       // input  stream
  OIOxdrout f_out(outp);                     // output stream
  GrayLevelImage * f = GrayLevelImage::readFrom(f_in);
  GrayLevelImage   g (f->SizeX(),f->SizeY());
  EdgeImage        h (f->SizeX(),f->SizeY());
  (*filter)(*f,g);                           // low-pass filter on input
  (*edgdet)(g,h);                            // detect edge elements
  SegObj s;                                  // to hold the results
  (*lindet)(h,s);                            // connect edge elements
  if (verb.isSet())
    cout << "Storing results" << endl;
  s.storeOn(f_out);                          // store on stream
  return(0);                                 // close files, clean up, exit
}
```
219

EdgeDet, and LineDet are used for image processing operations and will be filled in the following chapters. The abstract declaration is already given here in Listing 181.

Listing 219 shows the main program. After processing the command line, an image object is read from an XDR stream. Images for intermediate results are created with the same dimensions and the input image is filtered with a filter operator object.

As in Listing 180, we do not exactly specify which operator will actually be used; we use a pointer to an operator class that can point to some object of its derived classes during runtime.

Edges detected in the filtered image are stored in an edge image. An edge detection object can be implemented, for instance, using algorithms of Chapter 15. Edge elements are combined into lines and stored in a segmentation object. The operator object for this purpose may be based on the methods discussed in Chapter 15 and Listing 188.

The program fragments in Listing 218–219 can be combined and extended with the classes introduced in previous chapters, to produce a nice, powerful, and easy-to-change image segmentation program.

Coming back to the question of how to integrate this program in an interactive environment, we extend the class `Parser` which inspects all arguments passed to the program. If a special argument is given to the program, such as `-__HELP__`, the parser will print all possible option strings, their explanation, and the number of arguments expected (here: `("input"`, `"input file",1),("output","output file",1),`and `("verbose","flag"`, `0))`. This output will have to be parsed by a `tcl` script which creates a window with a radio button labeled verbose and two input fields called input and output. Another button for help will call the program with argument `-help`. When the input fields are filled in, an execution button will call the program with the given data. This way, no functions for the GUI have to be linked to the program.

When a sequence of programs has to be combined as in Figure 24.1, we can create temporary output files of one program which are the input to the next program. More elegantly, we will create a pipe between the two processes. The first program writes to the pipe, the second reads from it. We can simply modify the `OIOxdrin` and `OIOxdrout` classes in such a way that they write to `stdout` or read from `stdin` if the filename passed to the constructor is `"-"`. We can then write commands like the following:

```
median -input input.file -output - | sobel -input output file
```

24.6 Display

Naturally, image processing objects will have to be displayed on a raster display. For this purpose, image processing programs can be linked with libraries for graphical user interfaces; this is required if user intraction is requested based on the display. Several toolkits exist that simplify programming of such tasks. One example is the Qt-library which has nice functions for displaying images [Dah98].

Programs that require no graphical interaction will not link such libraries. Only one program is required that reads arbitrary objects such as images or segmentation objects and stores them in a graphics file format that can be displayed with some viewer. All others just write their results to file. The basic structure of this converter is similar to the program in Listing 217: after command line processing, the program reads the $ἵππος$-object and dispatches to various conversion routines for raster data or segmentation objects. These informations will be converted to a format that is compatible with the graphics routine used for display.

As there are so many possible display programs and so many options for visualization, it is recommended to separate this task from image processing and analysis programs.

24.7 Computer Vision

We mentioned that the description of an image is the final goal of analysis. According to [Tru98], the basic problem of *computer vision* is to compute properties of the three-dimensional world from one or several images. This includes, e.g., 3-D reconstruction, object recognition, scene analysis, and motion detection. Possibly, a reaction of the vision system is expected. In

Figure 24.6: Stereo camera system used on the mobile system shown of Figure 1.2

the following paragraph we give a very general overview of these problems that can be used to extend the implementation introduced in the previous sections. A detailed discussion of computer vision problems can be found e.g. in [Tru98, Fau93].

Computer vision requires image processing which we did in many sections of the book. All those images are typically captured by a CCD-camera; they map the three-dimensional world to the two-dimensional image plane by a projection mapping; some examples of such projections have been shown in Sect. 1.6 and Sect. 3.9. In some cases the objects visible in the scene are flat and can be described by features in the 2-D image plane, such as in the case of the toys shown in Figure 20.10. 2-D processing is sufficient to solve these problems. Similar tasks can be found e.g. in industrial environments when parts have to be identified on a conveyor belt that have a stable position and differ in 2-D shape.

For other problems such as driving a car automatically, these features certainly are not sufficient. One well-established method to conclude some three-dimensional facts from the 2-D images is to copy biology further for technical vision (cmp. Chapter 1). 3-D impression is mostly caused by light and shading effects, motion, and stereo. Instead of one camera, two cameras are used in a so-called *stereo* camera. One such device is shown in Figure 24.6. One strategy is to segment both images, e.g. into points and lines and to match the resulting segmentation objects using a geometric relation as sketched in Sect. 12.7. When the position of the cameras and the parameters of the camera optics are known, the search area for a point to be matched can be constrained by geometric considerations. Indeed, the 2-D search is reduced to a 1-D search problem [Tru98].

24.8 Object Recognition

Another challenge in computer vision is to recognize objects in a scene and to determine their pose (position and orientation); the pose is characterized by a rotation (orientation) as in Fig-

24.8 Object Recognition

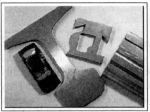  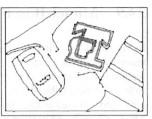

Figure 24.7: Localization of objects with heterogeneous background (left: gray-level image, middle: segmentation result, right: localized object)

  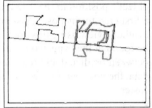

Figure 24.8: Localization of partially occluded objects and heterogeneous background (left: gray-level image, middle: segmentation result, right: localized object)

ure 12.5 and by a translation vector (position) that relate an object coordinate system to a reference coordinate system.

A statistical approach for object recognition and image analysis similar to the one described for speech understanding in Sect. 153 was described in [Hor96]. Features which can be detected in images were modelled taking into account the errors due to segmentation, occlusion, projection, and the object's pose. In particular, mixture densities (cf. Sect. 23.3) were used for this purpose. Each component of the mixture density characterizes the uncertainty of a single feature; the uncertainty of any image feature with unknown assignment is given by the convex combination of single densities. This sum results in a mixture probability density function that allows the computation of a probability for observing a certain feature. The parameters of the mixtures are estimated applying the EM technique introduced in Sect. 23.6. Object recognition is done by the Bayesian decision rule (Sect. 22.5). Pose parameters result from a maximum likelihood estimation (Sect. 7.3).

Figure 24.7 and Figure 24.8 show some scenes, where object localization is based on statistical methods using point features which result from image segmentation.

Only by an object–oriented implementation was this rather complex system kept modular with parts of it reused in other projects. In addition to the statistical models (Sect. 23.3) also algorithms for local and global optimization were provided as classes.

24.9 Model-Based Image Analysis

In Figure 24.1 we find the boxes "models" and "model generation". The idea here is to help understanding the contents of an image using some knowledge about the environment, the scenes, and the objects that we expect to find in the images. Knowledge on objects is typically called a model of the object. Ideally, models are generated from images automatically. They are stored and used as knowledge for image analysis. Using the ideas of Chapter 22 we can now consider training a classifier as the process of model generation; models serve, for example, as prototypes for a K-nearest neighbor classifier. But models in general are much more complex than a feature vector commonly used in pure pattern recognition.

As an example, let us assume that we search for a colored cube in the scene (such as the one in Figure 11.4). Based on color and histogram backprojection (Sect. 18.9) we can hypothesize the object's position in the 2-D image. The order of the color faces seen in the image can give us a first clue for its pose. Assuming that we have a cube at this position, we can now generate a synthetic view using this pose hypothesis (Sect. 12.6) and inspect the image, whether edges can be found at the expected position. Varying the pose estimate, we can minimize the differences between predicted and real edges in the image. If 3-D information is available, e.g. by stereo data, the pose parameters can be restricted further and the search for the optimal match is much easier.

In this example, our model was the geometric notion of a 3-D box. Such models are often collected in a so-called *model base* that is an *explicit representation* of the models, i.e. the models are provided as data to the program. Artificial intelligence provides various formalisms for the representation and management of such complex data, e.g., frames or semantic networks [Cre97].

This description is only a little more detailed than our first approach in Sect. 20.9; for it to work on real objects, the models and the hypotheses have to be more elaborate. Also, the computation of the optimal pose estimate is a complex search problem [Tru98]. We just wanted to motivate the reader to continue working on image analysis and demonstrate that we have outlined the fundamental tools and algorithms to make this task feasible.

Exercises

24.a Implement a method `storeOn` that handles revision numbers. Extend your class by one new member and increment the revision. Decode the revision upon reading the data and enable your new program to read old data, for which the new member will be initialized with a default value.

24.b Implement a class for image input from your frame grabber card. This should hide all hardware details — as in the case of speech input in Listing 76.

24.c Write a function that prints straight line segments in a graphics format you are familiar with (e.g., PostScript, `xfig`, etc.). Select lines from a segmentation object (`SegObj`) and write them to a file using your new routine.

24.d Complete the implementation of the class `Parser` in Listing 169.

24.9 Model-Based Image Analysis

24.e   Use the algorithms for line detection in Chapter 15 to fill in the classes for chain codes with data.

24.f   Invent a simple algorithm to convert a chain code into a polygon. Iterate along the chain code and approximate the current segment by a straight line. Whenever the approximation error exceeds a threshold, start a new line segment. Write a program which does this conversion from one segmentation object to another; the threshold should be given as command line argument.

24.g   Complete the definitions for the classes `Chain` and `ChainSeq` (Listing 194 and 191).

24.h   Complete the switch in Listing 29 for use in a chain code class.

24.i   Implement simple classes `OIOxdrin` and `OIOxdrout` to store and read arbitrary objects in a machine-independent format. Do not try to re-implement NIHCL, just provide sufficient functionality to read and write images using the same syntax as with NIHCL.

24.j   Compile your own small ANIMALS system. Provide the programs defined in 11.h, 15.f, 12.a, 12.b, 12.g, 12.h, 12.a, 12.b, 12.g, 12.h, 17.j, 17.k, 19.d, 20.f, and in Figure 24.2 with a common command line interface by the class `Parser` (Listing 169).

Part IV
Appendix

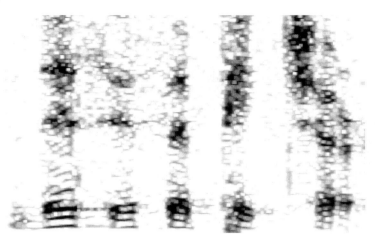

Erosion applied to spectrogram shown on page 199

In the appendix we list sources that can be used to complete the examples in the previous chapters. We describe how interested readers may access further information and request software via international computer networks. We will introduce basic software development tools.

```
struct OIOin {                          // dummy for object IO
    OIOin();  OIOin(istream&);
    OIOin& operator >> (int&);
    OIOin& operator >> (char*&);
} ;
struct OIOout {                         // dummy for object IO
    OIOout();  OIOout(ostream&);
    OIOout& operator << (int);
    OIOout& operator << (char*);
} ;
struct OIOxdrin  : public OIOin  { OIOxdrin(const char*);  };
struct OIOxdrout : public OIOout { OIOxdrout(const char*); };
typedef unsigned char byte;         // used very often
struct Represent {};                // used in HIPPOS
class Motor {} ;                    // for active vision
```
220

```
struct Set : public Object {        // use real Set from NICHL
    void add(Object&);
    void remove(Object&);
};
struct Integer : public Object { Integer(); Integer(int); };
ostream & operator<<(ostream&, Object&); /* shold call virtual function */
struct OrderedCltn : public Set {};
struct Bag : public Set {};         // container class
struct SeqCltn : public Set {};     // sequential Collection
struct Dictionary : public Set {    // use real Dictionary from NICHL
    addAssoc(Object&,Object&);
    Object *atKey(Object&);
};
struct Date : public Object { Date(); Date(int,char*,int); int year();
    int operator-(const Date&); };
struct LookupKey : public Object {
    Object& key();
    Object& value();
};
#define DO(obj,T,E) { T* E;   /* dummy, should use iterator */
#define OD           }        /* dummy */
```
221

This book was written with the LaTeX and TeX typesetting system. The pictures in this book were drawn with xfig (by Brian V. Smith), occasionally using clip art from Corel Draw. Pstricks (by Timothy Van Zandt) greatly simplified layout and formatting of the text.

In order to get a complete system from the source code fragments, the following definitions in Listing 220, have to be provided to the compiler. Listing 221 provides dummy definition for all the features of NIHCL that we have used in Chapter 16. Details are given in Sect. B.7.

Appendix A

Software Development Tools

In this appendix we describe some tools provided by the operating system Unix. First we introduce how teamwork is supported by file version and access control. Furthermore, some tools are explained for creation and management of huge program systems and the use of libraries.

A.1 Groups and ID's with Unix

Every user of a Unix system has a user name that is a textual equivalent of a unique user number (user ID, uid).[1] Users may be joint to groups, which also have a name and a number (group ID, gid). A user may be member of several groups; this is recorded in the file /etc/group. Upon login, the user is assigned to its uid and gid according to the file /etc/passwd.

Every file in the directory tree of the system is owned by a user. The uid is recorded with the file. The file is also assigned to a group[2]. Different rights may be granted to a particular file for the owner, the group, and all other users. Read, write, and execute permissions may be set or refused independently for all users (Figure A.1, see the manual entry for chmod). Defaults for the settings may be given (see the manual for umask). New files created inherit the user ID of the user creating the file. The group ID is set based on the group permissions of the directory that the new files resides in, and according to the list of groups that the user belongs to. The commands chown and chgrp allow changes of these settings.[3]

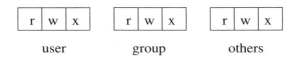

Figure A.1: Read (r), write (w), and execute (x) permissions with Unix

---
[1] As usual: there are exceptions to this rule.
[2] Try ls -l to see the user and group assignments of the file.
[3] Permission to use these commands varies between Unix-flavors.

On BSD systems, gid and uid of new files are set according to the settings of the current directory. On System 5, the user may also use the command `newgrp`.

A.2 Program Building with `make`

In the programming phase of a system, interfaces often have to be modified. Necessarily, adaption of other – dependent – modules should be done to preserve consistency. Programming environments and some operating systems such as Unix provide the powerful program `make`[4] to detect and update those modules that are out of date after such a change. This program `make` is useful for the development of small programs; it is even more necessary for large modular programs.

For example, you might have implemented a lot of modules that can be compiled separately into object code. In C/C++ those object files end in `.o`. In the linking stage several object files can be involved. Thus, the programmer has to make sure that a change of the object files will be followed by a new linkage of the program. The tool `make` supports the management of those dependencies. The implementor defines the file dependencies in a `Makefile` once, and describes the commands to be executed as well.

The file `Makefile` in the actual directory is read by the tool `make`. A `Makefile` can basically contain five different kinds of lines:[5] comments, target lines, command lines, macro definitions, and include lines. If something in the dependency graph has changed, i.e. the latest modification of a file is more recent than the modification time of files that depend on this target, the call of `make` will cause execution of all commands that are required for the update.

- dependencies:
  Dependencies describe how one file target depends on another file. The target specification starts on the first column of the `Makefile` and is followed by a colon. After the colon, a list of dependencies can be given.
  `target : list of files`
  If a target does not have any dependents specified after the separator ":" on the target line, all commands associated with the actual target are executed.

- commands:
  `<TAB> command`
  The lines including shell commands follow the target line and begin with a `<TAB>` symbol. The command lines can be continued across more than one line by ending each line with a backslash.

  Target lines with their subsequent command lines are called *rules*.

- Lines starting with a # are treated as comment lines.

Before we list more features, we give an example and explain the actions specified in the `Makefile`. We deal with a program `prog.c`, the related object file `prog.o` and an executable `prog`. These files are related as follows:

---
[4] Also included in most computer environments.
[5] See the manual for more types!

```
# Simple make file for building prog
prog    : prog.o
          cc -o prog prog.o
prog.o  : prog.c
          cc -c prog.c
```
222

- If the program `prog` has to be generated, it is necessary to produce the object file `prog.o`.
- If the file `prog.c` will be changed, `prog.o` has to be generated again.
- If the file object file `prog.o` is younger than `prog`, `prog` has to be linked.

A typical simple `Makefile` is shown in Listing 222. The execution of the program `make` without further arguments causes the first rule of the make file to be evaluated. By providing the target of generation on the command line, you can select special rules of the `Makefile`. For instance, the command `make prog` generates the executable program `prog`, assumed the actual version does not exist, yet. If you simply call `make prog.o`, only the compilation of `prog.o` is done. The command lines are normally printed before they are executed. Further options and facilities can be found in the Unix manual.

In the `makefile` we can define macros, use variables, and include files:

- The macro NAME is defined by `NAME=value`. Its value can be used by `$(NAME)`.
- Other files can be included by `include filename`.
- More variables exist which have special meaning, e.g. `$?` `$*` `$@` `$<` `$%`. Some of them we will use in the following examples. Refer to the manual for complete information on their meaning. The two varibales `$@` and `$?` are commonly used; they are handy shortcuts for the target and the dependent of the rule.

A.3 The Use of Libraries

Programs and modules developed by a team can result in many files that have to be written into an archive. For example, object files that have to be linked with other programs should be collected into one archive. Unix provides a tool that allows the generation and the management of those archives. The tool `ar -r file lib` will add or replace the file `file` in the library `lib` and `ar -d file lib` for deleting the file `file` from the library. The table of contents of the archive file can be printed using the command `ar -t lib`.

A single module *contained* in a library can also be a target of a `makefile` rule. The library name followed by the name of the module in parentheses has to be specified on the left side of a make–rule. This is of course different from specifying the library as a target; the date stamps of the modules are used, rather than those of the library file. In Listing 223 this feature is shown; the `make` variables `$@` and `$%` represent the library target and the module name.[6]

---
[6]Make has many more similar short forms for targets and dependents; see the manual for details!

```
LIB=mylib.a

$(LIB)(module.o) : module.c
    cc -o module.c
    ar -ruv $@ $%
```

A.4 Version and Access Control with `rcs`

RCS is very useful for teamwork. It allows easy sharing of code that is readable for all and writable for only one member of the group at a time. Let us asume you use a file called `file`. RCS will then create another file called `file,v` either in the current directory or in a subdirectory `RCS` if this is already present. The three basic programs for RCS are:

- `ci` (check in) which returns an edited version of `file` to the RCS file `file,v` and stores the changes,
- `co` (check out) which returns a saved version of `file,v` to `file`, Normally, this file will be read-only. If you supply the option `-l`, the file will be owned by you and you will have write access.
- `rcs` (revision control system) which does administration on `file,v`.

Their function is shown in Figure A.2. Common abbreviations in the diagram are `ci -u file` which is equivalent to the sequence

`ci file; co file;`

the command `ci -l file` stores the file and locks it. This is equivalent to

`ci file; co -l file.`

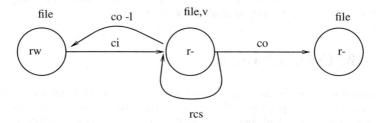

Figure A.2: RCS commands and file mode; the letters in the circles represent the file permissions.

Listing 224 shows a combination of `Makefiles` and `rcs`. The version information in this makefile is again inserted by `rcs`. In addition, `rcs` fills certain strings with values that can be used for documentation and information purposes. Further `rcs` tools inspect the version file; see the manuals for details on `rcsdiff`, `rcsmerge`, and `rlog`.

The file `file,v` can be manipulated by the `rcs` command. For example, the automatic update of the keyword strings such as `$Revision: $` or `$Id: $` can be suppressed by `rcs -ko`

```
# Makefile for use with rcs
# RCS will fill and update in the following strings
# $Revision: $
# $Author: $
# $Id: $
prog    : prog.o
          cc -o $@ $?
prog.o  : prog.c
          cc -c $?
prog.c  : prog.c,v
          co $?
```
                                                                    224

file. This is sometimes required, in particular, when files are locally managed by rcs and globally by another program called cvs which is a concurrent version control system [Fog99].[7]

A.5 Teamwork

We now describe the strategy for teamwork using rcs under Unix. First, ask the system manager to establish a group for your team. Every time you want to do group work you have to perform the following steps:

- Join the group
  In BSD systems this will be done by changing the current directory to one which belongs to the group.
  In System 5 system you will have to do an explicit change by newgrp.
- Set default write permissions to the group (using umask).
- If you start with a new project, create a subdirectory for the work with group ownership of the new group which has write permissions for the group.
- Use rcs for all files which are created or modified by the editor (i.e. source files, makefiles etc.).
- In your makefile
  - make sure that all group members have write permission to the files which are created during operation of make.
  - remove all temporary files after completing the target.

  Another option is to create all temporary files in your personal tmp directory and to use $(HOME)/tmp as directory prefix in your Makefile.

A.6 Shell

The Unix command line interpreters are powerfull programming languages that can be used to create batch files. They provide loops, conditional executions, subroutines, etc. Different

---
[7]This technique has been used for the TEX-source of this chapter, so the strings in Listing 224 are not expanded.

styles and syntax are required for the two most common interpreters csh and sh. The program make will use one of these programs to execute its commands.

Imagine that you want to train a classifyer from a large sample. This can be conveniently done running one program on many files sequentially. The files are selected in a loop of the shell script.

A.7 SED

A simple stream editor which is used to manipulate strings is available. The program is called sed. This is often useful to do simple replacement of strings in output created from image or speech processing, such as from the program in Exercise 11.h.

In our classifyer example of the previous section, some of the programs will produce more output than we want to use when we summarize the result of the training. We record all output and manipulate it by the stream editor automatically to produce the final text.

A.8 AWK

If simple string replacement is not sufficient, and additional compuation is required, the program awk is often more convenient than the sed program. The idea of awk is the same: read an input stream and convert its strings to the output according to some rules that are either given to awk on the commandline or in an awk program file.

Some informations in our classifyer example may be spread across many lines. This is hard to combine by sed. Using an awk program we can select such fragments.

A.9 Perl

More recently, the program perl has in many cases been used for purposes that formerly were written in awk or sed. The syntax of perl is similar to C. As perl is used as *the* programming language in web applications – cgi-bin scripts are usually written in this language, it is usefull to know this program as well.

When we want to do larger computations of the text of our classifyer, such as computing averages of numbers, do same calculations, etc., we can ask awk to do this for us. A syntax which is close to C might be easier to use – using perl.

Appendix B
Source Code and Tools

Various tools were mentioned in the book that can assist programming or pattern processing. Many of them are in the public domain and can be copied freely.

B.1 List of Tools

The NIHCL system which was used in Part II of the book is also available in the public domain with full source code.

The GNU tools are available at many places under the so called "copyleft".

The TeX macros for structograms can be found in ftp sites for TeX, at least in Germany.

The program `xfig` is a drawing tool for Unix. Segmentation results in this book have been converted to `xfig` graphics format and then to PostScript.

The system `Doxygen` provides automatic extraction of documentation from C++ source code. Class hierarchies as well as function definitions are commented and provided in various formats for query, such as `html`, `pdf`, and TeX.

The system CVS [Fog99] is available on many ftp sites. It is built on top of `rcs`.

B.2 Portable Image Format

A fairly simple format for image storage and transmission is well established in the internet. It is called the *Portable Image Format*. One option of this format encodes image data in printable characters, so that images can be transmitted by email easily so that bit orders on the various computers do not matter. For gray-level images, this format is very simple

```
P2
lines   columns
255
#       comment
p1      p2      p3   p4   ...
```

The start of the file (P2) is called the *magic number* and has to be written literally as in the example. Then come the image size and the number of possible gray-levels (usually 255, as in the example). Any line starting with a # is considered a comment and will be ignored when reading the file. Then come the pixels, line by line, pixel by pixel, as numbers such as 55 66 77 19 255 etc.

Various tools exist which read such images and manipulate them. They are all in the public domain and can be found in the internet. Together with these tools comes a library that includes functions for reading and writing such images.

B.3 How to get the sources

The programs NIHCL cdecl, xfig, etc. were mentioned in the text. They are all available for Unix only. In order to get them, connect to your nearest ftp site. Most of these programs should be available there.

All examples printed in this book are available in the internet and can be found on the page
    http://www5.informatik.uni-erlangen.de/~paulus/paho.html
They have been compiled and tested with g++.

B.4 Image Display

Various packages exist for the display and interactive manipulation of images on the screen. To list some of them that use the X11 windows system which is most common under Unix:

- xv
- ImageMagick
- gimp

These programs can also be found on ftp sites.

B.5 Course Material

If you want to use the book for teaching, you might want to get the program examples in source code (Sect. B.3). On the web page given in Sect. B.3 we also provide a PDF version of the that we use for teaching. They include all examples, figures, tables, and explanatory text. They can be found on the web page listed in Sect. B.3.

```
#ifndef BV_VERS
#define BV_VERS 1
#endif
#ifndef COLImg_VERS
#define COLImg_VERS 0
#endif
#ifndef EDGE_VERS
#define EDGE_VERS 1
#endif
#ifndef GLI_VERS
#define GLI_VERS 1
#endif
#ifndef IMAGE_VERS
#define IMAGE_VERS 1
#endif
```
`225`

B.6 Addresses

Dr.–Ing. Dietrich Paulus
Institut für Informatik
Lehrstuhl für Informatik 5 (Mustererkennung)
Martensstr. 3
D–91058 Erlangen
Germany
Phone: + 49 (9131) 85–27775
Fax: + 49 (9131) 303811
email: `dietrich@familie-paulus.de`
email: `joachim@horneggern.de`

B.7 Headers and Source Files

When you want to build your own system from the exercises and examples, you might start with the source code provided by ftp. Alternatively, you can use the examples in the book and compile your source files. The assignment of file names to the examples is shown in the tables on pp. 353. A list of programming examples and the corresponding page numbers can be found on p. 374. In order to compile the whole source, two files have to be created: Dictionary.h, Set.h that consist of one line: `#include "nihcl.h"`. Other files can be created from the examples given in the text as summarized in the tables on pp. 353. the listings given in the second column have to be concatenated to create the file given in the first column; the header files in the third column have to be included. In addition, all files include Listing 225 and the two files `stdio.h` and `stdlib.h`.

AtomLine.h	214	AtomObj.h
AtomObj.h	213	GeoObj.h HipposObj.h
ByteArray.C	112	OIO.h
ByteArray.h	103 104 105 106	OIO.h

ByteVector.C	99 101	ByteVector.h
ByteVector.h	98 100	OIO.h
Chain.C	192 195 197	Chain.h math.h
Chain.h	191 194	LineRep.h vector
ColorImage.h	141 111	GrayLevelImage.h OIO.h
Complex.C	92 94 121 122 123 124 125	Complex.h Matrix.h assert.h
Complex.h	120	math.h
DebugMacro.C	72 72	
Dictionary.C	161 162 176	Dictionary.h
Dictionary.h	221	Object.h
Edge.h	146 147 187 196	Chain.h OIO.h math.h
EdgeImage.h	148	Edge.h Image.h Matrix.h
FrameGrabber.C	119	GrayLevelImage.h
GeoObj.h	212	HipposObj.h Set.h
GrayLevelImage.C	142	GrayLevelImage.h
GrayLevelImage.h	140 144 110 211	Image.h Matrix.h
HipposObj.h	208 209	Dictionary.h
Histo.C	185	Histo.h
Histo.h	184 186	ipop.h
Image.h	139 210	HipposObj.h
ImageOps.C	118	Matrix.h OIO.h Options.h
LineRep.h	193 198	HipposObj.h PointXY.h
M.h	30	
M0.C	32	M.h
M1.C	31	M.h
Matrix.C	164 165	Matrix.h
Matrix.h	107 108 109 113 114 116 115 116	assert.h
Mean.C	183	ipop.h
OIO.h	220	stream.h
Object.C	153	Object.h
Object.h	152 154 154 155 156	OIO.h
Options.C	170	Options.h
Options.h	169	vector
PointXY.C	88	PointXY.h
PointXY.h	87	
SComplex.C	80 79	SComplex.h
SComplex.h	78	
SPointXY.C	77 18 55	SPointXY.h
SPointXY.h	17	
SegObj.h	215	GeoObj.h Set.h

B.8 Images

Segment.C	218 219	Options.h ipop.h	
Set.h	221	Object.h	
SpeechFrm.C	117 199	Matrix.h Object.h	
StreamEx.C	149 150 151	Image.h stream.h	
String.C	158 168 90 91 159	Object.h String.h string.h	
String.h	89		
TOptions.C	171	Options.h	
VecMed.C	177 178	ColorImage.h vector	
assocint.C	82	assocint.h	
assocint.h	81		
cassocint.C	85 84 86	cassocint.h	
cassocint.h	83		
classify.C	200 201 202 203 204 205 206	Matrix.h Object.h nihcl.h	
config.h	225		
datan2.C	145	math.h	
dist.C	179 180	GrayLevelImage.h	
dpdp.C	207		
hough.C	190	Edge.h Matrix.h math.h	
ipop.C	189	Edge.h ipop.h	
ipop.h	181 182 188 216	ColorImage.h EdgeImage.h SegObj.h	
math.C	73 74 75	math.h	
nihcl.h	221	Object.h	

B.8 Images

All test images used in the book can be downloaded from the web page given in Sect. B.3. Color images are provided wherever appropriate. As all images are included in the slides (Sect. B.5), you can compare your results of image processing algorithms with the ones computed from the algorithms in the book.

Appendix C

Formulas

C.1 Lookup Table Transformation

The solution of the system of equations on p. 224 is as follows:

$$\lambda_0 = a, \tag{C.1}$$

$$\begin{aligned}\lambda_1 = -\frac{1}{K}(&-255^3 b^2 e + 255^3 b^2 a + 255^3 d^2 c - 255^3 d^2 a - b^3 d^2 f + 255^2 b^3 e \\ &- 255^2 b^3 a - 255^2 d^3 c + b^3 d^2 a + b^2 d^3 f - b^2 d^3 a + 255^2 d^3 a) \end{aligned} \tag{C.2}$$

$$\begin{aligned}\lambda_2 = \frac{1}{K}(&255 b^3 e + b^3 da - 255 b^3 a - b^3 df - 255^3 be - d^3 ab + bd^3 f + \\ &255^3 ba + 255^3 dc + 255 d^3 a - 255^3 da - 255 d^3 c), \end{aligned} \tag{C.3}$$

$$\begin{aligned}\lambda_3 = -\frac{1}{K}(&255 b^2 e - 255 b^2 a + 255^2 dc - b^2 df + b^2 da \\ &-255 d^2 c - 255^2 be + 255^2 ba \\ &+d^2 bf - d^2 ba + 255 d^2 a - 255^2 da), \end{aligned} \tag{C.4}$$

where

$$K = 255 bd \left(-d^2 b + 255^2 b + 255 d^2 + b^2 d - 255^2 d - 255 b^2\right). \tag{C.5}$$

C.2 Marginal Density

The mixture

$$p(\boldsymbol{c}) = \sum_{\kappa=1}^{K} p(\Omega_\kappa) p(\boldsymbol{c}|\Omega_\kappa) \tag{C.6}$$

is a density function, since

$$\int p(\boldsymbol{c})\, d\boldsymbol{c} = \sum_{\kappa=1}^{K} p(\Omega_\kappa) \underbrace{\int p(\boldsymbol{c}|\Omega_\kappa)\, d\boldsymbol{c}}_{=1} = \sum_{\kappa=1}^{K} p(\Omega_\kappa) = 1 \; . \tag{C.7}$$

C.3 Identity

$$\sum_{l_1=1}^{n}\sum_{l_2=1}^{n}\cdots\sum_{l_m=1}^{n}\prod_{k=1}^{m}x_{k,l_k} = \sum_{l_1=1}^{n}\sum_{l_2=1}^{n}\cdots\sum_{l_{m-1}=1}^{n}\prod_{k=1}^{m-1}x_{k,l_k}\left(\sum_{l_m=1}^{n}x_{m,l_m}\right)$$
$$= \left(\sum_{l_1=1}^{n}x_{1,l_1}\right)\left(\sum_{l_2=1}^{n}x_{2,l_2}\right)\cdot\ldots\cdot\left(\sum_{l_m=1}^{n}x_{m,l_m}\right)$$
$$= \prod_{k=1}^{m}\sum_{l=1}^{n}x_{k,l} \quad .$$

C.4 Property of the H–Function

For the H–function $H(\widehat{\boldsymbol{B}}^{(i+1)}|\widehat{\boldsymbol{B}}^{(i)})$ the following inequality holds:

$$H(\widehat{\boldsymbol{B}}^{(i+1)}|\widehat{\boldsymbol{B}}^{(i)}) \leq H(\widehat{\boldsymbol{B}}^{(i)}|\widehat{\boldsymbol{B}}^{(i)}) \quad ; \tag{C.8}$$

this can be shown by a simple use of the definition of $H(\widehat{\boldsymbol{B}}^{(i+1)}|\widehat{\boldsymbol{B}}^{(i)})$:

$$H(\widehat{\boldsymbol{B}}^{(i+1)}|\widehat{\boldsymbol{B}}^{(i)}) - H(\widehat{\boldsymbol{B}}^{(i)}|\widehat{\boldsymbol{B}}^{(i)}) =$$
$$= \int p(\boldsymbol{Y}|\boldsymbol{X},\widehat{\boldsymbol{B}}^{(i)})\log p(\boldsymbol{Y}|\boldsymbol{X},\widehat{\boldsymbol{B}}^{(i+1)})\,d\boldsymbol{Y}$$
$$- \int p(\boldsymbol{Y}|\boldsymbol{X},\widehat{\boldsymbol{B}}^{(i)})\log p(\boldsymbol{Y}|\boldsymbol{X},\widehat{\boldsymbol{B}}^{(i)})\,d\boldsymbol{Y}$$
$$= \int \left(\log p(\boldsymbol{Y}|\boldsymbol{X},\widehat{\boldsymbol{B}}^{(i+1)}) - \log p(\boldsymbol{Y}|\boldsymbol{X},\widehat{\boldsymbol{B}}^{(i)})\right) p(\boldsymbol{Y}|\boldsymbol{X},\widehat{\boldsymbol{B}}^{(i)})\,d\boldsymbol{Y}$$
$$= \int \left(\log \frac{p(\boldsymbol{Y}|\boldsymbol{X},\widehat{\boldsymbol{B}}^{(i+1)})}{p(\boldsymbol{Y}|\boldsymbol{X},\widehat{\boldsymbol{B}}^{(i)})}\right) p(\boldsymbol{Y}|\boldsymbol{X},\widehat{\boldsymbol{B}}^{(i)})\,d\boldsymbol{Y} \quad .$$

Now we make use of the well-known inequality (cf. Figure C.1)

$$\log x \leq x - 1 \quad , \tag{C.9}$$

and get

$$\log \frac{p(\boldsymbol{Y}|\boldsymbol{X},\widehat{\boldsymbol{B}}^{(i+1)})}{p(\boldsymbol{Y}|\boldsymbol{X},\widehat{\boldsymbol{B}}^{(i)})} \leq \frac{p(\boldsymbol{Y}|\boldsymbol{X},\widehat{\boldsymbol{B}}^{(i+1)})}{p(\boldsymbol{Y}|\boldsymbol{X},\widehat{\boldsymbol{B}}^{(i)})} - 1 \quad ; \tag{C.10}$$

therefore,

$$H(\widehat{\boldsymbol{B}}^{(i+1)}|\widehat{\boldsymbol{B}}^{(i)}) - H(\widehat{\boldsymbol{B}}^{(i)}|\widehat{\boldsymbol{B}}^{(i)}) \leq \int \left(\frac{p(\boldsymbol{Y}|\boldsymbol{X},\widehat{\boldsymbol{B}}^{(i+1)})}{p(\boldsymbol{Y}|\boldsymbol{X},\widehat{\boldsymbol{B}}^{(i)})} - 1\right) p(\boldsymbol{Y}|\boldsymbol{X},\widehat{\boldsymbol{B}}^{(i)})\,d\boldsymbol{Y}$$
$$= \underbrace{\int p(\boldsymbol{Y}|\boldsymbol{X},\widehat{\boldsymbol{B}}^{(i+1)})\,d\boldsymbol{Y}}_{=1} - \underbrace{\int p(\boldsymbol{Y}|\boldsymbol{X},\widehat{\boldsymbol{B}}^{(i)})\,d\boldsymbol{Y}}_{=1} = 0 \quad .$$

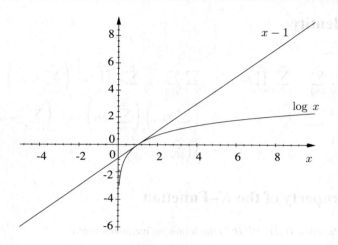

Figure C.1: Illustration of the inequality: $\log x \leq x - 1$

C.5 Lagrange Multiplier

Optimization problems in pattern recognition often have to be solved with constrained parameters. The introduction of Lagrange multipliers allows the computation of objective functions which include the predefined constraints. The following example shows the basic idea of this technique.

Discrete probabilities, for instance, have to sum up to one, i.e.,

$$\sum_{i=1}^{n} p_i \;=\; 1 \;.\tag{C.11}$$

$$\tag{C.12}$$

If we have to maximize the objective function

$$p(p_1, p_2, \ldots, p_n) \;=\; \sum_{i=1}^{n} a_i \, \log p_i \tag{C.13}$$

with respect to $p_1, p_2, \ldots, p_n$ where $a_i > 0$, $i = 1, 2, \ldots, n$, we maximize instead

$$p_{\text{Lagrange}}(p_1, p_2, \ldots, p_n) \;=\; \sum_{i=1}^{n} a_i \, \log p_i + \eta \left(\sum_{i=1}^{n} p_i - 1 \right) \tag{C.14}$$

where $\eta \in \mathbb{R}$ denotes the *Lagrange multiplier*. The maximum can be computed setting partial derivatives to zero, i.e.,

$$\frac{\partial p_{\text{Lagrange}}}{\partial p_i} \;=\; \frac{a_i}{p_i} - \eta \;=\; 0 \;.\tag{C.15}$$

C.6 Notation

By summing over all p_i, we get

$$\eta \sum_{i=1}^{n} p_i = \sum_{i=1}^{n} a_i \quad , \tag{C.16}$$

and due to (C.11)

$$\eta = \sum_{i=1}^{n} a_i \quad . \tag{C.17}$$

Using this result in above equation (C.15), we finally obtain

$$p_i = \frac{a_i}{\sum_{i=1}^{n} a_i} \quad . \tag{C.18}$$

C.6 Notation

We use the notation as suggested by many mathematical books and as used in many books on pattern recognition, speech processing, and in image processing. The notation is summarized in Table C.1.

Text	Explanation
`virtual`	programming code as well as keywords, class names, etc. is written in `teletype` letters
a	*scalar values* are written in mathematic font (italics)
x	*column vectors* are written lower case characters in bold mathematic font (italics)
A	*matrices* are written capital letters in bold mathematic font (italics)
A^T c^T	denotes transposed vectors and matrices.
a_{ij}	denotes the *matrix elements* and the matrix A can be written as $[a_{ij}]_{1 \leq i \leq N, 1 \leq j \leq M}$
$(A)_{ij}$	this notation is occasionally used to denote the element at position (i,j) in the matrix; this is useful when instead of A we have an expression (e.g. $(AA^T)_{ij}$).
$\mathbb{R}$	denotes *real numbers*
$\mathbb{C}$	denotes *complex numbers*
i	denotes $\sqrt{-1}$ for complex numbers
A	*sets* are like matrices written in capital letters and typed in bold face

Table C.1: Notation used in the book

Bibliography

Numbers after the reference indicate the pages where this citation is used.

[Ada83] Doglas Adams. *The Hitchhiker's Guide to the Galaxy.* Penguine Books, 1983. 10

[Aho74] A. V. Aho, J. E. Hopcroft, and J. D. Ullman. *The design and analysis of computer algorithms.* Addison–Wesley, Reading, MA, 1974. 143, 148

[Ale94] J. C. Alexander and J. Menon, editors. *Current Topics of Pattern Recognition Research*, volume 1. Research Trends, Trivandrum, India, 1994. 362, 365

[Alo90] Y. Aloimonos. Perspective approximations. *Image Vision and Computing*, 8(3):179–192, 1990. 12

[And58] T. W. Anderson. *An Introduction to Multivariate Statistical Analysis.* Wiley Publications in Statistics. John Wiley & Sons, Inc., New York, 1958. 257

[Arp92] R. B. Arps and W. K. Pratt, editors. *Image Processing and Interchange: Implementation and Systems*, San Jose, CA, 1992. SPIE, Proceedings 1659. 361, 362, 365

[Arv91] J. Arvo, editor. *Graphics Gems II.* The Graphics Gems Series, A Collection of Practical Techniques for the Computer Graphics Programmer. Academic Press, London, 1991. 361, 367

[Ary94] S. Arya, D. M. Mount, N. S. Netanyahu, R. Silverman, and A. Wu. An optimal algorithm for approximate nearest neighbor searching. In *Proceedings of the Fifth Annual ACM–SIAM Symposium on Discrete Algorithms*, pages 573–582, Arlington, Virginia, January 1994. SIAM. 296

[Bal82] D. H. Ballard and C. M. Brown. *Computer Vision.* Prentice-Hall, Englewood Cliffs, NJ, 1982. 243, 246, 267, 305

[Bau67] L. E. Baum and J. A. Eagon. An inequality with applications to statistical prediction for functions of Markov processes and to a model for ecology. *Bull. Amer. Math. Soc.*, 73:360–363, 1967. 310

[Bel61] R. E. Bellman. *Adaptive Control Process.* Princeton University Press, Princeton, 1961. 85

[Bel67] R. Bellman. *Dynamische Programmierung und selbstanpassende Regelprozesse.* R. Oldenbourg Verlag, München, Wien, 1967. 303

[Bel89] Z. W. Bell. A Bayesian/Monte Carlo segmentation method for images dominated by Gaussian noise. *IEEE Transactions on Pattern Analysis and Machine Intelligence*, 11(9):985–990, September 1989. 72

[Big89] N. L. Biggs. *Discrete Mathematics.* Clarendon Press, Oxford, 1989. 303, 305

[Bir83] G. M. Birtwistle, O. Dahl, B. Myrhang, and K. Nygaard. *Simula Begin.* Auerbach Publ. Inc., Philadelphia, PA, 1983. 101

[Bis95] C. M. Bishop. *Neural Networks for Pattern Recognition.* Clarendon Press, Oxford, 1995. 5, 83, 284

[Boo91] G. Booch. *Object Oriented Design.* Benjamin/Cummings, Redwood City, CA, 1991. 96, 101

[Bov87] A. Bovik, T. Huang, and D. Munson. The effect of median filtering on edge detection. *IEEE Transactions on Pattern Analysis and Machine Intelligence*, 9(2):181–194, 1987. 203
[Bre87] J. E. Bresenham. Ambiguities in incremental line rastering. *Computer Graphics and Applications*, 7(5):31–43, 1987. 133
[Bre88] P. Bremaud. *An Introduction to Probabilistic Modeling*. Undergraduate Texts in Mathematics. Springer, Heidelberg, 1988. 69, 70, 74
[Bre97] R. Breu, U. Hinkel, Ch. Hofmann, C. Klein, B. Paech, B. Rumpe, and V. Thurner. Towards a formalization of the unified modeling language. In Mehmet Aksit and Satoshi Matsuoka, editors, *ECOOP'97—Object-Oriented Programming*, 11th *European Conference*, volume 1241 of *Lecture Notes in Computer Science*, pages 344–366, Jyväskylä, Finland, 9–13 June 1997. Springer. 96
[Bro85] I. N. Bronstein and K. A. Semendjajew. *Taschenbuch der Mathematik*. Harri Deutsch, Thun, 1985. 139, 257
[Brü90] H. Brünig. Konzeption und Realisierung einer flexiblen Bildsegmentierung. Technical report, Dissertation, IMMD 5 (Mustererkennung), Universität Erlangen–Nürnberg, Erlangen, 1990. 2, 165, 206, 239, 241, 242
[Bub96] T. Bub and J. Schwinn. Verbmobil: The Evolution of a Complex Large Speech-to-Speech Translation System. In *Proc. Int. Conf. on Spoken Language Processing*, volume 4, pages 1026–1029, Philadelphia, Oktober 1996. IEEE Computer Society Press. 6
[Bun92] H. Bunke, editor. *Advances in Structural and Syntactic Pattern Recognition*, Series in Machine Perception and Artificial Intelligence, Singapore, 1992. World Scientific Publishing. 84, 85
[Bur83] P. J. Burt and E. H. Adelson. The Laplacian pyramid as a compact image code. *IEEE Transactions on Communications*, 31(4):532–540, 1983. 210
[Can86] J. F. Canny. A computational approach to edge detection. *IEEE Transactions on Pattern Analysis and Machine Intelligence*, 8(6):679–698, 1986. 249
[Cap91] R. Capelli. Fast approximation to arcus tangent. In Arvo [Arv91], pages 389–391. 170
[Car91] I. C. Carlsen and D. Haaks. IKS^{PFH} — concept and implementation of an object–oriented framework for image processing. *Computers and Graphics*, 15(4):473–482, 1991. 91
[Cha92] V. Chandran and S. Elgar. Position, rotation, and scale invariant recognition of images using higher order spectra. In *International Conference on Acoustic, Speech & Signal Processing*, volume 5, pages 213–216, San Francisco, March 1992. 274
[Che91] C. H. Chen. On the relationships between statistical pattern pecognition and artificial neural networks. *International Journal of Pattern Recognition and Artifical Intelligence*, 5(3):655–661, 1991. 322
[Chi83] R. Chien and C.-L. Yeh. Quantitative evaluation of some edge preserving noise smoothing techniques. *Computer Graphics and Image Processing (CGIP)*, 23:67–91, 1983. 203
[Cla92] A. F. Clark. Image processing and interchange — the imaging model. In Arps and Pratt [Arp92], pages 106–116. 120
[Coa91] P. Coad and E. Yourdon. *Object-oriented analysis*. Prentice Hall, Englewood Cliffs, NJ, 2nd edition, 1991. 96
[Cog87] J. M. Coggins. Integrated class structures for image pattern recognition and computer graphics. In K. Gorlen, editor, *Proceedings of the USENIX C++ Workshop*, pages 240–245, Santa Fe, NM, 9.-10. November 1987. 91
[Coo65] J. Cooley and J. Tukey. An algorithm for the machine computation of complex Fourier series. *Mathematical Computation*, 19(6):297–381, 1965. 137, 148
[Cre97] D. Crevier and R. Lepage. Knowledge-based image understanding systems: A survey. *Computer Vision and Image Understanding*, 67(2):161–185, August 1997. 340
[Dah98] M. K. Dahlheimer. *Programming with Qt*. O'Reilly, Köln, 1998. 337

[Dan90] P.-E. Danielsson and O. Seger. Generalized and separable Sobel operators. In H. Freemann, editor, *Machine Vision for Three–Dimensional Scenes*, pages 347–380. Academic Press, San Diego, 1990. 169

[Dav78] L. Davis and A. Rosenfeld. Noise cleaning by iterated local averaging. *IEEE Transactions on Systems, Man, and Cybernetics*, 8(9):705–710, 1978. 205, 206

[Dem77] A.P. Dempster, N.M. Laird, and D.B. Rubin. Maximum Likelihood from Incomplete Data via the EM Algorithm. *Journal of the Royal Statistical Society, Series B (Methodological)*, 39(1):1–38, 1977. 315, 316

[Den94] J. Denzler and H. Niemann. A two-stage real time object tracking system. In N. Pavešić, H. Niemann, D. Paulus, and S. Kovačić, editors, *3–D Scene Acquisition, Modeling and Understanding, Proceedings of the Second German–Slovenian Workshop*, Ljubljana, Slovenia, June 1994. IEEE Slovenia Section. 90

[Der91] R. Deriche. Optimal edge detection using recursive filtering. In *Proceedings of the 1st International Conference on Computer Vision (ICCV)*, pages 501–505, London, 1991. IEEE Computer Society Press. 249

[Dob91] M. R. Dobie and P. H. Lewis. Data structures for image processing in C. *Pattern Recognition Letters*, 12:457–466, 1991. 91

[Dud73] R. O. Duda and P. E. Hart. *Pattern Classification and Scene Analysis*. John Wiley & Sons, Inc., New York, 1973. 72, 80, 137, 169, 265

[Fah94] L. Fahrmeir and L. Tutz. *Multivariate Statistical Modelling Based on Generalized Linear Models*. Springer Series in Statistics. Springer, Heidelberg, 2 edition, 1994. 73

[Fal95] D. Falavigna. Comparison of different HMM based methods for speaker verification. In *Proceedings of the 4th Conference on Speech Communication and Technology*, pages 371–374, Madrid, 1995. 265

[Fan73] C. G. Fant. *Speech Sounds and Features*. MIT Press, Cambridge, Massachusetts, 1973. 276

[Fau93] O. Faugeras. *Three–Dimensional Computer Vision – A Geometric Viewpoint*. MIT Press, Cambridge, Massachusetts, 1993. 11, 12, 338

[Fog99] K. F. Fogel. *Open Source Development With CVS*. 1999. 349, 351

[Fre80] H. Freeman. Analysis and manipulation of lineal map data. In H. Freeman and G. G. Pieroni, editors, *Map Data Processing*, pages 151–168, New York, 1980. Academic Press. 251

[Fuk90] K. Fukunaga. *Introduction to Statistical Pattern Recognition*. Academic Press, Boston, 1990. 227, 296

[Gal91] D. Le Gall. MPEG: A video compression standard for multimedia applications. *Communications of the Association for Computing Machinery*, 34(4):47–58, April 1991. 120

[Gol83] A. Goldberg and D. Robson. *Smalltalk-80: The Language and its Implementation*. Addison-Wesley, Reading, MA, 1983. 101

[Gol97] G. H. Golub and H. A. van der Vorst. *Closer to the solution: Iterative linear solvers*. Clarendon Press, Oxford, 1997. 248

[Goo69] N. Goodman. *Languages of Art. An Approach to a theory of symbols*. Oxford Univ. Press, New York, 1969. 3

[Gor90] K. E. Gorlen, S. Orlow, and P. S. Plexico. *Data Abstraction and Object–Oriented Programming in C++*. John Wiley and Sons, Chichester, 1990. 179, 181, 184, 185, 190

[Har88] R. Haralick and J. Lee. Context dependent edge detection. In ICPR 88 [ICP88], pages 203–207. 233

[Har92] R. M. Haralick and V. Ramesh. Image understanding environment. In Arps and Pratt [Arp92], pages 159–167. 91

[Has94] A. Hasegawa. Image recognition by neural networks. In Alexander and Menon [Ale94], pages 237–250. 322

[He91]   Y. He and A. Kundu. 2–D shape classification using hidden Markov models. *IEEE Transactions on Pattern Analysis and Machine Intelligence*, 13(11):1172–1184, 1991. 315
[Hec82] P. Heckbert. Color image quantization for frame buffer display. *Computer Graphics*, 16(3):297–307, July 1982. 226
[Hor74] S. L. Horowitz and T. Pavlidis. Picture segmentation by a directed split-and-merge procedure. In *Proc. 2nd International Joint Conference on Pattern Recognition*, pages 424–433, Kopenhagen, 1974. 261
[Hor93] J. Hornegger and D. Paulus. Detecting elliptic objects using inverse Hough–transform. In *Image Processing: Theory and Applications*, pages 155–158. Elsevier, Amsterdam, 1993. 246
[Hor96] J. Hornegger. *Statistische Modellierung, Klassifikation und Lokalisation von Objekten*. Shaker Verlag, Aachen, 1996. 315, 339
[Hou62] P. V. C. Hough and A. Arbor. Method and means for recognizing complex patterns. Technical report, US Patent 3069654, 1962. 243
[Hu97]   J. Hu and H. Yan. Polygonal approximation of digital curves based on the principles of perceptual organization. *Pattern Recognition*, 30(5):701–718, May 1997. 254, 260
[Hua90] X. D. Huang, Y. Ariki, and M. A. Jack. *Hidden Markov Models for Speech Recognition*. Number 7 in Information Technology Series. Edinburgh University Press, Edinburgh, 1990. 275, 320
[Hue73] M. H. Hueckel. A local visual operator which recognizes edges and lines. *JACM*, 18:634–647; erratum in Vol. 21, p. 350, 1974, 1973. 232
[ICP88] *Proceedings of the 9th International Conference on Pattern Recognition (ICPR)*, Rom, 1988. IEEE Computer Society Press. 362, 365
[Jac92] I. Jacobson, M. Christenson, P. Jonsson, and G. Oevergaard. *Object-Oriented Software Engineering: A Use Case Driven Approach*. Addison-Wesley, Wokingham, 1992. 96
[Jäh93] B. Jähne. *Digital Image Processing — Concepts, Algorithms, and Scientific Applications*. Springer, Heidelberg, 1993. 6, 270
[Jak94] A. Jaklič, A. Leonardis, and F. Solina. Object–oriented analysis and design of image segmentation package. In 3rd *Electrotechnical and Computer Science Conf. ERK*, volume B, pages 23–26, Portorož, Slovenia, 1994. 91
[Jel98] F. Jelinek. *Statistical Methods for Speech Recognition*. MIT Press, Cambridge, Massachusetts, 1998. 80, 84, 299, 305, 315
[Jen85] K. Jensen and N. Wirth. *Pascal User Manual and Report*. Springer-Verlag, New York, 1985. 33
[Joh87] M. E. Johnson. *Multivariate Statistical Simulation*. Probability and Mathematical Statistics. John Wiley & Sons, Inc., New York, 1987. 129
[Joh93] R. Johnsonbaugh and M. Kalin. *Applications programming in ANSI C*. Macmillan, New York, 2 edition, 1993. 17
[Kan90] K. Kanatani. *Group–Theoretical Methods in Image Understanding*. Springer, Heidelberg, 1990. 132
[Kan93] K. Kanatani. *Geometric Computation for Machine Vision*. Number 37 in Oxford Engineering Science Series. Clarendon Press, Oxford, 1993. 12
[Kem97] M. Kempe. Ada 95 reference manual, 1997. http://lglwww.epfl.ch/Ada/rm95. 102
[Ker78] B. W. Kernighan and D. M. Ritchie. *The C Programming Language*. Prentice-Hall Software Series, Englewood Cliffs, NJ, 1978. 17
[Kle95] R. Klette and P. Zamperoni. *Handbuch der Operatoren für die Bildbearbeitung*. Vieweg, Braunschweig, 2 edition, 1995. 134
[Knu73] D. E. Knuth. *The Art of Computer Programming*, volume 2: Seminumerical Algorithms. Addison–Wesley, Reading, MA, 1973. 36, 129

[Koe96]   D. Koelma. *A Software Environment for Image Interpretation*. PhD thesis, Faculteit der Wiskunde, Informatica, Natuurkunde en Sterrenkunde, Amsterdam, 1996. 91

[Kro79]   L. I. Kronsjö. *Algorithms: Their Complexity and Efficiency*. John Wiley & Sons, Inc. John Wiley & Sons, Inc., Chichester, 1979. 148

[Leh99]   T. M. Lehmann, C. Gönner, and K. Spitzer. Survey: Interpolation methods in medical image processing. *IEEE transactions on medical imaging*, 18(11):1049–1075, November 1999. 213

[Luo94]   A. Luo. *Helligkeitsbasiertes Rechnersehen zur direkten Ermittlung räumlicher Eigenschaften*. Shaker Verlag, Aachen, 1994. 203

[Lyo97]   Douglas A Lyon and Hayagriva V. Rao. *Java Digital Signal Processing*. M&T Books, M&T Publishing, Inc., 501 Galveston Drive, Redwood City, CA 94063, USA, November 1997. 102

[Mac81]   R. Machuca and A. Gilbert. Finding edges in noisy scenes. *IEEE Transactions on Pattern Analysis and Machine Intelligence*, 3(1):103–111, 1981. 203

[Mao92]   J. Mao and A. K. Jain. Texture classification and segmentation using multiresolution simultaneous autoregressive models. *Pattern Recognition*, 25(2):173–188, 1992. 279

[Mar76]   A. Martelli. An application of heuristic search methods to edge and contour detection. *Comm. ACM*, 19:335–345, 1976. 242

[Mar80]   D. Marr and E. Hildreth. Theory of edge detection. *Proceedings Royal Society London B*, 207:187–217, 1980. 165, 175, 233

[Mar82]   David Marr. *Vision: A Computational Investigation into the Human Representation and Processing of Visual Information*. W.H. Freemantle, San Francisco, 1982. 84

[McL96]   G. J. McLachlan and T. Krishnan. *The EM Algorithm and Extensions*. Wiley Series in Probability and Statistics. John Wiley & Sons, Inc., New York, 1996. 305, 315

[Moo79]   R. K. Moore. A Dynamic Programming Algorithm for the Distance Between Two Finite Areas. *IEEE Transactions on Pattern Analysis and Machine Intelligence*, 1(1):86–88, 1979. 305

[Mor96]   H. P. Moravec. Robot spatial perception by stereoscopic vision and 3D evidence grids. Technical Report CMU-RI-TR-96-34, The Robotics Institue, Carnegie Mellon University, Pittsburgh, Pennsylvania 15213, September 1996. 262

[Mun92]   J. Mundy, T. Binford, T. Boult, A. Hanson, R. Veveridge, R. Haralick, V. Ramesh, C. Kohl, D. Lawton, D. Morgan, K Price, and T. Strat. The image understanding environments program. In *Image Understanding Workshop*, pages 185–214, San Diego, CA, Jan. 1992. 91

[Mus96]   D. R. Musser and A. Saini. *STL tutorial and reference guide*. Addison-Wesley, Reading, Mass., 1996. 179, 191

[Nag79]   M. Nagao and T. Matsuyama. Edge preserving smoothing. *Computer Graphics and Image Processing (CGIP)*, 9:394–407, 1979. 204

[Nev80]   R. Nevatia and R. Babu. Linear feature extraction and description. *Computer Graphics and Image Processing (CGIP)*, 13:257–269, 1980. 231, 234, 238, 239, 240, 241

[Nie74]   H. Niemann. *Methoden der Mustererkennung*. Akademische Verlagsgesellschaft, Frankfurt, 1974. 259

[Nie83]   H. Niemann. *Klassifikation von Mustern*. Springer, Heidelberg, 1983. 5, 14, 72, 75, 80, 81, 83, 84, 143, 148, 219, 266, 279, 280, 284, 286, 290, 292, 301

[Nie90a]   H. Niemann. *Pattern Analysis and Understanding*, volume 4 of *Springer Series in Information Sciences*. Springer, Heidelberg, 1990. 7, 8, 14, 86, 87, 88, 89, 137, 211, 265, 267, 270, 275, 279, 283, 299, 305, 322, 323

[Nie90b]   H. Niemann, G. Sagerer, S. Schröder, and F. Kummert. ERNEST: A Semantic Network System for Pattern Analysis. *IEEE Transactions on Pattern Analysis and Machine Intelligence (PAMI)*, 9:883–905, 1990. 91, 99, 192

[Nöt90]   E. Nöth. *Prosodische Information in der automatischen Spracherkennung, Berechnung und Anwendung*. Niemeyer, Tübingen, 1990. 88
[Opp75]   A. V. Oppenheim and R. W. Schafer. *Digital signal processing*. Prentice-Hall, Englewood Cliffs NJ, 1975. 148, 152
[Ost91]   W. Osten. *Digitale Verarbeitung und Auswertung von Interferenzbildern*. Akademie Verlag GmbH, Berlin, 1991. 273
[Ous94]   J. K. Ousterhout. *Tcl and the Tk toolkit*. Addison-Wesley, Reading, Mass., 1994. 335
[Pap91]   A. Papoulis. *Probability, Random Variables, and Stochastic Processes*. Electrical Engineering: Communications and Signal Processing. McGraw–Hill, New York, 3 edition, 1991. 69
[Pau92a] D. Paulus. Object oriented image segmentation. In *Proc. of the 4th Int. Conf. on Image Processing and its Applications*, pages 482–485, Maastrich, Holland, 1992. 327
[Pau92b] D. Paulus. *Objektorientierte und wissensbasierte Bildverarbeitung("Object–oriented and knowledge based image processing")*. Vieweg, Braunschweig, 1992. 88, 91, 123, 262, 325, 326, 327
[Pau92c] D. Paulus and H. Niemann. Iconic–symbolic interfaces. In Arps and Pratt [Arp92], pages 204–214. 326, 327
[Pau94]   D. Paulus and H. Niemann. Object–oriented programming for image analysis. In Alexander and Menon [Ale94], pages 185–204. 91
[Pip88]   J. Piper and D. Rutovitz. An investigation of object-oriented programming as the basis for an image processing and analysis system. In ICPR 88 [ICP88], pages 1015–1019. 91
[Pos90]   S. Posch. *Automatische Bestimmung von Tiefeninformation aus Grauwert-Stereobildern*. Deutscher Universitäts Verlag, Wiesbaden, 1990. 267
[Poy92]   C. A. Poynton. An overview of TIFF 5.0. In Arps and Pratt [Arp92], pages 150–158. 5, 120
[Poy95]   C. A. Poynton. colorspace-faq, May, 28 1995.
          http://www.inforamp.net/ poynton/Poynton-colour.html. 122
[Pra80]   M. Prager. Extracting and labeling boundary segments in natural scenes. *IEEE Transactions on Pattern Analysis and Machine Intelligence*, 2(1):16–27, 1980. 206
[Pra91]   W. K. Pratt. *Digital Image Processing*. John Wiley & Sons, Inc., New York, 2 edition, 1991. 128
[Pra95]   W. K. Pratt. *The PIKS Foundation C Programmers Guide*. Manning, Greenwich, 1995. 120
[Pre70]   J. M. S. Prewitt. Object enhancement and extraction. *Picture Processing and Psychopictorics*, pages 75–149, 1970. 169, 232
[Pre92]   W. H. Press, B. P. Flannery, S. Teukolsky, and W. T. Vetterling. *Numerical Recipes - the Art of Numerical Computing, C Version*. Cambridge University Press, Cambridge, 2 edition, 1992. 56, 152, 257
[Pri93]   L. Priese and V. Rehrmann. On hierarchical color segmentation and applications. In *CVPR93*, pages 633–634, 1993. 261
[Rab88]   L. R. Rabiner. Mathematical foundations of hidden Markov models. In H. Niemann, M. Lang, and G. Sagerer, editors, *Recent Advances in Speech Understanding and Dialog Systems*, volume 46 of *NATO ASI Series F: Computer and System Sciences*, pages 183–205. Springer, Heidelberg, 1988. 137, 265, 310, 312
[Ram72]   U. Ramer. An iterative procedure for polygonal approximation of plane curves. *Computer Graphics and Image Processing (CGIP)*, 1:244–256, 1972. 260
[Ras92]   J. R. Rasure and M. Young. Open environment for image processing and software development. In Arps and Pratt [Arp92], pages 300–310. 91
[Red84]   R. A. Redner and H. F. Walker. Mixture densities, maximum likelihood and the EM algorithm. *Society for Industrial and Applied Mathematics Review*, 26(2):195–239, 1984. 293
[Rim91]   R. D. Rimey and M. Brown. Controlling eye movements with hidden Markov models. *International Journal of Computer Vision*, 7(1):47–65, January 1991. 6

[Rip96] B. D. Ripley. *Pattern Recognition and Neural Networks*. Cambridge University Press, Cambridge, 1996. 5, 83, 266, 284

[Rit86] X. Ritter, P. Gadev, and J. Davidson. Automated bridge detection in flir images. In *Proceedings 8th Int. Conf. on Pattern Recognition*, pages 862–864, Paris, 1986. IEEE Computer Society Press. 232

[Rob77] G.S. Robinson. Edge detection by compass gradient masks. *Computer Graphics and Image Processing (CGIP)*, 6:492–501, 1977. 231

[Ros82] A. Rosenfeld and A. Kak. *Digital Picture Processing*. Academic Press, New York, 1982. 233

[Rum91] J. Rumbaugh. *Object-oriented modeling and design*. Prentice-Hall, Englewood Cliffs, NJ, 1991. 96

[Sag97] G. Sagerer and H. Niemann. *Semantic Networks for Understanding Scenes*. Advances in Computer Vision and Machine Intelligence. Plenum Press, New York and London, 1997. 86

[Sar94] K. B. Sarachik. An analysis of the effect of Gaussian error in object recognition. PhD thesis, Department of Electrical Engineering and Computer Science, Massachusetts Institute of Technology, AI Lab., Cambridge, Massachusetts, 1994. 72

[Sch77] J. Schürmann. *Polynomklassifikatoren für die Zeichenerkennung*. R. Oldenbourg-Verlag, München, 1977. 287, 290

[Sch78] J. Schürmann. A Multifont Word Recognition System for Postal Address Reading. *IEEE Transactions on Computers*, 27:721–732, 1978. 6

[Sch90] N. Schneider. *Kantenhervorhebung und Kantenverfolgung in der industriellen Bildverarbeitung*. Fortschritte in der Robotik, 6. Vieweg, Braunschweig, 1990. 35

[Sch95] E. G. Schukat–Talamazzini, J. Hornegger, and H. Niemann. Optimal linear feature transformations for semi–continuous hidden Markov models. In *Proceedings of the International Conference on Acoustics, Speech, and Signal Processing (ICASSP)*, volume 1, pages 369–372, Detroit, Mai 1995. IEEE Computer Society Press. 315

[Ser88] J. Serra. *Image Analysis and Mathematical Morphology*. Academic Press, London, 1988. 203

[She86] J. Shen and S. Castan. An optimal linear operator for edge detection. *Computer Vision, Graphics and Image Processing (CVGIP)*, 5:109–114, 1986. 250

[She88] J. Shen and S. Castan. Further results on drf method of edge detection. *Proc. Computer Vision, Graphics and Image Processing, Miami*, 6:223–225, 1988. 250

[Shi87] Y. Shirai. *Three–Dimensional Computer Vision*. Springer, Heidelberg, 1987. 176

[Shl88] S. Shlaer and S. J. Mellor. *Object-oriented systems analysis*. Yourdon, Englewood Cliffs, NJ, 1988. 96

[Smo99] B. Smolka, M. Szezepansik, and K. Wojciechowski. Random walk approach to the problem of impulse noise reduction. In K.-H. Franke, editor, *5. Workshop Farbbildverarbeitung*, pages 43–50, Ilmenau, 1999. Schriftenreihe des Zentrums für Bild- und Signalverarbeitung e.V. Ilmenau. 204

[Spr79] M. D. Springer. *The Algebra of Random Variables*. Wiley Publications in Statistics. John Wiley & Sons, Inc., New York, 1979. 129

[ST95] E. G. Schukat-Talamazzini. *Automatische Spracherkennung – Grundlagen, statistische Modelle und effiziente Algorithmen*. Künstliche Intelligenz. Vieweg, Braunschweig, 1995. 14, 72, 91, 265, 267, 268, 269, 275, 277, 280, 299, 305, 315

[Str97] B. Stroustrup. *The C++ Programming Language, 3nd edition*. Addison-Wesley, Reading, MA, 1997. 18, 22, 61, 64, 67, 102, 109, 154, 162, 180, 181, 191, 194, 197

[Swa91] M. J. Swain and D. H. Ballard. Color indexing. *International Journal of Computer Vision*, 7(1):11–32, November 1991. 227

[Tal93]   R. Talluri and J. K. Aggarwal. Position estimation techniques for an autonomous mobile robot – a review. In C. H. Chen, L. F. Pau, and P. S. P. Wang, editors, *Handbook of Pattern Recognition & Computer Vision*, pages 769–801, Singapore, 1993. World Scientific Publishing. 6

[Tan96]   M. A. Tanner. *Tools for Statistical Inference: Methods for the Exploration of Posterior Distributions and Likelihood Functions*. Springer Series in Statistics. Springer, Heidelberg, 3 edition, 1996. 73, 292, 305

[The89]   L.W. Therrien. *Decision, Estimation, and Classification*. John Wiley & Sons, Inc., New York, 1989. 266

[Tru98]   E. Trucco and A. Verri. *Introductory Techniques for 3–D Computer Vision*. Prentice Hall, New York, 1998. 11, 337, 338, 340

[Udu91]   J. K. Udupa and G. T. Herman. *3D Imaging in Medicine*. CRC Press, Boca Raton, 1991. 6

[Vap96]   V. N. Vapnik. *The Nature of Statistical Learning Theory*. Springer-Verlag, Heidelberg, 1996. 284

[vdH94]   F. van der Heijden. *Image Based Measurement Systems*. John Wiley & Sons, Chichester, 1994. 245

[Von98]   E. Vonk, L. C. Jain, and R. P. Johnson. *Automatic Generation of Neural Network Architectures Using Evolutionary Computation*. Advances in Fuzzy Systems – Applications and Theory. World Scientific Publ. Comp., New York, 1998. 305

[Wal90]   G. Wallace. Overview of the JPEG (ISO/CCITT) still image compression standard. In *Electronic Image Science and Technology*, pages 97–108. SPIE Proceedings 1244, Santa Clara, CA, Feb. 1990. 120

[War97]   V. Warnke, S. Harbeck, E. Nöth, and H. Niemann. Topic spotting using subword units. In *Proceedings des 9–ten Aachener Kolloquiums "Signaltheorie" Bild- und Sprachsignale*, pages 287–290, Aachen, 1997. 265, 267

[Wat85]   M. S. Waterman. Dynamic programming algorithms for picture comparison. *Advances in Applied Mathematic*, 1(6):129–134, 1985. 305

[Weg87]   P. Wegner. Dimensions of object–based language design. *OOPSLA '87 Conference Proceedings, SIGPLAN*, 22(12):168–182, 1987. 96

[Wel94]   S. T. Welstead. *Neural network and fuzzy logic applications in C/C++*. John Wiley & Sons, Inc., New York, 1994. 322

[Wu83]   C. F. J. Wu. On the convergence properties of the EM algorithm. *The Annals of Statistics*, 11(1):95–103, 1983. 317

[Wu91]   X. Wu. Efficient statistical computations for optimal color quantization. In Arvo [Arv91], pages 126–133. 227

[Wys82]   G. Wyszecki and W. S. Stiles. *Color Science: Concepts and Methods, Quantitaive Data and Formulae*. John Wiley & Sons, Inc., New York, 2 edition, 1982. 122

[XDR88]   Sun Microsystems Inc., Stanford. *RFC External Data Representation Standard: Protocol Specifications*, sun os 4 manuals, network programming, part 2 edition, 1988. 334

[Yam81]   G. Yamg and T. Kuang. The effort of median filtering on edge location estimation. *Computer Graphics and Image Processing (CGIP)*, 15:224–245, 1981. 203

[You96]   S. Young, J. Jansen, J. Odell, D. Ollason, and P. Woodland. *The HTK Book*. Entropic Cambridge Research Laboratory Ltd., Cambridge, 1996. 300

[Zam91]   P. Zamperoni. *Methoden der digitalen Bildverarbeitung*. Vieweg, Braunschweig, 1991. 251, 254

[Zim96]   W. Zimmer and E. Bonz. *Objektorientierte Bildverarbeitung*. Carl Hanser Verlag, München, 1996. 91

List of Figures

I	Test image	3
1.1	Graphics and image analysis	6
1.2	Simple and complex patterns	8
1.3	Facial images	9
1.4	Human ear	10
1.5	Part of the utterance "The pan galactic gurgle blaster"	11
1.6	The pinhole camera model	11
1.7	Perspective and orthographic projection	12
1.8	Human eye	12
1.9	A/D-conversion	13
1.10	Sampling and quantization	14
1.11	D/A-Conversion	15
2.1	From source code to executable programs	19
2.2	Declaration inside blocks	27
3.1	Cycle of software development	30
3.2	Structogram: sequence	33
3.3	Structogram: loops	33
3.4	Structogram: condition	34
3.5	Function, its linear approximation, and table look-up	37
5.1	Synthetic images	50
7.1	Frequencies and distribution of gray-levels	71
7.2	Gaussian densities	72
7.3	Random generator for normally distributed variables	74
7.4	Exponential distribution	76
7.5	2–D Gaussian density	78
8.1	Processing simple patterns	84
8.2	System structure for pattern analysis	87
8.3	Image segmentation into lines and corners	88
8.4	Abstract levels for image segmentation	88
8.5	General structure for pattern analysis systems	89
II	Edge strength	93

9.1	Object–oriented software engineering techniques	96
9.2	Abstract data types	98
9.3	Inheritance for numbers	100
11.1	Internal representation of a two-dimensional array.	116
11.2	Color, Gray-Level, and Range image	119
11.3	Binary images	121
11.4	Color image channels	122
11.5	Image matrices in main memory	123
12.1	Examples of synthetic images	128
12.2	Examples of pixel noise for different parameter values	129
12.3	Gaussian and salt-and-pepper noise	131
12.4	Views of a polyhedral object	132
12.5	Rotation of unit vectors in 3–D	132
12.6	Geometry of single stereo images	133
12.7	Simple texture generation	134
12.8	Texture	135
13.1	Linear combinations of trigonometric functions	138
13.2	First three summands of a Fourier series	140
13.3	Superposition of the Fourier functions	141
13.4	Continuous function and its Fourier transform	142
13.5	Application of the convolution theorem	143
13.6	Principle of the FFT	149
13.7	Fourier transformed image	150
13.8	High and low pass filter in Fourier domain	151
13.9	Result of high- and low-pass filter	151
14.1	Small hierarchy of geometric shapes	156
14.2	Hierarchy of image classes	161
15.1	Step edge and edge in real image	165
15.2	Intensity function in a real image	166
15.3	Edge and derivatives	167
15.4	Edge orientation and gradient	168
15.5	Masks for computation of the central differences	169
15.6	Masks for Sobel and Prewitt operator	169
15.7	Discrete directions and quantization	171
15.8	Discrete direction function	171
15.9	Gradient image from gray-level image	174
15.10	Robert's image: strength and orientation	174
15.11	Masks for the Laplace operator	175
15.12	Laplace image	176
15.13	Gradient image from color image	177

16.1	NIHCL class tree	181
IV	Pattern Analysis etc.	199
17.1	Linear filters	202
17.2	Rank-order operations	204
17.3	Smoothed-median-filter	204
17.4	Color median filter	206
17.5	Masks for edge preserving smoothing	206
17.6	Edge preserving and KNN filters	207
17.7	Conditional average filtering	207
17.8	Examples for magnifications	208
17.9	Bilinear interpolation	213
17.10	Comparison of scaling methods	213
18.1	Bimodal histogram threshold	218
18.2	Discriminant threshold	219
18.3	Entropy threshold	221
18.4	Multi-thresholding	222
18.5	Linearization of discrete distributions	222
18.6	Results of linearization	223
18.7	Local histogram equalization	224
18.8	Correction of gray-levels	225
18.9	Local histogram equalization	225
18.10	Median cut image	227
18.11	Histogram back-projection algorithm	228
18.12	Histogram back-projection examples	229
19.1	Masks for the Robinson operator	232
19.2	Result of Robinson operator	232
19.3	Masks for the Nevatia/Babu-operator	232
19.4	Result of Nevatia/Babu operator	233
19.5	Thresholds for binarization	234
19.6	Edge thinning	235
19.7	NMS image	235
19.8	NMA image	236
19.9	Chain code definition	238
19.10	Line following according to Nevatia/Babu (1)	239
19.11	Line following according to Nevatia/Babu (2)	240
19.12	Line following according to Nevatia/Babu (3)	241
19.13	Hysteresis algorithm (1)	241
19.14	Hysteresis algorithm (2)	242
19.15	Hysteresis algorithm (3)	242
19.16	Points to be inspected for gap closing	243
19.17	Image and Laplacian image	243
19.18	Principle of Hough transform for lines	244

19.19 Lines detected with Hough transform 245
19.20 Hough transform for circles 247
19.21 Orthogonal projection 248
19.22 Canny line detection (1) 249
19.23 Canny line detection (2) 250

20.1 Chain code processing 254
20.2 Rotated line 255
20.3 Uniformly distributed chain code directions 256
20.4 Area of a chain code: principle 258
20.5 Area of a chain code: structogram 258
20.6 Neighborhood 259
20.7 Contour tracking 260
20.8 Polygon-approximation of a chain code 261
20.9 Color region segmentation 262
20.10 Toy Animals 263

21.1 Decomposition of speech signals into frames 267
21.2 Speech signals of short utterances 269
21.3 Linear regression to compute average slopes 269
21.4 Speech signal of the utterance: "this is one word" 271
21.5 Logarithmic spectrum using rectangular windows 272
21.6 Logarithmic spectrum using Hamming windows of varying size 272
21.7 Logarithmic spectrum using Hann windows 272
21.8 Narrow and wide band spectrogram 273
21.9 Synthetic image and its spectrum 274
21.10 Computation of cepstral features 275
21.11 Mel scale 276
21.12 Triangular filters for 25 frequency groups 277
21.13 Speech production: the vocal tract 278
21.14 Model spectrum 280
21.15 Spectrum and model spectrum using Hamming windows 281
21.16 Classification of speech signals 281

22.1 Two classes in a one-dimensional feature space 287
22.2 Two classes in a two-dimensional feature space 287
22.3 The principle of the Bayesian classifier 291
22.4 Scalar discrete feature probabilities 292
22.5 Voronoi diagram 296
22.6 Class hierarchy for classifiers and features 297

23.1 Single word recognition 300
23.2 The utterance "pattern recognition" of three different speakers 301
23.3 Two speech signals representing the word "word" 302
23.4 Assignment of features: a graph search problem 303
23.5 Dynamic programming approach 304

23.6	From geometric distance measures to density functions	307
23.7	Assignment of observed and reference features	308
23.8	The handwritten word *minimum*	309
23.9	Forward algorithm	311
23.10	Hidden statistical processes	313
23.11	Examples of different topologies	314
23.12	EM-algorithm	317
23.13	Class hierarchy for density functions	321
24.1	Data flow in an image analysis system	326
24.2	Data flow for line segmentation	327
24.3	NIHCL and HIPPOS	329
24.4	Top of image processing class hierarchy	329
24.5	Segmentation objects	332
24.6	Stereo camera head	338
24.7	Localization of objects	339
24.8	Localization of partially occluded objects	339
V	Line approximation	343
A.1	Cycle of software development	345
A.2	RCS commands and file modes	348
C.1	Illustration of the inequality: $\log x \leq x - 1$	358

List of Tables

2.1	Format control strings	22
3.1	Look-up table for function approximation	38
4.1	Bit operations on integer values	42
4.2	Logical operators	43
5.1	Operations on pointers	54
7.1	Axioms of probability theory	70
13.1	Some properties of the Fourier transform	142
14.1	Access rules of base class members	155
15.1	Offsets for approximation	172
19.1	Flags for structure edge	236
20.1	Rules for smoothing chain codes	254
24.1	Data flow for line segmentation	328
C.1	Notation	359

List of Programs

1 — 20	46 — 56	91 — 108	136 — 159	181 — 215
2 — 21	47 — 56	92 — 109	137 — 159	182 — 215
3 — 22	48 — 57	93 — 109	138 — 160	183 — 215
4 — 23	49 — 57	94 — 109	139 — 160	184 — 226
5 — 23	50 — 57	95 — 110	140 — 160	185 — 226
6 — 23	51 — 59	96 — 110	141 — 161	186 — 226
7 — 24	52 — 60	97 — 110	142 — 161	187 — 237
8 — 24	53 — 61	98 — 111	143 — 162	188 — 237
9 — 25	54 — 61	99 — 112	144 — 162	189 — 237
10 — 26	55 — 61	100 — 112	145 — 170	190 — 244
11 — 26	56 — 62	101 — 112	146 — 172	191 — 251
12 — 27	57 — 62	102 — 113	147 — 172	192 — 252
13 — 27	58 — 63	103 — 116	148 — 173	193 — 253
14 — 28	59 — 63	104 — 116	149 — 180	194 — 253
15 — 28	60 — 63	105 — 117	150 — 180	195 — 253
16 — 38	61 — 64	106 — 117	151 — 180	196 — 254
17 — 39	62 — 64	107 — 118	152 — 183	197 — 257
18 — 40	63 — 64	108 — 118	153 — 183	198 — 261
19 — 40	64 — 65	109 — 118	154 — 183	199 — 268
20 — 41	65 — 65	110 — 120	155 — 184	200 — 282
21 — 41	66 — 65	111 — 122	156 — 184	201 — 285
22 — 42	67 — 66	112 — 124	157 — 185	202 — 293
23 — 42	68 — 66	113 — 124	158 — 186	203 — 293
24 — 43	69 — 67	114 — 124	159 — 186	204 — 298
25 — 44	70 — 67	115 — 125	160 — 187	205 — 298
26 — 44	71 — 67	116 — 125	161 — 188	206 — 322
27 — 45	72 — 68	117 — 126	162 — 189	207 — 324
28 — 46	73 — 73	118 — 130	163 — 189	208 — 328
29 — 47	74 — 73	119 — 135	164 — 190	209 — 330
30 — 47	75 — 76	120 — 145	165 — 190	210 — 331
31 — 47	76 — 92	121 — 145	166 — 190	211 — 331
32 — 48	77 — 103	122 — 145	167 — 191	212 — 332
33 — 49	78 — 104	123 — 146	168 — 191	213 — 332
34 — 50	79 — 104	124 — 146	169 — 192	214 — 333
35 — 51	80 — 104	125 — 148	170 — 193	215 — 333
36 — 51	81 — 105	126 — 154	171 — 194	216 — 333
37 — 52	82 — 105	127 — 154	172 — 194	217 — 334
38 — 52	83 — 106	128 — 155	173 — 195	218 — 336
39 — 52	84 — 106	129 — 156	174 — 195	219 — 336
40 — 53	85 — 106	130 — 156	175 — 196	220 — 344
41 — 53	86 — 107	131 — 157	176 — 197	221 — 344
42 — 54	87 — 107	132 — 157	177 — 205	222 — 347
43 — 54	88 — 107	133 — 157	178 — 205	223 — 348
44 — 55	89 — 108	134 — 158	179 — 212	224 — 349
45 — 55	90 — 108	135 — 158	180 — 212	225 — 353

Index

abstract data type, 97
access
    control, 348
    to member, 154
accumulator, 244–246
active vision, 90, 194, 209
Ada, 102, 196
allocation, 52, 53, 114, 335
    array, 115
    strategy, 189
ANIMALS, 325, 326
ANSI–C, 17, 62
artificial intelligence, 83, 89
`atan2`, 169, 170, 177
`atof`, 28, 65, 67
`atoi`, 25, 28, 50, 65, 67
autocorrelation, 269
autostereogram, 133, 134
awk, 350

base class, 97, 157
    access, 154
    private, 154
    protected, 154
    public, 154
Bayes
    Classifier, 290, 306
    decision rule, 291, 306
    error, 285
Bellman principle, 303
binarization, 217
bipartition, 218, 220
bispectrum, 274
bit field, 42
block, 267
`bool`, 42
`break`, 45, 46
`byte`, 54

C–beautifier, 33
CASE, 30
cast, 111, 157
    const, 196
    dynamic, 196

reinterpret, 196
catch, 63
`catch`, 45
CCD camera, 7, 10, 119, 129, 207
CD, 82
chain code, 238, 251
    conversion, 260
    length, 257
    smoothing, 254
`char`, 23
chi-square-test, 256
class, 96, 100
    abstract, 100
    `AffineDist`, 214
    `Bag`, 187, 285, 321
    base, 97
    `Chain`, 251, 254
    `ChainSeq`, 251
    `Class`, 182
    `Collection`, 187
    `ColorImage`, 121
    `complex`, 145
    `Date`, 186
    declaration, 105
    design, 113
    `Dictionary`, 188
    `Edge`, 233, 236
    `EdgeImage`, 173, 233
    `GeoObj`, 331
    `GrayLevelImage`, 96
    hierarchy, 153
    `HipposObj`, 328, 329
    `Histogram`, 225
    `Image`, 173, 329, 330
    image hierarchy, 160
    instance, 95, 96
    library, 179
    `LineRep2D`, 250
    `Stack`, 187
    `Matrix`, 97, 117, 330
    `Number`, 100
    `Object`, 182, 188, 328

    `OIOxdrin`, 334
    `OIOxdrout`, 334
    `OrderedCltn`, 187
    `PointXY`, 39
    polymorphic, 158
    `RelObj`, 329
    `Represent`, 329
    `SegObj`, 332
    `SeqCltn`, 187, 321
    `Set`, 187
    `Stack`, 187
    `String`, 186, 188
    `StrLineSeg`, 250
    template, 117
    `Time`, 183, 186
    `vector`, 111
classification, 83, 283, 299
    architecture, 84
    numerical, 84
    syntactical, 84
classifier, 264, 283
    consistent, 285
    speech, 299
clients, 99
color, 7, 13, 29, 121, 122, 160, 176, 177, 217, 226, 227, 261, 286, 326, 330
    space, 122
command line, 24–26, 28, 32, 57, 58, 105, 130, 192, 193, 326, 335, 336, 341, 346, 347
compilation
    conditional, 105, 252
compiler, 18
complex
    logarithm, 274
    number, 137, 145
    spectrum, 274
consistency, 285
const, 21
`const`, 111

constructor, 106, 115
    default, 106
    reference, 106
`continue`, 45
contrast, 223
conversion, 109
    operator, 109
    pointer, 59
convolution, 201
    continuous, 143
    discrete, 168
correlation coefficient, 208
covariance, 77
cpp, 18
CSC, 261
cumulative distribution, 70, 223
CVS, 34, 351

data
    abstraction, 96
    flow, 325
debugger, 68
decision function, 283
declaration, 20, 26
    extern, 46
    global, 26, 27
    local, 27
definition, 20
delegation, 99, 173
`delete`, 53, 107
density, 71, 290–292
    Cauchy, 82
    Gauss, 71, 297
    mixture, 79
    Poison, 297
depth, 11
derivation, 98, 153
    private, 154
    protected, 154
    public, 154
    syntax, 153
derivative, 166
    discrete, 166
    partial, 167
description

individual, 86
destructor, 107, 156, 158
DFT, 144
discriminant analysis, 219
distribution
    exponential, 76
    Gaussian, 72
    uniform, 75
do, 44
`double`, 23, 117
Doxygen, 351
doxygen, 34
durability, 96
dynamic
    binding, 101, 158
    programming, 89, 303
    time warping, 299, 300
`dynamic_cast`, 24, 162

edge
    detection, 165
    image, 165
    mask, 166
    orientation, 167
    strength, 167
efficiency, 102, 113, 214
EM
    algorithm, 315–318, 320
    key-equation, 316
encapsulation, 103
energy, 269
entropy, 80, 220
    conditional, 317
enumeration, 40
environment, 7
erosion, 343
estimation
    maximum likelihood, 312
Euclidean distance, 285, 295, 306
Euler's formula, 139
exception, 43, 111, 188
    handler, 45
    NIHCL, 188
exit, 26
`exit`, 20, 24, 107, 111

Expectation maximization
    algorithm, 315
`explicit`, 110, 196
exponentiation, 23, 72
external data formats, 119
external data representation,
    →XDR 375

`fclose`, 22
feature, 85, 265
    cepstral, 274
    statistical, 80
`fflush`, 23, 68
FFT, 148
`fgets`, 67
file
    access, 21
    extensions, 18
filter, 151, 201
    K nearest neighbor
        averaging, 205
    conditional average, 206
    dilatation, 203
    edge preserving, 204
    erosion, 203
    Gaussian, 203
    high-pass, 150, 233
    linear, 202
    low-pass, 150, 151, 203, 210
    mean, 202
    median, 203
    morphological, 203
    non-linear, 203
    separable, 203
    smoothed median, 203
`float`, 23, 117
`fopen`, 22, 25
`for`, 44
formant, 277
forward algorithm, 311
Fourier
    2–D transform, 150
    analysis, 270
    fast transform, 148
    series, 138

series complex, 141
short time transform, 271
transform, 142, 233
fprintf, 23, 24
frames, 266
frequency domain, 265
friend, 193, 251
fscanf, 67
ftp, 352
function, 25
    argument, 19, 25
    call, 19
    definition, 25
    density, 71, 136
    even, 139
    extern, 66
    inline, 65, 104
    intensity, 165
    odd, 139
    overloading, 63, 97
    pointer, 66, 214
    pure virtual, 159, 293, 321
    static, 66
    virtual, 158, 293, 321

gamma correction, 224
gaps, 241
Gauss
    density, 71, 72, 291, 293, 306, 315, 321
    distribution, 72
    filter, 249
    noise, 129
generalization property, 284
generating function, 210
geometric distortion, 210
gimp, 352
GNU, 2, 120, 351
goto, 32, 33, 43, 45
gradient, 167

handler, 45
hash, 187, 188
Hidden-Markov-Model, 79, 88, 91, 299, 305,
310–312, 314, 315, 320, 321, 323
    continuous, 315
    discrete, 315
    ergodic, 314
    left right, 314
HIPPOS, 326–330, 332–334, 337
hierarchy, 328
histogram, 217, 221, 225, 256, 270, 314, 321
    bi-modal, 217
    equalization, 223
    global equalization, 221
    linearization, 222
    local equalization, 223
HMM, 322, 323, →also Hidden-Markov-Model 375
Hough transform, 243, 245, 334
HSL, 122
hypertext, 5

if, 43
image
    binary, 121, 152, 216, 217, 259, 270, 283, 330
    intensity, 115, 117, 118, 174, 175, 233, 326
    polymorphic processing, 211
    pyramid, 210
    range, 118
    segmentation, 86, 214, 231, 251, 259, 325, 328, 329, 333
    single stereo, 133
    sub, 123, 267
    synthetic, 127
ImageMagick, 352
include, 18
incomplete data estimation, 315
independence
    statistical, 79, 308–310
information, 80, 316
    complete, 316
    hiding, 34, 97, 103, 105
    missing, 316
    observed, 316
inheritance, 96, 98, 153
    multiple, 98, 161, 328
    simple, 98
initialization, 317
    array–, 52
int, 23
interlace, 207
interpolation
    bilinear, 212
isA, 182
isEqual, 119, 182, 187
istream, 179
iterator, 187

Java, 102
    virtual machine, 102
JPEG, 5, 120, 267, 273

Khoros, 91
knowledge base, 89

Lagrange multiplier, 319, 358
LaTeX, 2, 344
learning, 84, 284, 305, 312, 322, 323
    supervised, 284, 285
    unsupervised, 284, 285, 312
Levinson recursion, 279
library, 347
line
    characteristic, 14
    detection, 231
    digital linear, 255
linear
    composition, 138
    predictive coding, 277
    reconstruction, 208
linearization, 222
linkage
    type-safe, 62

local connectivity, 238
logarithm
    complex, 274
long, 23
longjmp, 45
look-up table transform, 224
loop, 33, 44
    do, 44
    for, 33, 44
    until, 33
    while, 33, 44
LPC, 277
    spectrum, 280

macro, 65, 184
magnification, 208
Mahalanobis distance, 294
main, 24, 57, 182
Makefile, 346, 347, 349
mangling, 62, 63
marginalization, 79, 307
mask, 201
matching, 89, 301, 315
Matrix, 191
matrix, 49, 56, 96, 115, 130,
        132, 144, 173, 175,
        321, 328
    rotation, 132
    Vandermonde, 146
maximum likelihood, 73, 80,
        290, 291, 293
maximum likelihood
        estimation, 73, 317,
        318
mean, 71, 73, 306, 320
mean-square error, 247
Mel
    cepstrum, 276
    spectrum, 276
Mel scale, 276
memory leak, 190
message passing, 96, 158
method, 96, 103
metric, 295, 297
missing information
        principle, 315

mixture
    Gaussian, 80
mixture density, 299, 305,
        309, 339, 356
model, 340
    cepstrum, 280
    spectrum, 280
model base, 340
module, 97
moments, 74
MPEG, 5, 120
multi-threshold, 220, 228
multimedia, 5
mutable, 196

namespace, 60
nearest neighbor, 295, 299,
        300
neighborhood, 238, 259
NIHCL, 107, 179, 181–192,
        196, 197, 260, 285,
        321, 328–330, 332,
        334, 335, 341, 344,
        351, 352
NMA, 235
NMS, 234
noise
    Gaussian, 129, 204
    pixel, 128
    salt-and-pepper, 130
noisy rows, 207
normalization, 84

object, 96, 105
    file, 346
    input, 185
    output, 185
    persistent, 334
    pointer, 157
    polyhedral, 131
    static members, 182
object-oriented
    classification, 100
    paradigm, 95
    programming, 17
OIOin, 182

OIOout, 182
OOA, 95, 101
OOD, 95
OOP, 95
operation
    bit, 41
    pointer, 52
    shift, 41
operator
    (), 212
    <<, 179, 180
    Canny, 249
    color edge, 176
    color Sobel, 177
    comparison, 42
    delete, 335
    delete, 53
    hierarchy, 214
    Huckel, 232
    index, 112
    Kirsch, 232
    Laplace, 175, 241, 259
    logical, 43
    Nevatia-Babu, 232, 235
    new, 114, 335
    new, 53, 106
    not, 107
    overloading, 97, 109
    Prewitt, 169, 232
    Robert's Cross, 173, 177
    Robinson, 232
    scope resolution, 40
    Sobel, 169, 233
    virtual inline, 214
ostream, 179

pattern, 7
    analysis, 6, 83, 86
    complex, 8
    geometric, 128
    recognition, 6, 83
    recognition software, 29
    simple, 8
    understanding, 89
perception, 5
perl, 350

phoneme, 274
pitch, 277
pixel, 115
planning, 90
pointer, 51
polygons, 260
polymorphism, 96, 97, 101,
    109, 158, 187, 212,
    216
  weak, 101
polynomial, 138
PostScript, 2, 340, 351
pre-processing, 84
predictor coefficient, 279
`printf`, 22, 68
private
  base, 161
  base class, 154
  data, 105
  protected, 161
probability
  axioms, 69
  degenerated, 81
  space, 69
problem domain, 7
procedure, 25
projection, 10
  orthogonal, 247
  orthographic, 12
  perspective, 12
protected, 105, 154
  base class, 154
prototype, 306
pseudo color, 122
pseudo-inverse, 246, 248, 279
Pstricks, 344
public, 105
  base, 161
  base class, 154
PUMA, 326
pyramid
  Gaussian, 210

quantization, 5, 13, 14
  color, 226

random
  variable, 69, 307
  vectors, 77, 308
random variable
  continuous, 71
  discrete, 69
rcs, 34
`readFrom`, 184, 334
real-time, 35, 90, 123, 145,
    147, 190, 209
reference, 189
`reinterpret_cast`, 24,
    59
relative frequency, 70, 314
relative smoothness, 270
repeat, 68
resolution hierarchy, 209
`return`, 25, 104, 107
RGB, 121
Robinson operator, 231
root of unity, 144

sampling
  rate, 14
  theorem, 15
sampling rate, 14
sampling theorem, 139, 209
`scanf`, 67
scope, 26
scope resolution, 40
segmentation, 214, 325
  image, 86
  object, 332
  points, 262
`short`, 23
signal processing, 6
signal-to-noise ratio, 13, 81,
    203
Simula, 101
single stereo images, 133
singular value decomposition,
    248
`sizeof`, 54, 172
slices, 191
slides, 352

Smalltalk, 101, 102, 181,
    182, 186
software
  comment, 32
  development, 30
  documentation, 33
  efficiency, 35
  layout, 32
  teamwork, 97
  tools, 35, 345
source files, 353
spatial domain, 265
spectrogram, 199, 271, 343
spectrum, 271
  complex, 274
  power-, 271
speech
  record, 9
  signal, 268
  synthetic, 127
  top level loop, 92
splitting
  function, 286
  line, 286
  point, 286
  polynomial, 287
`sscanf`, 67
Standard Template Library,
    →STL375
`static_cast`, 24
`stderr`, 22
`stdin`, 22
`stdio`, 20–22
`stdout`, 22
steepest ascent, 167
stereo, 267, 338
STL, 103, 107, 179, 186–189,
    191, 192, 196, 197,
    261
`storeOn`, 182, 184, 334
`storer`, 184
stream, 179, 334
string, 55
`string`, 191
struct, 153

struct, 39, 103
structogram, 33
structure
    tag, 39
subclass, 98
subimage, 80, 123, 126, 202, 261, 267, 273
superclass, 98
SVD, 289, →also singular value decomposition 375
switch, 46
symbolic description, 8, 325
syntax, 17

template, 99, 117
texture, 127, 270
thinning, 233
this, 104
threshold, 217, 233
    hysteresis, 239
    least square, 217
throw, 45
TIFF, 5, 120
time stamp, 97
training, 284
transform
    cosine, 275
    Fourier, 209
    Hough, 243, 334
try, 45
type, 96
    cast, 24
    declaration, 59
    explicit conversion, 23
    implicit conversion, 23
    parametric, 99
    specifier, 60
typeid, 195

UML, 96, 98, 99
uncertainty, 89
unified modeling language, →UML 375
union, 153, 154
union, 41

Unix
    ar, 347
    chgrp, 345
    chmod, 38, 345
    chown, 345
    compress, 120
    gid, 345
    groups, 35
    make, 35, 38, 346
    makefile, 38
    newgrp, 35
    passwd, 345
    rcs, 35, 38, 348
    uid, 345
    umask, 35, 345, 349
Unix, 2, 4, 21, 22, 24, 33, 35, 64, 103, 120, 345–347, 349, 351, 352, 380
using, 195

variable
    auto, 60
    class–, 182
    const, 60
    member, 39, 96
    reference, 60
    register, 60
    static, 27, 60
variance, 71, 73
vector, 49
vector quantization, 227, 286
vector space, 138
video camera, 10
views, 131
virtual
    destructor, 163
    base class, 161
    function, 158
visualization, 15
Viterbi, 323
Viterbi algorithm, 312
vocal tract, 277
void, 25
volatile, 196
Voronoi

cell, 296
diagram, 298
partition, 296

while, 44, 68
window, 201
    function, 271
    Hamming, 267
    Hann, 267

XDR, 327, 334
xfig, 340, 344, 351, 352
xv, 352
XYZ, 122

zero-crossing, 74, 80, 166, 174, 241, 268, 270, 279, 282